*The publisher and the University of California Press Foundation
gratefully acknowledge the generous support of the
George Gund Foundation Imprint in African American Studies.*

The Racial Muslim

The Racial Muslim

WHEN RACISM QUASHES RELIGIOUS FREEDOM

Sahar Aziz

UNIVERSITY OF CALIFORNIA PRESS

University of California Press
Oakland, California

Library of Congress Cataloging-in-Publication Data
Names: Aziz, Sahar F., author.
Title: The racial Muslim : when racism quashes religious freedom /
    Sahar Aziz.
Identifiers: LCCN 2021008760 (print) | LCCN 2021008761 (ebook) |
    ISBN 9780520382282 (cloth) | ISBN 9780520382299 (paperback) |
    ISBN 9780520382305 (epub)
Subjects: LCSH: Muslims—United States—Social conditions. |
    Islamophobia—United States. | Religion and politics—United States.
Classification: LCC E184.M88 A95 2022 (print) | LCC E184.M88 (ebook) |
    DDC 305.6/970973—dc23
LC record available at https://lccn.loc.gov/2021008760
LC ebook record available at https://lccn.loc.gov/2021008761

30   29   28   27   26   25   24   23   22   21
10   9   8   7   6   5   4   3   2   1

For Sohair and Fathi, with deep gratitude
for the countless sacrifices you made for us.

CONTENTS

ACKNOWLEDGMENTS

When I first began writing this book, a colleague advised me that it would write itself. Having created a detailed outline and argument, I thought it an odd statement at the time. Five years later, after thousands of hours of research, writing, and workshopping, I now appreciate the wisdom of these words. The book-writing process is truly an intellectual and personal journey that leads to a destination unpredictable at the start.

I would not have completed the journey without the love and support of my husband. There are too many times to count when he took on a disproportionate share of work in our busy household when I needed more time to write or was traveling to workshop drafts of the manuscript. He was my intellectual sounding board when I struggled with an idea or needed a reviewer of the multiple rounds of drafts. His love and support is a daily nourishment to my soul. I am also blessed to have in my three children vocal cheerleaders and loyal drill sergeants. They regularly asked me how many pages I had written and repeated the advice I gave them about staying focused and never giving up on one's dreams. During our daily walks to his elementary school, my youngest son would lay out my writing schedule for the day and remind me that he would check if I finished my work after he returned from school. My dearest Amira, Yusuf, and Sherif, you bring joy and meaning to my life every day. I hope our journey together taught you that with hard work and persistence you can accomplish your goals.

My parents' lives and sacrifices for me and my siblings are the inspiration that gave me the stamina to complete this book project. Immigrating from Egypt with minimal material resources, their sheer willpower and devotion to their children carried us through many personal and financial challenges. Nothing was just handed to them, and everything they earned required double the work and double the credentials of their peers. My gratitude for the grit, love, pride, and work ethic they instilled in me cannot be overstated. Thank you, Fathi, for raising me to be a fighter, a critical thinker, and a strong female leader. Thank you, Sohair, for teaching me kindness, empathy, strength, and persistence. Heaven truly is at the feet of our mothers.

This book's journey allowed me to cross paths with many brilliant academics who graciously offered their candid, critical, and insightful feedback on draft chapters. I was privileged to be invited to a writing retreat hosted by Kimberly Crenshaw where I presented the seeds of the book idea. The comments I received from Kimberly Crenshaw, Devon Carbado, Khaled Beydoun, Justin Hansford, Paul Butler, Priscilla Ocen, and Luke Harris were invaluable in the development of the book's theoretical frame. I also greatly benefited from the critiques of early drafts by Amna Akbar, Shirin Sinnar, Ramzi Kassem, Maryam Jamshidi, and Daryl Li at a convening of critical national security scholars at CUNY Law School.

I am deeply indebted to Katherine Franke, whose intellectual boldness and passion are not only contagious, but set a high bar for us to strive to meet. She graciously welcomed me as a fellow at her Center for Gender and Sexuality Law at Columbia Law School, where I received valuable feedback on early drafts from Bernard Harcourt, Melissa Murray, Jamal Greene, Seyla Benhabib, Olatunde Johnson, Joseph Massad, and Kendall Thomas.

I am also thankful to Amaney Jamal for hosting a workshop at Princeton University comprised of esteemed academics who provided invaluable feedback. Professor Jamal embodies the kind and generous intellectual we should all strive to be. I am grateful to Deepa Kumar, Sylvia-Chan Malik, Arun Kundnani, Zain Abdullah, and Tanya Hernandez not only for their candid feedback and critiques at the workshop but also for their excellent scholarship that informs my work. The book also benefited from law faculty feedback on draft chapters at colloquia at Cornell University, Wake Forest University, St. John's University, and Rutgers Law School. I could not have found better editors than Maura Roessner, Madison Wetzell, Francisco Reinking, and David Peattie, whose guidance, patience, and enthusiasm were instrumental in bringing the book to the world.

Rarely does one have the good fortune to find a mentor as supportive and generous as Gerald Torres. His keen intellect, wit, and trailblazing scholarship in critical race theory has inspired a generation of his former law students, including me. From the beginning of my entrance into legal academia, Professors Adrien Wing and Neal Gotanda have been stalwart supporters whose generous mentorship has been invaluable and for which I am deeply grateful. My work has benefited tremendously from the leadership and scholarship of a generation of women of color law professors including Angela Onwuachi-Willig, L. Song Richardson, Cheryl I. Harris, Deborah N. Archer, Danielle M. Conway, Adrienne Davis, Meera E. Deo, D. Wendy Greene, and Natsu Taylor Saito.

I am also fortunate to work at Rutgers Law School, where social justice is prioritized under the visionary leadership of Chancellor Nancy Cantor and where I have the privilege of working with brilliant scholars committed to social justice. At Rutgers I received critical feedback on earlier drafts from Elise Boddie, David Troutt, Jon Dubin, Twila Perry, Alexis Karteron, Norrinda Hayat, and Taja-Nia Henderson. Instrumental in each phase of the research process were the excellent librarians at Rutgers Law School including Caroline Young, Rebecca Kunkel, Jootaek Lee, Marjorie Crawford, and John Joergensen. A special thanks to my former Texas A&M and Rutgers law students who provided excellent research assistance: Pati Candelaria, Sabah Abbasi, Reem Moussa, Kyle Carney, Brian Bailey, Dina Mansour, Travis Gasper, and Joseph Carr.

Finally, I would be remiss not to admit that the vitriol of Islamophobes (whether in liberal or conservative circles) motivates me to fight hatred with knowledge, to counter ignorance with education, and show through my life's work the strength and agency of Muslim and Arab women. My faith reminds me that when I see an evil, I must change it with my deeds, my words, and my heart. I pray the words in this book will inspire a generation of people, regardless of their faith, to speak out and resist anti-Muslim racism in their cities and countries. For it is when we stay silent and do nothing that oppression reigns.

FOREWORD

Anti-Muslim racism, or Islamophobia, is often ascribed to the political fallout from the September 11, 2001, terrorist attacks. To the contrary, the notion of an Islamic threat and a clash of civilizations has been perpetuated for decades by political events in the Muslim world and the West, as well as statements by government leaders, policy makers, and commentators in the media. Overlooked by many are these prescient comments by Edward Said in the early 1980s.

> For the general public in America and Europe today, Islam is "news" of a particularly unpleasant sort. The media, the government, the geopolitical strategists, and—although they are marginal to the culture at large—the academic experts on Islam are all in concert: Islam is a threat to western civilization. Now this is by no means the same as saying that only derogatory or racist caricatures of Islam are to be found in the West.... What I am saying is that negative images of Islam are very much more prevalent than any others, and that such images correspond not with what Islam "is"...but to what prominent sectors of a particular society take it to be: Islam and the West: A Clash of Civilizations? Those sectors have the power and the will to propagate that particular image of Islam, and this image therefore becomes more prevalent, more present, than all others.[1]

The 1990s provided the backdrop for the dramatic increase in Islamophobia after 9/11, as reflected in the writings of Bernard Lewis and Samuel Huntington and his clash of civilizations theory. Magazines, newspaper articles, and editorials warned of Islam's war with the West and its incompatibility with democracy. Islam increasingly came to be seen as a triple threat, political, civilizational, and demographic, feeding a notion of an impending clash between Islam and the West. Huntington concluded that

"Islam has bloody borders and so are its innards." Belief in an impending clash between the Muslim world and the West was reflected in American and European media headlines and television programs.

Al-Qaeda's attack and destruction of the World Trade Center in New York City and the Pentagon unleashed an exponential increase in anti-Islam and anti-Muslim racism, bigotry, discrimination, and violence in the United States and Europe, with national and global consequences. The 9/11 attacks shaped US Muslims' identity in popular culture, reinforcing a culture war that had an impact on Muslim civil liberties. Islam and Muslims, not just Muslim extremists and terrorists, were cast, in many cases demonized, as the radical "other" in the media: in political commentary and cartoons, in the portrayal of villains in movies and television shows, and in the explosion of social media websites and diatribes—all with international and domestic consequences. Domestically, this was manifested in the explosive growth of Islamophobia and anti-Muslim attitudes and behavior that fostered discrimination, hate speech, and violence and domestic policies (antiterrorism legislation and regulations, government surveillance and monitoring) that have threatened the civil liberties of millions of Muslims.

The media provided a platform not only for information and balanced reporting but also for anti-Islam and anti-Muslim statements by political leaders, commentators, and a host of "preachers of hate." Far Right political and religious commentators wrote and spoke out publicly about Islam and Muslims, asserting with impunity what would never appear in mainstream broadcast or print media regarding American Jews, Christians, and established ethnic groups. The Quran was compared to *Mein Kampf*. Conservative commentators engaged in hate speech. Ann Coulter, for example, stated, "We should invade their countries, kill their leaders and convert them to Christianity."[2] Michael Savage opined on his widely distributed radio show "The Savage Nation," "I think these people [Arabs and Muslims] need to be forcibly converted to Christianity.... It's the only thing that can probably turn them into human beings." President George W. Bush's distinction between Islam and Muslim extremists was overshadowed by the statements of prominent members of Congress and the hardline Christian Right like Pat Robertson, Franklin Graham, Jerry Falwell, John Hagee, and Rod Parsley.

A major study by Media Tenor, *A New Era for Arab-Western Relations*, found a shocking disparity of coverage in its analysis of 975,000 news stories published between 2001 and 2011 in US and European media outlets. In

2001, 2 percent of all news stories in the Western media presented images of Muslim militants, while just over 0.1 percent presented stories of ordinary Muslims. In 2011, the numbers were 25 percent and 0.1 percent, respectively. The net result over the ten-year period was a significant increase in coverage of Muslim militants but no increase in the coverage of ordinary Muslims.

By 2015, Islamophobia had become normalized according to the Media Tenor 2015 report, "Coverage of Islam" (January 1–December 31, 2015). After more than a decade of steady escalation, 2015 witnessed the all-time highest level of negative coverage. Specifically, the report found (1) in television media coverage of religious protagonists, over 80 percent covered Islam and in a negative light; (2) in the United States, the United Kingdom, and Germany, nine of ten articles about Islam were negative; (3) coverage of Muslim protagonists focused on the Islamic State (IS) and other "Islamist" terrorist networks (e.g., Al-Qaeda, Boko Haram, Taliban, al-Shabaab); (4) the increased coverage of mainstream Muslims also tended to be negative (more than 50 percent of reports); and (5) the vast majority of stories on Islam or Muslims focused on war and conflict. To put the media bias into perspective, a study released in November 2015 by 416 Labs, a Toronto-based consulting firm, found that the *New York Times* portrayed Islam and Muslims more negatively than alcohol, cancer, and cocaine, among other benchmarked words.

Islamophobic rhetoric by American politicians both reflected and validated the negative media coverage. In the 2016 presidential primary battles, for example, Donald Trump, Newt Gingrich, Ben Carson, Ted Cruz, and Marco Rubio resorted to targeting Islam and Muslims in seeking to mobilize broad-based support for their candidacy. Trump, the leading Republican candidate, advocated a freeze on all Muslim immigration, as well as the monitoring or even the forced closure of American mosques. The result? Trump soared in the polls.

Sahar Aziz, in *The Racial Muslim*, masterfully demonstrates that while 9/11 is a critical historical juncture in the racialization of Muslims, a comprehensive understanding of the extent to which anti-Muslim racism is rooted in American society requires an awareness of the often-overlooked deep historical roots of Anglo-Saxon Protestant nativism and White supremacy. Her argument provides a unique perspective and understanding of the myths of American and European religious pluralism that reveals America's historic failure to live up to them in their engagement of "the other," religiously, culturally, and civilizationally.

In this meticulously researched book, Aziz demonstrates that despite similarities to other religious minorities like Catholics, Mormons, and Jews, there are deep and distinct differences in the racialization of Muslims due to European Orientalism, American imperialism in Muslim-majority countries, xenophobia, and, finally, the September 11 attacks that sealed the entrenchment of the Racial Muslim in American race politics. While Jews, Catholics, and Mormons would eventually be regarded as part of America's newfound Judeo-Christian tradition, the legacy of Orientalism and Christian theology, especially missionary theology, excludes Islam from American national identity. The result, as Aziz notes, is "a weaponization of religion to perpetuate racial inequality without appearing to contradict religious freedom principles." Just as the crown (Western colonial powers) and the cross (Western missionaries) justified European colonialism with its slogans, "the white man's burden" (Britain) and "a mission to civilize" (France), 9/11 and the use of the phrase "[global] war on terrorism" became a justification for a war on Islam and Muslims used by some Western governments, media, and Islamophobic authors and websites.

In challenging popular mythic history about America's religious freedom norms, *The Racial Muslim* offers an important and comprehensive analysis of the historical roots and development of the racialization of Muslims. Aziz's in-depth research boldly shows the extent to which the war on terrorism has degenerated into a war on Islam and Muslims and produced a securitized racial Muslim identity contrary to American religious freedom principles. At a time when the United States and Europe are facing serious political challenges caused by White supremacist Christian nationalism and consequent threats to religious pluralism, *The Racial Muslim* is essential reading.

John L. Esposito, Professor of Religion, International
Affairs, and Islamic Studies and Founding Director
of the Prince Alwaleed Center for Muslim-Christian
Understanding, Georgetown University

Introduction

AS WE SHUFFLED OUT OF CLASS, the tension in the air was palpable. Instead of the usual sounds of law student chatter, the halls were eerily quiet. I walked toward the lobby, noticing a large congregation of students huddled around the television. I heard gasps at the replays of two commercial airplanes crashing into the World Trade Center. What happened on that Tuesday of my second week of law school is etched in my memory forever. It was the day I went from being racially ambiguous to racially threatening.

I joined my classmates in shock at the sight of buildings crumbling, people fleeing, and emergency personnel hauling away dead bodies covered in blood and dust. We oscillated between listening intently to the newscasters and speculating about what was happening. How could this have happened? Who was flying those airplanes?

As television stations replayed the horrific scenes alongside analysts providing facts piecemeal, a theme was beginning to emerge: this may have been a terrorist act, not an accident. And the suspected perpetrators were Arab Muslim men. The stares of my classmates felt like lasers.

I quickly left the law school as my mind turned to the safety of my mother, who wore the Muslim headscarf. I feared the backlash would be violent. I worried she would be attacked at the large public hospital where she worked. I also worried about my father, whose first name is Mohamed and who speaks with a heavy foreign accent. Would their coworkers accost, or worse, assault, them out of a desire for revenge? Would they be afraid to go to work, to the grocery store, to the mosque? Would we be blamed for these atrocious criminal acts? Our lives in America as invisible minorities were over. We were now Racial Muslims.

That day changed the trajectory of my legal career in ways I could never have predicted. No longer would my professional goal be to work on rule of law in Egypt, where I was born and from where my family had immigrated. I had enrolled in law school, despite my parents' wishes that I be an engineer or a doctor, out of an idealistic commitment to the fundamental rights enshrined in the US Constitution. The freedom of speech, association, assembly, and religion were rights I knew were not available in all countries. Hearing stories of my parents' experiences that caused them to leave their family and home behind to resettle in a new land with a different language and religion made me appreciate that freedom is not free.

The intense backlash against Muslims after 9/11, however, caused me to postpone any plans to travel to the Middle East to work with local civil society organizations to further the rule of law and defend human rights. A more existential issue now faced me, my family, and my faith community in the United States.

Everything, ranging from our mosques and charities to our travel and dress, was under scrutiny. American media now associated all things related to Islam with terrorism and threats to national security. My faith in the American legal system would be put to the test as I defended the rule of law right here in the United States.

. . .

"The New York Police Department Gathered Intelligence on 250-Plus Mosques, Student Groups in Terrorist Hunt," read the Associated Press headline on August 24, 2011.[1] Investigative reporters had uncovered a massive multiyear surveillance program wherein the NYPD was intentionally spying on tens of thousands of Muslims in the Tri-State area. What many of us in the civil rights community had long suspected was now confirmed: simply being Muslim was sufficient to attract the invasive scrutiny of the state.

But how could this happen in a country that prides itself on privileging religious freedom, both in law and in society? Where was the public outcry opposing the state's targeting of a religious minority in ways that chilled their right to religious freedom? Surely, spying on a house of worship constitutes the most direct infringement on this cherished First Amendment right.

Having advocated for the civil rights of Muslims for nearly a decade, I thought through different legal theories to challenge the NYPD surveillance program. My research led to me Title VI of the 1964 Civil Rights Act—a law that restricts recipients of federal funding from discriminating in their provision of services. Local and state police departments are among the largest recipients of federal funds from the US Departments of Justice and Homeland Security.[2] I thought I was on to something that could avoid the lacuna of the equal protection doctrine that thus far had failed to protect Muslims from post-9/11 discrimination.

Each time a Muslim plaintiff challenged national security practices on First, Fourth, Fifth, or Fourteenth Amendment grounds, courts dismissed the claims because the plaintiff could not prove the government intended to discriminate on the basis of the plaintiff's religion. Instead, courts accepted government claims that its policies and practices were rationally aimed to secure the nation, not target Muslims. Since the US Supreme Court ruling in *Washington v. Davis* in 1976, proving a disparate adverse impact on a minority group has been insufficient to win a Fourteenth Amendment equal protection claim.[3] Thus, a Title VI statutory claim offered a potential alternative litigation strategy.

There was one problem, though: the text of Title VI. The statute reads, "No person in the United States shall, on the ground of *race, color, or national origin*, be excluded from participation in, be denied the benefits of, or be subjected to discrimination under any program or activity receiving Federal financial assistance."[4] Religion is glaringly absent as a protected class under Title VI. Muslims, thus, are unprotected by the statute.

Muslim identity is not a race in any phenotypical sense. Indeed, Muslims are the most racially diverse faith community in the United States, composed of African Americans and immigrants from more than seventy-five countries.[5] Their diversity makes it hard for a lawyer to prove that a particular race or national origin, as required by Title VI, is the grounds on which national security practices are directed at Muslims.

And yet what we are witnessing in the post-9/11 era is a type and degree of profiling and targeting more closely resembling the racial discrimination historically experienced by African American, Native American, and Asian American communities (of all faiths). Muslims are being treated as a race, and more specifically, a suspect race, rather than as a religious minority to be protected from persecution. For that reason, government officials and members of the public—who may in fact believe in religious freedom norms—do not view targeting Muslims in national security and immigration practices as a threat to religious freedom.[6]

Herein lies the genesis of this book. With the goal of making a legal claim to stop police surveillance of Muslim communities, my research led me to a more fundamental question with much broader implications for all Americans. Is our stated commitment to religious freedom meaningful? Does it apply equally to all faith communities? If so, then how can we explain the systematic subordination of Muslim communities, including physical attacks on and surveillance of their houses of worship, under the guise of national security? The explanation, I believe, lies in the racialization of a minority religious group—a process with a protracted and checkered history in the United States.

This book interrogates how and why a country where religious freedom is a founding principle in law and societal norms produces such overt prejudice and discrimination against Muslims. How does the critical mass of Americans in the twenty-first century that holds unfavorable views of Muslims reconcile such mistreatment with the nation's (and their own) commitments to religious freedom?[7] More pointedly, how do Christian religious conservatives who decry assaults on their own religious freedom justify their support, as shown in numerous polls, for state practices that infringe on Muslims' religious freedoms?[8]

I proffer that the explanation lies in how racism intersects with religion to racialize a religion's followers and consequently excludes them from the panoply of religious freedom protections. Put simply, racialization causes a faith community's religious freedoms to be circumscribed or denied altogether. The ways in which particular religious communities are racialized depend on both domestic and international factors unique to that group. For this reason, I limit my analysis to the experiences of immigrant Muslims. That is because the domestic factors contributing to the racialization of African American Muslims is starkly different, though certainly overlapping, from the domestic factors racializing Muslims who immigrated primarily from the Middle East, North Africa, and South Asia. Similarly, relations between the United States and immigrant Muslims' countries of origin influence their treatment legally and socially in the United States in ways that do not impact African American Muslims.

My intervention is twofold. First, I argue that the racialization of immigrant Muslims is grounded in a racial-religious hierarchy, as opposed to just a racial hierarchy, to socially construct a racialized Muslim identity. Second, I offer a typology of what I call the Racial Muslim that explains why some immigrant Muslims are more likely to be targeted than others by private and government Islamophobia. Four factors converge to racialize Muslims to produce the Racial Muslim: (1) White Protestant supremacy, (2) xenophobia arising from coercive assimilation into Western European cultural norms,

(3) Orientalism, and (4) American empire in Muslim-majority countries. I explore how each of these factors interacts politically, socially, and discursively to define the characteristics attributed to Racial Muslims that in turn legitimize their systematic subordination.

The scholars Deepa Kumar and Nazia Kazi have critically examined how race intersects with empire in the racialization of Muslims, which I build on in my deeper examination of how religion, religious beliefs, and religious practices also racialize a group within the United States.[9] Scholars on Arab American identity, such as Nadine Naber, Amaney Jamal, and Moustafa Bayoumi, examine how religious affiliation influences Arab racial identity placements and how mainstream American society views Arab Americans.[10] The work of other scholars who have insightfully examined the intersection of race and religion, such as Tisa Wenger, does not extend to Muslims in the United States; and Erik Love's important work, *Islamophobia and Racism in America*, is limited to an exploration of Islamophobia exclusively through the lens of American racism.[11]

The existing literature, thus, does not examine in detail the central role religion plays and how it racializes diverse immigrants encompassed in the Racial Muslim construct.[12] And no books have yet presented an in-depth comparative analysis between the racialization of immigrant Muslims today and other religious minorities in the past. In this regard, I merge and expand on the important work of these scholars by showing how empire, American race/racism, xenophobia, *and* religion interact to racialize immigrant Muslims in the post-9/11 era.

The co-constitutive nature of religion and race means neither identity exists in isolation but rather interacts to produce a racial-religious hierarchy.[13] Religious identity in certain contexts functions as a racial marker. The literature on racial and ethnic formation, although richly developed, does not adequately incorporate the role of religion in producing socially constructed racial hierarchies, or what is known as the racialization of religion.[14] Likewise, the literature on religious freedom tends to overlook the dispositive role that race plays in the subordination of religious minorities. The social construction of Whiteness is shaped as much by religious identity as it is by skin color, hair texture, facial features, and other phenotypical characteristics.[15]

To fill these gaps in the literature, I proffer a theoretical framework to explain why Islamophobia—the systematic fear of Muslims and Islam[16]—has become entrenched in American race politics and in turn produces anti-Muslim racism on individual and structural levels.[17] My theoretical framework aims to explain the causes of a phenomenon, or more specifically, a paradox: overt private and state discrimination against a religious minority in a country that privileges religious freedom in both law and society.

To be sure, the Racial Muslim construct cannot explain every individualized experience or exception. Nor do I claim direct causation between the four macro factors in my theoretical frame and anti-Muslim racism. Instead, this book explains how the multiple, complex factors intersected in the past to produce systematic discrimination by the state, political elites, and members of the public against immigrant Muslims in the United States in the post-9/11 era.

THE RACIAL MUSLIM TYPOLOGY

The September 11 terrorist attacks finalized a transformation of Muslim identity that had been in the making for decades and was grounded in European Orientalism. Immigrant Muslims historically have been presumed to be Arabs and vice versa. As a result, Middle Eastern attire, the Arabic language, and Arab-presenting physical markers are combined with real or imputed Muslim beliefs to create a racial identity.[18] Put simply, to be Middle Eastern is to be presumed Muslim and vice versa. After the September 11 attacks, the racial markers of Muslim identity became tied to Al-Qaeda, ISIS, the Taliban, or Hamas. Persons who looked, dressed like, or had the same names as terrorists profiled in the media were collectively treated as Racial Muslims. Moreover, people of South Asian origin—whether Hindu, Sikh, Christian, or Muslim—joined Arabs in being "Muslim-looking."

By definition, Racial Muslims do not experience full religious freedom protections afforded to religious minorities. Nor are they considered to have an American national identity, even if they were born in the United States or possess US citizenship. Rather, Racial Muslims are a suspect race, permanent foreigners, and national security threats who warrant exclusion, purging, or incarceration to protect real (White Judeo-Christian) Americans. Their mere presence on US soil poses a national security threat.

Like any persons who are attributed a socially constructed racial identity, Racial Muslims are not all treated the same by the government or private actors. Building on Mahmoud Mamdani's "good Muslim, bad Muslim" frame, I propose that the performative and social construction of the Racial Muslim is hierarchical, not dichotomous.[19] Mamdani argues that the US government's "good Muslim" aligns geopolitically with the United States. For example, during the 1980s, some political Islamists such as the Afghan mujahideen and Saudi Arabian Salafists were "good Muslims," whereas others such as Khomeini and his Islamist supporters were "bad Muslims," deemed enemies of the United States.

I expand on this dichotomy by arguing that the severity and extent of state and private acts of racialization vary depending on the Racial Muslims' religious practices, political beliefs, and assimilation as defined by Anglo-Protestant social norms. Accordingly, the Racial Muslim comprises an internal hierarchy that determines which Muslims are most and least likely to be targeted by private and state anti-Muslim racism. The hierarchy is shaped by a Muslim's levels of religiosity and political dissent. Hence a religious political dissident Muslim is likely to experience the harshest forms of anti-Muslim racism, while a secular, politically mainstream or apolitical Muslim is likely to be tolerated as a "good Muslim." While skin color, hair texture, facial features, and other phenotypical traits still affect the racialization process, phenotype is subsumed by the now-racialized Muslim identity. Put another way, a White-presenting immigrant practicing Muslim named Mohamed cannot escape Islamophobia or anti-Muslim racism in the post-9/11 era.

Two international factors interact with two domestic factors to produce this outcome. American imperial designs and Orientalism interact with coercive assimilationism of immigrants and White Protestant supremacy. The interplay of these four factors produce five typologies of the Racial Muslim: (1) Religious Dissident, (2) Religious, (3) Secular Dissident, (4) Secular, and (5) Former Muslim. The typology partially explains the interplay between the state's prioritization of certain Muslims in national security enforcement, on the one hand, and individual identity performances by Muslims seeking to avoid the material and dignitary harms arising from racialization, on the other.[20]

Secularism and support for American militarism in Muslim-majority countries signify higher levels of assimilation into White Christian normalcy.[21] The Secular Racial Muslim thus is the least threatening, both for liberal elites and for religious conservatives. In contrast, Islamic beliefs and practices coupled with dissent against American foreign policy make him a Religious Dissident Racial Muslim targeted for surveillance, prosecution, deportation, denaturalization, and private discrimination. The Former Racial Muslim, meanwhile, serves as a native informant who legitimizes repression of the other four categories of Racial Muslims.

Religious Dissident Racial Muslim

Muslims experiencing the most harm from Islamophobia and national security practices are the political dissidents (as defined by the US government and American elites) who practice Islam. Accused of terrorism, barbarity, and inassimilability, the Religious Dissident Racial Muslim is the prime target of government antiterrorism operations, frequently discriminated against at work and in public, and portrayed in the media as a threat to American security.[22] In vociferously challenging American empire abroad and racism at home, Religious Dissident Racial Muslims attract government repression, which in turn chills other devout Muslims, who remain silent about their dissenting political views and hide their religious beliefs.[23] The result is a coercive depoliticization and secularization of immigrant Muslims in exchange for less discriminatory treatment.

Religious Racial Muslim

Less dangerous, though still subject to heightened state scrutiny and public suspicions, is the Religious Racial Muslim, who is either apolitical or supports mainstream politics particularly with regard to US policy in Muslim-majority countries.[24] Even though Muslims in this category do not challenge the political status quo, their religiosity alone prompts state scrutiny and public suspicions. Praying five times a day, fasting during Ramadan, growing a beard or wearing a hijab, socializing with other religious Muslims, attending Islamic school, and regularly attending a mosque triggers government suspicion. Just being religious makes a Muslim vulnerable to recruitment by Islamic terrorist groups, according to this racialized reasoning. The Religious Racial Muslim's visible religious identity and lifestyle also triggers suspicions by neighbors and coworkers influenced by right-wing Islamophobic conspiracy theories of Muslims as a fifth column or Trojan horse waiting to Islamicize America from within.[25]

Secular Dissident Racial Muslim

More palatable to mainstream White Judeo-Christian America but still racialized as outsiders are Secular Dissident Racial Muslims. They are secular in lifestyle but hold dissident political views. Even though Secular Dissident Racial Muslims may not practice their faith, their political views are still attributed to a nominal Muslim identity. Opposition to American foreign policy, especially regarding Muslim-majority countries and the Israel-Palestine conflict, and antiracist domestic activism marks an immigrant Muslim as disloyal.[26] That they are not overtly practicing Muslims (e.g., secularized in lifestyle) assures the government of the unlikeliness of recruitment by Islamic terrorist groups. But their support for Black Lives Matter, undocumented immigrant rights, and Palestinian human rights makes them nefarious Muslims who strategically hide their orthodox religious views as part of an anti-American conspiracy. In the end, they are treated as suspect Muslim immigrants who should be investigated, deported, and prosecuted as punishment for challenging White supremacy at home and American imperialism abroad.[27]

Secular Racial Muslim

The most palatable and least dangerous Muslim is secular and politically mainstream or apolitical. Secular Racial Muslims identify as Muslim but do not practice their religion of birth, believe American culture is colorblind, and support American foreign policy. Secular Racial Muslims—commonly referred to as moderate Muslims—attempt to pass as not Muslim to avoid discrimination. The Secular Racial Muslim is the manifestation of the model minority who works hard, doesn't complain, believes America is the best country in the world, secularizes their lifestyle according to Anglo-Protestant norms, and joins majoritarian condemnations of dissident and religious Muslims.[28]

Secular Racial Muslims are the exception that liberal and conservative Islamophobes point to when arguing that they do not believe all Muslims are terrorists. If only all Muslims lived and assimilated like the Secular Racial Muslim, goes the narrative propagated by liberals and moderate conservative Americans, then Islamophobia would not be such a serious problem. Hence Muslims are to blame for the rise in anti-Muslim bigotry. In the end, Secular Racial Muslims stand the highest chance of becoming honorary Whites should American national identity expand from Judeo-Christian to Abrahamic—a topic I explore in the final chapter of this book.

Former Racial Muslim

Finally, the ideal Muslim for White Judeo-Christian normativity is the Former Racial Muslim who converts from Islam (preferably to Protestantism) and serves as a native informant.[29] Former Muslims such as Ayaan Hirsi Ali, Wafa Sultan, and Nonie Darwish are frequently invited to give media interviews and public presentations to religious conservative audiences where they validate claims that Islam is violent, evil, misogynist, and antithetical to Western civilization.[30] Meanwhile, secular liberals point to female Former Racial Muslims and Secular Racial Muslims to validate their belief that Muslim women need saving by the West.[31] The Former Racial Muslim's portrayals of Islam as misogynistic convince Christians that they are not racist in concluding the "Islamic world" is illiberal and violent.[32] The Former Racial Muslims' role as validators of Islamophobia evinces the permanence of their racialized Muslim identities, notwithstanding their formal departure from the faith. Although their tokenized status allows them to escape the worst consequences of anti-Muslim racism, Former Racial Muslims are still racial outsiders.

THEORETICAL UNDERPINNINGS OF THE RACIAL MUSLIM

The terms *Religious* and *Secular*, as I use them in the typologies discussed above, are not intended to be objective descriptors but rather ascriptive terms based on Anglo-Protestant normativity that dominates American culture and race politics at a particular time. For example, a Muslim who wears a headscarf, has a beard, or prays the daily prayers is perceived as religious in mainstream American society today. In contrast, a Muslim who drinks alcohol, engages in premarital sex, or associates exclusively with non-Muslims is perceived as secularized and modern. Whether that person is in fact religious or secular according to Islamic tenets is not what determines where they fall in the Racial Muslim typology. Rather, it is how they are perceived by those doing the racializing. Those perceptions in turn determine how a Muslim is treated by coworkers, neighbors, friends, and members of the general public—as well as the US government.

Similarly, if one falls within the Religious Racial Muslim and the Secular Racial Muslim typologies, one is not a political dissident as perceived by mainstream American society. This often translates into being either uncritical or supportive of liberalism, American empire, and neoliberal economic policies. Should mainstream politics change in the future, so too will the boundaries of what constitutes a dissident in the Racial Muslim typology. Whether a particular Muslim is treated as a (nondissident) Religious Racial Muslim or (nondissident) Secular Racial Muslim by the government or private actors is determined by mainstream Judeo-Christian norms, which fluctuate over time depending on domestic and international developments. Put another way, I am not making claims as to what Islam really is or what a Muslim actually believes but rather what the US government and the American public perceive Islam and Muslims to be—which can be dispositive in the racialization of Muslim identity.

I begin the intellectual journey by historicizing the racialization of religion in the United States because in American society religious freedom has always been circumscribed by race. In examining the experiences of Jews, Catholics, and Mormons from the turn of the twentieth century until World War II in chapters 2, 3, and 4, I illustrate how immigrants have always had to conform to Anglo-Saxon Protestant norms, language, and lifestyles in order to access socioeconomic privileges and legal rights of first-class citizenship.[33] Thus, structural assimilation through English-only rules, staunch individualism, and capitalism undergirds American national identity.[34] Immigrants, in turn, are expected to divest their foreign language, culture, dress, and lifestyle.[35] They are also expected to "Protestantize" their faith in ways that translate into a secularization and individualization of their religious communities. Failure to do so results in stigmatizing and discriminatory responses at best or in physical exclusion and criminalization at worst.

Four phenomena explain the historical racialization of Muslims before and after the September 11 attacks: (1) White Christian dominance, (2) American empire, (3) imputation of racial attributes based on religious beliefs and practices, and (4) racialized borders of religious freedom.

White Christian Dominance

Early American Protestant leaders perpetuated Europeans' depictions of Muslims as violent and blasphemous. Tellingly, the famous American Protestant theologian Jonathan Edwards attacked Islam by comparing it to Roman Catholicism.[36] He described both religions as kingdoms erected by the devil to oppose the kingdom of Christ. Because Islam was purportedly established through violence, Edwards claimed, Christ would destroy it as one of the forces of the devil at the battle of Armageddon. Indeed, the demise of Islam was a sign of the second coming of Christ for some American Evangelicals—a belief that motivates contemporary Evangelicals' support for Israel's dehumanization of the Palestinians.[37]

During the formation of the American Republic, Islam was also deployed as a political foil. For example, Thomas Paine's book *Common Sense* contrasted America's status as an "asylum for liberty" with Islam's despotic empire of superstition and fanaticism.[38] Although Thomas Jefferson emphasized that "Mahometans" should be protected under his vision of religious freedom, as Denise Spellberg's book, *Thomas Jefferson's Quran*, meticulously demonstrates, Jefferson's commitments to religious pluralism were never tested.[39] The only Muslims in America at the time were enslaved Africans not considered fully human under law.[40] John Adams and Thomas Jefferson referred to each other as "Oriental despots" and "Mahometans" as derogatory epithets during the 1800 presidential election, revealing the extent to which Islam was the antithesis of American notions of liberty and freedom.[41]

In chapters 5 and 6, I demonstrate how the association of Islam with violent barbarism predated the September 11 attacks. As far back as the Crusades, Europeans portrayed Islam as an evil threatening Christian civilization.[42] Remnants of European Orientalism and colonialism in the "Old World" combined with racism, settler colonialism, and xenophobia in the "New World" still shape contemporary American culture. Entrenched Orientalist stereotypes of people from the Middle East, therefore, contribute to the redefinition of Islam as an aggressive political ideology antithetical to Christianity in the post-9/11 era.[43]

American Empire

Racialization of Islam as an evil and violent ideology combined with American coercive assimilationism do not fully explain the social construction of the Racial Muslim. American hegemony in the Middle East after World War I required a narrative that morally justified military interventions in Muslim-majority countries. As expansion of its global influence became a priority in the second half of the twentieth century, the US government took great interest in controlling the large oil reserves of Saudi Arabia and other Middle Eastern countries.[44] Meanwhile, Europe's dissolution of the Ottoman Empire after World War I and mounting pogroms in Eastern Europe triggered mass migration and land purchases by European Jews seeking a permanent homeland in Palestine with little regard for the rights of indigenous Palestinians.

In 1948, when President Harry S. Truman became the first head of state to recognize the state of Israel after Jewish militias violently expelled approximately 700,000 Palestinians, America dealt a decisive blow to Palestinian aspirations for self-determination.[45] During an era when indigenous populations around the world were fighting European colonial powers for their independence, US support for Israel—which became nearly unconditional after 1967—coupled with US extraction of oil in the Persian Gulf established the United States as an imperialist nation in the Middle East.[46] Since then, the United States has been a major player in regional geopolitics through economic and military aid to dictator allies, business dealings, military interventions, and covert intelligence operations against Arab nationalist leaders.[47]

To persuade Americans of the need for foreign interference, the government needed to persuade them that Arabs (incorrectly presumed to all be Muslim) and Muslims were a threat to national interests.[48] Thus, when the Organization of Arab Petroleum Exporting Countries (OPEC) proclaimed an oil embargo to protest US support for Israel during the 1973 war with Egypt, the media portrayed Arabs as greedy, backward sheikhs seeking to destroy the US economy. And when Iranians rose up in the tens of millions to overthrow the US-supported shah of Iran in 1979, American politicians condemned them as angry, irrational mobs, as opposed to revolutionaries seeking a regime that served their interests. Few Americans knew of the shah's repressive policies and mass corruption (with US assistance) that prompted Iranians to revolt. Nor did they differentiate between Farsi-speaking Iranians and Arabic-speaking Arabs in the collective punishment of Middle Eastern immigrants in the United States.

All the while, the US media and politicians portrayed Palestinian resistance fighters as irredeemably irrational, bloodthirsty terrorists rather than an occupied people fighting for self-determination and human rights. The First Gulf War, during which the United States defended Kuwait against Iraqi invasion, was sold to Americans as necessary to stop Saddam Hussein's despotic transgressions—despite US military aid to Hussein during the Iran-Iraq War in the 1980s.[49]

Each time the United States engaged militarily and politically in the Middle East, stereotypes of Arabs and Muslims as irrational, violent, and backward were reified in American culture. So, when the 1995 Oklahoma City bombings shocked Americans across the country, media pundits presumed Arab Muslims were the perpetrators.[50] That the bomber turned out to be a Christian White nationalist, Timothy McVeigh, did not alter the entrenched stereotypes of Muslims. Nor did it cause Americans to suspect all Americans who are White and Christian as prone to right wing extremism.

Racial Attributes Imputed by Religion

Double standards lie at the heart of racialization. Members of the dominant racial-religious group are treated and judged by their individual actions, whereas members of subordinated groups are presumed guilty based on the misdeeds of a few individuals who share their religious identities or national origins. For example, Palestinians and Iranians abroad are labeled terrorists, so too are Palestinian Americans and Iranian Americans, unless each can individually prove otherwise. Doing so requires taxing identity performances that appease coercive assimilationism and pressures to secularize.

In chapter 7, I show how the racialization of religion applies to Muslims. I interrogate why Christian conservatives who hate Muslims do not believe they are betraying religious freedom principles when they support Muslim travel bans, oppose the construction of mosques, or approve singling out Muslims in countering terrorism.[51] They reconcile the contradictions by redefining Islam, by placing it outside the purview of religion. To them, Islam is not a religion but a political ideology.[52] Islam is not holy; it is man-made by savages.

As a result, defaming, harassing, and attacking Muslims is not un-American or antithetical to religious liberty principles. To the contrary, it is as rational as rounding up Japanese Americans after the attack on Pearl Harbor—when the US government determined they were godless pagans incapable of being loyal to a liberal, democratic America.[53] Law in the post-9/11 era is instrumental in creating racial projects comparable to Japanese American internment that make policy, shape state action, and affect Muslims' daily personal interactions.[54]

This leads to an exploration of how law is deployed to normatively exclude Muslims from the realm of legally protected religion, which I address in chapters 8 and 9. Both religious conservatives and secular liberals, under the leadership of George W. Bush, Barack Obama, and Donald Trump, adopted national security policies subordinating Muslims, albeit to different degrees.[55] The securitization of Muslim identity through state actions that violate Muslims' civil liberties and rights are deemed politically justified by the American public.[56] Private acts that would otherwise be viewed as religiously discriminatory are rationalized as patriotic vigilance or unfortunate consequences of necessary national security policies.

Racialized Borders of Religious Freedom

My theoretical frame, thus, begs the question, what is the future of the Racial Muslim? Is it a permanent fixture in American race politics or a temporal construction that will dissipate over time? Will Muslims' call for a new Abrahamic national identity to replace the current Judeo-Christian identity succeed in bringing (some) Muslims into the fold of Whiteness and, by extension, first-class citizenship? Will Muslim identity become deracialized insofar as an individual's phenotypical traits determine how they are socially raced: White, Brown, Asian, or Black? Or will Muslim identity be a racial marker that permanently bars immigrant Muslims (alongside African American Muslims, who collectively experience second-class citizenship on account of their Blackness) from the full dignitary and material benefits of citizenship?

These questions animate the final chapter of the book as I examine the responses of Racial Muslims, ranging from neoliberal multicultural interfaith initiatives to progressive cross-racial coalitions confronting systemic racism. Although calls for a new Abrahamic American national identity may decrease discrimination against (some) immigrant Muslims, a new exclusionary racial boundary will harm followers of non-monotheistic faiths. Anticipating this peril, a growing number of young American Muslims have joined cross-racial solidarity movements seeking to eliminate America's racial-religious hierarchy and privileging of Whiteness.[57] They recognize that replacing Judeo-Christian identity with Abrahamic identity merely continues the systemic racialization of religion.

THE LIMITATIONS OF THEORIZING THE RACIALIZATION OF MUSLIMS

Historicizing and contextualizing the pervasive discrimination against Muslims in the post-9/11 era defies a tidy analysis along lines of religious freedom or racial bigotry. Without looking at how race and religion work together, we cannot understand how Muslims are racialized, including those whose phenotype presents as White. An examination of discrimination against Muslims in the United States is further complicated by their rich diversity of race, ethnicity, class, and immigration status. Although the total Muslim population is in dispute because the US Census does not track religious affiliation, estimates range from four million to six million, making Muslims approximately 1 percent of the US population.[58]

Muslims are the most racially diverse faith community in the United States. Contrary to popular belief, Arabs make up a minority of Muslims, at only 30 percent, while 75 percent of Arabs in the United States are Christian.[59] Approximately 30 percent of Muslims are African American, 30 percent are Middle Eastern and North African (classified as White in the US Census), 30 percent are South Asian, 5 percent are Latino, and 5 percent are multiracial.[60] Notably, 70 percent of Muslims are immigrants or children of immigrants due to changes in US immigration laws in 1965 that lifted Asian exclusion laws that had applied to Muslims outside of Europe.[61] Thus 80 percent of Muslim immigrants are naturalized US citizens.[62]

Muslims are also politically and religiously diverse.[63] Although they overwhelmingly identified as Republican before 9/11, less then 15 percent vote Republican today.[64] Among the majority who vote as Democrats, some Muslims are centrist liberals, while a growing number who came of age in the post-9/11 era identify with the progressive wing of the Democratic Party.[65] Likewise, levels of religiosity fall on a wide spectrum, from practicing Muslims to secularized Muslims whose mosque attendance and prayer is limited to being a "Eid Muslim," similar to an Easter Christian or a Hanukkah Jew.

For these reasons, no single book can adequately theorize the experiences of state and private discrimination against such diverse communities. This book is no exception. The most glaring limitation is my purposeful focus on immigrant Muslims who arrived on US shores after 1965. Although I take into account how the racialization of African American Muslims has shaped the racialization of immigrant Muslims (see chapters 3, 5, and 6), I agree with Sylvia Chan-Malik, and Zain Abdullah that the racialization of African American Muslims is intertwined with the enslavement of Africans, of whom approximately 30 percent were estimated to be Muslim.[66] I also concur with Edward Curtis in his assessment that African American Muslims are racialized as Black first, resulting in their Black identity intersecting with their Muslim identity to create experiences of private and state discrimination uniquely different from those of immigrant Muslims.[67]

While both immigrant and African American Muslims suffer subordination arising from White Christian dominance, different factors shape their racialization and consequent forms of discrimination. The root cause of discrimination against African American Muslims lies largely in the legacies of slavery that produced Jim Crow segregation laws, lynchings, mass incarceration, school-to-jail pipelines, and the extreme poverty of Black inner-city ghettos.[68] In contrast, discrimination against immigrant Muslims is animated largely by Orientalism, American empire in Muslim-majority countries, xenophobia, and theologically based Islamophobia. A book about anti-Muslim racism that merges the experiences of immigrant and African American Muslims thus risks erasure of the important, nuanced distinctions between the two groups' past and present subordination.

Furthermore, my examination of European Orientalism and American empire is focused exclusively on the Middle East and North Africa. Although the complex relationship between Europe and the Indian subcontinent shapes the stereotypes and treatment of the hundreds of millions of Muslims in South Asia, US political and economic engagement with Muslim-majority countries in the Middle East and North Africa in the twentieth century has had a disproportionate impact on the racialization of immigrant Muslims in the United States regardless of their national origin. In the post-9/11 era in particular, the way in which anti-Muslim racism operates does not distinguish between a Muslim of Pakistani, Indian, Bangladeshi, North African, or Middle Eastern descent. The Racial Muslim is a homogenizing social construct defined by the past and current relations of the United States with the Middle East.

Gender also plays an instrumental role in how a Muslim is racialized. For example, Muslim men disproportionately bear the brunt of national security and immigration practices because of the masculinized stereotypes of Muslims as terrorists, despotic, violent, and misogynistic.[69] While women can also be racialized as violent, as was the case with the so-called Brides of ISIS that triggered state scrutiny of devout Muslim women,[70] Muslim women wearing headscarves tend to be especially vulnerable to hate crimes. Moreover, many private actors of violence against Muslims target women wearing headscarves because they may be perceived to be associated with male terrorists and sympathetic to terrorism by virtue of their religious identity. Perceptions that women are too weak to defend themselves physically make Muslim women especially vulnerable to racial violence.[71]

Nonetheless, the political, economic, and social factors shaping the social construction of the Racial Muslim develop within systems of hypermasculinity and patriarchy. Thus, I use the male pronoun in reference to the Racial Muslim while acknowledging that females are also Racial Muslims. I leave it to others to expand on the intersection of race and gender in the social construction of the Racial Muslim.[72]

Like any book taking on controversial contemporary topics through a normative lens, this book is likely to attract opposition by members of groups that benefit from existing racial-religious hierarchies. One form of such opposition may be critiques of my use of terminology relating to normative concepts whose definitions are perennially in dispute within and across disciplines. For these reasons, my intervention is not to develop an authoritative definition of religion, religious freedom, or race. Rather, I aim to provide a theoretical, normative framework that attempts to explain why and how Muslims are discriminated against on account of their religious identities (whether nominal or substantive) in the post-9/11 era. For this reason, a clarification of my use of terminology is warranted.

A CLARIFICATION OF TERMINOLOGY

Numerous concepts undergird my argument, many of which are contested within the scholarly literature. Thus, a clarification on how I use those concepts is in order. First, I am not taking a position as to what constitutes a Muslim, Islam, or religion. I take at face value a person's or community's identification as Muslim while acknowledging that non-Muslims, such as Sikhs, Hindus, and Arab Christians, are mistaken for Muslims based on stereotypes portrayed in the media and public discourse. While there is a robust literature on what constitutes religion, my analysis accepts Islam as a religion for purposes of examining the limitations of normative and legal protections of religious freedom in the United States. My analysis is based on ascriptive definitions of what constitutes Islam and Muslim identity.[73]

Second, *race* is a social construction, not a biological fact, that has real-life material consequences. Accordingly, I adopt Eduardo Bonilla-Silva's definition of race as "an organizing principle of social relationships that shapes the identity of individual actors at the micro level and shapes all spheres of social life at the macro level."[74] That is, racism arises from racialized social systems in societies where "economic, political, social, and ideological levels are partially structured by the placement of actors in racial categories or races."[75] The classification of people based on racial groups arises from cognitive processes entrenched in social interactions, not from biological differences.[76] Put simply, race is the social construction that transforms the ideology of racism into biological racism.[77]

In applying a structural racism analysis, I adopt Derrick Bell's "Black-White paradigm" and Joe Feagin's "white racial frame," which argue that Blacks are permanently at the bottom of the American racial hierarchy and Whites are permanently at the top.[78] Racial stratification according to the Black-White paradigm causes "different races to experience positions of subordination and super-ordination in society and develop different interests."[79] Races at the bottom of the hierarchy are depicted as savage, uncivilized, and unfit for self-government; races at the top are depicted as civilized, liberal, and democratic.[80] The systemic analytical approach differs from the social psychology approach that characterizes racism as an individual phenomenon arising from prejudice and stereotypes.[81] To combat racism, according to the social psychology approach, individuals need to be educated in order to change their minds about how they perceive and treat particular races. In contrast, systemic racism that legitimates conquest, colonization, enslavement and neocolonial labor immigration requires a deracialization of the structures, laws, and policies on which a society is built in order to decrease racism.

My theoretical framework takes the systemic racialization theories one step further to argue that the American racial hierarchy is more accurately described as a racial-religious hierarchy. Phenotypical race in American society has been and continues to be a central factor in the placement of people in a racialized social system.[82] However, religion also plays a dispositive role in racialization. This has always been true for Blacks, who were racialized as heathen and inferior based on biblical stories labeling them as the children of Ham cursed into slavery.[83] It was also true for religious minorities such as Jews, Catholics, and Mormons in the nineteenth century and first half of the twentieth and for Muslims today—albeit for different reasons and with different material harms.

The most obvious implications of the systemic Black-White paradigm for Muslims is the racialization of African American Muslims first as Black, with their Muslim identity racializing them as a particularly dangerous type of Black person, as witnessed by the government's treatment of the Nation of Islam during the Cold War era. In contrast, immigrant Muslims and their descendants, who are the primary focus of this book, are foreigners first;

their Muslim identity then racializes them as terrorists and uncivilized. As a result, America's diverse immigrant Muslim communities find themselves facing bigotry in overtly religious terms.

My use of *racialization* adopts the definition proffered by Robert Miles: "a dialectical process by which meaning is attributed to particular biological features of human beings, as a result of which individuals may be assigned to a general category of persons which reproduces itself biologically."[84] Sets of characteristics viewed as inherent to members of a group because of their physical or cultural traits are consequently ascribed to them. Put another way, when a religion is racialized, the religious beliefs and practices of the adherents are associated with cultural traits, which in turn are surrogates for biological traits.[85]

Islamic tenets, regardless of whether practiced or believed in fact, impute to Muslims inherent cultural traits that operate biologically to make them inferior in a White Judeo-Christian supremacist society. For example, believing in (nonviolent) jihad, polygamy, Sharia, hijab, fasting, hajj, and the Prophet Muhammad is associated with a Muslim's purported innate sense of despotism, savagery, and illiberalism. For both religious conservatives and secular liberal elites, these religious beliefs and practices cast Muslims as outsiders to American national identity; more specifically, it casts Muslims as suspected terrorists. A purported "Muslim culture" is taken as fixed, deterministic, and essentialist such that Islamophobia collapses into scientific racism. A Muslim woman's covering of her hair and body confirms Americans' beliefs that Islam is misogynistic, which then prompts calls to "save Muslim women" by means of imperial projects.[86]

I use the term *religious freedom* frequently throughout the book as the most obvious (though not exclusive) civil right denied to Muslims as a result of racialization. My usage of the term is not limited to a narrow legal definition as determined by a court of law pursuant to the First Amendment of the US Constitution or a statute. Religious freedom also entails the absence of fear, stigma, or material punishment for openly practicing one's religion. For Muslims, religious freedom includes building and attending mosques, praying at work, wearing a hijab, donning a beard, sending children to Islamic schools, having Muslim names, operating and donating to Muslim charities, establishing Muslim civil society, and marrying and divorcing according to Islamic tenets—without public censure or government persecution. Not having to downplay or hide one's Muslim identity from fear of physical, economic, or dignitary harm is also an index of religious freedom.

Finally, I acknowledge the lively debate as to whether *anti-Muslim racism* or *Islamophobia* most accurately describes the systemic subordination of Muslims in the post-9/11 era. My analysis treats Islamophobia as a causal factor in the outcome of anti-Muslim racism.[87] That is, anti-Muslim racism is the operationalization of Islamophobia. *Islamophobia* first became a term of art in a 1997 report by the Runnymede Trust's Commission on British Muslims and Islamophobia titled "Islamophobia: A Challenge for Us All."[88] Defined in the report as "the dread, hatred, and hostility towards Islam and Muslims perpetrated by a series of closed views that imply and attribute negative and derogatory stereotypes and beliefs to Muslims," Islamophobia results in practices that discriminated against Muslims through myriad state and private mechanisms, which fall under the rubric "anti-Muslim racism." Anti-Muslim racism, thus, occurs because Islam is portrayed as "1) monolithic and static; 2) separate and 'other,' not sharing the values of other cultures; 3) irrational, primitive and inferior to the West; 4) aggressive, violent and implicated in a clash of civilizations; 5) an ideology used to promote political and military interests; 6) intolerant towards western critiques; 7) deserving of the discriminatory practices towards and exclusion of Muslims; and 8) making anti-Muslim hostility natural and normal."[89]

Critics of the term *Islamophobia* argue that it does not contest racial hierarchy but rather incorporates the rhetoric of color-blindness and the post-racial paradigm by adopting the individualized social psychology view of how prejudice works. As such, Islamophobia suggests "individual fears and anxieties that can be alleviated and overcome if one meets a Muslim, or reads the Qur'an, or comes to know something of Islam."[90] This in turn causes Muslims to seek model minority or honorary White status rather than eradicate the systematic racial-religious hierarchy subordinating Black and Brown communities in the United States.

My concern here is not so much whether to use *Islamophobia* or *anti-Muslim racism* as it is to adopt a theoretical framing that explains the material consequences of the systematic racialization of Muslims. I take the position that engaging in Islamophobia that restricts Muslims' religious freedom and other civil rights is a product of systemic racism. My working definition of *Islamophobia* and *anti-Muslim racism*, thus, is an exaggerated fear of, hatred of, and hostility to Islam and Muslims by the state and the public as a result of imputed inferior biological and cultural traits based on religious identity *that produce* systemic bias, discrimination, marginalization, and exclusion of Muslims from social, political, and civic life.[91]

. . .

What I hope to accomplish in this book is to demonstrate that religion has always shaped and continues to shape American conceptions of race and that racism circumscribes religious freedom. After the September 11 attacks, all Muslims became raced as outsiders to American (White Judeo-Christian) national identity regardless of identity performance, class, religiosity, and phenotype. Some Muslims resist their racialization by attempting to shift national identity to an Abrahamic one, thereby emulating efforts by Jews and Catholics to make America a Judeo-Christian nation a century earlier. But such efforts shortsightedly leave intact the racial-religious hierarchy by continuing the subordination of non-monotheistic faiths, which I explore in chapter 9.

If national identity expands to include Muslims, then an individual's phenotype, class, assimilation, and national origin—as opposed to Muslim identity—will determine their place in the racial-religious hierarchy.[92] If their physical traits and skin color sufficiently resemble Europeans', subgroups of Muslims will experience the same opportunities for racial transformation into Whiteness as did the Jews, Catholics, and Mormons during the second half of the twentieth century. Some immigrant Muslims and all African American Muslims, however, will be raced as non-White on account of their skin color and physical features.

While class certainly exacerbates or mitigates harms arising from racialization, class does not eliminate the role of race as a master category of the social, economic, and political order.[93] Indeed, class tends to facilitate some Muslim Americans' assimilationist responses to racialization as they become the "moderate" Secular Racial Muslims buttressing the criminalization of "extremist" Religious Dissident Racial Muslims.

Of course, this triggers another question: why would or should immigrant Muslims seek to be White, honorary White, or a model minority through accommodationist identity performance rather than challenge American racism on its face?[94] To be sure, I am not arguing that Muslims should normatively seek to become White or honorary White. Rather, I am arguing that so long as the United States retains a predominantly White Judeo-Christian national identity, Muslims will remain outsiders who cannot attain the full dignitary, legal, and material benefits of citizenship. The solution is to change our national identity to reflect the diversity of races, cultures, and religions of Americans and to eliminate the ensuing racial-religious hierarchy that privileges those at the top. Until then, each community and each generation will continue to wrestle with how to define its identity in a racialized society where one's ascribed race affects her material and dignitary rights.[95]

Two decades after that momentous day in 2001 that changed the lives of so many people, the US government and members of the public have yet to stop punishing American Muslim communities collectively for the criminal acts of nineteen foreign hijackers who claimed to kill in the name of Islam. Irrespective of the future of American race politics, and Muslims' place in it, this book is a humble attempt to equip scholars, advocates, and policy makers with a deeper understanding of why a religious minority faces such blatant discrimination in a nation that prides itself on, and legally privileges, religious freedom. When we acknowledge the disconnect between our ideals and our practices, only then can we fulfill our aspirations for a pluralistic and more inclusive American society.

ONE

When American Racism Quashes Religious Freedom

The guiding hand of providence did not create this new nation of America for ourselves alone, but for a higher cause: the preservation and extension of the sacred fire of human liberty. This is America's solemn duty.

PRESIDENT RONALD REAGAN,
Bicentennial Celebration of the US Constitution (September 17, 1987)

AMERICA IS A BASTION OF RELIGIOUS FREEDOM, a land where persecuted religious minorities find refuge from the tyranny of the majority. So goes the narrative that is taught in schools across the nation and that permeates American culture.[1] And yet Muslims in America have found religious freedom in practice more myth than reality.

Law enforcement agencies surveil mosques, Islamic schools, and Muslim-owned businesses. The US government scrutinizes Muslims' personal associations, travel, and religious practices. Following the government's lead, private citizens distrust Muslim neighbors, coworkers, and customers. As a result, Muslims have experienced unprecedented levels of discrimination at work and schools, as well as mosque vandalizations and hate crimes.[2]

That Muslims are experiencing overt discrimination at a time when contestation over religious liberty is a national issue brings into sharp relief the fact that religious freedom is not equally available to all faiths. Conservative Evangelical Christians decry a secular assault by liberal elites with regard to contraception, abortion, same-sex marriage, and religion in schools, yet many simultaneously support state practices that quash Muslims' religious freedoms.

This begs the question, Why, for a critical mass of Americans, are Muslims' rights to be safe in their mosques, wear their religious garb without fear of discrimination, and live as first-class citizens not subject to religious freedom protections? And why do the same people who defend religious freedom for Christians simultaneously support violating the civil rights of Muslims?

The explanation, I argue, is that Muslims are treated like a suspect race, not a religious minority. In turn, Islam is placed in the realm of politics, and more specifically, national security, not religion. State and private discriminatory practices contrary to American religious freedom ideals are considered rational and patriotic. This racialization of Muslims has had devastating effects on the lives of millions of people in the United States.

Donald J. Trump's ascendance to the presidency of the United States exposes the thinness of America's commitment to religious freedom and the deep entrenchment of racism. Trump campaigned and won on his bravado, guised as "Patriot Talk," that ranged from calling for the United States to register Muslims in a database and barring them from entering the country to mass surveillance of mosques and calling on Muslims to spy on each other.[3] His right-wing Christian base saw no contradictions between such overtly anti-Muslim policies and their commitments to religious freedom.[4]

Such overt religious animus today demonstrates the enduring legacy of the racialization of religion in American society—an understudied topic in legal and social science literature. Accordingly, this book problematizes American religious freedom by interrogating how and why a country where religious liberty is a founding principle produces such overt prejudice and discrimination against Muslims. How do Americans in the twenty-first century who hold unfavorable views of immigrant Muslims reconcile their suspicions with the nation's commitments to religious freedom? Exploring how American racism has historically quashed religious freedom offers some insight into this vexing question.

As the United States was founded as a White Protestant settler nation dependent on the labor of enslaved peoples, its social hierarchies are shaped first and foremost by phenotypically defined race.[5] A person's skin color, hair texture, facial features, and national origin determine where they fit in American racial categories.

Because Whiteness is intertwined with (Protestant) Christianity, religion also works to racialize people. An ethos that liberty, equality, and self-governance are inalienable rights of Anglo-Saxon Protestant settlers pursuing their Manifest Destiny has long animated American religious freedom norms.[6] Indeed, Anglo-Saxon triumphalism bolstered the Puritans' belief that they were God's chosen people on a religious pilgrimage to create a Christian nation in the New World without regard for the rights or freedoms of Native peoples, enslaved peoples, and non-Christians.[7] These settlers believed God granted favor to them to inherit America, and in return they would establish a Christian Protestant nation.[8] Simultaneously, Whiteness (socially constructed and expanded over time) protects the status of economic and political White elites at the expense of racial minorities.[9] And Christian identity is an indicator of Whiteness, particularly as it applies to legal and normative citizenship.

Thus, the narrative that a Protestant White majority committed to rational, enlightened principles of religious pluralism such that persons of different faiths could coexist in harmony and learn from each other is more aspirational than reality.[10] Intolerance of religions deemed a threat to Anglo Protestantism has been entrenched in American culture since its founding,[11] whether it was Catholics who were legally discriminated against in state constitutions or Jews suspected as saboteurs. Historically, full religious freedom was reserved for White Protestants.

The racialization of immigrant Muslims in the contemporary era demonstrates the extent to which Christianity continues to be intertwined with Whiteness, both for religious conservatives and for liberal secularists. Indeed, one-third of (religious conservative) Americans today hold steadfast to an ethnoculturalism based on their belief that one must be Christian to truly be an American.[12] Meanwhile, secular liberal Americans racialize immigrant Muslims not necessarily because they are not Christian, but for failing to adhere to modernity's transcendence beyond religiosity. Muslim religiosity as perceived by secular liberals is a threat to American liberalism.

Accordingly, I argue that a Protestant—later expanded to a Judeo-Christian—identity is integral to America's predominantly White national identity. Whether being Judeo-Christian is interpreted by religious conservatives as ascribing moral goodness or by liberal elites as ascribing secular goodness, not following the New or Old Testament makes Muslims outsiders. Until this national identity changes to include other faiths, Muslims will continue to suffer the negative consequences of non-White racial status.

To be sure, my exploration of the relationship between Muslim identity and Whiteness is not intended to argue that Muslims should seek to be White. Quite the contrary: I argue that the racialization of Islam as violent, illiberal, uncivilized, and anti-American dooms all Muslims to a lower societal caste regardless of their individual beliefs, lifestyles, and accomplishments. This is because Whiteness is linked to an individual's optimum access to opportunity, resources, wealth, and dignity in the United States. As the legal scholar Cheryl I. Harris contends, Whiteness is a property that imbues a higher status in society.[13] By showing how this phenomenon impacts immigrant Muslims, this book argues for dismantling the privileges associated exclusively with Whiteness.

THE MYTH OF AMERICAN RELIGIOUS LIBERTY

The ways in which religious groups are racialized in the United States vary according to the particular religion's relationship with Protestantism and Whiteness. Whether before the courts in citizenship proceedings, legislatures in segregation laws, or the executive branch in national security policy, religion has long been a surrogate for identifying threats to the colonists' and Founders' vision of a free White Protestant nation.[14] That is, a religion's interaction with the dominant Christian ideology at a particular historical moment shapes the racialization process and its material consequences for adherents of a minority faith.[15]

Initially limited to mainline Protestantism, American Christian identity later expanded to include Catholics, albeit after decades of anti-Catholic discrimination.[16] Jews, who are considered White today, were not socially White when their Eastern European immigrant ancestors arrived on America's shores more than a century ago, leading to significant anti-Semitism.[17] At a time when American national identity was firmly rooted in Anglo-Saxon Protestantism, both Catholics' and Jews' religious beliefs effectively darkened their skin color and imputed to them inferior biological traits.

After World War II, with the expansion of American national identity to a Judeo-Christian one, Jews were granted full cultural citizenship, as opposed to only legal citizenship.[18] With the inclusion of Jews and Catholics in the national identity came their transformation from inferior non-Anglo-Saxon "races" to culturally assimilable ethnic Whites. This path to first-class citizenship, however, was not available to African Americans, Native Americans, and Asian Americans. Their phenotype and skin color permanently exclude them from legal and social Whiteness—even if they convert to Christianity.

During the drafting of the US Constitution, both the Federalists and the Anti-Federalists advocated for separation of church and state.[19] Skeptical of institutional religion, the Founders agreed on the need to prohibit government assistance to religious authorities in order to prevent infringements on individuals' freedom of conscience, a concept that culminated in the establishment clause.[20] Meanwhile, the free exercise clause gave religious authorities and individuals the right to pursue their religious beliefs without government interference.[21] The protection of worship of White Protestant sects without government intervention—while not protecting other faiths practiced by those deemed racially inferior—undergirds American religious freedom.[22]

Notably, significant numbers of Americans at the time opposed the official separation of church and state as antithetical to their Protestant beliefs. They litigated, protested, and legislated to embed Christianity in law and governance. A culmination of these efforts starting in the colonial era involved repeated attempts by the National Reform Association (formerly called the Christian Amendment Movement), comprising eleven Protestant denominations, to demand a change to the preamble to the US Constitution to read:

> We the people of the United States, humbly acknowledging Almighty God as the source of all authority and power in civil government, the Lord Jesus Christ as the Ruler among the nations, and His revealed will as the supreme law of the land, in order to constitute a Christian government and, in order to form a more perfect union, establish Justice, insure domestic tranquility, provide for the common defense, promote the general welfare, and secure the inalienable rights and the blessings of liberty, and the pursuit of happiness to ourselves, our posterity, and all the people, do ordain and establish this Constitution for the United States of America.[23]

In 1864, that proposal failed, but subsequent political disputes over women's suffrage, funding of parochial schools, public school science curricula, and abortion have centered on the attempt to infuse Protestant Christian values in public life.

Notwithstanding the Founders' reliance on secular Enlightenment norms in developing America's governing principles, Protestantism dominates American political life and social structures until the present day.[24] Indeed, Alexis de Tocqueville's work on American democracy insightfully observed that the United States was a country that proclaimed its separation of church and state, and yet "there is no country in the world where the Christian religion retains a greater influence over the souls of men than in America."[25] His words still ring true today in many parts of the United States.

Race also dominates American social structures. Christian arguments morally justified the US government's subjugation of Native Americans and enslavement of Africans. In conjunction with pseudoscientific theories of eugenics and phrenology, Christian theology supported claims that Africans,

Native Americans, and Asians were uncivilized, barbaric, and unfit for self-governance.[26] That a sizable number of enslaved Africans were Muslims only confirmed Whites' beliefs in their inferiority.[27]

Race making thus plays a potent role in othering groups domestically and in empire building abroad. Through an ideologically and politically driven process, non-Whites are classified in racial terms to justify conquest, colonization, enslavement, indentured servitude, and exploitation.[28] According to Michael Omi and Howard Winant's racial formation framework, race is a master category in America around which power and wealth are distributed.[29] Race is therefore a key marker of difference that creates hierarchies that inform social structures, shape institutions, and distribute resources. Likewise, Eduardo Bonilla-Silva notes that race is a "social fact" similar to gender and class that exists wherever a racial structure is in place.[30] Ultimately, racialization is the process by which social and political meanings are attributed to particular biological features.[31]

In America, White Christian elites control racialization by ascribing different meanings and values to particular races, based on historical and contemporary circumstances, in ways that preserve White dominance at the top of the racial-religious hierarchy and non-Whites, Blacks in particular, at the bottom.[32] Certain physical and cultural differences signify inferiority or superiority in intelligence, capabilities, and worth.[33] As such, inferior biological, behavioral, and moral traits are assigned to non-Whites.[34]

When race interacts with religion, inferior biological traits become intrinsically associated with certain religious beliefs or the lack thereof. Intellectual inferiority, laziness, violence, barbarism, licentiousness, despotism, and being unfit for self-government have been associated with specific religions, such as Islam, Judaism, Catholicism, and non-monotheistic belief systems. White Christian elites deem these inferior traits a threat to the American Calvinist ethic that espouses industry, morality, frugality, enterprise, and individual liberty.[35] For these reasons, some American Protestants saw no contradiction between their faith and the enslavement, oppression, deportation, exclusion, and labor exploitation of, or denial of citizenship to, followers of non-Protestant religions.[36]

Racialization of religion not only reinforces the privileging of Protestantism (later expanded to Judeo-Christian) in American society but also bolsters White dominance.[37] Over time, religious justifications have been conflated with purported scientific theories of race to justify conquest and subordination of those deemed inferior.[38]

Although today's liberal elites claim that secularism and religious pluralism have supplanted Protestantism, the national identity to which immigrants are expected to assimilate is still defined by Anglo-Saxon Protestant norms.[39] What Robert N. Bellah termed "civil religion" incorporates Protestant norms into secular, nationalist beliefs, rites, and understandings that foster a collective identity.[40] For liberal secularists, civil religion centers the "American way of life," an idea that rallies the public when the nation is under attack.

For religious conservatives, Christianity does (and should) define American national identity. A telling example is then–Texas governor George W. Bush's declaration of June 10, 2000, as "Jesus Day."[41] Later, as president of the United States, Bush acted on his commitment to a Christian America through faith-based initiatives that funneled public funds to religious groups engaged in social services.[42]

Mirroring American colonial narratives grounded in European Orientalism, religious conservatives today deploy Christian theological portrayals of Muslims as violent, heathen, and antithetical to American democracy to justify excluding them from religious freedom protections. Muslims, in turn, become legitimate targets of myriad national security practices that infringe on their religious practices, threaten their liberty, and purge them from American soil.[43]

Muslims' racialized identities are in stark contrast to Americans' association of Christianity with peace, civilization, charity, and forgiveness, notwithstanding a historical record of violence in the name of Christianity.[44] That Christianity is treated as normal and Islam as aberrant causes wayward Christians to be treated as individuals while Muslims' wrongdoings represent the threat of the entire group. When Muslims are targeted by the national security and military-industrial complex, religious freedom is not under threat.[45] This racial logic underpins the social construction of the Racial Muslim.

The Racial Muslim construct collapses myriad ethnic and religious groups—including Armenian, Berber, Chaldean, Afghan, Pakistani, Druze, Sikh, Muslim, Persian, and Arab—into a single racialized identity that is "Arab-looking" and in the post-9/11 era looks like Osama bin Laden.[46] The Racial Muslim also includes male Sikhs, who are mistaken for Muslim because of their religiously mandated turbans. It conflates Arab with Muslim identity because of their names and phenotype. Hence Syrians, Turks,

Lebanese, or Palestinians (both Christian and Muslim), who in the past may have phenotypically passed as socially White, are now racialized as dangerous, suspect outsiders similar to the darker-skinned Pakistani, Yemeni, North African, and other immigrants from Muslim-majority countries.[47] After 9/11, religion does the work of phenotype and national origin to racialize millions of people in the United States.

Like other subordinated groups, the Racial Muslim moves up or down the racial-religious hierarchy depending on the political, social, and economic circumstances of the time. As I discuss in chapters 4 and 5, the othering of immigrant Muslims has fallen under myriad discursive constructs such as "the Arab," "the Moor," "the Turk," or "the Mahometan"—all of which connote inferiority and threat to the White Protestant.[48] In the post-9/11 era, the Racial Muslim is racialized as the extremist, jihadist, terrorist, and permanent foreigner but never the citizen, patriot, veteran, philanthropist, or some other favorable identity associated with Americanness.

· · ·

Inclusion of religious identity in notions of Americanness is itself a racial project. Being a member of the Judeo-Christian tradition brings with it a certain degree of material and dignitary privilege. A Christian or Jew who is also a racial minority makes one less threatening than minorities who belong to other faith traditions or have no faith at all.

In contrast, recent studies find that negative perceptions of Muslims are shifting from association with terrorism to being perceived as a cultural threat to American values.[49] Islamophobia situates Muslims outside the cultural mainstream on account of their religious identity.[50] As the rate of terrorism by Muslims remains low in the United States, the salience of politicians' accusations that Muslims do not support religious tolerance, gender equality, or democracy increases. These narratives, though complementary, stand in contrast to narratives that Muslims are security threats—the dominant stereotype for more than fifteen years after 9/11.

The interchangeable use of *culture* and *race* associated with Muslim religious identity does not refute the racialization process. It merely imputes immutability to culture. This neo-racism grounded in cultural racism is consistent with the racialization of Jews, Catholics, and Mormons a century ago, which I discuss in chapter 3.[51] Their religions purportedly produced a biological (and cultural) incapacity to practice the liberty, freethinking, and self-governance necessary for first-class citizenship in America. Just as Jews, Catholics, and Mormons sought to transition from being outsiders in America, many immigrant Muslims today want to prove that Islam is culturally compatible with Anglo-Protestant normativity.

Although the grounds and processes of racialization of Muslims are unique, the racialization of minority religions is not. Policies banning and expelling Muslim bodies harken back to a checkered history of religious persecution of Jews, Catholics, and Mormons. These practices also remind us of the role religion played in racializing Asian Americans, Native Americans, and African Americans, to which I now turn.

TWO

——————

The Color of Religion

The right to freedom of religion undergirds the very origin and existence of the United States. Many of our Nation's founders fled religious persecution abroad, cherishing in their hearts and minds the ideal of religious freedom.

INTERNATIONAL RELIGIOUS FREEDOM ACT

RELIGION IS ACCORDED A PRIVILEGED STATUS in American law and society.[1] Allowing people to practice their faith freely without government interference or private discrimination is a distinctive characteristic of a free society. In practice, however, not all religions have been granted these protections in the United States.[2] Congregants first had to be fit for self-governance to be eligible for religious freedom.[3] Being Protestant and White afforded one the full panoply of individual liberties in American society, while non-Whites and non-Protestants were presumed incapable of self-governance.[4]

As such, race played a crucial role in determining which religions were afforded social and legal protections from discrimination. A closer look at the racialization of religion in American history illuminates why Muslims, a religious minority, face systemic discrimination in the post-9/11 era, notwithstanding the privileging of religious liberty. Racialization also explains why some Americans who identify themselves as Christians committed to religious freedom do not believe it is un-American for the government to target Muslims in surveillance and antiterrorism enforcement, much less for the public to suspect all Muslims of disloyalty.

MANIFEST DESTINY: CIVILIZING NATIVE AMERICANS AND ENSLAVING AFRICANS

Racial constraints on religious freedom can be traced to the Puritans' motivations for leaving England.[5] They came to the New World to practice their religion without fear of persecution.[6] They also came to colonize the land pursuant to what they believed was a covenant with God that entailed civilizing the purportedly savage natives.[7] Deploying divine justifications of conquest similar to Christopher Columbus's proclaimed God-ordained destiny to discover new lands, the Puritans who founded the Massachusetts Bay Colony believed they were children of God with a holy mandate to create a utopian society.[8] This founding generation believed America was an enchanted land, the "city on a hill" where God commanded them to foster and protect Protestantism, which they deemed to be pure Christianity.[9] However, when theirs was the dominant religion in New England, Puritans became more religiously intolerant.[10] As thousands of Protestant congregations worshipped freely in the American colonies, religions deemed heathen, cultish, or false according to Protestant theology were ineligible for religious freedom protections.[11]

This White Protestant notion of Manifest Destiny has since animated America's national identity.[12] Indeed, more than half a century after the United States won its independence from Britain, Herman Melville succinctly articulated what his compatriots have believed since the nation's founding: "We Americans are peculiar, chosen people, the Israel of our time. We bear the ark of the liberties of the world. God has predestined, mankind expects, great things from our race; and great things we feel in our souls."[13]

Conquest and Forced Conversion of Native Americans

When the Puritan settlers arrived in America, they found that the Native peoples not only looked different but also practiced unfamiliar religions. Although a diverse group with differing views on the separation of church and state, Puritans had no qualms about exploiting, appropriating, and dominating Native Americans—whom they believed were heathens and pagans.[14]

Puritans interpreted Native Americans' religions as evil or no religion at all.[15] Either interpretation confirmed their belief that the Native peoples were uncivilized savages. Governor John Harvey of colonial Virginia, for example, declared the Native peoples were savages with "only a general residency there, as wild beasts in the forest."[16] Similarly, Governor John Winthrop of the Massachusetts Bay Colony cited Genesis 1:28 to tell his constituency they were justified in taking the land: the Natives had failed to "be fruitful, and multiply, and replenish the earth, and subdue it."[17] Land theft, criminalization of Native American religious ceremonies, and forced conversion to Christianity were deemed necessary to civilize the indigenous popula-tion.[18] Therein can be found the genesis of White Christian supremacy in the United States.[19] Nearly two centuries later, the US Supreme Court in *Johnson v. McIntosh* validated this reasoning when it ruled that Native Americans did not have property rights unless and until they had fully assimilated into White Christian society.[20] Notably, prior to the mid-twentieth century, ref-erences to Christianity implied Protestantism.

A series of colonial charters confirmed these Protestant pronouncements, among them the Third Charter of Virginia of 1612, which dedicated the col-ony to "the propagation of the Christian Religion, and Reclaiming of People barbarous, to Civility and Humanity."[21] The Act Declaring Who Shall Be Slaves (1670) stated that "all servants not being christians, being imported into this country by shipping," and An Act to Repeal a Former Law Making Indians and Others Free (1682) declared that "negroes, moors, mullatos, and others borne of and in heathenish, idolatrous, pagan and Mahometan parent-age and country have heretofore, and hereafter may be purchased, procured, or otherwise obtained as slaves." The Declaration of Proposals of the Lord Proprietor of Caroline (1663) announced "a pious and good intention for the propagation of the Christian faith amongst the barbarous and ignorant Indians."[22] And the Charter of Rhode Island and Providence Plantations (1663) sought to pursue "with peaceable and loyal minds [the] sober, serious, and religious intentions...[of] the gaining over the conversion of the poor ignorant Indian natives."[23]

This worldview infiltrated teaching in public schools in the eighteenth century. Lessons included preaching and prayers for freedom from "delusion of the Devil, the malice of the heathen [Native Americans], the invasions of our enemies, and mutinies and dissensions of our own people."[24] Conquest, enslavement, and disenfranchisement were grounded in a religious logic of spreading Christianity and civilization in a barbaric land.[25]

Thus, it was the "white man's burden" to deculturize and civilize Native Americans.[26] The Indian Removal Act of 1830, for example, authorized the federal government to confiscate all Indian land east of the Mississippi River and forcibly evacuate Native American residents.[27] President Andrew Jackson justified displacing Indians by pointing to the superiority of Anglo-American "liberty, civilization, and religion" over the barbarous ways of the Native Americans.[28]

These so-called civilizing projects purposefully mandated converting Native American children to Protestantism. The US government abducted them under the color of law to boarding schools, where they were prohibited from practicing their tribal religions, speaking their indigenous languages, and seeing their families.[29] Meanwhile, Native American tribes who converted to Protestantism and assimilated to Anglo-Saxon culture received preferential treatment relative to other tribes.[30]

A case in point is the "Five Civilized Tribes," comprising the Cherokee, Chickasaw, Choctaw, Creek (Muscogee), and Seminole. They were considered civilized by the Anglo-Protestant settlers in part because they had religiously converted, established constitutional government structures, and adopted European economic, educational, political, and social institutions acceptable to the settlers' worldview.[31] In exchange for their partial assimilation, these tribes received preferential treatment in land allotments and treaty negotiations.[32]

In contrast, in 1883, the U.S. Department of the Interior banned "heathenish" Indian dances, as part of its efforts to convert Native Americans to Christianity.[33] Tisa Wenger's work describes how this affected the Ghost Dance, which had few practitioners at the time of the religious ban.[34] The Ghost Dance was popularized in 1889 in Nevada by a Paiute prophet named Wovoka and soon became practiced throughout the Great Plains. Wovoka, who had encountered Catholics and Mormons, preached that the Ghost Dance would bring a new era of peace and harmony—a theme found in Christian millennialism. This message was particularly appealing to the Lakota and other tribes that were dissatisfied with the Bureau of Indian Affairs' (BIA's) mismanagement, mistreatment, and breach of treaties that resulted in severe poverty on the reservations. When local Whites and military officials witnessed the large number of Native Americans dancing, they feared a massive revolt was imminent. Citing national security justifications, government officials cracked down on the Ghost Dance.

Recognizing the salience of religion in White American society, Native American chiefs invoked religious freedom in their defense of the Ghost Dance and other indigenous religious practices. For example, a group of Pawnee leaders wrote to US Commissioner of Indian Affairs Cato Sells, asserting, "Our Messiah or Ghost Dance is a religion that we think a great deal of, for through it, we found the white man's Christ, and the Book of Revelation of the New Testament furnishes us much of our ceremony whereby we worship the great spirit of Heaven."[35] Similarly, a Blackfeet tribal representative compared the need for three days to celebrate the Medicine Dance to Christianity's Holy Week. He wrote, "These gatherings are to us as Easter is to white people. We pray, and baptize our babies only instead of water we paint them."

That Native American leaders felt compelled to analogize their religious practices to Christian practices evinces the extent to which indigenous practices had to comport with Christianity (and Protestantism in particular) in order to be preserved.[36] Despite these efforts, however, the US government continued to criminalize the Ghost Dance according to the BIA's Religious Crimes Code of 1883,[37] and violators were subjected to fines, forced labor, loss of rations, and prison time.[38]

Ingesting peyote was another Native American religious practice banned by the US government. Again, proponents compared peyote to Christian practices, such as ingestion of the holy sacrament, that allow Indians to talk with Jesus.[39] Peyote leaders testified before the US House Committee on Indian Affairs in 1918 that ingesting peyote was their way of "praying to God....We use it like people going to church."[40] To persuade government officials that they were bona fide Christians, the peyote practitioners legally incorporated as the Native American Church, whose aim was to promote "the Christian religion with the practice of the Peyote Sacrament as commonly understood and used among the adherents of this religion."[41]

But the US government refused to grant the Native American Church religious freedom protections because in a predominantly Protestant nation, Native American practices had always been deemed superstition and heathenism, not religion. Accordingly, the BIA determined that peyote and the various dances impeded Indians' civilizational progress.[42] It was not until decades later, in 1978, that Congress passed the American Indian Religious Freedom Act, giving Native American religions legal protections.[43]

The label "heathen" did not apply just to Native Americans, but to people who did not worship the one true God, as determined by Anglo-Saxon Protestants.[44] In the case of Africans, Americans justified their enslavement based on their Christian beliefs that Africans were godless heathens with no souls.[45]

Forced Conversion of Enslaved Africans

From the time the first Europeans settled North America until the late nineteenth century, most White Americans believed they were chosen by God to rule over Africans, whose dark skin they believed was the curse of Ham.[46] According to the biblical story, when Ham, the youngest of Noah's three sons, sees his father naked, Noah curses the descendants of Canaan, Ham's son, to perpetual servitude. European and American Christians believed Black people, and more specifically Africans, were the descendants of Ham. Noah's curse, thus, condemned Blacks to slavery. That is, Blacks were inferior, evil, and heathen because their land of origin, Africa, was the "Dark Continent," a place lacking civilization and culture. As Sylvester Johnson notes, "The deeper issue behind racism and racialism…was not slavery but identity and existence."[47]

The Noahic account became the foundation of the three major races underpinning the American racial taxonomy: White, Yellow, and Black.[48] To be American was to be White and the people of God. Religion and race thus became intertwined in justifying the enslavement of Blacks. Put simply, God had ordained Anglo-Protestant supremacy.[49]

Moreover, White Americans believed that slavery helped Africans by exposing them to the gospel of Jesus Christ through their masters and Anglo-Protestant cultural norms.[50] Despite religiously grounded opposition by Quakers and other Christian minorities, the prevailing view was that Africans were not human because they purportedly lacked souls. Hence slavery continued for centuries without contradicting mainstream Christian morality.[51]

Christians' belief in the inferiority of Africans mirrored the racialization of Native Americans and was similarly integrated into colonial laws. In a 1690s preamble to a South Carolina slavery law, for example, White lawmakers referred to the enslaved Africans as "of barbarous, wild, savage natures, and…constitutions, laws and orders, should in this Province be made and enacted, for the good regulating and ordering of them, as may restrain the disorders, rapines and inhumanity, to which they are naturally prone and inclined."[52] Likewise, the slave codes passed in the late seventeenth century emphasized skin color and religion as that which divided the superior from the inferior.[53] White settlers associated enslaved Africans' non-Christian religions with real or imagined inferior racial characteristics.[54]

While converting enslaved Africans to Protestantism was deemed necessary to civilize them, their race was considered too indelibly inferior to deserve liberty.[55] As far back as 1667, Virginia passed a law stating, "It is enacted that baptism does not alter the condition of the person as to his bondage or freedom."[56] South Carolina followed suit in 1690 when it legally prohibited a slave from becoming free on conversion to Christianity.[57]

Notably, a sizable number of enslaved Africans were Muslims, which only confirmed colonialists' beliefs in their heathenism.[58] However, if an African

Muslim slave could read Arabic, he was labeled an Arab—inferior to Whites but superior to Blacks—because White slave owners deemed Africans incapable of becoming literate.[59] According to this European supremacist logic, northern Africa belonged to the Asiatic world, which although inferior to Europe, was superior to Africa in the minds of American slaveholders. Nonetheless, Muslim slaves' black skin and heathen souls made them permanently unfit for self-government.[60] Similar claims are made today against Islam as a violent political ideology incompatible with democracy, the topic of chapter 7.[61]

Although being Christian was not necessary for attaining legal citizenship, being socially raced as White was.[62] As a result, the millions of European Jewish and Catholic immigrants who were White by law did not receive the social, economic, and political privileges of Whiteness.[63]

THE CONFLATION OF SCIENTIFIC RACISM AND RELIGION

Two waves of mass immigration between the mid-nineteenth century and the early twentieth century triggered a White nativist backlash similar to today's xenophobia against Latinos, Muslims, and Asian immigrants.[64] Between 1830 and 1930, approximately 38 million immigrants came to the United States.[65] Nearly 16 million of them arrived between 1900 and 1930. In 1920, immigrants and their children made up 76 percent of New York's population, 72 percent of Chicago's, and 69 percent of Cleveland's. This major influx of immigrants was composed primarily of Eastern European Jews, Irish Catholics, and Italian Catholics.[66] By the second decade of the twentieth century, Southern and Eastern Europeans were immigrating at twice the number of the "English speaking races."[67]

Some American elites embraced the newcomers under a burgeoning notion of religious pluralism, as evinced in the 1893 World's Parliament of Religions in Chicago. But most politicians, clergy, and citizens feared that America's Protestant, Anglo-Saxon purity was under threat.[68] The Ku Klux Klan, established in the 1860s to terrorize newly freed black slaves, reemerged in the 1920s to proclaim Catholics and Jews a threat to America. In contrast to the covert Klan of the 1860s and 1870s, the Klan in the early 1900s reemerged in mass public events, recruiting advertisements in newspapers, and electing members to political office.[69] With Anglo-Protestant nativism anxiety at fever pitch, Klan membership peaked in the mid-1920s, at an estimated four million members in over forty-three states, primarily in the North and West.[70]

The Klan conflated White nationalism with religion in defense of a Protestant America.[71] Its slogan, "Native, white, Protestant supremacy," attracted primarily lower- and middle-class White Protestant males in the North, as well as African Americans.[72] Similar to German Nazism and Italian Fascism, the Klan's White supremacist ideology proclaimed that America must remain Anglo-Saxon and Protestant in accordance with its Manifest Destiny.[73] For example, a Klan minister in Maine described the organization as "the rising of a Protestant people to take back what is their own."[74] The Klan incorporated Protestant churches and Evangelicalism into its core mission. Invocation of religious terminology labeling White Protestants as pure and godly and non-Whites and non-Protestants as impure, ungodly, and traitorous attracted an estimated forty thousand Protestant ministers to join the Klan. Notably, the same racial-religious logic is fueling a rise in Evangelical Christian, White supremacist groups today whose targets are Muslim, Jewish, Latino, Black, and LGBTQ communities. Some of these Evangelical Christian groups also claim that God chose Donald J. Trump for a providential mission to racially purify America.[75]

The tens of millions of Southern and Eastern European immigrants who came to work in American cities during the Industrial Revolution changed the demographics of urban life.[76] In the 1890s, for example, nearly 70 percent of residents in the largest cities were Southern and Eastern European immigrants. By 1910, nearly 7 percent of the American population was foreign born, and by 1920, first- or second-generation immigrants made up nearly 25 percent of the population.[77] A growing nativist movement maligned both waves of immigrants—from Ireland, Germany, and Scandinavia in the first and Italy and Russia in the second—as lower castes of Whites than the Anglo-Saxon Protestant majority.[78]

The new immigrants' different languages, "Old World" customs, and non-Protestant religions triggered nativist fears of the so-called mongrelization of the Anglo-Saxon race.[79] The notion of a unified, unvariegated White race unraveled. Similar to the discourse racializing enslaved Africans and Native Americans, the American media portrayed these Eastern and Southern European immigrants as savage, barbarian, and treacherous.[80] The large influx of Catholics and Jews, in particular, triggered mainline Protestants' fears that their political and economic hegemony was under threat.[81]

Immigration thus became an existential concern among America's intellectual and political elite.[82] The narrative that "old stock" Americans were being pushed aside by less civilized and mentally inferior races from the lowest stratum of European society fueled scientific racism.[83] Social scientists and the government developed a hierarchy of races within and at the borders of Whiteness that categorized groups based on skin color, geographic origin, mental ability, and religion.

The nativists demanded a curb on immigration from Eastern and Southern Europe, similar to President Trump's and his White nativist supporters' contemporary calls to stop so-called chain migration from non-European nations, and most explicitly Muslim-majority countries.[84] Failure to curb immigration would lead to the "race suicide" of American "old stock," warned the nativists, among them, Presidents Theodore Roosevelt, Jr., Woodrow Wilson, and Calvin Coolidge.[85] Wilson's belief in the superiority of European civilization caused him to support the racial segregation of African Americans and immigration restrictions. Similarly, Coolidge stated in a popular magazine, "Biological laws tell us that certain divergent people will not mix or blend. The Nordics propagate themselves successfully. With other races, the outcome shows deterioration on both sides."[86]

Government officials relied on the work of sociologists such as Edward A. Ross, who in 1901 wrote the seminal article, "The Causes of Race Superiority," to draw distinctions between superior Europeans, those of Anglo-Saxon and Nordic descent, and inferior Europeans, those of Slavic, Latin, Iberian, and Jewish descent.[87] A taxonomy of European races mixed eugenics with biblical reasoning wherein a person's geographic origin, skin tone, *and* religion were attributed levels of intelligence, physical health, and moral and political characteristics.[88] Although legally White, Hebrews, Iberians, Levantines, Alpines, and Slavs could be socially White on condition that they assimilate into Northern European Protestant culture.[89] Ultimately, race became a means to rationalize the exclusion of certain groups from obtaining rights, economic opportunity, and legal as well as social equality.[90]

Due in part to their religious beliefs, Catholics from Ireland, Italy, and Germany and Jews from Eastern Europe were assigned racial traits inferior to those of Anglo-Saxons.[91] One report, for example, found that "83 percent of the Jews, 80 percent of the Hungarians, 79 percent of the Italians, 87 percent of the Russians were classified as Feebleminded."[92] Sixty percent of Jews were classified as Morons. Political elites of the time also believed Jews were unfit for citizenship because they were antisocial and antidemocratic by nature.[93] The same justifications for unequal treatment of African Americans and Native Americans on religious grounds of savagery and other inferior traits were now being deployed against Eastern and Southern European immigrants.[94]

An 1890 report by Carl Campbell Brigham, a Princeton University professor, titled *A Study of American Intelligence*, ranked Russian, Italian, and Polish immigrants at the bottom of the intelligence scale, just above African Americans.[95] Another professor, Ellwood P. Cubberley, in his 1909 book, *Changing Conceptions of Education*, distinguished between the inferior new immigrants of Southern and Eastern Europe and the superior earlier immigrants from Northern Europe. He stated, "These southern and eastern Europeans are a very different type from the north European who preceded them. Illiterate, docile, lacking in self-reliance and initiative and not possessing Anglo-Teutonic conceptions of law, order and government, their coining has served to dilute tremendously our national stock, and to corrupt our civic life."[96] Policy makers used such reports to argue for the need to restrict immigration in order to prevent the dilution of the (Northern European) White race in America.[97]

In the *Dictionary of Races or Peoples*, produced in the 1911 Dillingham Commission's Report on Immigration, forty-five races were counted entering the United States, of which thirty-six were indigenous to Europe.[98] Among the races identified was the South Italian, who is "an individualist having little adaptability to highly organized society"; the Sicilian, who is "vivid in imagination, affable, and benevolent, but excitable, superstitious, revengeful"; and the Slav, who is "depressed, melancholy, and fatalistic," as well as careless "as to the business virtues of punctuality and often honesty."[99] The Immigration Restriction League submitted a report to the Dillingham Commission in support of restricting immigration because "a considerable proportion of the immigrants now coming are from races and countries... which have not progressed, but have been backward, downtrodden, and relatively useless for centuries."[100]

Like today, immigration policy was a race issue. Relying on eugenics, the Dillingham Commission's Report recommended that immigration from Southern and Eastern Europe be severely curtailed because of racial difference and inassimilability.[101] Thirteen years later, in 1924, at the Second International Congress of Eugenics, a prominent eugenicist succinctly summarized the logic behind racial formation: "All men are born with equal rights has been confused with the political sophistry that all men are born with equal character and ability to govern themselves and others, and the educational sophistry that education and environment will offset the handicap of heredity." As a result, the American nativist movement labeled Celts, Italians, Hebrews, and Slavs an inferior stock of Whites that warranted their exclusion from American shores.[102]

Scientific racism's effect on immigration policy culminated in strict national origin quotas in the 1924 Immigration Act, which severely curbed immigration from Southern and Eastern Europe, as well as Asia, for the next forty years. In congressional debates preceding passage of the law, government reports demonstrated the anti-Semitic motives behind restrictions on Eastern European immigrants. For example, the director of consular service, Wilbur J. Carr, released a report warning that 350,000 to 5 million Jews who were "filthy[,] ... often dangerous in their habits[, and] ... lacking any conception of patriotism or national spirit" would flood the United States if immigration restrictions were not imposed.[103] Such reports were validated by academics such as Robert Ward, a Harvard professor who founded the Immigration Restriction League. Ward warned Congress of imminent Jewish mass immigration.

The deluge of anti-Semitic and anti-Catholic appeals succeeded. The 1924 Immigration Act limited the total number of immigrants to approximately 150,000 per year and restricted immigration from Eastern and Southern European countries to a mere 2 percent of American residents from each country as recorded in the 1880 US Census.[104] Because most Eastern European Jews and Southern European Catholics immigrated after 1880, the law prescribed larger allocations for immigrants from Northwestern Europe.[105] As a result, for the next forty years, 70 percent of immigrants would come from the United Kingdom, Ireland, and Germany.[106] The immigration law also prohibited entry of non-White persons ineligible for citizenship, which targeted Japanese, Chinese, and other Asians but also restricted immigration from the Middle East, as I discuss in chapter 4.[107]

Immigration laws successfully halted immigration from Asia and significantly slowed immigration from Eastern and Southern Europe.[108] The combined quota of Poland, Russia, Romania, and the Baltic countries hit Jewish immigrants particularly hard. For instance, the fixed national origin quota of 9,443 was a fraction of the 100,000 Jews who immigrated annually before World War I.[109] Less than 3 million Eastern and Southern European immigrants came between 1930 and 1960, as compared to 9 million in the first decade of the twentieth century.[110] Not until passage of the 1965 Nationality and Immigration Act were Asians, including people from the Middle East and North Africa, permitted to immigrate in substantial numbers to the United States.[111] As a consequence, nearly 70 percent of Muslims in America today are foreign born or children of immigrants, making them a prime target for the new wave of White nativism in the post-9/11 era.[112]

· · ·

In trying to understand the contemporary racialization of Muslim identity, the historical treatment of Africans and Native Americans is instructive for understanding the role that religion played, along with phenotype, to justify their enslavement and near annihilation, respectively. The history of Jewish and Catholic immigrants from Europe brings into sharper relief the role of religion in the racialization process. These communities were legally White, similar to Muslims from the Middle East and North Africa today; however, their religions socially raced them as a threat to the Anglo-Saxon Protestant national identity. Consequently, the arrival of millions of Jews and Catholics coupled with international events—World War I, the rise of Communism, and World War II—paradoxically resulted in both their systemic discrimination and their entrance into Whiteness. I now turn to the racialization of Jews, Catholics, and Mormons to illustrate the troubling similarities between an era of blatant White Protestant nativism over a century ago and the current rise of White Judeo-Christian nativism racializing Muslims today.

THREE

Racialization of Jews, Catholics, and Mormons in the Twentieth Century

THE TWENTIETH CENTURY BEGAN with nativist fervor. Religion was at the forefront of debates on whether the millions of new European immigrants were "fit for self-governance"—a euphemism for race.[1] Large numbers of Irish Catholics prompted fears of popery, as Protestants claimed the hierarchy of the Roman Catholic Church with an infallible pope at the top contradicted American principles of liberty and freethinking.[2] Likewise, mass migration of Eastern European Jews triggered nativist anxiety of the so-called Hebrew race corrupting American society. And, Mormons' polygamous marriages caused the White Protestant majority to disparage them as "American Mohammedans."

Contrary to popular perceptions that religion is a sacred space (both figuratively and literally), America's checkered history of xenophobic, exclusionary immigration policies against these new European arrivals demonstrates how religious identity serves as a proxy for racial identity. Taking a closer look at how the religious identities of Jews, Catholics, and Mormons were racialized historically is instructive for the contemporary racialization of immigrant Muslims. Both in the past and present, the racialization of religion serves the political purpose of excluding, expelling, and discriminating against the targeted minority.

RACIALIZING JEWS: THE HEBREW RACE

American anti-Semitism is steeped in Christian theology. English Protestants brought with them the Old World trope of Jews as Christ killers.[3] Similar to Orientalist depictions of Muslims in eighteenth- and nineteenth-century America, Protestant polemicists racialized Jews as innately evil and deceitful because they did not accept Jesus Christ as the messiah.[4] Some went so far as to claim that the persecution of Jews was divine retribution for the murder of Jesus Christ.[5]

Due to their small numbers during the colonial era—fewer than two thousand—Jews were spared the high level of persecution they endured in Europe.[6] Indeed, George Washington recognized the "children of the Stock of Abraham" when he made his famous statement that the government "gives to bigotry no sanction, to persecution no assistance."[7] Until the 1870s, most Jews were highly educated and affluent immigrants from Central Europe.[8] German, French, and English Jews were willing to change their habits of dress, language, dietary practices, and even way of worshipping to comport with Protestant normalcy and thereby were more readily accepted into the American mainstream.[9]

However, when the number of Jews grew dramatically starting in the late-nineteenth century, so too did bigotry against them.[10] At a time when rapid industrialization, urbanization, and mass immigration were unnerving the dominant White Protestants, Jews became associated with the purported hordes of inferior White races overtaking America.[11] That this new wave of Jewish immigrants were indigent only exacerbated White Protestant nativism.

Although European Jews were legally White, the US government treated them as a distinct race on account of their religion and their mixed origins from North Africa and the Middle East.[12] The American scientific community in the late nineteenth century described Jews as "Hebrews," a separate racial type with different biological characteristics.[13] The US Census considered expanding its racial classification in 1910 to categorize immigrant races, including Jews, but reversed course after successful lobbying by the American Jewish Committee.[14]

Some government officials categorized Jews as a mixed race that had interbred with Black Africans during the Diaspora.[15] This conclusion was based on some scientists' claims that Semites originated in Africa.[16] Similar to the "one drop" rule for Blacks, Jewish religious identity thus was ascribed irredeemable biological traits arising from their impurity of blood.

The alleged biological inferiority translated into cultural inferiority. The media described Jews as clannish, separatist, parasitic, pushy, dishonest, and agents of Bolshevism.[17] The US government and political elites deemed Jews undesirable immigrants, inassimilable, and threats to American democracy.[18] Jews' communal lifestyle, wherein they rarely married outside their religious communities, reinforced mainstream claims that they were a distinct and inassimilable racial group.[19]

Such racialization rarely went beyond fiery sermons when Jewish immigrants numbered in the thousands.[20] But when the Jewish population increased from approximately fifty thousand in 1850 to more than three million in 1920, most of whom were Eastern European, White nativists deployed theologically based racism in claiming they were Judaized Mongols and Chazars.[21] Hyperbolic depictions of their bulging eyes, protruding sensual lips, hooked noses, and animal-like jaws permeated the American media in the first half of the twentieth century. These physical depictions only reinforced Anglo-Saxon Americans' convictions that Jews should be treated like a separate (inferior) race on account of their religious beliefs and practices.[22]

Racialization of Jews also manifested in conspiracy theories holding that Jews' clannishness and economic competitiveness aimed to eliminate Anglo-Saxon Protestants, mirroring the clash of civilization theories portraying Islam as a threat to Western civilization.[23] For example, the Missouri lawyer and Methodist layman Orville Jones claimed in 1892 that Jews deserved to be persecuted because of their "persistent determination...to practice fraud, extortion, and especially usury."[24] Jones cloaked his anti-Semitism in religious rhetoric as he warned that Jews were expanding their influence into the nations of Christendom to recruit Christians in their "crime against civilization."[25] This racial-religious rhetoric would rear its ugly ahead again in the 1990s but this time targeting Islam and Muslims when Samuel Huntington's clash of civilizations theory called for stopping Muslim immigration to the United States, as I discuss in chapter 6.[26] Indeed, Islamophobia mirrors anti-Semitism in its conflation of religious, ethnic, and cultural prejudices.[27]

American elites interpreted Jews' economic or educational success not as a result of ability but rather as a plot to displace Anglo-Saxon Protestants from what was rightfully theirs.[28] With Jews comprising nearly one of every four New Yorkers and 8 to 10 percent of the populations of Philadelphia, Boston, and Baltimore, the revived Ku Klux Klan of the 1920s described Jews as greedy, money-grubbing merchants out to swindle consumers.[29]

Publications such as "The International Jew" and the *Protocols of the Learned Elders of Zion* promoted anti-Semitic narratives of Jews trying to take over the world.[30] The *Protocols of Zion*, originally published in 1903 in Russia, framed Christian Gentiles as victims of a Jewish conspiracy to achieve world domination.[31] The belief that Jewish financiers were conspiring to defraud Europeans and Americans of their livelihoods permeated the highest levels of the US government by 1919.

Despite attempts by some American elites such as Nathaniel Shaler, dean of Harvard's Lawrence Scientific School (now the Harvard John A. Paulson School of Engineering and Applied Sciences), to show that Jews were closer to Anglo-Saxons than to Negroes and Native Americans, Jews remained suspect outsiders during the first half of the twentieth century.[32] The increase in Hebrew schools, Jewish libraries, and free legal services for immigrants fleeing from pogroms in Europe only confirmed White Americans' suspicions of Jewish separatism.[33] These people without a country, according to White Protestant nativists, had no loyalty to the United States or solidarity with their fellow Americans.[34] Rather, their loyalty was presumed to be only to other Jews.

Anti-Semitism was not merely rhetorical; it was also violent.[35] During the depression of the late nineteenth century, for example, Jewish families and businesses were attacked by night riders.[36] Two decades later in 1915, the lynching of Leo Frank in Georgia brought to light the deep roots of anti-Semitism.[37] Convicted of murdering a fourteen-year-old Christian girl, Frank was sentenced to hang.[38] When the governor of Georgia commuted Frank's sentence to life in prison, the public outcry led to Frank's lynching by vigilante White supremacists.[39] While the lynching of Jews is not commensurate with the systematic racist violence inflicted on African Americans, Jews' subjugation to the most violent form of American racism evinces the extent to which they were treated as outsiders.[40] By the Great Depression, more than one hundred anti-Semitic groups existed.[41] Like the surge in Islamophobic organizations after 9/11, their activities contributed to the spread of anti-Semitism among the public.[42]

Among the most virulent anti-Semites was Henry Ford, founder of the Ford Motor Company. His newspaper, *Dearborn Independent*, published British anti-Semitic articles that blamed Jews for a number of social problems.[43] In a ninety-one-article series titled "The International Jew: The World's Problem," Ford blamed Jews for international Communism, the two world wars, and race mixing.[44] In 1921, "The International Jew" described the "Jewish question" as the "oriental infection" of American culture.[45] Consequently, anti-Semitism was a rational form of self-defense against a

The Ford International Weekly

THE DEARBORN INDEPENDENT

One Dollar   Dearborn, Michigan, May 22, 1920   Five Cents

The International Jew:
The World's Problem

"Among the distinguishing mental and moral traits of the Jews may be mentioned: distaste for hard or violent physical labor; a strong family sense and philoprogenitiveness; a marked religious instinct; the courage of the prophet and martyr rather than of the pioneer and soldier; remarkable power to survive in adverse environments, combined with great ability to retain racial solidarity; capacity for exploitation, both individual and social; shrewdness and astuteness in speculation and money matters generally; an Oriental love of display and a full appreciation of the power and pleasure of social position; a very high average of intellectual ability."
—The New International Encyclopedia.

FIGURE 1. The article that signaled the beginning of Henry Ford's seven-year hate campaign against the Jews. Collections of the Henry Ford Museum, Greenfield Village.

fifth column—another theme permeating Islamophobic rhetoric in the post-9/11 era.

By 1938, one poll found that 35 percent of Americans believed Jews were to blame for the pogroms and other atrocities committed against them in Europe; and nearly 50 percent of Americans held low opinions of Jews.[46] Tellingly, the same unfavorable opinions of Muslims pervade American society nearly one hundred years later. A 2017 Pew Research poll, for example, found that 50 percent of Americans think Islam is not part of mainstream America and only 48 percent express warm feelings toward Muslims, as compared to 65 percent toward mainline Protestants.[47]

Anti-Semitism in the first half of the twentieth century affected fraternization, employment, education, housing, and business.[48] Jews were barred from certain hotels and neighborhoods.[49] Some Anglo-Protestant home owners and realtors excluded Jewish home buyers and renters from certain neighborhoods in New York City, such as Park Slope and Brooklyn Heights.[50] And many Jews lost their businesses when the Ku Klux Klan targeted them in Americanization campaigns calling for exclusive support of

White Protestant businesses.[51] Western Union and the New York Telephone Company refused to hire Jews. By 1942, more than 30 percent of job advertisements preferred Christian applicants. Unsurprisingly, second-generation American Jews, many of whom were secularizing as part of their assimilationist process, anglicized their names and hid their Jewish identity in order to obtain employment.[52]

For socially mobile Jews, anti-Semitism manifested in social and educational exclusion.[53] Due in large part to the high cultural value Jewish immigrants placed on education, the number of Jewish students in universities was disproportionately higher than their representation in the general population. Claiming Jews were unathletic, too academically competitive, and incapable of integrating into university social life, a sizable number of faculty members and students supported quotas to limit Jewish enrollment.[54] Jewish student enrollment at Columbia reached 40 percent in 1919, causing the university to impose quotas on Jews and admissions criteria that favored affluent Protestant students.[55] Harvard followed suit in 1922 when it imposed a 15 percent limit on the admission of Jewish students.[56] As a result, the number of Jewish students dropped from 40 percent to 22 percent at Columbia within two years.[57] Notwithstanding the decline in Jewish students, six of the nine editors of the *Columbia Law Review* were Jewish in 1930 because of their superior academic performance. Their social status as racial outsiders resulted in punishment, rather than reward, for their success.[58]

However, Jews were not the only religious minority singled out for unfavorable treatment in the twentieth century. The burgeoning population of Irish and Italian Catholics were also perceived as interlopers by White Protestant America.

CATHOLICS, POPERY, AND THREATS
TO AMERICAN DEMOCRACY

Discrimination against Catholics in America dates back to the colonial era.[59] Anti-Catholic prejudice arose from long-standing political conflicts between Catholics and Protestants in Europe. The Wars of Religion in the sixteenth and seventeenth centuries created deep-seated tensions between adherents of the two faiths.[60] Protestants brought with them to the New World their suspicions of the Catholic Church, which were as theologically rooted as they were political.

Some Protestants believed Catholics were the contemporary Amalekites. In the Old Testament, the Amalekites were related by blood to the Jews but attacked Jews when they were fleeing Egypt. According to the biblical story, God then commanded the Jews to annihilate the Amalekites.[61] The English Reformation depicted Catholics as duplicitous Amalekites who were the enemies of Protestants.[62] The Puritans marshaled these prejudices in campaigns against Catholics in North America.

Notably, the Puritans' religious intolerance centered on eliminating popery in the colonies while religious nonconformists under the umbrella of Protestantism proliferated. Presbyterians, Baptists, Quakers, and other dissenting Protestant churches clashed with Puritans' constricted interpretations of Christianity. Quakers were whipped and hung, Baptists were expelled, and religious dissenters were treated like a plague threatening God's chosen people. As the number of dissidents grew exponentially, religious pluralism gained a foothold in colonial laws by necessity. But full religious liberty was still limited to Protestants, whereas minimal religious tolerance was granted to Catholics and other Christians.[63]

American colonial politicians were also deeply distrustful of Catholicism. Self-government emerged as a fundamental value distinguishing the New World from the Old. Thus religions with hierarchical leadership such as Catholicism, Anglicanism, and Lutheranism (and later Mormonism) were antithetical to Protestant notions of individual liberty.[64] American Protestants viewed Catholics, in particular, as tyrannical and backward—a similar smear hurled at Muslims today.[65] Politicians imported anti-Catholic laws from England, such as Maryland's Act to Prevent the Growth of Popery within This Province, that denied Catholics numerous civil rights in the state where the largest number of Catholics lived during the eighteenth century.[66] In seventeenth-century Virginia, Catholic clergy were banned.[67]

The colonies also required religious tests for citizenship.[68] New York's Ministry Act of 1693 required a resident Protestant minister in every town who was paid from tax assessments and imposed a religious test for holding public office that excluded Catholics.[69] In some colonies, Catholics were prosecuted and sometimes executed.[70] By 1791, when the First Amendment was passed, twelve states required religious tests in order to hold public office and five paid salaries of Christian ministers from taxes.[71] At the time, Catholics were under 1 percent of the population, evincing that anti-Catholicism was primarily an importation of European prejudices, not an outgrowth of local conditions.[72]

Anti-Catholic discrimination continued after the founding of the nation, notwithstanding the US Constitution's separation of church and state, because the federalist system permitted state constitutions to retain their Protestant preferences while limiting First Amendment religious freedom and establishment rights to federal government action.[73] It was not until the mid-1900s that states became legally bound by federal law to treat all religions the same.[74] As a result, some states did not grant Catholics full citizenship rights.[75] The constitutions of North Carolina,[76] South Carolina,[77] and New Jersey,[78] for instance, required a person to be Protestant in order to hold public office.[79] New Jersey's first constitution prohibited discrimination only against Protestants until 1844.[80] In New York, Catholics were not granted citizenship until 1821.[81] Georgia's colonial charter also withheld religious freedom from Catholics.[82]

Before the mid-nineteenth century, when the Catholic population was negligible, anti-Catholicism was driven by ideology rather than demographic realities. After three million Catholics from Ireland and Germany immigrated to the United States between 1846 and 1855, Protestant nativism surged. The additional four million Catholic Italians and two million Poles who immigrated to the United States between 1880 and 1920 bolstered the resurgence of the Ku Klux Klan.[83]

Hundreds of magazines and newspapers, such as *The American Protestant Vindicator* and *Downfall of Babylon*, published anti-Catholic works between 1830 and 1860.[84] Books also were published in which the authors fomented hatred of Catholics. In 1835, Samuel R. B. Morse, inventor of Morse code, published the book, *Foreign Conspiracy Against the Liberties of the United States*, in which he labels Catholics infidels and foreigners in the United States—the same labels used today to describe Muslims by Islamophobes.[85] *Romanism and the Irish Race*, published in 1879, echoed this sentiment: "A republican form of government implies freedom and self-reliance...[which are] extinguished in Romanism, as flame goes out in carbonic acid."[86] Josiah Strong, a famous Congregationalist missionary, in his widely read 1885 book, *Our Country*, described Catholic European immigrants as slavish to authority and superstitious.[87] According to Strong, Catholics lacked the independent and critical thinking needed to become self-governing Americans.[88] Their religious beliefs made them a feebler race than the Anglo-Saxon Protestants, whose rightful place was to rule America.[89]

Notably, anti-Catholic discourse in the eighteenth and nineteenth centuries associated the Roman Catholic Church with Islam. Roman Catholicism

FIGURE 2. The American Pope, Udo J. Keppler (1894). Cornell University—PJ Mode Collection of Persuasive Cartography.

and Islam were considered a dual threat to Christianity, whose demise would play a central role in the end of days and the return of the messiah.[90] For example, Eric Tobias Bjorck, a Lutheran leader in New York, proclaimed, "The Scripture speaketh of Two great Anti-Christs, one in the West, the other in the East.... [O]ne is called Mahomet, or Gog and Magog,...the Other is the pope."[91] According to this logic, Catholics were unfit to be Americans because their loyalty was to the pope, not the elected government of the United States. Their theocratic values made them ineligible for self-governance and thus incapable of being patriotic and democratic.[92]

The Irish, Polish, and Italian Catholic immigrants were largely poor peasants escaping famine and depressed economic conditions.[93] The Irish and Italians toiled in unskilled jobs in northern port cities, and the Poles worked primarily in coal mines, meatpacking plants, and steel mills in the Midwest. German Catholic farmers immigrated largely to farming communities in the Midwest. Thus the new parishes were led by priests from abroad who conducted services in German, Italian, or English.[94] By 1869, nearly a third of American priests were German speakers who conducted services in German. Although German immigration did not stir up as much backlash as Irish and Italian immigration, retention of the German language and culture agitated the growing Protestant nativist movements. The Catholic Church thus became a threatening symbol of rising immigrant power.[95]

A series of violent confrontations between Protestants and Catholics in the 1830s culminated in the destruction of a Catholic convent in Boston.[96] In Philadelphia, Catholics' homes and churches were set on fire by a Protestant mob in 1844.[97] Each year, Protestants celebrated Orange Day, commemorating the defeat of the Catholic King James II by the Irish Protestant William of Orange. The 1869 Orange Day celebrations turned into riots in New York City, resulting in the deaths of dozens of Irish Catholics in sectarian fights between Catholics and Protestants.[98] In the next year's Orange Day celebrations, sixty-one Catholics died in a conflict with state police and militia.[99] The media coverage of the events characterized the Irish Catholics as a savage mob, demons, and incarnate devils.[100]

Two decades later, American nationalism arising from the Spanish-American War of 1898 was depicted as a conflict between so-called triumphant Anglo-Saxon Protestantism and decadent, authoritarian Catholicism.[101] This framing of American liberty at war with foreign despots has consistently animated US conflicts with foreign states such that persons in America with ties to the foreign state are treated like a fifth column. Muslims are no exception, as White Christian nativists in the post-9/11 era allege Islam is in a civilizational conflict with the Judeo-Christian United States, which I explore in chapter 6.

As their numbers grew, Catholics created their own community organizations with a focus on establishing Catholic schools.[102] Bishops required every parish to have a Catholic grammar school, resulting in increased attendance, from approximately 400,000 children in 1880 to 1.7 million in 1920. The nationwide system of Catholic schools exacerbated tensions with Protestants, especially as the schools sought public funding.

Religious freedom litigation in the early to mid-twentieth century centered on whether separation of church and state doctrine prohibited public funding of busing, books, food, and other expenses for Catholic schools.[103] In the 1920s, the Ku Klux Klan condemned Catholics as a people whose separate parochial schools, foreign-born priests, and services in a foreign language threatened American Protestant national identity.[104] By practicing their religion, Catholics allegedly were secretly plotting to eliminate individual liberties—the same conspiracy leveled at Muslims in the post-9/11 anti-Sharia campaigns.[105]

The Klan pointed out that the teachings of the Roman Catholic Church were inconsistent with liberalism's principles of self-governance and thereby a threat to American democracy.[106] The Imperial Wizard proclaimed, "They vote, in short, not as American citizens, but as aliens and Catholics!"[107] Catholics would allegedly eliminate the foundational American principle of separation of church and state.[108]

The Klan also opposed Catholic schools on the grounds that children were being brainwashed to be loyal to the pope before the nation. The Klan sought to amend some state constitutions to require that all children attend only public schools that taught American patriotism through the lens of Protestant values.[109] When this failed, the Klan shifted its opposition to calling for loyalty oaths from teachers, mandating uniform textbooks for parochial and public schools, regulating all school texts through government commissions, granting students time for religious study, and requiring colleges to give credit for religious study only from authorized (Protestant) churches. Ultimately, the Klan sought to relegate Catholics, like Jews, to second-class citizens whose religious practices should be either prohibited or severely curtailed.

The Klan also accused Catholics of conspiring with Jews to take over America. In opposing the 1928 presidential candidate Al Smith, a Catholic, the Klan claimed that Smith's selection of Jewish Belle Moskowitz as his adviser was proof of a conspiracy against Protestants.[110] It was alleged that with Moskowitz's help, Smith would build a palace in Washington, DC, from which he would allow the papacy to take over America. Other nativist elements contributed to a whisper campaign comprising pamphlets, editorials, and sermons warning Americans to beware of a Catholic president whose loyalty would be to the pope in Rome, not to the US government.[111] Islamophobes led a similar campaign in 2008 alleging that Barack Obama was a secret Muslim who would nefariously Islamicize America from the White House.

Another virulently anti–Irish Catholic group calling for restrictive immigration and naturalization laws was the American Protective Association (APA),[112] which claimed a national membership of 2.5 million. The APA called for the removal of Catholics from public office and a prohibition on Catholics teaching in public schools.[113] APA members were required to take an oath to "do all in [their] power to retard and break down the power of the Pope[,] ... not countenance the nomination ... of a Roman Catholic for any office[,] ... [and] not employ a Roman Catholic."[114] The APA portrayed Anglo-Saxon Protestants as victims of a Catholic plot to take over the government.[115] It falsely claimed that 60 to 90 percent of government employees were Catholic and that the US Armed Forces were being "Romanized."

The more politically influential American Party, also known as the Know Nothing Party, was among the most vocal denouncers of Catholics. The Know Nothing Party declared Catholics inassimilable, perpetuating rumors that Catholics were unfit for self-government on account of their blind loyalty to the pope.[116] The anti-Catholic fervor won the Know Nothing candidates seats in local and state office in Massachusetts, New York, and other northeastern states in the 1854 elections.[117]

These suspicions took center stage a century later when the Catholic senator from Massachusetts, John F. Kennedy, ran for president of the United States. By the mid-twentieth century, almost a quarter of Americans believed Catholics would take over America.[118] Because of growing public concerns that his Catholic faith would require him to take orders from the Vatican and oppose the separation of church and state, Kennedy gave a high-profile speech in 1960 to a group of Protestant ministers assuring Americans that his loyalty to the United States was unwavering.[119]

The rise of the Klan, the APA, and the Know Nothing Party resulted in the publication of approximately sixty national anti-Catholic weekly papers in the period leading up to World War I.[120] The periodicals circulated the conspiracy that the Roman Catholic Church was trying to take over America.[121] For example, the Klan accused the Knights of Columbus, a Catholic fraternity and charity, of creating a secret militia to seize the United States government and exterminate Protestantism.[122] Islamophobes today make similar unsubstantiated claims that the Muslim Brotherhood, Muslim Student Associations, and Muslim civic leaders are plotting to take over America from within (see chapter 6).[123]

Irish Catholics bore the brunt of anti-Catholic prejudice. Their religious identity racialized them as a Celtic race, deemed inferior to and incompatible with the Anglo-Saxon race.[124] The media and elites portrayed the millions of indigent Irish Catholic immigrants as a race of savages and purposefully compared them to African Americans.[125] Ralph Waldo Emerson referred to them as "Paddies," a stereotype of the poor, drunk, and lazy Irishman, in contrast to the civilized and hardworking Anglo-Saxons.[126] Emerson went so far as to state that the Irish were not from the Caucasian race because they could not be trusted with freedom.[127]

As a result, Irish Americans faced discrimination in work, housing, and schools.[128] For example, a New York city job advertisement in the 1850s stated,

"Woman Wanted—to do general housework...English, Scotch, Welsh, German or any country or color except Irish."[129] Such bias contributed to mob violence against Irish people and the torching of Catholic churches.[130]

As anti-Catholicism peaked, another religious minority group, Mormons, faced blatant persecution. The experiences of Mormons, who are of Anglo-Saxon and Scandinavian descent, bring into sharp relief the role of religion in social constructions of race. Although legally and phenotypically White presenting, Mormons were racialized as inferior Whites, an in-between race, solely on account of their religion.[131]

MORMONS: THE AMERICAN MAHOMETANS

In 1820, Joseph Smith, who was to become the Mormons' prophet, claimed to have received a revelation that Protestants had misunderstood previous Christian revelations.[132] In 1830, Smith translated writings on golden plates that he claimed were inscribed with religious truths. The writings became the Book of Mormon, which Smith characterized as a religious history of the indigenous people of the Americas. Smith believed Mormons would build the city of Zion in the Americas as the biblical New Jerusalem. He preached that Native Americans were descendants of the ten lost tribes of Israel, thereby legitimating intermarriage between Mormons and Native Americans.[133]

As the number of Smith's followers grew, so too did anti-Mormon hostility. Mormons' missionary work set off alarms among Protestant missionaries, who feared that Christians would fall prey to what they believed to be a false religion.[134] Politicians warned that Mormons were undermining freedom in the American West as part of a plot to subvert the government.[135] Over the next three decades, violence forced Mormons to flee from New York to Ohio, Missouri, Illinois, and finally Utah, where they permanently established their religious communities.[136] Nativists destroyed a Mormon settlement in Missouri and killed seventeen Mormons in the Haun's Mill massacre of 1838.[137] Six years later, a mob of two hundred men murdered Joseph Smith in Carthage, Illinois.[138]

Protestants accused Smith of being a fraud who duped poor Whites.[139] The mainstream media described Mormons as infernal devils, miscreants, foreigners, and enemies of public peace. The majority of Protestants did not consider Mormons adherents of a real religion and went further to accuse Mormons of corrupting Christianity and brainwashing its followers. Mormons' conversion of Native Americans and Mormon–Native American marriages only fueled Protestant conspiracies that Mormons were plotting to take over the country. In the end, Protestants perceived Mormons as a domestic security threat.

Scientific racism further validated anti-Mormonism in the nineteenth century. Religion was instrumentalized by phrenologists and physiognomists who claimed that Mormons' brains were small, thereby making them more susceptible to the evils of polygamy.[140] As noted in W. Paul Reeve's work, one army doctor wrote of Mormons in his report to the US Senate following the Utah War, "The yellow, sunken, cadaverous visage; the greenish-colored eyes; the thick, pro-tuberant lips; the low forehead; the light, yellowish hair; the lank, angular person, constitute an appearance so characteristic of the new race, the production of polygamy, as to distinguish them at a glance."[141] The doctor concluded that Mormons' physical degeneracy was a result of their moral depravity.

Newspapers, political cartoons, novels, and other public documents depicted Mormons' bodies as physically distinct from the mainstream American population. Mormons were racialized as animalistic or devilish, with cloven feet and horns, mirroring the racialization of Jews and Native Americans.[142] In the late 1800s, political cartoons compared Mormons to Chinese, Japanese, Blacks, and Irish Catholics as a pressing political problem for America. That Mormons were equated with other groups deemed national security threats speaks to the powerful role of religion in racially distinguishing between Protestants and Mormons, notwithstanding their common Anglo-Saxon origins.

Mormons, ultimately, faced the same criticism leveled at Jews and Catholics: they were unfit for self-government—a euphemism for racial inferiority. The Mormons' prophet, Smith, articulated a vision of government that limited power to the godly whose authority superseded civil government, thereby granting a Council of Fifty the authority to govern all Mormons.[143] Mirroring antipapist propaganda at the time, Mormons' obedience to their church, even if it meant disobeying the federal government, rendered them a separate race incapable of democracy.[144] Protestants feared that Mormons would acquire sufficient power to take over the country, leading to sectarian violence. In 1857, suspicions reached a fever pitch, when President

James Buchanan dispatched federal troops to remove Brigham Young as governor of Utah.[145]

Tellingly, Mormons were called "American Turks" and the new "Mahometans" in America. Prophet Smith's theocratic cult was likened to the Turkish Sultanate.[146] Because many antebellum Protestant leaders believed that the Prophet Muhammad's claim of a divine mission was false, it followed that Islam was not a religion. Widely read critics dismissed Muhammad as an ambitious despot, not a prophet. Islam was a political ideology spread by the sword, not a divinely inspired religion, with which Muhammad allegedly pursued his authoritarian designs.[147] These same themes reemerged after 9/11 when Evangelical leaders and politicians declared that Islam is not a religion.[148]

Referred to as an American Mahomet, Joseph Smith was vilified by Americans as licentious, duplicitous, and conniving. Protestants were especially enraged by Mormon polygamy.[149] The practice confirmed Mormons' foreignness and susceptibility to despotism. Orientalized depictions of Joseph Smith portrayed him as a sexually depraved despot with a large harem of women held captive under his spell.[150] The multifamily Mormon households were likened to Turkish harems. Like "Mahometans," Mormon polygamists were described as callous patriarchs who exploited their wives for sex and produced an inferior race of children. Protestants also believed polygamy turned women into slaves and men into brutes.

The popular association of Mormonism with Islam validated accusations of imposture, arbitrary power, and infidelity.[151] Congressman Caleb Lyon of New York stated in 1854, "Point me to a nation where polygamy is practiced, and I will point you to heathens and barbarians. It seriously affects the Prosperity of States, it retards civilization, it uproots Christianity."[152] The US Supreme Court agreed in 1878: "Polygamy has always been odious among the northern and western nations of Europe, and, until the establishment of the Mormon Church, was almost exclusively a feature of the life of Asiatic and of African people."[153] Although the Mormon Church instructed its followers to abandon polygamy in 1890, Mormons' racialization as barbarian, savage, and uncivilized persisted until American national identity expanded to be Judeo-Christian in the mid-twentieth century.[154]

At the same time that anti-Mormonism was raging, Chinese and Japanese immigrants were facing increasing public hostility. Although much of the consequent discrimination was articulated in the language of phenotype and national origin, their non-Christian religions reinforced the permanent exclusion of Chinese and Japanese immigrants from legal Whiteness, thus barring them from US citizenship.

RELIGION AND THE RACIALIZATION OF ASIANS

The literature on the racialization of religion frequently overlooks the experiences of Asians. As the number of Chinese laborers grew in the late 1800s, so too did prejudice against them. The American public stereotyped the Chinese—pejoratively called Coolies—as superstitious, duplicitous, and secretive.[155] White Protestants considered Chinese customs, physical features, and foreignness permanent impediments to their ability to assimilate into White Protestant America.[156] As a result, local and state governments classified Chinese children in the South as Black and excluded them from the higher-quality White schools.[157]

Adherence to Confucianism and Buddhism was among the reasons the Chinese were deemed unfit for American citizenship.[158] In 1866, when Congress debated the naturalization of Chinese citizens, California Representative William Higby articulated his colleagues' sentiments when he proclaimed that "the Chinese are nothing but a pagan race."[159] An editor of a newspaper in Butte, Montana, summarized what many Americans felt at the time when he wrote, "The Chinaman's life is not our life, his religion is not our religion.... He belongs not in Butte."[160]

A decade later, in 1877, the sociologist Edward Meade expressed anti-Chinese prejudice in racial-religious terms in his speech to the Social Science Association of America: "He comes here as a laborer. He personifies the character in its absolutely menial aspect—the operation of fifty centuries of paganism, poverty, and oppression have made him—a mere animal machine."[161] Meade goes on to accuse the Chinese of lacking any morals because they practiced concubinage, smoked opium, and gambled. The alleged contempt of the Chinese for Western Christian civilization coupled with their loyalty to their Celestial Empire made them a threat to liberal democracy. Meade alleged that the Chinese "now confront us upon the shores of the Pacific with a host which, by force of numbers alone, is able to convert this broad land into a Chinese Colony, and the Valley of the Mississippi a new battle of the races." The next year, 1878, US senator Aaron A. Sargent called on his colleagues to stop Chinese immigration because their customs, way of life, and religion prevented them from assimilating into America's Anglo-Protestant society.[162]

To stop this so-called Yellow Peril, Congress passed the Chinese Exclusion Act of 1882, which barred Chinese citizens from immigrating to the United States.[163] The law was extended for another ten years in the Geary Act of 1892, which was upheld by the US Supreme Court in *Fong Yue Ting v. United States*.[164] Chinese immigrants already in the country could not become naturalized citizens until 1943.[165]

Some states went as far as prohibiting Asians from testifying in court against White people. The California Supreme Court upheld such laws after determining they were based on the reasonable suspicion that Chinese, raced as Mongolians, possess dangerous characteristics that make them untrustworthy.[166] Anti-Chinese racism reached the US Supreme Court in Justice John Marshall Harlan's dissent in *Plessy v. Ferguson* in 1896, in which he pejoratively wrote, "There is a race so different from our own that we do not permit those belonging to it to become citizens of the United States. Persons belonging to it are, with few exceptions, absolutely excluded from our country."[167]

Mounting anti-Chinese prejudice on the West Coast prompted California to pass the 1913 Alien Land Law Act, preventing immigrants from owning land. When Sikhs became successful farmers in the early 1900s, anti-Asian xenophobia expanded to include people from the Indian subcontinent, collectively categorized as Hindus in the US Census.[168] Congress then passed the 1917 Immigration Act, barring Indian, Chinese, and other Asians from immigrating to the United States.[169]

Japanese nationals were also targets of anti-Asian xenophobia. Although preferred over Chinese before immigration laws excluded all Asians, Japanese Americans' national origin combined with their Shinto and Buddhist faith proved fatal to their liberty when Japan attacked Pearl Harbor in 1941.[170] American Buddhist priests of Japanese descent were among the first to be rounded up for internment.[171] Regardless of citizenship status or the number of years they had lived in the United States, Japanese Americans were deemed disloyal and susceptible to recruitment by foreign agents.[172] General John L. De Witt, though admitting no sabotage had yet taken place, declared to a congressional panel in 1942 (using pejorative terms), "A Jap's a Jap; it makes no difference whether he is an American citizen or not. I have no confidence in his loyalty whatsoever."[173] The US government thus justified its extreme measure of internment on the grounds that the Japanese were an "enemy race."

That the Japanese practiced the purported pagan religions of Buddhism and Shintoism was further evidence of their disloyalty.[174] In the decades preceding World War II, for instance, Shintoism put many Japanese Americans under suspicion of treason because of the Shinto belief that the emperor of Japan was divine. Consequently, some Japanese stopped practicing their religions from fear of being labeled anti-American.[175]

In contrast, Italians, whose country of origin was also at war with the United States during World War II, were not interned, and their enemy alien designation was rescinded in May 1942. That Italians and Germans, who were legally White and predominantly Catholic, were not subjected to the same harsh treatment demonstrates that the further away a group's phenotype and religion is from Anglo-Saxon Protestantism, the lower they are in the racial-religious hierarchy.[176] It also cues the subsequent expansion of Whiteness to include previously disfavored Europeans.

It was not until the mid-1960s that the media and the government portrayed Asians as "model minorities," in what Claire Jean Kim calls *relative valorization*.[177] Juxtaposed to stereotypes of the lazy, militant, and inferior African American, the image of the Asian American in the media transformed into the hardworking, self-reliant, and docile immigrant.[178] As Cindy Cheng notes, the change in stereotypes arose from cultural pluralism during the Cold War and Asian Americans' efforts to prove their loyalty through assimilation and displays of Americanness.[179] Unlike African Americans, who were agitating, protesting, and litigating for equal rights, Asian Americans became model minorities in the American racio-religious hierarchy.[180] This potential transformation from a suspect race to a model minority, with the attendant political consequences, faces immigrant Muslims if efforts for an Abrahamic national identity succeed, which I address in chapter 10.

To be sure, Asian Americans (Christian or otherwise) are still lower in the racial-religious hierarchy than White Christians. For example, Asians' high levels of education, move to White suburbs, and cultural assimilation did not grant them entrance to Whiteness, as it did the Jews, Catholics, and Mormons of European descent. Rather, Asians were perceived as model minorities, simultaneously blamed for stealing Whites' educational and employment opportunities and held up to show the failures of the African American and Latino communities.

. . .

By exploring how religion racialized Jews, Catholics, Mormons, and Asians as socially non-White, this chapter argues that America's commitment to religious freedom historically is restricted to those categorized as socially and legally White. This American tradition of racializing religion is grounded in an American national identity shaped by Protestant settler colonialism, xenophobia, and anti-Black racism. The Americanization movement arising from fears of espionage during World War I pressured Southern and European immigrants to abandon their cultures and languages to comport with Protestant Anglo-Saxon norms.[181] Foreignness and non-Protestant religious identity signified a threat to national security.[182]

History is repeating itself as Muslims in the post-9/11 era are (mis)treated as racial groups such that repression of their religious practices is not considered a violation of American principles of religious freedom.[183] Through essentialist reductionism, all people who present as Arab-looking based on media images are homogenized as violent, threatening, and foreign. Consequently, some Sikh and Hindu Indians as well as Catholic Latinos are subject to anti-Muslim attacks because their brown skin, hair texture, and phenotypes are associated with a criminalized, Arab-looking Muslim identity.[184]

Just as domestic events have an impact on the racialization process—in this case, the arrival of tens of millions of non-Protestant immigrants—so too do international events. World War II and the early Cold War years were a watershed moment for both race and religion in America. The next chapter explores how the US government attempted to differentiate itself from Nazism and Communism by rejecting racism and religious bigotry that gradually led to an expanded White Judeo-Christian national identity.

On the one hand, the United States prided itself on being a nation of believers, in contrast to the atheist Communists, resulting in the addition of "one nation under God" to the Pledge of Allegiance in 1954.[185] On the other hand, America touted itself as a pluralist democracy, in contrast to its Soviet Communist enemy. Official state publications emphasized religious pluralism and condemned racial bigotry as antidemocratic. As a result, Whiteness had to expand to include Catholics, Mormons, and Jews. The domestic and international factors that contributed to the expansion of American identity from Protestant to Judeo-Christian provide the backdrop for understanding which factors socially construct Muslims as a suspect race.

FOUR

From Protestant to Judeo-Christian National Identity

THE EXPANSION OF AMERICAN WHITENESS

MOST WHITE AMERICANS TODAY do not identify with their countries of origin. Nor do they recognize the physiognomic differences between Slavs, Celts, Teutons, Hebrews, Iberians, Scandinavians, or Anglo-Saxons.[1] Instead, Whiteness now centers on a common European ancestry and Judeo-Christian identity. But this was not always the case.

For more than a century, American identity was defined by Anglo-Saxon culture and Protestantism.[2] As a result, European Jews, Catholics, and Mormons—who were legally White—could not attain the full social, political, and economic benefits of their legal status.[3] They were an "in-between race."[4] As a result, they experienced myriad forms of systemic discrimination arising from the racialization of their non-Protestant religions.

Starting in the 1930s, however, the religious identities and ancestry of Mormons, Catholics, and Jews no longer axiomatically excluded them from social Whiteness.[5] This social reconstruction (and expansion) of Whiteness arose from three phenomena. First, the transition from biological race to cultural ethnicity as a marker of difference among legally White groups allowed second- and third-generation Southern and Eastern European Americans to assimilate into Anglo-American normalcy. Second, a Judeo-Christian American religious identity countered domestic White Protestant nativism and Fascism and Nazism abroad. Finally, US competition with the Soviet Union for global hegemony during the Cold War required the United States to put into practice its rhetorical commitment to religious pluralism.[6]

Examining how these domestic and international developments socially reconstructed Whiteness to include Jewish-Protestant-Catholic identity informs how Muslims are racialized in the post-9/11 era. The previous chapter demonstrated how religion has been racialized historically, making the racialization of Muslims today not as extraordinary as it may appear. That is, religious freedom in America has always been confined by the race of the adherents. The further away from Whiteness, as both legally and socially constructed, the less religious freedom a group experiences.

After World War II, ethnicity, as opposed to race, became the primary differentiating characteristic between Americans of different European national origins.[7] As Richard Alba and Victor Nee note, "Ethnicity involves both social structure and the more elusive factors of subjective meaning."[8] For Americans of Irish, Italian, and Eastern European descent who were Catholic and Jewish, being labeled an ethnic group gave members an opportunity to become socially White on condition they assimilate into mainstream Anglo-Protestant culture and normativity.[9] Ethnic identity, therefore, granted a person agency not available to those ascribed a racial identity.

In contrast to immutable external characteristics ascribed to race, ethnicity describes a person's culture, which they can change through acculturation and assimilation.[10] An "ethnic White" can be rehabilitated through assimilation, whereas a racial non-White cannot, because race is deemed biological. This same discursive distinction between ethnicity and race affects Muslim identity. Will Muslim identity continue to be considered a subordinate racial trait, as is currently the case? Or will it be transformed into a purely religious identity that grants an individual Muslim agency to shape their racial identification based on ethnic origins, phenotype, and cultural assimilatory behaviors? Before examining these questions, which I address in chapter 8, a look back at the latter half of the twentieth century is illuminating.

In the case of Catholics and Jews, avoiding a separate racial category allowed them to assert their American identity themselves rather than have Anglo-Saxon Protestants with exclusionary political agendas impose it on them.[11] The newly coined "ethnic Whites" of the post–World War II era faced questions as to whether their religions were compatible with American democracy, mirroring contemporary debates on whether Islam is antidemocratic.[12] Their European ancestry granted them entrance into Whiteness on condition they adopt Anglo-Protestant norms in their lifestyles, associations, and religious practices.

Second- and third-generation Jews and Catholics accommodated these demands to show their loyalty and conformity to Anglo-American norms by abandoning their foreign cultures and languages.[13] When a sufficient number of them assimilated, the entire group was eligible to become socially White.[14] That they did not have to convert from their faith to belong to

American national identity demonstrates that in comparison to cultural or racial identity (which did require conversion), religious identity was privileged normatively.

These developments prompt numerous questions that remain salient today. Why did the social borders of Whiteness evolve to add Catholics, Jews, and Mormons to Christian normativity? Did religion become less relevant in defining Whiteness in general or only for some groups but not others?[15] As the September 11 attacks fade into the past, will immigrant Muslims with "White-passing" phenotypes be like Jews, Catholics, and Mormons and become subsumed under the category "White," representing another expansion of Whiteness, or will they be collectively othered as non-Whites regardless of their level of religiosity, individual phenotype, and assimilation? An examination of the social reconstruction of Whiteness in the mid-twentieth century informs the contemporary racialization of Muslims today and in the future.

THEORETICAL UNDERPINNINGS OF AMERICA'S COERCIVE ASSIMILATIONIST MODEL

When Anglo-American elites realized the tidal wave of immigrants from Eastern and Southern Europe was drastically changing the demography of the country, they focused their efforts on integrating these new immigrants into Anglo-Saxon Protestant culture.[16] To survive, the "American race," as defined by Anglo-Saxon ethnocentric notions of assimilation, would have to absorb and improve these allegedly inferior Europeans. Becoming an American, therefore, has always required immigrants to change their lifestyles, behaviors, clothing, diet, and language to comport with the norms and behaviors of Anglo-Protestant culture.[17] Immigrants also have to abandon any claims to racial distinctiveness, most specifically, any association with Blackness.[18] The African American poet and intellectual James Baldwin candidly described this process when he stated, "The American Dream is at the expense of the American Negro."[19]

While some immigrants may not have wanted to assimilate into White Protestant norms, the cost of failing to do so was prohibitively high. Assimilation granted access to the legal, political, social, and economic benefits of the majority group.[20] In stark contrast, for those racially categorized as Black, Native American, Mexican, Turkish, and Asian, their skin color, phenotype, and geographic origins barred them from legal Whiteness.[21] For these reasons, new immigrants from the Middle East sought entrance into Whiteness as they intentionally disassociated from Black and Asian identity (see chapter 5).[22]

In arguing that America is a coercive assimilationist society, I acknowledge that *assimilation* is a contested term.[23] In his theory of race relations, the University of Chicago sociologist Robert Ezra Park argued that all immigrant groups eventually assimilate into Anglo-American society.[24] He defined assimilation as "a process of interpenetration and fusion in which persons and groups acquire the memories, sentiments, and attitudes of other persons or groups, and, by sharing their experience and history, are incorporated with them in common cultural life."[25] Park's theory of assimilation represents the last stage of a "race-relations cycle" of "contact, competition, accommodation, and eventual assimilation."[26] As a result, immigrants abandon ties to their country of origin, speak only English, adopt Anglo-American attire, eat Anglo-American food, and break out of their ethnic enclaves.[27]

Building on Park's model, the sociologist Milton M. Gordon identifies four stages that follow assimilation: structural assimilation; large-scale intermarriage; ethnic identification with mainstream society; and the end of prejudice, discrimination, and value conflict.[28] Gordon's theory tellingly acknowledges that American culture, which serves as a reference point for immigrants and their children, can best be described "as the middle-class cultural patterns of, largely, white Protestant, Anglo-Saxon origins."[29]

Elliot Barkan offers a more elaborate model of acculturation, integration, and assimilation that comprises seven phases: contact, acculturation, adaptation, accommodation, integration, and assimilation.[30] The final stage is full membership in the dominant society and culture, which occurs when persons shed all the linguistic, cultural, and behavioral characteristics of their original ethnic group. Barkan defines assimilation as "a two-way process wherein the dominant society must be willing to accept the assimilation-prone individuals and those persons whom the core society is willing to accept must wish to assimilate." In doing so, Barkan admits that the core society is Anglo-American.[31] Both Park's and Barkan's classical assimilationist theories presume that descendants of immigrants eventually enter mainstream America as defined by Anglo-Protestant norms.

By contrast, the multiculturalists Alba and Nee challenge assimilationist theories by arguing that American society is amenable to a two-way exchange between the dominant Anglo-American culture and non-White or non-Christian cultures. They define assimilation as "the decline of an ethnic distinction and its corollary cultural and social differences" such that the American mainstream is defined as "that part of society within which ethnic and racial origins have at most minor impacts on life chances or opportunities."[32]

Rather than coerce immigrants to adhere to Anglo-American norms as a means of creating a cohesive national identity, according to Alba and Nee, American society offers more flexibility for ethnic groups to retain their distinctive cultures and languages and still be considered American.[33] If immigrants and their offspring learn English and assimilate in other ways, they can retain their culture of origin. America's melting pot thus allows for the coexistence of multiple cultures, in contrast to ethnocentric classical assimilationist theories.[34] According to Alba and Nee, assimilation is not a static or unchanging concept.

Critical race scholars, however, argue that the melting pot narrative is a myth. Entrenched White supremacy systemically coerces immigrants, enslaved peoples, and occupied peoples to abandon their cultures and replace them with the dominant culture of Anglo-Saxon Protestantism. Rejecting racism as merely a social problem caused by individual prejudices, sociologist Joe Feagin proffers the White Racial Frame as "a broad and persisting set of racial stereotypes, prejudices, ideologies, interlinked interpretations and narratives, and visual images" that establishes Whites' in-group superiority and non-Whites' out-group inferiority as the foundation of American politics, economics, and social relations.[35] For this reason, assimilation theory is unable to explain the permanent exclusion of Blacks from "mainstream" America, despite their presence for two centuries and the absence of ethnic or linguistic ties with the African nations from which they were abducted.[36]

According to Feagin, US law, politics, and social norms are structured through a White racial frame of reference to advantage Whites and disadvantage non-Whites.[37] As a result, only Whites are eligible to enjoy meaningful equality, justice, and liberty; meanwhile, the denial of rights to non-Whites is not perceived as contradictory to American values. The White Racial Frame explains why one terrorist attack by a Muslim triggers surveillance, investigation, and prosecution of Muslim communities, while White right-wing extremism does not incriminate White Christian communities en masse. As applied to Jews, Catholics, and Mormons, their entrance into social Whiteness did not upset the White Racial Frame. Rather, these immigrants accommodated it. The same would occur should American national identity expand to become Abrahamic, thereby encompassing assimilated Muslims.

My analysis adopts Feagin's White Racial Frame and Derrick Bell's Black-White paradigm while also accepting Alba and Nee's argument that ethnicity has replaced race as the trait that explains the differences among legally White groups starting in the mid-twentieth century.[38] But first ethnic identity has to change to assimilate into the dominant Anglo-Protestant norms. The assimilation of second- and third-generation Eastern and Southern European immigrants into American Protestant norms, for example, began the transition of Jews and Catholics to social Whiteness. Upon becoming White, some of their cultural practice could be integrated into American norms.[39]

The fusion of Protestantism-Catholicism-Judaism (what is now referred to as Judeo-Christian) into an American faith tradition sealed their membership in American identity. Mormons, who were of Anglo-Saxon and Nordic ancestry, were elevated to full Whiteness after they renounced polygamy and made public reassurances of their loyalty to the state.[40] By the last quarter of the twentieth century, race disappeared from the nomenclature describing people of various European origins as they socially transitioned from an in-between race to "ethnic Whites" to fully White.[41] Thus, the White Racial Frame persists, but coercive assimilationism allows some ethnic groups to become White while Blacks can never receive the full benefits of first-class citizenship.

These transformations in White identity explain why Arabs sought entrance to Whiteness through their own paths of assimilation during the twentieth century. As the next chapter explains, Arab immigrants' success depended largely on whether they were phenotypically White presenting—that is, European-looking—*and* Christian. Although international developments such as the Iranian Revolution, the Palestinian resistance, and the First Gulf War obstructed Muslims' path toward Whiteness, their racialization was sporadic and avoidable through assimilation. However, the September 11 terrorist attacks resulted in a permanent fall from Whiteness for both Arab Muslims and Arab Christians. Muslims of diverse ethnicities became national security threats. Put simply, their religion raced them.

THE TRANSITION FROM RACE TO ETHNICITY
AND THE EXPANSION OF WHITENESS

Prior to World War II, *race* and *ethnicity* were synonymous.[42] Both terms were used to describe biological traits and cultural characteristics of groups deemed inferior to Anglo-Saxon Protestant Americans. Physical features coupled with differences in language, social organization, diet, dress, and culture dictated a person's inherited propensities.[43] Religion also played a significant role in race making. Religious beliefs were evidence of racial distinctiveness from the dominant White group. Thus to be a "real American" in the first half of the twentieth century, one had to be Christian and more specifically Protestant.[44]

Not all citizens, however, could attain the full socioeconomic benefits of Whiteness.[45] Immigrants of European origin were divided into different races normatively even if they were all legally White. For example, Scandinavians, Dutch, and Celtic Protestants were eligible to assimilate into Whiteness, whereas Southern and Eastern Europeans were socially ascribed racial inferiority.[46] In addition to their different cultural practices, these new immigrants' non-Protestant religions were pointed to by Protestant Americans as evidence of inferior racial difference. Catholics' loyalty to the pope or Jews not believing in Jesus Christ marked Eastern and Southern Europeans as uncivilized and unfit for self-governance. Jews had long been presented as aliens in Christian Europe, a concept transplanted to Protestant America.[47] Jews living in the American South, for example, were grouped with Blacks, leading to open hostility against these new immigrants from Eastern Europe.[48]

It was not until after World War II, when Whiteness was socially redefined to include all groups of European ethnic origin and American identity expanded to a Judeo-Christian one, that Catholics, Mormons, and Jews were granted an opportunity to become first-class citizens.[49] The differences between Eastern and Southern European immigrants and Anglo-Saxon Americans became ethnic rather than racial. Because ethnicity was a difference based in culture, not biology,[50] Americans of Italian, Irish, and Eastern European ancestry had individual agency to assimilate into mainstream Anglo-American society—a choice unavailable to persons of non-European origin or outside of the Judeo-Christian tradition.[51]

Another prerequisite for becoming socially White was disassociation from Blacks.[52] Thus when Booker T. Washington in 1906 condemned lynching by comparing it to pogroms, some Jewish Americans refuted the comparison by praising the freedoms available in America and pointing out the criminality of the Negro.[53] Similarly, some Jewish Americans' support for disenfranchisement of Blacks in the first half of the twentieth century was a means of proving their racial loyalty to Anglo-American normativity, into which they sought acceptance.[54]

Not all Jews were silent about lynching and other racial violence against Blacks. Open support of Blacks' civil rights, however, played into the hands of Anglo-Protestant nativists' claims that Jews were sympathetic to the despised Negro, which corroborated anti-Semitic conspiracies of disloyalty. To receive the full benefits of social Whiteness, therefore, Jews and Catholics had to participate in the subordination of African Americans. Arguably, it was not until Jews felt more secure in their Whiteness in the decades after World War II that they became more assertive in their support for African Americans' civil rights.[55]

Although ethnicity and race are both social constructions deployed to distinguish groups from the dominant Anglo-Saxon American identity, ethnicity grants people agency in defining the attributes of their identity and their relationship with the dominant group.[56] The relationship can be cooperative, competitive, or outright conflictual, depending in large part on the extent of the ethnic group's willingness and ability to assimilate. Race in the United States, by contrast, is largely defined by physical characteristics and relatedness to African ancestry. Skin color, hair texture, lip size, and nose structure are evidence of how much African blood a person possesses, with even one drop making a person Black.[57] Each wave of new immigrants in the nineteenth and twentieth centuries was racialized according to this Black-White racial paradigm. Those closest to Whiteness in the racial-religious hierarchy received more material and dignitary benefits than those raced closest to Blackness.[58]

A case in point were dark-skinned Sicilians in the American South. When a group of Sicilians were lynched in Louisiana in 1891, the press justified the violence by highlighting their brutal nature arising from southern Italian culture and biology.[59] Three more Italians in Louisiana were lynched in 1896 as punishment for fraternization with Blacks.[60] In 1898, some delegates at the Louisiana state constitutional convention argued that Italians should be disenfranchised because they are "as black as the blackest negro in existence."[61] Similarly, when Greek immigrants were subjected to racial violence, it was justified by pejorative allegations of their "half n—" racial status.[62]

For the next three decades, Italian immigrants would be racialized as Black, making them subject to anti-miscegenation laws, Jim Crow laws, and other forms of racial discrimination. In 1914, a White farmers' association in Louisiana included Italians and Sicilians as ineligible for membership along with Japanese, Chinese, Mongolians, Asians, and Blacks.[63] Old stock Anglo-Saxon Americans derogatively referred to Italian Americans as wops, dagos, and guineas.[64] Some congressional leaders went so far as to seek to strip Italians of their legal status as Whites to match their social status as non-Whites, which would have denied them the right to naturalize as US citizens.[65] In response, European immigrants and their children sought racial inclusion in Whiteness through assimilation into Anglo-American culture and disassociation from Blacks.[66]

The politics of World War II offered the children and grandchildren of Eastern and Southern European immigrants an opportunity to prove their loyalty to the United States. Fighting in the armed forces against Nazism and Fascism in Europe, these second- and third-generation Americans became the "us" fighting "them" in Germany and Italy.[67] Many of them spoke only English, gave their children anglicized names, relinquished a communal lifestyle, and no longer had ties to their country of origin. Increased intermarriage further dissolved their ethnic differences, making it easier to blend into the dominant Anglo-Protestant culture.[68]

ASSIMILATING ETHNICITY INTO ANGLO-PROTESTANT NORMATIVITY

The usage of *race* and *ethnicity* began to diverge in the 1940s. The influential anthropologist Ruth Benedict's division of people into three races—Negroid, Mongoloid, and Caucasian—shaped policy and public perceptions.[69] Ethnicity, instead of race, distinguished the differences among Caucasians of European ancestry, who were deemed superior to the other two races. The loss of a separate racial classification was a gain in social status.

Similar to race, ethnicity is a social construct shaped by myriad factors such as ancestry, nationality, language, and culture that collectively create a sense of peoplehood.[70] Religion is an essential component in the formation of ethnic identity.[71] Religious affiliation created multiple communities among immigrants with the same national origin.[72] Irish immigrants, for example, formed separate communities along Protestant and Catholic lines. Their respective churches were a resource for socialization, communalism, and a space free of discrimination by mainstream Anglo-American society. Likewise, Italian, German, and French ethnic communities were defined in part by their shared Catholic religion.[73] Jews and Mormons also became distinct ethnic groups on account of their religious identity.

As religion intersected with ethnicity, new ethnoreligious identities formed. Members of these identities interacted with each other and with mainstream society, sometimes leading to full assimilation and sometimes restricting it. On the one hand, acculturated Jewish American leaders argued in the 1890s that Jews who had lived in the United States for two generations or more were no longer a distinct race, but still retained a global Jewish identity.[74] They could be members of the White race while still constituting a distinct Jewish ethnic group. For instance, in a speech to the Conference of Eastern Council of Reform Rabbis in 1915, one year before his nomination to the US Supreme Court, Louis Brandeis noted that "religion, traditions and customs bound us together, though scattered throughout the world. The similarity of experience tended to produce similarity of qualities and community of sentiments."[75] On the other hand, newer Jewish immigrants from Eastern Europe clung to the notion of a Jewish people distinct from Gentiles.

Ethnicity was continuously being reinvented based on social and political factors within and outside the group. Immigrants and Americans who belong to an ethnic group, therefore, have some agency in defining their group identity as they renegotiate their relationship with the dominant Anglo-American culture.[76] The more individuals within an ethnic group change their behavior, lifestyle, language, and overall culture to emulate the dominant culture, the less threatening the ethnic group is perceived by the public.[77] In turn, group members obtain more material and dignitary benefits as compared to other groups who are unwilling or unable to assimilate.

German Americans of the late nineteenth century are illustrative. German immigrants began arriving in the United States in the late eighteenth century, at which time they constituted less than 9 percent of the population. By the mid-1850s, Germans along with Irish immigrants accounted for nearly three-fourths of America's 2.2 million foreign-born persons.[78] In the nineteenth century, approximately one-third of German immigrants were Catholic, with the total reaching more than 1.2 million by 1900.[79] They lived in tight-knit communities, with church services, schools, and newspapers in German; and their marriages were mostly confined to other Germans.

Although deteriorating economic conditions in Germany were an impetus for German migration, Catholic Germans also left to escape religious persecution. In the 1870s and 1880s, the secular German imperial government fought with the Roman Catholic Church for control of educational and ecclesiastical appointments in what came to be known as the Kulturkampf. The May Laws of 1873 stripped the church of jurisdiction over German Catholics, abolished religious orders, and deposed bishops, resulting in the exodus of German Catholic religious leaders to the United States, where they created German Catholic communities.[80]

The new Catholic immigrants settled together in the Midwest and replicated their German way of life in their new home, including their religious practices. In contrast to their English-speaking Irish Catholic compatriots, German immigrants felt isolated in American Catholic churches. As a result, they created separate churches where priests offered services in German.[81] They built Catholic schools with lessons in German to avoid sending their children to secular public schools, which they perceived as godless. The German Catholic church discouraged its congregants from assimilating into Anglo-American norms it perceived as materialistic, hypocritical, vain, and immoral.

These German enclaves triggered Protestant nativism. Some states, including Wisconsin, passed laws requiring that English be taught in all schools, including parochial schools, for at least sixteen weeks a year.[82] At the turn of the twentieth century, millions of Catholics from Italy and Ireland were immigrating to the United States, triggering more anti-Catholic nativist backlash.[83] Rising animus toward Catholics merged with anti-German prejudice during World War I. Cities and states across America banned the German language, and German books were burned by vigilante groups.[84] Schools banned history books deemed pro-German.[85] Similar to the post-9/11 government targeting of Muslims on account of their shared religious identity with declared enemies of the United States, Germans were arrested under the Aliens Act of 1798 and the Espionage Act of 1917.

That the critical mass of Germans in the United States (though certainly not the majority) were Catholics during World War I contributed to the government's suspicion.[86] Over 250,000 Germans, both Catholic and Lutheran, were required to register at local post offices and carry identity cards because the state deemed them enemy aliens, a practice that remerged after 9/11 in the National Security Entry and Exit Registration System targeting Muslims.[87] State practices engendered private discrimination and violence. Private groups spied on and harassed German Americans. A German immigrant was lynched in Illinois in 1918.[88] The anti-German hysteria during this time reached such heights that a town in Ohio banned Beethoven's music.[89]

Analogous to Muslims seeking to shield themselves from Islamophobia after the September 11 attacks, German Americans proclaimed their allegiance to the United States and opposition to Germany in an attempt to avoid discrimination and harassment. Many German American newspapers shut down, and Catholic churches stopped holding services in German.[90] Institutional and commercial entities removed German from their names. German Americans anglicized their names and joined the military to prove their loyalty.[91] Native-born generations left farms and villages to live in the cities, where they forgot their mother tongue, enrolled their children in public schools, and joined the urban industrial milieu.[92] By the end of World War I, the number of German American institutions had fallen precipitously.[93]

To be sure, cultural assimilation did not eliminate class hierarchy. Nor did each ethnic group experience White Protestant normativity in the same way.[94] But the option of ethnic assimilation granted the privileges of Whiteness irrespective of class while denying those same privileges to more educated or wealthier Blacks, Asians, and other non-White groups.[95] Hence ethnicity allowed a group to define itself in terms of what it was not: Colored.[96]

EXPANSION OF WHITENESS IN A BLACK-WHITE RACIAL-RELIGIOUS HIERARCHY

Blacks, Native Americans, Mexicans, and Asians, whose differences were articulated in explicitly racial, as opposed to ethnic, terms remained permanently excluded from Whiteness and systematically subordinated.[97] Notably, the Christianiziation of African Americans peaked after Emancipation as Black churches gained greater institutional visibility and influence.[98] However, as Tisa Wenger's work shows, attempts by Black churches to overcome racism by pointing to their Protestant beliefs proved futile.[99] In the early 1900s, the predominantly Black American Methodist Church, for example, highlighted how conversion to Christianity civilized the former enslaved people. Many Black churches highlighted their congregants' accomplishments as "civilized moderns" who abandoned their African heathenism, thereby making them worthy of full American citizenship rights.[100] But converting to Christianity did not grant Blacks the legal and social equality they sought.

Indeed, anti-Black racism was so deeply entrenched that some White Protestants invoked it to justify segregation, including in churches.[101] Along with freedom of choice and association, White Christians (Protestants and Catholics) claimed that their sincerely held religious convictions mandated racial segregation in schools, neighborhoods, workplaces, and businesses.[102] This "segregationist folk theology" gave some White southerners moral license to defend Jim Crow laws as consistent with divinely ordained tenets to separate the races.[103] Religion-based claims are used today to securitize Muslims on grounds that Islam is evil and violent, more specifically, that Religious and Religious Dissident Muslims are national security threats (see chapters 6 and 7).

Obtaining the benefits of Whiteness requires loyalty to a racial-religious hierarchy that places Blacks and Native Americans at the bottom. Having been exposed to the underbelly of White supremacy as in-between races, the new "ethnic Whites" competing for jobs with Blacks and other racial minorities united in their support of racial segregation in housing, employment, and schooling as a means of preserving their newfound racial privilege.[104] They adopted and perpetuated stereotypes of Blacks as lazy, violent, and dependent on state welfare, notwithstanding significant housing and loan subsidies granted to European immigrant families after World War II.[105]

By the 1960s, Whites whose Italian and Irish grandparents had been victims of Anglo-Protestant nativist hate decades earlier now agreed with the scholars Nathan Glazer's and Daniel Patrick Moynihan's claims that cultural and racial deficiencies of Blacks, Native Americans, and Latinos explained why they were disproportionately poorer, less educated, and more likely to be incarcerated.[106] The onus of blame was on racial minorities, not a systemically racist society.

The transition from race to ethnicity in identity formation prompts the question of how European immigrants' non-Protestant religions ceased to race them as socially non-White and instead became a peripheral cultural aspect of their ethnic identity.[107] Why didn't coercive assimilation require religious conversion from Judaism, Catholicism, and Mormonism to Protestantism? One explanation is the social reconstruction of America's religious identity from a Protestant to a Judeo-Christian nation. This shift in national identity that now encompassed Catholics, Jews, and Mormons was a key to opening the door to Whiteness for tens of millions of Americans.[108] Exploring this history informs whether a shift to an Abrahamic identity is the prerequisite for some Muslims to attain first-class citizenship status.

RELIGIOUS PLURALISM AS AN ANTIDOTE TO NAZISM

International events shaped the racialization of Southern and Eastern European immigrants just as they have shaped the social construction of the

Racial Muslim. Prior to World War II, religion represented a ceiling on how high an immigrant group could move up the racial-religious hierarchy. No matter how much Irish or Italian Catholics assimilated into Anglo-American normativity, they could not move out of the inferior in-between racial category, though they would be ranked above Blacks, Native Americans, Asians, and Latinos.

Pointing to the three faiths' shared holy text, the Old Testament, proponents of a Judeo-Christian American identity argued that Protestants, Catholics, and Jews believed in American democratic principles of individual rights, freedom of expression, liberty, and brotherhood.[109]

Interfaith work, coupled with a spike in anti-Catholic bias during Al Smith's 1928 presidential campaign, culminated in the establishment of the National Conference of Christians and Jews (NCCJ) in 1927.[110] Composed of thirty-nine Christian and Jewish organizations, the NCCJ hosted a national discussion tour by a priest, a minister, and a rabbi aimed at promoting religious tolerance of Catholics and Jews.[111] The NCCJ included the American Jewish Committee, the American Jewish Congress, and the Anti-Defamation League, which expanded their work beyond anti-Semitism to opposing all forms of religious intolerance.[112] Jewish leaders such as Roger Williams Straus, Jr. played a key role in making the NCCJ the vehicle for bringing Protestants, Catholics, and Jews together. Straus was joined by other American Jewish intellectuals within the Reform Judaism movement who were opposed to the idea that Jews were a distinct racial or national group.[113] Instead, Reform Jews argued that Jews should be treated as loyal citizens of the countries in which they lived. In exchange for recognition as full members of American White society, Jews should dispose of obsolete and ritualistic practices as part of their adaptation to modernity.[114]

The Anti-Defamation League, established in 1913 after the lynching of Leo Frank, opposed racialized images of Jews in the media and the theater.[115] Before World War I, Jews claimed Whiteness based on assertions that Semites are members of the Aryan race. After World War I, Jews focused on religious commonalities between Jews and Christians in furtherance of a Judeo-Christian national identity. American Jews also defended Al Smith, a Catholic, as a means of combating Protestant hegemony in American political life and because Smith had cultivated Jewish support when he was governor of New York. Over 72 percent of Jewish voters cast their ballots for Smith in 1928.[116]

Meanwhile, the American Jewish Committee focused its efforts on declassifying Jews as a Hebrew race in immigration proceedings, which finally occurred in 1942.[117] Through their alliances with Irish and German Catholics—who were accepted as a White religious minority—Jews found support for their claim that they too should be treated as a White religious minority, not a separate race.[118] In 1940, when the US Census stopped asking whether a person or a person's parents were foreign born, Jewish and Catholic Americans were no longer legally differentiated from Anglo-Americans in this regard.[119] Courts also rebuffed attempts to impose Christian religious practices on schools and public life.[120] The famous footnote 4 of the Supreme Court's 1938 ruling in *United States v. Carolene Products Company* that established the heightened scrutiny test for laws targeting "discrete and insular minorities" included religious as well racial minorities.[121] But it would take decades of persistent advocacy to reverse public opinion; polls in the late 1930s and early 1940s showed that nearly two-thirds of Americans believed Jews were mercenary, clannish, pushy, crude, and domineering.[122]

World War II was a turning point in the expansion of Whiteness to include Americans of different European origins as well as some non-Protestant faiths. As the United States fought Nazism and Fascism in Europe, the nation was confronted with its own racism against Blacks—as well as Catholics and Jews.[123] Indeed, when President Franklin Roosevelt criticized Hitler's treatment of Jews, Hitler retorted, "Look at how you treat your Negroes. I learned how to persecute Jews by studying the manner in which you Americans persecute Negroes."[124] America's geopolitical interest in distinguishing itself from Nazism and Fascism further facilitated the discrediting of race and the adoption of ethnicity as a primary identifier for ethnic Whites.[125]

Americans who identified as people of faith called for national unity against Fascism in Europe.[126] Invoking religious freedom allowed Jews and Catholics to both retain their religious identities and claim a stake in American national identity. When challenging the American racial-religious hierarchy, Catholics sought equality with Protestants without connecting their subordination to that of Black Protestants or Latino Catholics. The Whitening of Jews and Catholics only entrenched the Black-White dichotomy that permanently subjugated African Americans.[127]

Meanwhile, in response to the rise of the Ku Klux Klan and other White nativist groups, religious and secular organizations promoted an inclusive vision of Americanism grounded in religious pluralism.[128] Most notably, the American Council Against Nazi Propaganda, the Friends of Democracy, the Council Against Intolerance in America, and the Common Council for American Unity were founded to redefine American national identity to be more racially and religiously inclusive of people of European ancestry. Interfaith coalitions and dialogues as an antidote to bigotry would reemerge after 9/11 between Muslims, Jews, and Christians. Muslims' current attempts to overcome Islamophobia through an expansion of American identity from Judeo-Christian to Abrahamic face resistance from right-wing Jews and Christians, who now belong to a contemporary American White nativist movement (see chapters 7 and 8).

The National Conference of Christians and Jews actively opposed Nazism by using the language of religious freedom and liberalism. As Nazis attacked Jews in Europe, NCCJ's leader, Straus, warned in *Religious Liberty and Democracy* that if the Nazis were not stopped, they would soon attack Catholics and Evangelical Protestants.[129] Put simply, Nazi anti-Semitism was an assault on all Judeo-Christian faiths.[130] Although most Americans were opposed to allowing Jewish refugees to enter the United States during an economic depression, Straus's message aligned with government propaganda contrasting US democracy with Nazi anti-Semitism.

That the United States had failed to open its borders to Jews fleeing from Hitler's final solution, admitting merely 110,000 Jewish refugees, became a source of national shame once the world discovered the gravity of the Holocaust.[131] Many White Anglo-Saxon Americans came to the realization that anti-Semitism was a cancer capable of destroying societies, including their own.[132] Adopting a Judeo-Christian identity became a mainstream political project.

Judeo-Christian America in the Post–World War II Era

Will Herberg's seminal 1955 book, *Protestant-Catholic-Jew*, sought to convince the American elite that religion had become an essential means of European immigrants' assimilation.[133] Herberg argued that the three religious identities had fused into a single Judeo-Christian tradition, that they were "expressions of an over-all American religion, standing for essentially the same 'moral ideals' and 'spiritual values.'" He argued further that Judaism had become "one of the three 'religions of democracy.'" Herberg's new American national identity notably excluded the approximately ten million African American Protestants, as well as a growing number of African American Muslims.[134] Although part of American society still perceived them as distinct ethnoreligious groups, Jews and Catholics were assimilating into Anglo-Protestant normativity. As a consequence, they became wealthier and more educated without converting from their religions.[135]

During the Cold War, when a focus of Americans was "godless Communism," America experienced a religious revival. More Catholic schools and churches were built in the 1950s than in the mid-nineteenth century.[136] Polls taken in 1952 and 1957 found that 75 percent of Americans said religion was "very important" in their personal lives and 81 percent said religion is the answer to the problems of the day, respectively.[137] To rally political support for the Cold War, Dwight D. Eisenhower held an annual "Back to God" campaign that connected belief in God to Americanism.[138] Congress added "under God" to the Pledge of Allegiance in 1954 and replaced *E pluribus unum* (out of many, one) with "In God we trust" on the Great Seal of the United States in 1956. Not coincidentally, it was at this time that Herberg declared Protestantism, Catholicism, and Judaism the religions of democracy.

Secularization and Class Mobility of Jews

Entrance into Whiteness, however, required assimilation and secularization. Jews in the postwar era, particularly among the middle and upper-middle classes, increasingly left Orthodox Judaism for Conservative or Reform Judaism.[139] Conservative Jewish spokespersons rejected the immigrant ghetto, which they believed was created by Orthodoxy transported from Eastern Europe.[140] Reform Judaism went further by rejecting the binding power of Jewish law. Taking the position that Judaism has changed over time with society, Reform rabbis interpreted Jewish tradition based on contemporary circumstances. Reform Judaism's universalistic approach to religion attracted second- and third-generation American Jews seeking to retain their Jewish identity without having to comport with Jewish laws that conflicted with their secular American lifestyles.[141] As a result, Reform congregations grew from 300 in 1943 to 656 in 1964 and to more than 800 in 1995.

A growing number of Jews blended their religious identity into their American national identity as their communal activities mirrored those of their Christian neighbors' church activities.[142] Starting in the 1920s, attendance at religious services and consumption of Kosher meat began to decline.[143] With each passing decade, Jewish identity became increasingly more cultural and secularized and less religious. For example, although

Yiddish fluency had disappeared among American-born Jews, Yiddish food and phrases and Jewish holidays connected the grandchildren of Eastern European immigrants to their Jewish identity.[144] As the number of Reform Jews increased significantly after World War II, American Judaism experienced a Protestantization.[145] American Jews wanted from their rabbis the inspirational sermon common in Protestantism. Rather than emphasize a reading of the Torah on Saturday morning or explicate Jewish law, American rabbis gave well-prepared lectures on social and political issues on Friday nights.[146]

Prior to the 1960s, marriage to Gentiles was perceived as a threat to Jewish survival. But as second- and third-generation American Jews integrated into mainstream White society, the rate of intermarriage—the litmus test of assimilation—soared.[147] For example, between one-third and one-half of Jews had a non-Jewish spouse in the 1980s, compared to only one of fourteen in the 1960s.[148] For interfaith marriages in which the father is Jewish, Judaism's matrilineal descent made their children non-Jewish. In response to these major demographic changes, the Reform Judaism movement accepted patrilineal descent in 1983, on the condition that the children of Jewish fathers were raised as Jews.[149] Meanwhile, increasing levels of intermarriage among Americans of European ancestry contributed to the decreasing relevance of national origin.[150] More than half of US-born Whites in the 1990s had spouses whose ethnic background was different from their own.[151]

Economic prosperity coupled with the lifting of Jewish quotas in medical schools, law schools, and universities significantly increased the number of Jewish professionals.[152] For example, only 1 percent of doctors were Jewish men before World War II. That number rose to 16 percent in the postwar generation.[153] The number of Jewish applicants to law school also increased between World War I and World War II. Because prestigious private law firms refused to hire them, Jewish lawyers created their own law firms, which today are among the largest and most prestigious in the nation.[154] Despite these challenges, Jews outpaced Italian Catholics in reaching middle-class status, notwithstanding the two groups' immigration to the United States at the same time. For example, in 1925, 13 percent of the Jewish workforce but only 2 percent of the Italian Catholic workforce had reached middle-class status.[155]

As the number of Jewish professionals rose, the number of Jewish small businesses that served a primarily Jewish clientele declined.[156] Jews moved to the suburbs, climbed corporate ladders, joined university faculties, and gradually increased among the ranks of elected officials.[157] Between 1950 and 1970, the percentage of Jewish professionals rose from 15 to 30 percent.[158] By the 1980s, Jews made up only a small percentage of America's working class.[159]

Jewish graduates of Ivy League colleges became indistinguishable from their Gentile colleagues in dress, mannerism, appearance, and speech patterns. After World War II, Jews were hired in large numbers in fields such as insurance, commercial banking, and automotive manufacturing, where they had historically faced employment discrimination.[160] Their social mobility and transition from urban ethnic communalism to suburban White lifestyles changed public opinion, such that by 1959, slightly more Americans would vote for a Jew than a Roman Catholic as president. Another poll in the same year found only 2 percent of respondents objected to having Jewish neighbors, in comparison to 20 percent in 1948.[161]

The media was also instrumental in countering anti-Semitism. Numerous Hollywood films in the 1940s portrayed Jewish characters in a positive light. Two films in particular, *Crossfire* and *Gentlemen's Agreement*, swayed public opinion to associate anti-Semitism with un-Americanness.[162] By 1962, 75 percent of Americans stated they would reject a presidential candidate solely on the grounds that he was anti-Semitic.[163] This was a dramatic change from 1918, when *The Races of Europe*, an essential work on race at the time, categorized Jews as a separate, inferior race.[164]

Class and Political Mobility of Catholics

Around the same time, Catholics' influence was also rising, particularly in politics.[165] The 1928 Catholic presidential candidate Al Smith, of Irish descent, won the twelve largest cities due in large part to the Catholic immigrant vote.[166] One of every four Americans and 45 percent of the northeastern states' population was Catholic by the mid-1900s, and Hollywood began depicting Catholics in a more positive light.[167] Catholics earned slightly higher salaries than Protestants and were just as likely to live in exclusively White suburbs.[168] Similar to the experiences of Jews, suburbanization became a vehicle for Catholic cultural assimilation into Anglo-American normalcy. That housing laws and redlining excluding Blacks, Latinos, and Asian immigrants from the suburbs did not include Jews and Catholics was further proof of their entrance into social Whiteness.[169]

The public's high esteem for religion in the two decades after World War II further contributed to the mainstreaming of Catholic religious life.[170]

Churches, cathedrals, and synagogues expanded their work to include civic recreation, youth programs, and social activities as part of the American way of life.[171] Catholic churches and schools whose attendees were primarily first- or second-generation Americans became a central part of the American cultural landscape. Consequently, nearly 70 percent of Catholics in 1963 disagreed with the statement, "Most Protestants are inclined to discriminate against Catholics."[172]

The admission of Catholics into social Whiteness culminated in 1960, when John F. Kennedy became the first Catholic elected as president of the United States.[173] Nonetheless, Kennedy felt compelled during his campaign to publicly state, "Whatever one's religion in private life may be, for the office holder, nothing takes precedence over his oath to uphold the Constitution and all its parts—including the First Amendment and the strict separation of Church and State," revealing persistent suspicions of Catholics' national loyalties.[174]

The deracialization of Catholic, Jewish, and Mormon religions changed portrayals of "good Americans" to include adherents of those faiths who were no longer raced as savage, despotic, or unfit for self-governance.[175] These social changes not only facilitated the assimilation of Jewish and Catholic identity into Anglo-Protestant norms but also contributed to what Robert Bellah described as America's "civil religion."[176] The replacement of Protestantism with a civil religion grounded in Judeo-Christian traditions and US nationalism expanded who could be considered a "real American" so long as they subscribed to certain fundamental beliefs, values, holidays, and rituals—in addition to those of their chosen religion.[177] The Pledge of Allegiance, the Fourth of July, the Bill of Rights and US Constitution, belief in God, and the superiority of American democracy constitute fundamental values of American civil religion. But civil religion did not affect the exclusion of those raced as non-White from American national identity, neither in the past nor in the present.

JUDEO-CHRISTIAN NORMATIVITY AND THE EXCLUSION OF NON-WHITES

The transition to religious pluralism within a Judeo-Christian framework did not end racism; it merely redefined its boundaries. Fervent anti-Black and anti-Asian racism was still intact.[178] More than seventy thousand Japanese

Americans were interned during World War II, while Italian Americans, whose nation of origin was also at war with the United States, escaped the same fate.[179]

As notions of religious pluralism normalized, the systemic discrimination against Blacks and other racial minorities became glaring. Legalized racial segregation and immigration restrictions targeted non-Whites, many of whom were also non-Christian. Seeking to merge the religious pluralism movement with the Civil Rights Movement, Martin Luther King Jr. invoked the language of Christian brotherhood and national unity to push for racial equality. His appeal in 1963 to the National Conference on Religion and Race prompted the inclusion of race in its conception of the brotherhood of man under God. To that end, they issued this statement: "We Americans of all religious faiths have been slow to recognize that racial discrimination and segregation are an insult to God, the Giver of human dignity and human rights. Even worse, we all have participated in perpetuating racial discrimination and segregation in civil, political, industrial, social and private life."[180] With the increased participation of religious organizations in the Civil Rights Movement, racial differences between Blacks and Whites eclipsed divisions between Protestants, Catholics, Mormons, and Jews.

Concerns with racism extended beyond civil society to the US government fighting the Cold War. The Soviet Union pointed to rampant anti-Black and anti-Asian racism in its claims that American democracy was a fraud. American racism became a national security issue. As a result, the United States needed to exude the moral high ground to obtain cooperation from non-European nations in its Cold War policy of Communist containment.[181] But the narrative that American democracy was superior to Communist dictatorship was not credible without civil rights reforms.[182] Nor could the US government credibly claim that American democracy brought freedom to all its citizens.

Partly in response to US international interests after World War II (and White violence against returning African American veterans), President Truman created the President's Committee on Civil Rights to explore how to strengthen and safeguard civil rights in the United States, focusing on African Americans.[183] The committee's final report, released in 1947, identified discrimination in employment, education, housing, social services, and voting as areas where federal government intervention was necessary. Truman consequently called on Congress to pass laws to protect civil rights for all or risk failure of efforts by the United States to be the leader of the free world.[184] It would take Congress two decades to pass federal civil rights legislation in 1964 and 1965.

When challenges to school segregation reached the US Supreme Court in 1954, the Department of Justice in an amicus brief justified its anti-segregation stance in this way: "The United States is trying to prove to the people of the world, of every nationality, race and color, that a free democracy is the most civilized and most secure form of government yet devised by man."[185] Efforts to pass civil rights legislation culminated when President Lyndon B. Johnson signed the landmark 1964 Civil Rights Act.[186] Tellingly, Johnson emphasized the law's historic significance in promoting a "more abiding commitment to freedom, a more constant pursuit of justice, and a deeper respect for human dignity."[187]

Simultaneous with pressures to implement racial equality were pressures to open up America's borders to immigration from Asia. After China joined the United States as an allied nation in World War II, President Roosevelt successfully pushed for repeal of the Chinese Exclusion Act in the 1943 Magnuson Act.[188] A decade later, Congress passed the 1952 McCarran-Walter Act, granting Asians the right to naturalize as citizens.[189] By 1965, all national origin quotas and immigration bars were lifted. The door was now open for immigrants from outside Europe, including Muslim-majority countries, to come to America in large numbers.

The use of national origin to determine who was fit to immigrate, however, was replaced with an individual's commitment to American democracy and rejection of Communism. The 1940 Alien Registration Act, also known as the Smith Act, granted the US attorney general authority to deport non-citizens suspected of subversive activities, resulting in the conviction of eleven leaders of the Communist Party.[190] A decade later when the Korean War began, the 1950 McCarran Act, also known as the Subversive Activities Control Act, authorized denaturalizations and deportations of thousands of US citizens suspected of supporting the world Communist movement. It was no coincidence that Jews and Asians—long suspected of disloyalty—were among those targeted by political witch-hunts that came to be known as McCarthyism, named for the staunch anti-Communist US senator Joseph McCarthy.[191]

Although membership in the US Communist Party was 30 to 40 percent Jewish during the Great Depression, the overwhelming majority of Jews at this time were Democrats. Nevertheless, White nativist groups claimed *Judeobolshevism*, a term coined by the Nazis, was being spread by Eastern

European Jews in the United States.[192] Indeed, some scholars argue the House Un-American Activities Committee was an anti-Semitic tool to target wealthy and influential Jews in Hollywood and government.[193]

Among the most high-profile cases was that of Julius and Ethel Rosenberg, charged, along with Harry Gold and David Greenglass, Ethel's brother, with transmitting classified information about the atomic bomb to the Soviet Union. For their testimony against the Rosenbergs, Gold and Greenglass received prison sentences. The Rosenbergs were executed on June 19, 1953.[194] Seeking to contain the anti-Semitic backlash—all the defendants were Jews—mainstream Jewish organizations such as the Anti-Defamation League, the American Jewish Committee, and Jewish War Veterans cooperated with the House Un-American Committee by making their files available.[195] They also refused to help the defendants out of fear they would be suspected by association.

Five decades later, Muslim American leaders would also find themselves in the government's crosshairs, as Muslim individuals and organizations were charged with terrorism in an aggressive domestic War on Terror. The same weaponization of immigration and criminal law to regulate and chill political activism of immigrants was replicated starting in the 1980s as the Cold War was winding down.[196] After the September 11 attack, practicing Islam became the most threatening subversive activity in the government's War on Terror—a racial project infused with religious animus.

. . .

The experiences of Catholics, Jews, and Mormons leads us back to the race question facing Muslims today: Does having a non-Judeo-Christian religious identity permanently bar immigrant Muslims from obtaining the full dignitary and social benefits of citizenship? So long as Muslim identity is racialized, the answer is likely no.[197] Meanwhile, African American Muslims will continue to be barred from first-class citizenship on account of entrenched anti-Black racism under America's Black-White racial paradigm.

Accordingly, this chapter explains how religious pluralism, civil rights reforms, and the lifting of national origin immigration restrictions occurred in large part due to international developments that made racial and religious equality a matter of national security.[198] As Derrick Bell argues, when there is a convergence of interests between the dominant White Christian elite and subordinated minority groups, the latter has some leverage to reform, though not eliminate, racialized social structures.[199] For Eastern and Southern European Jews and Catholics, interest convergence granted them entrance into social Whiteness. But it did not fundamentally change the racial-religious hierarchy propping up White Christian normativity that racializes immigrant Muslims in the post-9/11 era.

I now turn to the racialization of Muslims in America. While their story is similar to that of other immigrants, the differences loom large. Muslims arrived in the United States not only by immigrating from more than one hundred different countries, many of which were targets of American imperial designs, but also on ships carrying enslaved Africans beginning in the seventeenth century. Islam's association with categorically condemned heathens and savages from Africa merged with the importation of European Orientalism whose nemesis was the Mahometan Turk to produce a complex and fluid process of racialization. As a result, Muslim identity is socially constructed to merge immigrants and non-immigrants of various skin colors, ancestries, and phenotypes into an essentialized identity: the foreign, illiberal, and inherently violent Racial Muslim.[200]

FIVE

Social Construction of the Racial Muslim

EVEN MORE THAN CATHOLICISM and Judaism, Islam has historically been depicted as uncivilized, illiberal, and despotic. During the colonial era many Americans did not recognize Islam as a legitimate religion, considering it instead a false ideology followed by savages in Africa and the Orient.[1] This theme reemerged in the post-9/11 era to justify excluding Muslims from American religious freedom norms. Despite American school lessons on the sanctity of religious freedom, deporting, prosecuting, and discriminating against Muslims is part of a long history of nativism that reserves the full exercise of religious freedom for White Christians. As a result, pervasive stereotypes associating Islam with terrorism infect government counterterrorism practices and private citizens' (mis)treatment of Muslims.

Although the White nativist ideology that racialized Jews, Catholics, and Mormons in the twentieth century is deployed against Muslims today, racialization of Islam is distinct in various ways. Specifically, European Orientalism and American imperial ambitions in Muslim-majority countries placed immigrant Muslims permanently outside the national identity. Individual attempts to assimilate and secularize, primarily by Arab Muslims, proved futile for attaining the full benefits of citizenship. The September 11 attacks thus accelerated a racialization of Muslims that predated 2001, resulting in an entrenchment of the Racial Muslim in American race politics.

When immigrants from the Levant slowly began to arrive at the turn of the twentieth century in pursuit of economic opportunity, their affiliation with Islam (either as Muslims or as Christians governed by Muslim rulers) deemed them inassimilable non-Whites. Although Muslims did not immigrate in large numbers until changes in immigration laws after World War II, when they did arrive, they remained outsiders to America's newfound Judeo-Christian identity.[2]

The social construction of the Racial Muslim, thus, is informed by White Protestant supremacy, xenophobia, Orientalism, and American empire. The previous two chapters demonstrated the roots of White Protestant supremacy and xenophobia—phenomena that have affected all minority groups, albeit in different ways. I now turn to the third component: the racialization of Islam as uncivilized, pagan, and violent in Western Orientalist and Christian theological narratives. The result is the weaponization of religion to perpetuate racial inequality.[3]

EUROPEAN ORIENTALISM

The contemporary portrayal of Islam as a violent political ideology and a false religion is not a new phenomenon. Europe historically situated Islam as the antithesis of modernity and enlightenment, such that a clash with Western Christendom was inevitable.[4] Popular narratives that Islam is malevolent and "spread by the sword" were grounded both in European geopolitics and Christian theology.[5]

Since the First Crusade in 1095, European Christians viewed Islam's supposed propagation of ignorance, violence, and sensuality as a threat to Christianity's perceived light, knowledge, and reason.[6] The juxtaposition of enemy Islam to Christianity created a collective Christian identity, a political unifier, after centuries of fighting within Christendom.[7] As Tomaž Mastnak notes, Pope Urban II, who launched the First Crusade, "fixed the image of the Muslim as the focal point for Christian animosities."[8] With each Crusade's call on Christians to take back Jerusalem and the Holy Land, Muslims were described as barbarians.[9] As Europe came to represent the locus of Christendom, the Mahometan Turks became the enemy, and "exterminate the Turk in Europe" became a unifying slogan.[10] The Englishmen who founded the United States imported these prejudices into their settler colonial project.[11]

The West's historical domination, restructuring, and control of the Orient—what Edward Said called Orientalism—shapes the discourse, knowledge, and ideological framework through which Muslims are deemed inferior.[12] European art and literature depicted the Muslim Middle Easterner as fanatical, cruel, and degenerate, on the one hand, and exotic and hypersensual, on the other.[13] The positional superiority of the West over the East justified European imperialism, particularly in Muslim-majority areas and the Indian subcontinent.[14] For example, Orientalist stereotypes animated Napoleon's conquest of Egypt and Syria in 1798, the construction of the Suez Canal in the 1860s, and British colonization of Southwest Asia and Africa in the nineteenth and twentieth centuries.[15] According to colonialist logic, Anglo-Saxon tutelage was necessary to civilize people whose religion produced a backward culture. This same racialized reasoning undergirds America's claims after 9/11 that the War on Terror is necessary to protect the West from Muslim terrorists both within and outside the country.[16]

European literature also played an important role in Orientalism by depicting a corrupt, religiously zealous, exotic, and licentious Muslim world.[17] John Milton's *Paradise Lost*, published in 1741, for example, described Satan as an Ottoman sultan, and fallen angels were depicted as Muslim warriors. Voltaire's play *Fanaticism* used the Prophet Muhammad and Islam as the representation of fanaticism and intolerance.[18] Said's work demonstrates how European Orientalism portrayed Muslims as "fatalistic children tyrannized by their mind-set, their 'ulama, and their wild-eyed political leaders into resisting the West and progress."[19] Deemed antithetical to the Enlightenment, Islam embodied the inferiority of the so-called Orient.

Islam as a political enemy was also theologically grounded.[20] Throughout the Reformation, Protestants and Catholics portrayed Islam as evil and Mahometans as incapable of exercising human reason.[21] The English Protestant cleric John Foxe, in his 1563 *Book of Martyrs,* depicted Mahometan Turks as cruel despots whose atrocities against Christians were comparable to the Romans' violence centuries earlier.[22] During the nineteenth century, the English churchman Humphrey Prideaux claimed Islam was not a religion but rather a political scheme hatched by Muhammad to take over Arabia. In his influential 1808 book, *The True Nature of Imposture Displayed in the Life of Mahomet*, Prideaux argued that Islam was an imposter religion because it served carnal interests, was led by wicked men, used craft and fraud, and was spread by force.[23] Prideaux's book mainstreamed the notion that Prophet Muhammad was a militant zealot who forcibly spread his political ideology by the sword. This theme would later animate depictions of Muslims as terrorists in American political discourse starting in the 1970s. Notably, the demand for Prideaux's book in North America was so high that it was published in eight editions.[24]

The English Protestant elites who founded the United States would adopt European Orientalism in setting up Islam as the quintessential antidemocratic foil.[25]

AMERICAN ORIENTALISM: THE CONVERGENCE OF RELIGION, RACE, AND EMPIRE BUILDING

With the exception of the Barbary Wars in the early 1800s and enslavement of African Muslims, Americans had little contact with Muslims before World War II. Nonetheless, European Christian theological hostility to Islam influenced religious polemics during the American colonial era.[26] Discursive hostility to Muslims originated in American missionaries' accounts of Jerusalem and other Muslim cities during the formative period of the modern Middle East.[27]

As the historian Thomas Kidd's work demonstrates, American eschatological writings of the nineteenth century predicted the destruction of the Roman Catholic and Islamic powers as a sign of the end of times.[28] Thomas Wells Bray, a respected Evangelical minister in Guilford, Connecticut, cited Prideaux in his 1780 dissertation: "By cruel tyranny and over-bearing power, did that vile impostor Mahomet set up and propagate a false religion, which has been one of the greatest plagues to the Christian religion, and filled all the eastern world with error and thick darkness, like the smoke of a bottomless pit."[29]

Similarly, the prominent American theologian Jonathan Edwards described Islam as one of the great kingdoms the devil erected to oppose the kingdom of Christ, along with Roman Catholicism.[30] As part of his post-millennialism ideology, Edwards believed that the second coming of Christ would destroy Islam in the battle of Armageddon and that a Christian America was specially chosen for God's kingdom to exist thereafter.[31] Samuel Langdon, a Congregationalist pastor and former Harvard president, claimed the devil was the source of Muhammad's revelations. Ultimately, the multitude of theological vilifications of Islam influenced the White Protestant men who would establish the new American republic.[32] By the end of the American Revolution, Kidd notes, American theologians had "a clear place for Islam in their visions of the last days, characterized Muhammad as an imposter, and deplored Muslim polities as despotic."[33]

American missionary work in the Middle East and North Africa became the means by which Americans undertook the "white man's burden" to civilize and liberate Muslims as a global extension of Manifest Destiny.[34] White Protestants believed their race and religion was superior to that of the Mahometan Turks.[35] American missionaries traveling to the Middle East in the mid-1800s returned with accounts that further racialized Muslims as men "of unrestrained passions, full of falsehood and blasphemy."[36] They believed these "Orientals," whether Muslim or Christian, needed to be saved by the West—a recurring theme of American Orientalism up to the present day.[37]

The Barbary Wars and Christian Slavery

Notwithstanding political and theological discursive hostility to Muslims, the American government had minimal interactions with Muslim-ruled states. With the conclusion of the American Revolution in 1783, American ships were no longer protected by the British navy.[38] Thus American ships and crew were vulnerable to capture on the high seas. Between 1784 and 1816, Barbary pirates captured at least thirty-six American merchant ships and one naval ship, resulting in the enslavement of four hundred to seven hundred (White) American men.[39]

The Barbary regencies ruled present-day Morocco, Algeria, Libya, and Tunisia, from which they prowled the Mediterranean, seizing European merchant ships. The Christian crew members became captives until their rulers paid a hefty ransom or until the captive converted to Islam. Barbary ships also sent bands of armed pirates to kidnap people from the coasts of Southern Europe.[40] To protect their ships from piracy and their crews from enslavement, European rulers entered into treaties that required an annual tribute to the Barbary Regencies. The tributes became a substantial source of income, such that nothing short of a war would stop the piracy.[41]

Stories of egregious abuse and enslavement of the White Christian crew members by Muslim captors terrorized American readers. Freed slaves told of miserable conditions and hard labor in a hostile, foreign land, where their Muslim masters reminded the Christians of their inferiority on a regular basis.[42] For example, one former captive recounted witnessing the torture, beheadings, and merciless persecution of slaves on account of their Christian faith, which the pirates claimed was "bigotry and superstition" and in disregard of the "true doctrine of God's last and greatest prophet, Mahomet."[43]

The piracy ultimately led to two wars between the United States and the Barbary powers in 1801 and 1815, inspiring a new genre of Barbary captivity plays. Susanna Rowson's 1794 *Slaves in Algiers* and David Everett's 1817 *Slaves in Barbary* portrayed Turks and Arabs as savage beasts.[44] Christian slaves were compared to the ancient Israelites seeking to escape from the oppression of the pharaoh in Egypt.[45] That White Christians were the slaves of Muslim heathens was the ultimate humiliation for Protestant Americans.[46] Although stridently opposed to the enslavement of White Christians by Muslims, Americans justified the enslavement of Africans based on Christian theological notions that Blacks were racially inferior.[47] That nearly a third of the Africans were Muslims only further justified the racist logic.[48]

Although Barbary piracy against the United States ended by the mid-nineteenth century, the image of the Muslim savage became a staple in Christian polemics and American culture.[49] Protestant leaders compared Islam and Catholicism, condemning both as threats to American Christendom, thereby parroting what the German Protestant reformer Martin Luther declared in the fifteenth and sixteenth centuries: "The person of the Antichrist is at the same time the pope and the Turk."[50]

Kidd's work details how Judge Samuell Sewall, the Puritan lay leader Anne Hutchison, and the influential preachers Cotton Mather, Edward Taylor, and Eric Tobias also associated Islam with the Antichrist by comparing Muhammad to the pope.[51] In *The Mohammedan Missionary Problem*, published in 1879, the Presbyterian missionary Henry Jessup depicted Muslims in present-day Lebanon as wild beasts and thirsty for the blood of Christians.[52] Jessup presciently declared that "in the conflict between civilization and barbarism Islam must be the loser." The same narratives would resonate among Americans in the years following the attacks of September 11, 2001.

Islam as the Antithesis of American (Protestant) Democracy

While America's Protestant founders disagreed vehemently on myriad political matters, one issue found consensus: Islam was the antithesis of their democracy grounded in Protestantism.[53] As Denise Spellberg's work demonstrates, however, notwithstanding his distrust of Islam, Jefferson, a Deist, believed Muslims should be protected under his universalistic notions of religious freedom.[54] Jefferson quoted John Locke in proclaiming to his fellow countrymen that "neither Pagan nor Mahamedan nor Jew ought to be excluded from the civil rights of the Commonwealth because of his religion."[55] That the only Muslims in the United States at the time were enslaved Africans limited the effect of his lofty rhetoric to abstract principles of religious freedom that did not bear out in practice. Indeed, American slave owners prohibited their Muslim slaves from practicing their religion while forcing them to convert to Christianity.[56] American Orientalism was also manifested in literature and art. As early as 1776, Thomas Paine's best-seller, *Common Sense*, situated Islam as a foil for his vision of an American Republic based on reason and liberty, not superstition and monarchy.[57] William Guir's *The Life of Mahomet*, published in 1861, portrayed Muhammad as a fraud who created a false religion for ignorant and lustful barbarians in Arabia.[58]

Mark Twain's book *The Innocents Abroad*, published in 1869, describes his tour of the Holy Land. Twain portrays Muslims and Ottomans as "a people by nature and training filthy, brutish, ignorant, unprogressive, [and] superstitious."[59] The book was wildly popular, with nearly 100,000 copies sold. Similarly, the American author Washington Irving confirmed to his readers the inability of Muslims to self-govern. In his biography of the Prophet Muhammad published in 1897, *Mahomet and His Successors*, Irving concludes that adherents to Islam were better suited for theocratic or autocratic rule—in sharp contrast to Protestants' free and democratic America.[60]

In the 1850s, the American artist Hiram Powers renewed Americans' anxieties over Christian slavery when he sculpted the *Greek Slave*. Depicting a young Christian virgin taken captive by Muslim Turks, the sculpture symbolized the clash of civilizations, with American freedom and Christian purity positioned against Turkish brutality and Muslim heathenism.[61] Nearly a century later, in 1921, the movie *The Sheik* portrayed Arabs as lusting after the White female lead.[62] The same motif remerged in David Friedman's 1968 movie, *The Lustful Turk*, which portrayed Turks as barbaric, lustful, and unrestrained as they sexually devour the innocent White (Christian) female. Not coincidentally, gendered racialization of Muslim men mirrored those of Black men as sexual predators of White women.[63] Comparing non-Whites to Blacks was a common tool used to racialize immigrants; people from the Middle East were no exception.

CHRISTIAN IDENTITY AS A PATH TO
US CITIZENSHIP FOR ARABS

Before World War II, the number of immigrant Muslims in the United States was nominal. American Orientalism had minimal practical domestic consequences, with one exception: the legal status of approximately 150,000

Christian immigrants from Syria and Lebanon.[64] These immigrants perplexed judges presiding over naturalization applications as US law permitted only White persons to become citizens.[65] Did the litigants' Christian religion from the eastern Mediterranean make them civilized and assimilable Whites such that they qualified for American citizenship, or did their status as subjects of the Muslim Ottoman Empire make them uncivilized and inassimilable non-White Turks? The courts' inconsistent findings demonstrate the role that religion played in racing Arab immigrants in America, a phenomenon that informs the social construction of the Racial Muslim today.

Until national origin quotas were lifted in 1965, Muslims were treated as either inferior foreigners in lands far away or militant African Americans.[66] The few Muslim immigrants from the Ottoman Empire were largely invisible, numbering in the mere tens of thousands, at a time when more than ten million Jews and Catholics were emigrating from Eastern and Southern Europe.[67] Magazines such as *National Geographic* and *Harper's* depicted Arabs and Turks as an exotic people lagging in modernity and cultural sophistication.[68] American artists such as Miner Kilbourne Kellogg and Edward Troye painted Middle Eastern vistas populated by primitive Bedouins and exotic, despotic peoples.[69]

Outside the public spotlight and of European origin, Bosnian, Albanian, Polish, and Lithuanian Muslim communities sprang up in New York and Chicago in the first decade of the twentieth century.[70] Albanian Muslims opened the first mosque built by immigrants in 1915 in Massachusetts.[71] Other European Muslim immigrants built mosques in Ross, North Dakota; Highland Park, Michigan; and Cedar Rapids, Iowa, in the 1920s and 1930s.[72] As Muslims from the Levant slowly trickled in, the number of mosques gradually increased. For the most part, immigrant Muslims remained invisible as a religious minority, at a time when Jews and Catholics faced pointed religious bigotry and African American Muslims were treated as a domestic security threat.[73]

The Racial Ambiguity of Syrian Immigrants in the Early Twentieth Century

Starting in the late 1870s, a slow stream of migrants from Mount Lebanon, Palestine, and Syria sought economic fortune in the United States.[74]

Intending to return home with the fruits of their labor, these predominantly Orthodox Christian migrants peddled goods throughout the United States. As word spread of their success, economic migration from the immigrants' home villages accelerated. The desire to send remittances, accumulate wealth, and eventually return home to establish businesses motivated this first wave of migrants.

The longer the Arabic-speaking Levantines stayed, however, the less likely they were to return to their villages in the Ottoman Empire.[75] Although reliable data are not available, scholars estimate that the apex of Syrian migration occurred in 1913, when around 150,000 Syrian immigrants lived in the United States. Approximately 22,000 Syrians were naturalized US citizens in 1920, and that number grew to 40,000 in 1930. By 1940, an estimated 200,000 Syrian immigrants and Syrian Americans had permanently settled in the United States, with their largest numbers in New York, Boston, Chicago, Cleveland, and Detroit.[76]

Due to their small numbers, particularly as compared to Catholic and Jewish immigrants, the first generation of Christian Syrians seldom experienced prejudice on account of their ethnic identity.[77] Naff explains that Syrian peddlers quickly learned English and assimilated into Anglo-American society because of their frequent interactions with Americans.[78] The experience of Muslims, who made up only 10 to 15 percent of Syrian immigrants, mirrored those of their Christian compatriots.[79] They assimilated by anglicizing their names, marrying White Christians, and enlisting in the US military. Some even converted to Christianity.[80] Pressures to assimilate into Anglo-Protestant culture also led to the loss of the Arabic language by the second or third generation.

Meanwhile, Syrian immigrants' legal status was in flux. During the nineteenth century, the US government categorized any subject of the Ottoman Empire as coming from "Turkey in Asia."[81] In 1899, however, the Bureau of Immigration changed the racial classification of people from the Levant to "Syrian," to distinguish them from Greeks, Turks, and Armenians, who were also ruled by the Ottomans. This new category had no relation to identity formation in their homelands.[82] No one identified as an Arab or a Syrian.[83] Instead, a person's religion was the primary distinguishing factor in a majority-Muslim society, followed by the region, town, village, or city of origin. Over time, these predominantly Christian immigrants found that their common Arabic language, emphasis on family honor and generosity, and similar foods gave them a shared Syrian identity within America's complex racial and ethnic landscape.[84] They eventually self-identified as Syrian.

As Syrians' ties to the United States strengthened, they sought citizenship because it bestowed multiple benefits, including the ability to travel easily between the United States and Syria and the right to purchase property, own businesses, and vote.[85] However, the Naturalization Act of 1790 limited naturalization to free White persons, of good character, and living in the United States for two years.[86] After the Bureau of Immigration legally categorized Syrians and Palestinians as Caucasian in its 1899 racial classifications, they had little difficulty naturalizing.[87] Local political bosses seeking votes from immigrants assisted Syrians to quickly obtain citizenship in exchange for political loyalty.[88] Syrian economic mobility also contributed to their attempts to become legally White. By the second generation, many Syrians had entered the ranks of the middle class.

However, as xenophobia and White nativism against Southern and Eastern European immigrants escalated in the early 1900s, Syrians found themselves caught in the crosshairs. In 1909, the US government classified Syrians as Mongoloid.[89] Within a decade, their racial status had shifted from Caucasian to Asian. At a time when four schemas—biology, phenotype, common knowledge, and geographic origin—complicated racial categorizations, naturalization cases produced different definitions of Whiteness across the country.[90] Anti-immigrant politicians used the newly created Bureau of Immigration and Naturalization (BIN) to decrease the number of naturalizations.[91] Under the pretext of eliminating fraud, corruption, and low standards for admission, Congress ordered the BIN to heavily scrutinize naturalization applications, with an unfavorable bias against non-Europeans and non-Christians.[92]

Syrians who challenged the BIN's denial of naturalization faced judges' subjective assessments, further demonstrating the incoherence of Whiteness as a racial category.[93] Courts struggled to identify the races of persons from West Asia and the eastern shores of the Mediterranean. Syrian litigants deployed their Christian identity to prove they were fit to be US citizens and specifically to argue they were White. The xenophobia permeating American society at the time conflicted with favoritism toward Christians, producing mixed results. Cases in 1909, 1910, and 1915 held that Syrians were White "Asiatics" or Caucasians, while cases in 1913 and 1914 found them to be non-White Asians, buttressing the fact that race is socially constructed.[94]

With material and dignitary interests at stake, Syrians aggressively contested their legal racial status. As Khaled A. Beydoun notes, societal perceptions that Islam was a pagan faith and a heathen foil caused Syrian litigants in naturalization cases to highlight their Christian religion to distinguish themselves as civilized and fit for self-government, in contrast to the uncivilized and illiberal Muslims.[95] Some Arab litigants, for example, pointed to the 1891 law barring polygamists or persons who admit their belief in polygamy as evidence of Congress's intent to bar Muslims, not Christians, from the eastern Mediterranean.[96] Syrian Christians, thus, emphasized their connection to the Holy Land and belief in Jesus Christ.[97] Whatever differences Syrians may have had with respect to American society were attributable to culture, not race. And they assured the courts that as Christians, they were assimilable into Protestant Anglo-American society, in contrast to Muslims.

Because so many of the Arab litigants "looked White" after centuries of intermarriage, some judges were not persuaded by the US government's simplistic claims that people from western Asia were not White. For example, in 1909, the US District Court in Oregon ruled in favor of granting naturalization to a Syrian Christian applicant, Tom Ellis.[98] Although the court found Ellis to be White, the district attorney argued that he was not the right kind of White person because American citizenship was reserved for "only of the white persons who, from tradition, teaching, and environment, would be predisposed toward our form of government, and thus readily assimilable with the people of the United States."[99]

Invoking the same unfit for self-government tropes used against Jewish and Catholic immigrants, government lawyers emphasized the cultural inferiority and despotism of the Ottoman Empire from whence Ellis came. The court rejected this reasoning and found the "word 'White,' ethnologically speaking, was intended to be applied in its popular sense to denote at least the members of the White or Caucasian race of people." The court reasoned, "If there be ambiguity and doubt, it is better to resolve that doubt in favor of the Caucasian possessed of the highest qualities which go to make an excellent citizen, as the applicant appears to be, and withal drawn to and well disposed toward the principles and policies of this government."[100] It was not immaterial that Ellis's Maronite Christian identity distinguished him from the Mahometan Turks ruling his homeland.[101]

In the next two years, two federal courts, in *In re Najour* (1909) and *In re Mudarri* (1910), accepted the Christian Syrian litigants' classification as Caucasian as a basis for determining their legal Whiteness.[102] The judge in *Najour* was not persuaded by the government's emphasis on the applicant's darker, walnut complexion as a basis for determining race. So long as the litigant is Caucasian, they qualified as "free white persons" within the definition of the naturalization laws. Furthermore, the court rejected the government's attempts to disqualify Najour, a Christian Syrian, on account of "the fact that the applicant was born within the dominions of Turkey, and was heretofore a subject of the Sultan of Turkey."[103] Similarly, in *Mudarri* the court held that although "Syrians by race are probably of a blood more mixed than those who describe themselves as Armenians,... the older writers on ethnology are substantially agreed that Syrians are to be classed as of the Caucasian or white race."[104]

A blow to Syrians' naturalization efforts came in 1910 when the US Census classified people from the eastern Mediterranean as Asiatics.[105] Christian Syrians were now at risk of being racially equated with non-White Mohammaden Turks, Buddhist Chinese, and Hindu Indians—all racial descriptors based in part on a religious identity.[106] Although skin color, hair texture, and facial features allowed some Syrians to phenotypically pass as White, their legal status as subjects of the Muslim Ottoman Empire deemed them Asians.[107] No longer did being classified as Caucasian suffice to qualify as legally White. Syrians now had to prove they were European.[108]

As the court in *Ex parte Shahid* in 1913 stated, "The meaning of free white persons is to be such as would naturally have been given to it when used in the first naturalization act of 1790. Under such interpretation it would mean by the term 'free white persons' all persons belonging to the European races, then commonly counted as white, and their descendants. It would not mean a 'Caucasian' race."[109] The court found that the mixing of European, Arabian Mahometan, Mongolian, and Turkish blood barred Syrians from qualifying as "free white persons" under the naturalization statutes. European habitancy and descent became some courts' primary standard for determining the litigant's White racial status. Christian identity certainly worked in favor of litigants, but as *Shahid* demonstrates, it was not dispositive.

However, in 1915, the Fourth Circuit Court of Appeals in *Dow v. U.S.* looked to congressional intent in the 1790 Naturalization Law to find that although the question of Whiteness centered on European origin at the time, the Syrians "were so closely related to their neighbors on the European side of the Mediterranean that they should be classed as white, [and] they must be held to fall within the term 'white persons' used in the status."[110] Notably, George Dow referred to the 1911 Dillingham Report of the Immigration that found Syrians belong to the Semitic branch of the Caucasian race, in contrast to their Turkish rulers, who were categorized under the Mongolian race.[111] Little did Dow know at the time that his argument that Syrians should be treated like European Jews based on the historical connections between Jewish and Christian people would be mirrored by American Jews' calls for a Judeo-Christian American national identity a decade later, after World War I.[112]

In 1923, the US Supreme Court affirmed that being Caucasian was insufficient to qualify an applicant as White. In *United States v. Bhagat Singh Thind*, the Indian applicant, a Hindu, could prove he was anthropologically Caucasian, but the Court rejected his naturalization application by replacing the scientific inquiry rule with the common knowledge rule.[113] A dark-skinned Indian, even if anthropologically Caucasian, simply could not be White. Not until Congress amended immigration laws in 1943 and 1946 would Asians be permitted to immigrate and naturalize.[114] Rather than challenge racism, Christian Syrians followed what many immigrants seeking to evade American racism did: they emphasized their Christian identity and Caucasian origins.[115] For example, prior to the *Thind* ruling, a prominent Syrian leader stated in 1909 in a letter to the editor of the *New York Times*, "The Syrians are very proud of their ancestry and believe that the Caucasian race had its origin in Syria, that they opened the commerce to the world, and that Christ, our savior, was born among them."[116] But such reassurances fell on deaf ears in areas where White nativism was ubiquitous.

In 1914, North Carolina senator Furnifold McLendel Simmons called Syrian immigrants the "degenerate progeny of the Asiatic hoards [and]... the spawn of the Phoenician curse" in his opposition to immigration. Syrian children were called camel jockeys, dirty Syrians, and Turks.[117] A Syrian family's home in Marietta, Georgia, was destroyed, allegedly by the Ku Klux Klan, in 1923.[118] In 1929, a Syrian grocer, Nola Romey, was lynched in Lake City, Florida, a few weeks after Pennsylvania's US senator David A. Reed condemned Syrians as "the trash of the Mediterranean."[119] Each time such racial violence occurred, Syrian elites viewed it as racial misidentification and attempted to distinguish themselves from African Americans and Asians.[120]

Jewish and Armenian immigrants from the Ottoman Empire also began to lose their naturalization cases. The US government argued that inhabitants of western Asia and the eastern Mediterranean were Asiatic.[121] In response, Armenians and Sephardic Jews emphasized their religions and Semitic origins to contest the new laws. One example of such advocacy occurred in a stinging letter in 1909 by the Board of Delegates on Civil Rights of the Union of American Hebrew Congregations to the secretary of labor arguing that the denial of naturalization to Christians and Jews "would, if living, exclude David and Isaih [*sic*] and even Jesus of Nazareth himself."[122]

Syrian Christians, Armenian Christians, and Sephardic Jews were not challenging the inclusion of Turks as racially Asiatic and Mongoloid. Rather, they were arguing that Christian and Jewish Ottoman subjects were racially superior to Muslim Ottoman subjects on account of their Christian religion and European ancestral ties. In doing so, they perpetuated the imputation of racial traits based on religious beliefs.

A case in point is *In re Halladjian*. Four Armenian applicants won their naturalization claims in 1909 because "in the warfare which has raged since the beginning of history about the eastern Mediterranean between Europeans and Asiatics, the Armenians have generally, though not always, been found on the European side. . . . By reason of their Christianity, they generally ranged themselves against the Persian fire worshipers, and against the Mohammadens, both Saracens and Turks."[123] Fifteen years later, Armenian litigants in *United States v. Cartozian* adopted this argument when claiming that their Christian religion deemed them civilized and assimilable Whites, as opposed to the Mongoloid and semicivilized Turks who practiced polygamy.[124] In the end, Armenians' Christian faith was a proxy for assimilability and White racial belonging.[125]

The same reasoning, however, worked against a Yemeni applicant in *In re Ahmed Hassan* in 1942.[126] Even though Yemen is outside the Asiatic Barred Zone, the court stated, "it is well known that they [Arabians] are a part of the Mohammaden world and that a wide gulf separates their culture from that of the predominantly Christian peoples of Europe."[127] The court disregarded the Asiatic Barred Zone as evidence of congressional intent to exclude people of the Arabian Peninsula from the racial definition of Asian, thereby demonstrating the work done by religion to socially construct race. That is, the clear geographically based legal definitions were supplanted by Arabians' Muslim religion to deny them citizenship.

It was not until 1944 that courts would recognize Arabs as legally White, when America had deepening economic interests in the Middle East. In *Ex parte Mohriez*, a local representative of the Immigration and Naturalization Service recommended that the court grant the petitioner citizenship because the US government "regards Arabs, at any rate if born outside the [Asiatic] Saudi Arabian Barred Zone, as white persons eligible for citizenship."[128] At the time, legal Whiteness included the eastern Mediterranean because those people were a race of "Asiatics whose long contiguity to European nations and assimilation with their culture has caused them to be thought of as of the same general characteristics."[129] The *Mohriez* court highlighted that "the Arab people stand as one of the chief channels by which the traditions of white Europe, especially the ancient Greek traditions, have been carried into the present."[130]

This rare positive portrayal of Arab culture was paradoxically consistent with European Orientalism, which limited favorable depictions of Arabs to those carrying forward the ancient civilizations to Europe. The fallen cultures of contemporary Arabs, therefore, were valued only to the extent that they had provided Europe with benefits in the past. More pertinent to the time of the *Mohriez* decision was the US government's courting of Saudi Arabia, now a major oil producer. At least five American multinationals were drilling oil wells in Saudi Arabia and other Arab countries.[131] By the mid-twentieth century, Saudi Arabia would be an American ally in its opposition to Communism and Arab nationalism in the Middle East.[132]

Although Arabs became legally White, their Muslim identity excluded them from social constructions of Whiteness—much as had happened with Jews and Catholics in the first half of the twentieth century. As Arab nationalism inspired populist, anti-Western colonial movements, Muslim identity became increasingly associated with violence and anti-Americanism. These racial-religious associations, however, did not arise exclusively from European Orientalism. The roots of American Islamophobia also lie in the legacy of American slavery and anti-Black racism.

AMERICAN ORIENTALISM AND ANTI-BLACK RACISM

Around the same time when Syrians and Turks began migrating to the United States after the American Civil War, four million newly freed Blacks faced a backlash of discrimination from angry Southerners. "Black codes" controlled African American labor and terrorized Black communities. Jim Crow laws enforced segregation between Blacks and Whites. The violence and discrimination ultimately prompted more than six million African Americans, starting in 1916, to migrate from the rural South to cities in the Northeast and Midwest in what has come to be known as the Great Migration.[133]

In two of these cities, Chicago and Newark, a new Black Liberation movement developed that appropriated Islamic identity as a rebuke to White Christian supremacy. Organizations such as the Nation of Islam (NOI), founded in 1930 in Detroit, and the Moorish Science Temple, founded in 1913 in Chicago and later renamed the Moorish Science Temple of America, called on Blacks to "revert" to Islam, their forefathers having been stripped of their African Muslim identities by their Protestant slave masters. The NOI flipped the script of White supremacy—which deemed Blacks heathens and Whites people of God—by declaring White people the heirs of Satan.[134] As a result, the NOI advocated for Black separatism in America's White supremacist society. The sociopolitical ideology they taught, however, had little resemblance to the world religion of Islam followed by their forefathers who came on slave ships from West Africa.[135]

African Muslims in the Antebellum Era

Enslaved African Muslims arrived on US shores in the early eighteenth century.[136] Comprising an estimated 10 to 20 percent of enslaved persons, Muslims came mostly from West Africa where Islam had been an established religion for centuries.[137] The religion had spread peacefully as indigenous traders, clerics, and rulers interacted with the Arabian merchants who traveled to the region frequently selling their goods.[138]

Sylviane Diouf's work examines the various means by which Africans became enslaved. While some were kidnapped by slave traders, most Africans were enslaved as a result of conflicts between African tribes wherein the winners took the losing tribes' members as captives. Some kept them as their own slaves, while others sold the captives to European transatlantic slave traders.[139] Muslim captives were no exception. As the demand for slaves by Europeans increased, so too did the profitability of selling war captives into the transatlantic slave trade. Armed conflicts in West Africa eventually supplied the largest number of enslaved Africans to the New World. Indeed, some conflicts were driven purely by the economic incentive to capture and enslave large numbers of people, bringing an African tribal ruler the latest weapons from Europe and large sums of money.

As the transatlantic slave trade expanded and became more profitable, enslavement became a common form of punishment for crimes. Now enslaved, African convicts could be sold to the Europeans. Seeking to generate more funds, guns, or other goods offered in exchange for slaves, African rulers expanded the categories of crimes punishable by enslavement, including debtors unable to repay their creditors.[140] Famine was another driver in the local slave trade. Some people pawned themselves into slavery to wealthy Africans in order to have enough to eat, only to later be sold to the Europeans because their African slave owners could no longer afford to feed them, among other reasons.

Notably, Muslims were religiously prohibited from selling other Muslims.[141] This proscription, not always followed by African Muslims at the time, limited the number of African Muslims sold into the transatlantic slave trade. It also caused some war captives to convert to Islam to avoid enslavement. Nevertheless, Muslim men were sold into slavery when their tribes lost wars. Diouf notes that enslaved Muslim men of present-day Senegal from the Fulani, Wolof, Mandingo, and Tukulor tribes were sent to Mexico, Peru, and Colombia. Despite having different languages and customs, their common religion united them in these far-off lands and in some cases allowed them to mobilize revolts against their Spanish slave owners.

Enslaved Muslims stood out among the slaves in their literacy in Arabic.[142] Because their religion emphasized reading and learning, Muslims in West Africa had a higher literacy rate than non-Muslims. Small schools taught memorization and recitation of the Quran, and higher-level schools taught Arabic so that students could read the Quran and understand the tenets of the faith. Consequently, many of the Muslims brought to the United States (and other parts of the New World) could read the Quran and continued to practice their faith. Some of them were well-traveled, cosmopolitan, and multilingual urban men.

The most well-known of these men are Omar ibn Said, Job ben Solomon, and Ibrahima abd al Rahman, who came from learned and leading families in their tribes. They left testimonies of their faith in their Arabic writings of Quranic text. Their Muslim names and attire distinguished them to the extent that some Whites called them "Mohammadens" or "Moors," whom Whites considered superior to Blacks but nonetheless still heathen.[143]

Among the most famous is Ibrahima abd al Rahman, an African prince and military general captured in war and sold to British slave traders, who transported him to New Orleans. Until he was freed more than forty years later, al Rahman worked as an enslaved person on Thomas Foster's tobacco plantation in Natchez, Mississippi, where he had to pretend to be a Christian.[144] Al Rahman retained his knowledge of Arabic by tracing the letters in the sand of the plantation. His regal behavior, literacy in Arabic, and fluency in five languages eventually led a southern journalist to name him "Prince" and to conclude that al Rahman could not be an African but rather was a Moor.[145] After being freed, al Rahman returned to Africa, where he reverted to his Muslim identity.[146]

Despite the large number of African Muslims enslaved in the United States, Islam was eventually extinguished among their heirs.[147] Three factors led to this outcome. First, White Protestant slave owners believed Islam was a false religion created by the devil such that most prohibited their slaves from practicing it. Second, all enslaved African people were subject to coerced conversion to Christianity as a means of saving their purportedly heathen souls. They were given European names and prohibited from giving their children African or Muslim names. Protestant preachers taught the slaves that Islam was one of the primitive African pagan practices that must be shed in order for their souls to be saved. They instructed slaves, and eventually freed Blacks, to shed all remnants of their purportedly heathen African origins through conversion to Christianity. Although some slaves incorporated their Muslim beliefs into their Christian practices or only pretended to convert, Muslims' inability to practice their communitarian religion accomplished what the slave owners wanted: the elimination of Islam among Blacks in America.

Finally, even those Muslims who secretly practiced their faith could not pass it on to their children or grandchildren due to the sale of their offspring.[148] Rarely could a Muslim man find a Muslim spouse, raise the children Muslim, and keep the children long enough to pass on the religion. Absent Islamic schools and religious leaders, American-born African slaves could not learn how to recite their Quranic prayers or the tenets of the faith without parental teaching.

Thus what kept Islam in America during the antebellum era was the continuous arrival of enslaved Africans.[149] When the last African-born Muslims died in the early twentieth century, Islam as practiced in West Africa effectively disappeared within African American communities. Around the same time, however, a new political movement was growing that would appropriate Islam as a Black Liberation ideology against White supremacy and the myriad legacies of slavery. The domestic backlash would merge anti-Black racism with Orientalism.

Islam and the Black Nationalist Movement

It was not until the 1920s that Islam became associated with militant Blackness and political radicalism.[150] The dangerous, disobedient, and violent Black Muslim was a racial trope separate from the foreign, despotic, and uncivilized Mahometan Turk. But as African Americans fought to dismantle Jim Crow laws and Arab nationalists fought against American imperialism in the Middle East and North Africa, the two racial constructs began coalescing. The association of Islam with violence, heathenism, and savagery—whether by immigrant or African American Muslims—was now a domestic racial ideology. European Orientalism merged with anti-Black racism.

Religion played a vital role in the perseverance and resilience of African Americans, both during and after slavery, in the face of White supremacy. While most African Americans were Protestant, a group of newly freed slaves rediscovered Islam in their search for liberation from White supremacy.[151] Some came into contact with Muhammad Sadiq, a spiritual leader of the Ahmadiyya Movement in India who traveled to the United States to proselytize Islam.[152] Sadiq highlighted that Islam was a universal religion that treated all people equally during his frequent and dynamic public speeches about Islam's antiracist tenets. Between 1920 and 1940, Sadiq undertook extensive missionary work, resulting in five thousand to ten thousand American converts, half of them African Americans.[153] Among Sadiq's followers were famous musicians such as Ahmed Jamal, Sahib Shihab, Art Blakely, Talib Dawud, and Lynn Hope.[154]

That Sadiq came to the United States in the 1920s, during the resurgence of the Ku Klux Klan and other White nativist movements, made his message all the more attractive to African Americans. Moreover, Sadiq supported Marcus Garvey's Universal Negro Improvement Association (UNIA), which sought to establish an independent country in Africa as a refuge from White racism.[155] Sadiq's message that people of Asian and African descent were both victims of European imperialism caused some UNIA members to convert to Islam. In the January 1923 issue of the first Muslim publication in the United States, the *Moslem Sunrise*, Sadiq called on African Americans to join Islam.

> My Dear American Negro... the Christian profiteers brought you out of your native lands of Africa and in Christianizing you made you forsake the religion and language of your forefathers—which were Islam and Arabic. You have experienced Christianity for so many years and it has proved to be no good. It

is a failure. Christianity cannot bring real brotherhood to the nations. Now leave it alone. And join Islam, the real faith of Universal Brotherhood, which at once does away with all distinctions of race, color and creed.[156]

As more African Americans were targets of racial violence and experienced racism in employment, housing, education, and public accommodations, the newly founded Nation of Islam and the Moorish Science Temple drew from parts of Islamic doctrine to advocate for Black nationalism.[157] Noble Drew Ali, born Timothy Drew, established the first Moorish Temple in Newark, New Jersey, in 1913. Drew Ali proclaimed that African Americans were "an olive-skinned Asiatic people who were the descendants of Moroccans."[158] He called on African Americans to abandon their Christian slave identities, claiming they were ancestrally Muslim Moors, not Negroes.[159] Drew Ali used symbols, texts, and attire from Muslim societies at the time, including the fez and turban.

But Drew Ali's self-appointment as a prophet of Allah was considered heresy to the few thousand Muslim immigrants from the Ottoman Empire and the Indian subcontinent, thereby limiting his membership primarily to African Americans. His approximately thirty thousand followers established temples in Philadelphia, Baltimore, Richmond, Lansing, Chicago, and Milwaukee, among other cities.[160] Drew Ali mirrored Marcus Garvey in his promotion of Black nationalism and economic independence from mainstream White society.[161] Although its following was in the mere tens of thousands, the Moorish Science Temple was the predecessor to the Nation of Islam (NOI)—a much larger and more influential Black nationalist movement that would attract aggressive US government suppression.

NOI founder Fard Muhammad claimed to be Allah incarnate; and Elijah Muhammad, Fard Muhammad's disciple, was Allah's messenger. They offered African Americans who migrated to Chicago from the South an alternative identity wherein they were racially superior to Whites. According to the NOI, White people were devils engineered by an evil scientist.[162] Christianity, thus, was the religion of White oppressors used to indoctrinate African Americans to accept their inferior status. Taking from the UNIA's message, the NOI taught its members self-help and promoted a racially uplifting message that emphasized Black solidarity, Black capitalism, and racial separatism. The NOI's most famous convert, Malcolm X, became a leading voice for Black empowerment during the 1950s and 1960s Civil Rights Movement.[163]

FIGURE 3. Elijah Muhammad listens as Malcolm X speaks (1961). Frank Scherschel/The LIFE Picture Collection via Getty Images.

Due in large part to Malcolm X's charisma and tireless proselytizing, the NOI expanded tenfold from 1956 to 1961, to between fifty thousand and seventy-five thousand members.[164] Most of their new recruits were in unemployment lines and impoverished inner-city ghettos; however, some middle-class African Americans also joined the NOI. Many of the converts to the Nation of Islam did so as a rebuke to the White and Christian mainstream responsible for systemic racism. This pairing of Black consciousness and Islam was a consistent feature of American racial politics prior to the large migrations of Muslims from the Middle East, North Africa, and South Asia after 1965.[165]

It is worth noting immigrant Muslims' rejection of followers of the Nation of Islam. The immigrants found the belief that Fard Muhammad was God and Elijah Muhammad the son of God sacrilegious. A core tenet of Islam is the belief that God is not human and that Muhammad was his final prophet. Moreover, NOI members, like Moorish Science Temple followers, did not prostrate themselves when praying. Nor did they practice any other of the five pillars of Islam.[166] Upon hearing Malcolm X at public lectures, a Sudanese Muslim graduate student publicly criticized the NOI as heretical. Yahya Hayari published an editorial in the October 27, 1962, edition of the *Pittsburgh Courier* stating, "Mr. Elijah does not believe in or teach Islam. What he teaches in the name of Islam is his own social theory." Hayari concluded, "All those that follow him should know that they are being led straight to Hell."[167]

On July 15, 1964, the *Chicago Defender*, a Black newspaper, published a story about the influential Egyptian Muslim League's disagreement with "the anti-white, anti-Christian, anti-Jew, and anti-integration preachments of America's Black Muslims." In a rare personal response, Elijah Muhammad forcefully proclaimed, "Neither Jeddah nor Mecca have sent me! I am sent from Allah and not from the Secretary General of the Muslim League. There is no Muslim in Arabia that has authority to stop me from delivering this message that I have been assigned to."[168]

It was not until the majority of followers of the NOI converted to Sunni Islam in the 1970s, following Elijah Muhammad's son Warath Dean Muhammad, that African American Muslims came into more frequent contact with immigrant Muslims. Although national origin, language, and race segregated American Muslim communities, African American Muslim and immigrant Muslim leaders gradually increased their collaboration.

African Americans' deployment of Islam as a political liberatory ideology made them uniquely threatening to the US government.[169] Beginning in the 1930s, the FBI surveilled and investigated the Moorish Science Temple, the Nation of Islam, and the UNIA as purportedly radical movements.[170] Internal memos communicated the FBI's belief that the NOI was a national security threat. Elijah Muhammad's correspondence in the late 1950s with Arab Nationalist Egyptian President Gamal Abdel Nasser cast more suspicion on Black Muslims' national loyalty.[171]

During World War II, for example, the FBI believed that African American civil rights activists were colluding with the Japanese, which led to mass surveillance of African American dissidents under the code name RACON.[172] To circumvent legal prohibitions against targeting religious groups, the FBI labeled the Nation of Islam and the Moorish Science Temple cults and violent ideologies—the same framing by right-wing Islamophobes in the post-9/11 era whose primary targets are immigrant Muslims. Further marginalizing the NOI was the deployment of Christianity as a moral justification for the civil rights of African Americans by mainstream Black organizations such as the Southern Christian Leadership Conference. Even African American Christian leaders deemed Black Muslims too militant.[173] Local police departments also set up special forces to surveil and infiltrate Nation of Islam temples, especially in New York, where Malcolm X was based.[174]

FBI director J. Edgar Hoover's animosity to socialist and Communist activists merged with his deep distrust of Black nationalists in a series of counterintelligence programs known as COINTELPRO. In a 1967 memo, Hoover initiated COINTELPRO-BNHG, a counterintelligence program targeting groups designated "Black Nationalist Hate Groups."[175] He instructed his twenty-three field offices to "expose, disrupt, misdirect, discredit, or otherwise neutralize the activities of Black nationalist, hate-type organizations, their leadership, spokesmen, membership, and supporters."[176] Across the country, FBI agents set out to create discord among Black nationalist groups, including the Revolutionary Action Movement, the Black Panthers, and the Nation of Islam.

The FBI planted false stories in the media to discredit leaders and undermine efforts to recruit African American youth.[177] Americans were misled to believe NOI members' first loyalty was to their religious "cult" rather than to the United States—the same accusation leveled at Catholics and Mormons to justify their persecution at the time and the same accusations leveled at Muslims after 9/11.[178] Pretextual prosecution of Black Muslim leaders also became a tool to weaken the Black nationalist movement. For example, the federal government convicted Elijah Muhammad for dodging the draft in 1943, along with two hundred other Black nationalists during World War II.[179] The famous boxer and NOI member Muhammad Ali was convicted in 1967 for refusing to be drafted into the military.[180]

Around the same time, Muslim citizens in the newly formed nation-states in the Middle East, whose borders were drawn by the British and French in the 1916 Sykes-Picot Agreement, were agitating for independence. The ensuing revolutions coupled with the emergence of the Cold War with the Soviet Union prompted the United States to compete for global hegemony. With that came confrontation with Arab nationalism, which would become a foil in US Middle East policy. Stereotypes of the despotic and Mahometan Turk converged with the militant Black Muslims to create the Arab (Palestinian) terrorist trope—the precursor to today's Muslim terrorist trope and the topic of the next chapter.

. . .

The September 11, 2001, terrorist attack did not begin the social construction of the Racial Muslim; it accelerated and deepened the ongoing processes of racialization. The English settlers who established the United States of America brought with them Orientalist beliefs of the so-called Mahometans as uncivilized and barbaric. The Protestant ideological foundations of American identity considered the Mahometan Turks heirs to an Islamic civilization antithetical to Christianity going as far back as the Crusades.[181] The importation of European animus toward Islam merged with American racism against Blacks (and other racial minorities) to racialize immigrant Muslims in the twentieth century.

Starting in the late 1960s, America's growing hegemony in the Middle East faced stiff resistance by Arab nationalist rulers and a predominantly Muslim populace. The consequence was the centering of the irrational and bloodthirsty Arab in the racialization of Muslims in the United States.[182] America's foreign policy in the Middle East over the following four decades would delegitimize Muslims' political aspirations for self-determination by characterizing their resistance as indicia of racial inferiority, savagery, and most saliently—terrorism.

SIX

American Orientalism
and the Arab Terrorist Trope

PRIOR TO WORLD WAR II, Islam was a distant threat.[1] With Muslim-majority lands occupied by European powers, the US government's interactions with them were limited to deploying ambassadors whose reports reified the Orientalist view that "history does not record a single instance of successful constitutional government in a country where the Mussulman religion is the state religion."[2] Although such derogatory portrayals circulated among the intellectual elite, the average American was preoccupied with more pressing domestic economic concerns in the first half of the twentieth century.

This began to change when Muslim immigrants arrived in sizable numbers after 1965, when national origin immigration quotas were lifted, and the United States competed with the Soviet Union for client states in the Middle East and North Africa.[3] The same structural racism buttressing domestic oppression of Blacks, Native Americans, and Asians would soon be deployed against immigrant Muslims. However, the means by which racism occurred, as well as the material consequences, were unique to Muslims' immigration history and the geopolitical context of the time.

Like that of other immigrants, Muslims' racialization in America was shaped by the political and military conflicts between the United States and their countries of origin.[4] Religion would also play a crucial role in the racialization of Muslims in ways that morally justified America's pursuit of political, economic, and military domination abroad and securitization of Muslims at home. Although not always explicitly stated, a clash of civilizations narrative informed laws governing the US government's treatment of immigrant Muslims in the second half of the twentieth century.

Grounded in European Orientalism, American Orientalism took on a life of its own as hegemonic geopolitics merged with domestic racial-religious hierarchies. In the first half of the twentieth century, American Orientalism produced contradictory state policies toward Arabs. On the one hand, Henry King and Charles Crane, appointed by President Woodrow Wilson to head the 1919 mission to Palestine, opposed the Balfour Declaration out of support for Arab self-determination.[5] On the other hand, President Wilson's secretary of state, Robert Lansing, interpreted Arabs' violent struggle for self-determination as illegitimate.[6] Tellingly, Lansing did not believe all races deserved self-determination. He bluntly stated on the eve of the Versailles Conference in 1918, "The more I think about the President's declaration as to the right to 'self-determination,' the more convinced I am as to the danger of putting such ideas into the minds of certain races.... Will it not breed discontent, disorder and rebellion? Will not the Mohammadens of Syria and Palestine, possibly of Morocco and Tripoli rely on it?"[7]

After World War II, America's national security priorities were twofold: control the oil reserves in the Middle East, which constituted one-third of the world supply, and prevent the Soviet Union from expanding its global influence.[8] This new world order prompted academic, policy, and journalistic interest in the so-called Arab people, Islam, and the Middle East.[9]

Predominantly White male academics and journalists reinforced European Orientalist tropes of Arabs and Muslims as irrational, despotic, and uncivilized. They erroneously used "Arab" to refer to Persians, South Asians, Sikhs, Sephardic Jews, and anyone whose physical appearance was stereotypically Arab-looking.[10] No longer were Muslims a distant threat for European colonialists to manage.[11] They were now America's problem, as it sought to commandeer Muslim-majority lands as client states in the Cold War.[12] The Racial Muslim construct was emerging.

Seven international and domestic crises, in particular, contributed to the social construction of the Racial Muslim: (1) the establishment of Israel in 1948; (2) the 1967 Arab-Israeli War; (3) the 1973 Arab oil embargo; (4) the 1979 Iranian Revolution; (5) the First Gulf War in 1990; (6) the 1993 bombing of the World Trade Center; and (7) the September 11, 2001, terrorist attacks.[13] After each event, the American media intensified its coverage of political conflicts in the Middle East. Arabs (incorrectly presumed to all be Muslim) were portrayed as violent, irrational, and antidemocratic.[14] The

Racial Muslim trope expanded beyond the uncivilized, despotic, and imperialist Turk (which was Europe's problem) to the violent, irrational, and radical Arab (now America's problem).[15]

When the Soviet Union fell in 1990, American policy makers warned that Islam would replace Communism as the global threat to US national security.[16] The first post–Cold War decade began what the September 11 attacks finalized: the association of terrorism with Muslims first and Arabs second. During the Cold War, however, the quintessential "terrorist" was Arab first and Muslim second. More specifically, he was Palestinian.

ZIONISM AND THE DEHUMANIZATION OF PALESTINIANS

European colonies across the world agitated for independence at the turn of the twentieth century. The Middle East and North Africa, previously ruled by the Ottomans, were no exception. Among them were Palestinians, governed by the British based on the Sykes-Picot Agreement that drew artificial borders between French- and British-controlled territories.[17] As more Jews fled from pogroms in Eastern Europe to Palestine, they purchased land using foreign funding as part of a European Zionist settler project.[18] The British allowed the mass land purchases, notwithstanding that Jewish landowners' refusal to sell land to Palestinians only heightened communal tensions. Consistent with global colonialist policies, pitting Arabs and Jews against each other strengthened British domination over Palestine.[19]

But Palestinian protests in 1929 and 1936 against the Zionist settlers' expanding influence prompted the British to restrict Jewish migration and land purchases pursuant to the British White Paper of May 1939.[20] For the next two decades, Jewish leaders in Europe and the United States lobbied their respective governments to allow more Jews to escape violent anti-Semitism in Europe and immigrate to Palestine.[21] The objective was to create a Jewish state in Palestine as the permanent solution to centuries of oppression of Jews in Europe.[22] Despite its lofty goal of providing Jews with a permanent homeland where they would no longer face centuries of European anti-Semitism, Zionism became instrumental in dehumanizing Palestinians in American politics and culture.

At the start of World War II, the American Zionist movement's efforts to establish the state of Israel was gaining momentum. By 1945, magazines and televisions projected into American homes images of Jewish corpses stacked on top of each other and emaciated bodies of Holocaust survivors. Of the nearly one million displaced people, more than 250,000 were stateless Jews seeking to immigrate to Palestine.[23] As Americans realized the gravity of their nation's failure to help Jewish refugees during the Holocaust, many Christians believed it was their moral obligation to support a Jewish homeland—and what better place than the Holy Land?[24]

The Holocaust bolstered Zionists' claims that only a Jewish state could prevent centuries of European pogroms that culminated in a genocide.[25] Indeed, support for Israel became a unifying force among an increasingly diversifying American Jewish population. Despite theological disputes among Orthodox, Conservative, and Reform Jews, they all agreed that supporting Israel was imperative for the survival of Judaism. Zionism thus became a surrogate for Judaism.

Although American Jews had experienced a surge in anti-Semitism during the wave of White nativism in the early 1900s, their racial Whitening within the domestic racial-religious hierarchy granted them membership in America's newfound Judeo-Christian national identity. This translated into more political influence over time. After 1945, Jewish Americans emerged as a voter base courted by politicians.[26] In 1948, when Israel was created, leaders of the nearly five million second-generation American Jews mobilized to successfully pressure the Truman administration to recognize the state of Israel.[27]

When Israel won the 1967 Six-Day War against Jordan, Syria, and Egypt, dues-paying membership in the American Israel Public Affairs Committee (AIPAC) boomed.[28] Jewish political activity intensified each subsequent year, such that by 1972, a Democratic presidential candidate who did not support Israel, as George McGovern discovered, would be abandoned by the majority of American Jewish donors who subscribed to the Zionist project in the Middle East.

Meanwhile, Arabs, numbering in the mere hundreds of thousands before 1965, had minimal political clout. President Harry S. Truman responded bluntly to British officials who criticized his favoritism for Israel: "I have to answer to hundreds of thousands who are anxious for the success of Zionism. I do not have hundreds of thousands of Arabs in my constituents."[29] Most Arabs at the time were Christian and second- or third-generation Americans seeking to assimilate into Whiteness. Many had abandoned their language, given their children anglicized names, and distanced themselves from international politics.

In 1948, European Jewish immigrants to Palestine established the state of Israel in a war that forcibly evicted more than seven hundred thousand indigenous Palestinian Muslims and Christians to Jordan, Lebanon, and other neighboring states.[30] The US media portrayed citizens of the newly recognized Jewish state as industrious and brave. Often compared to the hardworking Puritans who founded "God's American Israel," Israelis would bring civilization and democracy to the backwardness of the Muslim Orient.[31] This comparison of Jews to Puritans fleeing religious persecution in Europe further humanized them to a guilt-ridden American public.

The Arab Palestinians, in contrast, were depicted in pictures and text as irrational barbarians when they defended lands on which they had lived for centuries.[32] Some American Zionists exploited these dehumanizing stereotypes to coin the slogan, "pay a dollar, kill an Arab," to raise funds in support of Israel.[33] American narratives of the 1948 war depicted Jews as a people who deserved a state of their own after enduring centuries of persecution that culminated in the extermination of six million Jews in the Holocaust. Meanwhile, Palestinians were depicted as a small number of primitive people with no valid claim to the land.[34]

Simultaneous with this dehumanization of Palestinians, Hollywood produced movies about the plight of Jews during the Holocaust. The 1978 television miniseries, *The Holocaust,* featuring Meryl Streep as Anne Frank, was so popular that it won eight Emmy awards.[35] Streep's performance in *Sophie's Choice*, a haunting film about a Holocaust survivor having to choose which of her two children would be sent to Auschwitz, earned her an Oscar for Best Actress.[36] While educating Americans about the atrocities of the Holocaust was an important public service, it came at the expense of the human rights and self-determination of indigenous Palestinians.

As Steven Salaita's work shows, the racialization of Palestinians mirrored that of Native Americans, portrayed as heathens with no right to a land "discovered" by White people. Coupled with theological justifications, as Thomas Kidd's work demonstrates, Protestant leaders during the twentieth century believed American imperialism in the Middle East was ordained by God, which entailed support of Israel.[37] American Evangelicals, dispensationalists in particular, propagated the clash of civilizations narrative to their followers, both in pursuit of large-scale Muslim conversions and because of a religious belief that Jews must return to Palestine in order for the Messiah to arrive.[38]

Manifest Destiny took on a global dimension under the auspices of

Zionism.[39] As early as 1917, the Methodist Evangelist leader Rev. Henry Clay Morrison (not to be confused with the 19th-century Tennessean Methodist bishop Henry Clary Morrison) announced that the pending collapse of the Ottoman Empire would bring the end of times and the rise of the Antichrist.[40] In the 1930s, the Evangelical leader Rev. Charles S. Price told his followers that the Bible ordained that Palestinians be removed from Palestine so that the children of Israel could rebuild the temple where the Dome of the Rock now stood. Keith Brooks, editor of *Prophecy* magazine, stated in 1936 that the "Arab and Moslem world is not only anti-Semitic, but is out and out anti-Christ." By 1974, the American Evangelist, Rev. Billy Graham was arranging conferences with more than two thousand Christians, focused on aiding Jews in the Arab-Israeli conflict.[41]

That European Jewish settlers in the twentieth century were raced as Whites, notwithstanding the prevalence of American anti-Semitism, demonstrated America's changing national identity from Protestant to Judeo-Christian, discussed in chapter 4. In contrast, Palestinians (incorrectly presumed to all be Muslims) were raced as unenlightened barbarians whose political grievances were illegitimate in the face of European Jews' claims.[42] The racial Whitening of Jews occurred simultaneously with Arabs' (both Christian and Muslim) transition from racial ambiguity to non-White foreign threats—a key facet of the Racial Muslim construct.[43]

THE IRRATIONAL ARAB NATIONALIST

At the intersection of three continents and with more than 60 percent of the world's oil reserves, the Middle East became a vital strategic location. As Britain's regional influence waned, the United States competed with the Soviets to be the new Western hegemon.[44] However, the mid-twentieth century witnessed a wave of independence movements across the world, including in the Middle East. Nationalist leaders such as Mohammad Mossadegh of Iran, Gamal Abdel Nasser of Egypt, and Hafez al-Assad of Syria defied US hegemonic interests in the region.[45]

Notwithstanding its rhetorical commitments to self-determination, the US government dismissed Arabs' aspirations for independence as illegitimate.[46] Tellingly, a 1949 CIA report concluded that Arabs are "non-inventive and slow to put theories into practice" and capable of "astonishing acts of treachery and dishonesty."[47] Presidents Truman, Eisenhower, Kennedy, and

Johnson all had in common the belief that Arabs were unpredictable, explosive, and backward.[48]

Eisenhower's aversion to Arab nationalists like Nasser arose in part from a conviction that Arabs "simply cannot understand our ideas of freedom or human dignity."[49] Demonstrating the potency of race in the American psyche, President Lyndon B. Johnson compared Palestinians and Arab nationalists to treacherous Indians, while he likened Israelis to the noble Texan freedom fighters.

Despite its recognition of Israel in 1948, the United States sided with Egypt in 1956 when Israel (with the help of France and Britain) attempted to capture the Suez Canal.[50] However, when Nasser and Assad were defeated in the 1967 war, the United States shifted its Middle East policy more fully in support of Israel.[51] As the Cold War spread around the world, US government officials saw Israel as a client state that could serve as a bulwark against the spread of Arab nationalism and Communism in the Middle East.

The spread of Nasserism across the region threatened Saudi Arabia, Jordan, Iraq, and Iran, whose leaders were American lackeys.[52] The CIA leveraged regional conflicts to develop client states in Saudi Arabia, Jordan, and Iraq. In Iran, the CIA orchestrated a coup against the democratically elected nationalist Mohammad Mossadegh in 1953. Gamal Abdel Nasser, the charismatic president of Egypt, would prove more difficult to eliminate. Wildly popular across the Middle East for his anti-imperialist stance, Nasser snubbed the United States when he met with Yugoslavia's President Josip Broz Tito and Communist China's Premier Zhou Enlai. He defiantly refused to support a secret Anglo-American initiative that would grant Arab recognition of Israel's right to exist in exchange for territorial concessions by Israel.[53] When Nasser accepted Soviet military equipment and interest-free loans in exchange for Egyptian cotton, the United States realized Nasser was driven by his vision of a strong Egyptian state with regional hegemony that would not bow to US dominance.[54]

President Eisenhower's chief strategist on psychological warfare called on the US government to use Islam as a vehicle to mobilize Muslims against godless Soviet influence and secular Arab nationalist leaders.[55] In 1957, a working group of intelligence and defense officials in the Eisenhower administration published the *Inventory of U.S. Government and Private Organization Activity Regarding Islamic Organizations as an Aspect of Overseas Activity*, which concluded that Islam was more compatible with Christianity than Communism such that it could be deployed to rally support in the Cold

War.[56] The CIA agreed that the United States should deploy religion to fight Communism by supporting the Muslim Brotherhood and other political Islamists who opposed the secularism of Arab nationalist leaders.[57]

The "Islam strategy" would eventually lead to America's financial support of Osama bin Laden's mujahideen in Afghanistan against the Soviet Union—the same ones who later planned the September 11 terrorist attacks in New York City.[58] When it benefited US interests, the United States sent military aid to the mujahideen and Osama bin Laden, calling them "freedom fighters" against the Soviet Union in Afghanistan.[59] But as soon as they were no longer useful to the United States, that is, after the fall of the Soviet Union, the same group of mujahideen—Al-Qaeda—was designated a terrorist group.[60] After 9/11, all political Islamists would be grouped together in the Muslim terrorist trope, leading to the criminalization of the Religious Dissident Racial Muslim and the Religious Racial Muslim, which I discuss in chapters 7 and 8.

US concerns with Arab nationalism were reinforced in 1972 when President Ahmed Hassan al-Bakr, a staunch Ba'athist, nationalized Iraqi oil fields without compensating the US-based companies Exxon and Mobil.[61] The Middle East soon became a focal point of Cold War politics and militarism. Entangled in this global conflict was the Palestinians' struggle for self-determination and resistance to the creation of Israel.

THE (PALESTINIAN) ARAB TERRORIST TROPE

Starting in the 1960s, the quintessential terrorist trope in American culture was the Arab Palestinian.[62] The Palestinian Liberation Organization's violent resistance, whether through plane hijackings, the massacre at the 1972 Munich Olympics, or the 1983 bombing of US Marine barracks, was rarely framed as part of a broader political conflict over land and indigenous political rights. Instead, Western media described the violence as a civilizational conflict with bloodthirsty terrorists who could be stopped only through violent elimination.[63] Palestinian savagery, according to this narrative, originated in the long-standing clash of civilizations between the Muslim Orient and Western Christendom.[64] Had the violence been placed in historical and political context, Americans would have had to face the reality that their government supported a settler colonial country that, similar to the US, had dismissed the land and political rights of the indigenous population.[65]

When Israel occupied the Sinai, the Golan Heights, the West Bank, and Gaza in the 1967 war, Arabs in America organized protests and called on businesses to divest from Israel.[66] Pamela Pennock's work shows the increasingly leftist turn of Arab American organizations after the occupation of Palestine. The concurrent rise of Black nationalism brought together Third World nationalist Arab Americans and leftist and African American activists. Although Arab American leftists were a growing minority within the Arab American community, alliances with Black nationalists along with support for the Palestinian liberation movement marked Arab immigrants (regardless of their religion) as radical, subversive, and anti-Semitic. Moreover, the Palestinian-Israeli conflict was depicted in the American media and churches as the fulfillment of a biblical prophecy and a fight between David and Goliath, thereby giving the US government license to target Arab activists.[67] Mirroring the experiences of leftist Eastern European Jews during the Red Scare, Arab political activists became increasingly surveilled, deported, and prosecuted by US law enforcement—setting the stage for racialized national security enforcement after 9/11.[68]

The Palestinian terrorist trope informed domestic racial projects that involved the surveillance, special registration, deportation, and prosecution of Arab American individuals and organizations opposed to US Middle East policy.[69] Political cartoons, eerily similar to those that demonized Jews and Mormons in the early twentieth century, portrayed Arabs as aggressive, scheming, and beastlike. As Peter Gottschalk and Gabriel Greenberg note, during the 1973 oil crisis, "Arabs were given large misshapen noses, facial hair, furry eyebrows, and generally vile and sly countenances."[70]

Arabs learned firsthand that American individual freedoms were circumscribed by race, religion, and international politics.[71] After members of Black September, a Palestinian resistance organization, killed Israeli Olympic athletes in Munich in 1972, the Nixon administration launched Operation Boulder.[72] The FBI spied on Arab communities, tapped their phones, and gathered intelligence on their political activities. The Cabinet Committee to Combat Terrorism established by President Richard Nixon in 1972 oversaw FBI surveillance of Fatah, Black September, and the Popular Front for the Liberation of Palestine operatives in the United States with a particular interest in their suspected infiltration of Arab American organizations.[73] The three-year program led to the screening of at least 3,500 Arab students and visitors and the deportation of hundreds of Arab immigrant activists on technical immigration irregularities.[74] Meanwhile, in retaliation for US sup-

FIGURE 4. Political cartoon
of OPEC and Arabs holding
Americans over a barrel of oil
(1974). *Washington Star.*

'YOU MAY FORCE US TO DO SOMETHING ABOUT THIS!'

port of Israel in the 1973 war with Egypt, Arab members of OPEC imposed an oil embargo. Anti-Arab prejudice surged. As angry Americans waited in long lines at gas stations, the US government exploited the oil crisis to scapegoat Arab regimes for the nation's economic recession.[75]

At the same time, well-established and politically influential American Zionist organizations contributed to portrayals of Arabs in general, and Palestinians in particular, as bloodthirsty terrorists and anti-Semites whose violence was driven by an irrational hatred of Jews.[76] The organizations called on the US government to increase its scrutiny of Arab university students mobilizing around Palestinian rights. According to a 1972 report in the *Washington Post* and an article in the *Chicago Tribune* in 1975, Israeli officials and the Anti-Defamation League exchanged information with US officials about Arabs living in the United States, especially activists sympathetic to Palestinian rights.[77] The US government's and the media's depiction of Arab Americans' dissent as antidemocratic and anti-Semitic built on European Orientalism's racialization of Middle East Muslims as illiberal, violent, and uncivilized.[78] These portrayals would later dominate media coverage of the post-9/11 War on Terror.

REFRAMING POLITICAL VIOLENCE: FROM
INSURGENCY TO TERRORISM

US officials' attribution of terrorism committed by Muslims to Islam was facilitated by a shift in Western states' treatment of political violence. Prior to the 1970s, Western policy makers and intellectuals treated non-state political violence as insurgency grounded in material grievances.[79] But as Palestinian liberation groups' violence against the Israeli occupation crossed borders into Europe, Western countries considered terrorism a form of psychopathology that violated universal norms.[80] In turn, terrorists were characterized as evil, irrational, pathological, and fundamentally different from the United States and its state allies whose violence was morally justified. The idea that political violence arose out of legitimate, resolvable grievances was rejected outright. Instead, all violence by non-state actors against the United States and Europe was condemned as terrorism equivalent to an illegitimate act of war.[81]

Terrorism also replaced insurgency discursively. As Lisa Stampnitzky's work demonstrates, the number of terrorism conferences increased from one to five per year from 1972 to 1979. Attendees at terrorism conferences grew exponentially, from 8 in 1972 to 436 in 1978.[82] But no profession or academic discipline of terrorism existed. The unstructured nature of terrorism studies rendered the discourse unbound by the mature discipline of experts with formal training and research credentials. Consequently, a cottage industry of ideologues and journalists misrepresenting their expertise unduly influenced Western security policy.[83] This cadre of so-called terrorism experts propagated views not subjected to rigorous peer review and infected by racial, religious, and cultural biases.[84] The consequences would prove devastating for the civil rights of Arab and Muslim activists in the United States, whose dissident political views and religious identities axiomatically made them suspect.

Beginning in the 1980s, another paradigm shift occurred when the United States began treating terrorism as war rather than as a crime. An influential international conference in Jerusalem in 1979, hosted by future Israeli prime minister, Benjamin Netanyahu, gathered high-level government officials from the United States and Israel.[85] The organizers sought to persuade attendees, including the future president George H. W. Bush, that the Soviet Union was supporting international terrorism as part of its Cold War strategy. In seeking to change the discourse on terrorism, Netanyahu and his

Israeli analysts discredited Palestinian insurgents seeking self-determination, claiming instead that they were terrorist proxies of the Soviets' goal to destroy democracy.[86] Accordingly, Palestinian insurgents were purportedly part of a global assault on Western civilization, democracy, and freedom.

The implication was clear: the United States was at war with the Palestinian resistance movement.[87] As a result, the Reagan administration adopted the terror network theory, associating Arab political groups with Soviet conspiracies to attack American democracy. The US Department of Justice (DOJ) devised secret contingency plans to intern Arab and Iranian "alien terrorists." A 1986 DOJ document, "Alien Terrorists and Undesirables: A Contingency Plan," designated a detention camp location to intern tens of thousands of Arab American students in the United States.[88] Although the contingency plan was never implemented, its existence demonstrates the lengths to which the US government was willing to go, notwithstanding this nation's shameful history of interning Japanese Americans in the 1940s.

The case of the Los Angeles Eight put a spotlight on the government's association of Arabs with terrorism. Eight political activists, seven of whom were Palestinian, were placed under surveillance for three years, from 1987 to 1990, as part of an antiterrorism investigation.[89] Their fund-raising and activism for the Popular Front for the Liberation of Palestine attracted the attention of the US government, which equated pro-Palestinian activism with terrorism.[90] The government sought to deport the Palestinian activists pursuant to the McCarran-Walter Act, which criminalizes association with any organization that "advocated for world Communism."[91] This was the same law used to deport Jewish leftists during the era of McCarthyism. After two decades of litigation, an immigration judge ruled in 2007 that the US government had violated the defendants' constitutional rights.[92]

By the mid-1990s, terrorism by Muslims became the global threat that replaced Communism.[93] American pundits and politicians, looking for a new enemy, replaced the Red Scare with the so-called Green Menace.[94] No longer useful as American proxies to fight the Soviets, Osama bin Laden and Al-Qaeda were the face of the new enemy. Once portrayed as freedom fighters in America's global war on Communism, these mujahideen who formed Al-Qaeda in the 1990s now opposed US military presence on Saudi Arabian soil. They were the new enemies in America's burgeoning War on Terror. Muslims who engaged in political violence were no longer insurgents; they were savages to be killed in warfare.[95] The Arab (Palestinian) terrorist trope was morphing into the Muslim terrorist trope.

Although the Arab terrorist trope implied a Muslim connection, it was not until the 1979 Iranian Revolution (also known as the Islamic Revolution) and the Iran Hostage Crisis that the American public directly linked Islam with terrorist violence.[96] Following two years of populist protests and strikes, the US-backed shah of Iran was forced into exile in early 1979. Ayatollah Khomeini, who became Iran's Supreme Leader, railed against Westernization and American imperialism, calling it a plague that was corrupting and enslaving Iran. His revolutionary slogan, "Neither East, nor West—Islamic Republic!," appealed to lower- and middle-class Iranians.[97]

A bulwark against the spread of Communism in the Middle East, Muhammad Reza Shah's secular government had worked closely with the US government during the Cold War. Thus the arrival of an Islamic, anti-American theocracy was a seismic blow to US Cold War policy.[98] Few government officials had anticipated the Iranian Revolution, much less planned a response. The political crisis took immediate urgency when Iranian students overtook the US embassy in Tehran and held fifty-two American diplomats and citizens hostage for more than a year.

American audiences received daily doses of television coverage portraying Muslims in general, and Iranians in particular, as terrorists.[99] Nationally, news anchors such as Walter Cronkite of CBS and Frank Reynolds of ABC attributed the Iran Hostage Crisis to Muslims' hatred of America. Images of blindfolded Americans paraded by their Iranian captors enraged Americans.[100] Again, Islam was equated with savagery, vengeance, and evil.[101] Major newspapers published articles with titles such as "The Islam Explosion" and "Militant Islam: The Historic Whirlwind," arguing that wherever there was war, murder, and protracted conflict Islamic fundamentalism was present.[102] Political cartoons portrayed Iranians and Muslims as crazy, backward, and violent.[103] The American media inundated its readers with the message that a new era of holy war was emerging between Judeo-Christian America and Islamic Iran. This narrative would expand to all Muslims after 9/11.

In 1979, President Jimmy Carter declared a national emergency in Executive Order 12170, prompting law enforcement to suspect all Iranians in America.[104] Iranian nationals, most of whom were Muslim graduate students at the time, were required by law to register at the Immigration and Naturalization Service. Anyone out of status was immediately deported; those who were permitted to stay were closely surveilled as potential national

FIGURE 5. Protest in the United States against the Iranian Hostage Crisis (1979). Marion S. Trikosko.

security threats.[105] Meanwhile, a wave of Jewish Iranians fleeing the new Khomeini regime was granted asylum in the United States, further evincing the role of religion in determining the level of threat posed by a particular (non-White) race.[106]

Following the Iranian Revolution, negative public opinion of Iranians— and by extension, Muslims—nearly tripled, from 37 percent in the late 1970s to 91 percent in 1989.[107] Although the most immediate consequence of the Iranian Revolution was the collective punishment of Iranians in America, the longer-term effect was a gradual shift from the Arab Palestinian terrorist trope to the Muslim terrorist trope as a global threat.[108]

Just as international events shaped American perceptions of Muslims, so too did domestic politics. The American Evangelical Moral Majority, headed by the Rev. Jerry Falwell Sr., was spearheading a political campaign against a perceived tide of secularism in the United States. Falwell's 1980 best-selling book, *Listen America!*, opposed religious pluralism because it would pave the way for Muslims, Hindus, and other religious minorities to shape public policy.[109] Likewise, the Rev. Pat Robertson, the popular Evangelical leader of the Christian Coalition, deployed Judeo-Christian identity in the 1990s as a tool of exclusion when he asked rhetorically, "How dare you maintain that

FIGURE 6. Paid advertisement on Metropolitan Transit Authority (MTA) buses in New York, "Support Israel. Defeat Jihad" (2012).

those who believe in Judeo-Christian values are better qualified to govern American than Hindus and Muslims? My simple answer is, Yes, they are."[110]

The convergence of Orientalism and Zionism funded anti-Muslim racism after 9/11, which I address in chapter 7. For example, one explicit attempt to associate terrorism with Palestinians and Muslims was on display in a 2012 advertising campaign on New York, Washington, DC, and San Francisco subways and buses that warned Americans, "In any war between the civilized man and the savage, support the civilized man. Support Israel. Defeat Jihad."[111]

The label "terrorist sympathizer," which had for decades vilified Arabs and Palestinians, was now weaponized to imply that all Muslims in the United States were inassimilable.[112] And those who were critical of US Middle East policy, including its unconditional support of Israel—the Religious Dissident Racial Muslim—were especially dangerous.

FROM COLD WAR TO THE CLASH OF CIVILIZATIONS

The last decade of the twentieth century was a turning point in American Orientalism. During the 1980s, America's intervention in Muslim-majority countries came through support of particular regimes and organizations, such as Saddam Hussein in the Iran-Iraq War and Al-Qaeda in Afghanistan, within a bipolar Cold War global order.[113] In 1990, Vice President Dan

Quayle presciently warned in his speech at the US Naval Academy, "We have been surprised this past century by the rise of communism, the rise of Nazism and the rise of radical Islamic fundamentalism.... I am sure we'll be surprised again in the future. Though we may be surprised, let us always be prepared."[114]

As it had done in other proxy wars with the Soviet Union, the United States provided nearly $3 billion in arms and funding to non-state fighters in Afghanistan, self-described as Islamic mujahideen.[115] But when the Soviet Union pulled out of Afghanistan and collapsed soon thereafter, the global threat was no longer Communism. Islam now became the menace impeding American global hegemony. And Al-Qaeda and the mujahideen went from being freedom fighters to terrorists.[116]

In 1990, at the same time that the Soviet Union was dissolving, Saddam Hussein invaded Kuwait. Having spent half a trillion dollars fighting Iran with American support, Iraq was deeply in debt.[117] President George H. W. Bush dispatched more than 500,000 US troops to the Persian Gulf in a conflict he described as a military crusade.[118] He reiterated this point in a 1992 speech: "In the Persian Gulf we fought for good versus evil.... America stood fast so that liberty could stand tall. Today, I want to thank you for helping, America, as Christ ordained, to be a light unto the world."[119]

Bush would not be the only one to describe the Gulf War in religious terms. Self-identified Islamist resistance groups—including Al-Qaeda, Hamas, and Hezbollah, which had replaced Arab nationalists in opposing Western hegemony—called on Muslims to fight the Christian invaders. Militant groups leveraged economic and political malaise in the region to recruit disaffected young men who believed that but for US support, their repressive authoritarian leaders would fall. Despite Saddam Hussein's notoriety as a brutal dictator, the images of American tanks in Saudi Arabia triggered Muslim populist angst. Public opinion turned sharply against the United States as most Arab citizens saw the US military not as liberators but as occupiers seeking to steal Arabs' oil and occupy Islam's two holiest cities. That the Persian Gulf's authoritarian leaders were propped up by the US government lent further credibility to the pan-Islamist resistance groups' claims that Islam was under attack.

The most vocal dissident was Osama bin Laden, who had received military aid from the United States in the 1980s to fight the Soviets in Afghanistan. After the Gulf War, he set his sights on liberating Saudi Arabia from American domination. Bin Laden condemned the Saudi monarchy for allowing a Christian army to set up bases so close to the holy cities of Mecca and

Medina. To him, the American war in Kuwait was part of a grand scheme by Christians seeking to control the Islamic world.

Bin Laden's clash of civilizations worldview was shared by conservative American elites.[120] Weeks after the Gulf War, Bernard Lewis, a British Orientalist teaching at Princeton, published his influential article, "The Roots of Muslim Rage," in the widely read *Atlantic* magazine. Lewis argued that Muslims' opposition to America was symptomatic of Islam's purported enmity for secularism and modernity.[121] Muslims' political grievances were categorically attributed to Islamic fundamentalism—an irrational fusion of religion with politics that could not be reasoned with.[122]

Lewis warned Americans that Islamic civilization has clashed with Christendom for more than a millennium: "It should by now be clear that we are facing a mood and a movement far transcending the level of issues and policies and the governments that pursue them. This is no less than a clash of civilizations—the perhaps irrational but surely historic reaction of an ancient rival against our Judeo-Christian heritage, our secular present, and the worldwide expansion of both." Lewis perpetuated stereotypes of Arabs as inferior, describing early Zionists in Palestine as a sophisticated culture amid the savagery of Arab society.[123] His work would be repackaged for popular consumption after the September 11 attacks in his two widely read books, *What Went Wrong: The Clash between Islam and Modernity in the Middle East*[124] and *The Crisis of Islam: Holy War and Unholy Terror*.[125] Lewis contended that Islam, not the postcolonial Western hegemonic political order, was to blame for the autocracy and political violence in Muslim-majority countries.[126]

Three years later, in 1993, Harvard professor, Samuel Huntington, penned his provocatively titled article in *Foreign Affairs*, "The Clash of Civilizations?," arguing that the next global conflict would be between the West and Islamic states.[127] Building on the chorus of American Zionists claiming Muslims were a growing security threat, Huntington rebuked post–Cold War optimistic visions of a peaceful world order based on multilateral internationalism and universal values.[128] Instead, he essentialized Islam as possessing an unchangeable core that made its followers incapable of accepting modernity and democracy, in contrast to Protestantism's democratic ideals.[129] Not coincidentally, these were the same racial tropes deployed against Catholics and Jews to justify restricting their immigration earlier in the twentieth century.

Moreover, Huntington's theory of the clash of civilizations conflated and homogenized the diverse cultures of Muslim-majority countries. This is clearly illustrated by his oft-cited statement, "Islam's borders are bloody and so are its innards. The fundamental problem for the West is not Islamic fundamentalism. It is Islam, a different civilization whose people are convinced of the superiority of their culture and are obsessed with the inferiority of their power."[130] Whatever conflict or violence emanated from Muslim-majority countries, therefore, was directly attributable to Islam, as opposed to a complex combination of social, political, and economic factors shaped in large part by US and European support for dictators in the Middle East.[131] Effectively, Huntington treats Muslims as biologically incapable of practicing democracy, liberalism, and modernity—themes that emerged from the Bush administration's justification of war abroad and violations of the civil liberties of Muslims in the United States.

Huntington's and Lewis's theories circulated widely within Christian Evangelical circles. Robert Morey's influential 1992 book, *The Islamic Invasion*, rang a false alarm that the presence of millions of Muslims in America was part of a planned invasion.[132] Harking back to the anti-Chinese, anti-Semitic, and anti-Catholic rhetoric of the early twentieth century, Morey condemned Muslims as inassimilable, uncivilized, and a fifth column. A decade later, in 2002, the Southern Baptist leader William Wagner's book, *How Islam Plans to Change the World*, adopts Huntington's clash of civilizations theory to scare his followers into believing that American Muslims are attempting to conquer the United States from within.[133]

These war cries, however, were not novel. Rather, they rehashed the ideas of an earlier American Orientalist, Basil Mathews, literary secretary of the World's Alliance of the YMCA, who in 1926 published his book, *Young Islam on Trek: A Study of the Clash of Civilizations*.[134] In it, Basil claimed that Islam was a military ideology and that its creed was conquest by the sword.[135] The world was still divided into "us" versus "them," but now "they" were Islamic fundamentalists—a euphemism for religious and dissident Muslims who would be treated as the most vexing Racial Muslims after 9/11.

While Presidents George H. W. Bush and William J. "Bill" Clinton rejected Huntington's clash of civilization theory and Lewis's Muslim rage theory, some members of Congress embraced them. In 1993, the Congressional Task Force on Terrorism and Unconventional Warfare of the House Republican Research Committee, led by an Israeli American, Yossef Bodansky, authored "The New Islamist International." This report was "a result of several years of research and analysis of the trends in the spread of Islamic fundamentalism into the Sunni Muslim world and the overlapping relationships between the various fundamentalist terrorists groups."[136] The Task Force declared, "there has been a significant increase in Islamist terrorism, subversion, and violence[,] ...the escalation of an Islamic Jihad against the 'Judeo Christian world order.'" The report effectively reinforced Lewis's and Huntington's claims that Islam was the new global threat replacing the Red Scare of Communism. American journalists made similar claims. Six months after the Task Force report and one month after Huntington's theory entered the mainstream, Judith Miller's article in *Foreign Affairs*, "The Challenge of Radical Islam," mimicked right-wing Evangelicals' assertions that Islam was a threat to America.[137]

Neoconservatives took the clash of civilizations theory to another level by equating Islam with Fascism and Communism.[138] They shifted the focus from the international to the domestic, with the intent to persuade law enforcement to target Muslims and Arabs in the United States as a means of quashing pro-Palestinian activism. Daniel Pipes, a self-proclaimed terrorism expert, argued in his 1990 article, "The Muslims are Coming! The Muslims are Coming!," that Islamic terrorists had infiltrated the United States.[139] The 1993 World Trade Center bombings galvanized Pipes, among others, to disseminate the theory of a clash of civilizations to American elites.

In 1994, Pipes founded the Middle East Forum (MEF), which publishes the *Middle East Quarterly*, a pseudo-academic journal warning of the growing threat from Islam and Muslims.[140] He opposed US alliances with Arab states and called for military intervention in Iran. Most notably, Pipes was among the most vocal purported experts who blamed Arabs and Muslims for the 1995 Oklahoma City bombings, only to be proven wrong when the government confirmed that the perpetrator was Timothy McVeigh, a disgruntled White Christian male veteran.[141] Tellingly, the media did not conduct an inquisition into the faults of Christianity.[142]

But Pipes was not the only Zionist neoconservative to conclude that Muslims were to blame for the Oklahoma City bombing. Steven Emerson, who directs the Investigative Project on Terrorism, also went on national television to point a finger at Muslims. This was not the first time Emerson propagated anti-Muslim messaging. In his 1995 documentary, *Terrorists Among Us: Jihad in America*, aired on the mainstream television program *Frontline*, Emerson asserted that Muslim Americans were plotting a terrorist attack in the United States.[143] He associated Islam with anti-Semitism by showing scenes of bloodshed and havoc after suicide bombings in Israel. His propaganda film warns American viewers of Muslim-led conspiracies to bomb innocent, unsuspecting Americans.[144] An Associated Press investigation into these claims revealed that the FBI evidence used in the documentary had been falsified.[145]

Prior to the September 11 attacks, Daniel Pipes, Steven Emerson, and other anti-Muslim ideologues had limited influence among mainstream media and policy makers.[146] Their outlandish equation of Islam with terrorism often fell on deaf ears in US halls of power. That would change on September 11, 2001, when the Racial Muslim became entrenched in American race politics.

. . .

The evolution of American Orientalism in the second half of the twentieth century demonstrates the significance of global geopolitics in shaping domestic racial-religious hierarchies. The September 11 attacks confirmed Gary Gregg's five common negative perceptions of the Arab Muslim world: (1) despotism and strife stem from a tribal mentality equipped with modern weapons; (2) a "code of honor" monopolizes the Middle Eastern psyche and subverts modernization; (3) Islamic fatalism breeds inaction and stalls development; (4) the momentum of tradition resists modernization; and (5) terrorism springs from fanaticism in Arab culture and the Arab psyche.[147] These perceptions inform the different categories of Racial Muslims, with Religious and Dissident Muslims most likely to be stereotyped as dangerous and irrational, and secular and nonpolitical Muslims most likely to be tokenized as model minorities.

Over the course of the twentieth century, Arabs in the United States went from being an obscure minority advocating for legal Whiteness, with varying success, to a growing perceived foreign threat. Incorrectly presumed to all be Muslim and mistakenly including Persian Iranians, the Arab in the second half of the twentieth century was raced as the quintessential terrorist in media, films, and policy making. Immigrant Muslims' treatment in the United States, thus, was precariously dependent on events in their countries of origin. Each time an international political crisis occurred, Muslims in the US experienced varying levels of temporal backlashes, after which they could return to being a relatively invisible religious minority in their daily lives.[148] Although the Racial Muslim was under formation for decades, it became entrenched in American race politics after September 11, 2001. I now turn to the myriad ways in which the War on Terror effectively became a War on Muslims, putting to the test America's commitments to religious freedom.

SEVEN

Fighting Terrorism, Not Religion

WHEN NINETEEN HIJACKERS crashed two airplanes into the World Trade Center, Americans were primed to criminalize Muslim identity. Religion, rather than ancestry or phenotype, had become the dominant trait racializing people from the Middle East, North Africa, and South Asia—including those misidentified as Muslim. This transformation of Muslim identity into a racial identity has led to myriad assaults on Muslims' religious freedoms. Similar to the racialization of Jews, Catholics, and Mormons a century ago, adherence to Islam imputes inferior biological and cultural traits to its followers. That is, to be Muslim is to be presumed to possess a pathology of violence, fanaticism, and despotism antithetical to (Christian) religious norms.[1]

After the September 11 attacks, Islamic practices such as jihad, Sharia, *salaat* (the five daily prayers), hijab, and Ramadan were maligned as threatening to America's Judeo-Christian national identity. Even though most Americans did not understand these concepts, the constant rhetoric in the media associating Islam with terrorism caused Americans to view Muslims as a suspect race who posed a security threat. The more religious and dissident a Muslim acted, the more severe the material and dignitary consequences of racialization.

Although Islam was viewed with suspicion long before 2001, the stereotypes ebbed and flowed based on international events. As I discuss in chapters 4 through 6, American Orientalism in the twentieth century contributed to news stories, films, and books that portrayed Middle Eastern–looking men as angry, violent, and viscerally anti-American. Arabs, incorrectly presumed to all be Muslims, were associated with bloodshed, intolerance, and cultural backwardness. But the anti-Muslim protagonists

FIGURE 7. Front page of the *Washington Post,* September 12, 2001.

remained on the fringe of public discourse, or their political impact was limited to conservative elites.

Thus, to convince a large swath of Americans to discriminate against a religious minority, Islam had to be redefined as a violent political ideology. And this is precisely what politicians, news media, films and television series, and a burgeoning, well-funded Islamophobia industry did after the 9/11 attacks.

FRAMING ISLAM AS A VIOLENT
POLITICAL IDEOLOGY

Six days after the terrorist attacks, President George W. Bush visited a mosque and declared, "The face of terror is not the true faith of Islam. That's not what Islam is all about. Islam is peace."[2] Three months later, at an Eid celebration, Bush highlighted the similarities between Islam, Judaism, and Christianity, the three largest world faiths. He hinted at an Abrahamic national heritage when he advised his audience "to remember how much we have in common: devotion to family, a commitment to care for those in need, a belief in God and His justice, and the hope for peace on Earth."[3] In direct contradiction to these statements, however, Bush implemented a Middle East foreign policy centered on the presumption that Muslims are a despotic people whose use of violence is irrational and terroristic. Indeed, Bush's signature "Freedom Agenda" sought to spread freedom by means of military intervention and occupation in Afghanistan and Iraq. The heathens had to be civilized by force, resulting in the merging of a Cold War mind-set with American Orientalism.

As the Bush administration's neoconservatives schemed to depose President Saddam Hussein—whom they had supported just fifteen years earlier in the Iran-Iraq War—Bush's rhetoric invoked apocalyptic language appealing to his Evangelical Christian right-wing base. In his 2002 State of the Union, Bush declared that his doctrine of preemption would animate the US occupation of Iraq abroad and increase targeting of Muslims at home.

> These enemies view the entire world as a battlefield, and we must pursue them wherever they are. So long as training camps operate, so long as nations harbor terrorists, freedom is at risk. And America and our allies must not, and will not, allow it. . . . But some governments will be timid in the face of terror. And make no mistake about it: If they do not act, America will.[4]

Bush reiterated this preemption doctrine in a West Point commencement speech six months later: "If we wait for threats to fully materialize we will have waited too long. . . . We must take the battle to the enemy, disrupt his plans and confront the worst threats before they emerge."[5] The drumbeats of an impending war in Iraq were getting louder.

Political commentary justified the War on Terror by evoking a religious crusade between Christianity's good and Islam's evil. Countless articles, books, and media outlets portrayed Islam as a violent political ideology, thereby legitimizing state violence against Muslims. For example, in the four months after the September 11 attacks, the *New York Times* published articles with the following titles: "Barbarians at the Gate," "This Is a Religious War," "Defusing the Holy Bomb," "The Core of Muslim Rage," and "A Head-On Collision of Alien Cultures."[6]

Government discourse reinforced the good versus evil narrative that permeated the media. According to the 2006 US National Security Strategy, "From the beginning, the War on Terror has been both a battle of arms and a battle of ideas—a fight against the terrorists and against their murderous ideology."[7] Vice President Dick Cheney invoked Orientalist discourse in a 2007 speech to the American Israel Public Affairs Committee.

> The terrorists value death the same way you and I value life. Civilized, decent societies will never fully understand the kind of mindset that drives men to strap on bombs or fly airplanes into buildings.... [T]he only option for our security and survival is to go on the offensive, facing the threat directly, patiently and systematically, until the enemy is destroyed.[8]

Rather than acknowledge the role of Western countries in propping up authoritarians who perpetuate political repression, economic disparities, and corruption that triggers non-state violence, US government officials blamed Islam.[9] Federal prosecutors shared the belief that Islam is "both a religion and a political-social ideology."[10]

In a civil case involving local opposition to the construction of a new mosque in Murfreesboro, Tennessee, the plaintiffs' lawyers insisted that Islam is a political ideology, not a religion, and therefore the Muslim defendants could not rely on the First Amendment protection of freedom of religion.[11] Frank Gaffney, director of the Center for Security Policy who later become a senior adviser to Donald Trump, was called as an expert witness to testify on behalf of the plaintiffs that Sharia was incompatible with American values.[12] These arguments may have appealed in the court of public opinion, but they failed in the court of law.[13] The US Department of Justice's amicus brief reminded the court, "The plaintiffs' claim that Islam is not recognized by the United States is false and no authority sustains such an idea. Freedom of assembly and religion is literally the foundation of this country."[14] Unfortunately, not all Americans share this view when it comes to Muslims.

The casting out of Islam from the realm of religion in a country that privileges religious freedom normatively was not the first time a religious minority faced overt discrimination.[15] As I discuss in chapters 2 and 3, American religious freedom was historically circumscribed to Protestant Whites. Only later did it expand to Catholics, Jews, and Mormons, and this was after protracted domestic advocacy, demographic changes, and international developments that transformed the national identity from Christian to Judeo-Christian.

That Jews, Catholics, and Mormons are now included in an expanded definition of Whiteness and American national identity does not eliminate the racialization of religion; it merely redefines it. The same tropes of inassimilable, antidemocratic immigrants who are unfit for self-governance are still deployed but for a different religious minority in the racial-religious hierarchy.

Today, Muslims find themselves near the bottom of this hierarchy, due not only to a single terrorist attack but also to a gradual entrenchment of American Orientalism that transformed into systemic Islamophobia after 2001. Orientalism exoticizes and infantilizes Muslims, while Islamophobia and anti-Muslim racism securitizes and criminalizes them as existential threats to the nation's security. Similar to the racialization of Blacks during the antebellum and Jim Crow eras, Christian theological arguments underpin the racialization of Muslims.

AMERICAN EVANGELICALS CAST OUT ISLAM

Theological attacks against Islam surged after 9/11. Conservative Evangelical leaders, seeking to prove the truth of Christianity and the fallacy of Islam, proclaimed spiritual warfare and described Islam as an ideology of war intent on killing Christians and Jews.[16] Echoing Orientalist tropes, their sermons have repeatedly associated Islam, Muslims, and the Prophet Muhammad with terrorism, war, savagery, and despotism.[17] After 9/11, religious or dissident Muslims are presumed to be anti-Semitic, anti-Christian, and anti-American.

Despite efforts by moderate Evangelical and mainline Protestant leaders to condemn Islamophobic rhetoric, the Far Right Christian leadership, which proudly boasts its Zionist allegiance, openly demonizes Islam and defames the Prophet Muhammad. In an interview on the televangelist Pat Robertson's 700 Club, Rev. Jerry Falwell said, "These Islamic fundamentalists, these radical terrorists, these Middle Eastern monsters are committed to destroying the Jewish nation, driving her into the Mediterranean, conquering the world. And we are the great Satan. We are the ultimate goal."[18] A year later, Falwell called the Prophet Muhammad "a terrorist...a violent man, a man of war." As the founder of the Moral Majority, an influential Evangelical political movement, Falwell's words on the Christian Broadcasting Network reached millions of Americans.[19]

Likewise, in 2002, Reverend Jerry Vines, who had served as president of the Southern Baptist Convention, warned his sixteen million followers that the Prophet Muhammad was a "demon-possessed pedophile."[20] Paul Weyrich, co-founder of the "Moral Majority" with Paul Falwell, and William S. Lind, director of the Center for Cultural Conservatism, jointly authored a booklet titled *Why Islam Is a Threat to America and the West,* wherein they argue that Muslims "should be encouraged to leave. They are a fifth column in this country."[21] In 2003, Pat Robertson called the Prophet Muhammad "an absolute wild-eyed fanatic" and a killer.[22] Thirteen years later, in 2016, Robertson called on Belgium and France to stop Muslim immigration, which he called an infection, and condemned Obama for allowing Muslims to immigrate to the United States.[23]

Franklin Graham, son of the famous Evangelist Billy Graham and a family friend of George W. Bush, called Islam a "very wicked and evil religion."[24] Graham's condemnation of Islam earned him the Daniel of the Year Award in 2002 from *WORLD,* a magazine that "reports the news from a Christian worldview."[25] More than a decade later, in 2014, Graham's views had not changed; he stated that Islam has always been and continues to be "a religion of war."[26] Graham also peddled the conspiracy theory that Obama was a secret Muslim assisting American Muslims to take over the government, "which eventually will lead to persecution of Christians and Jews in America."[27]

What came to be known as the "birther movement" against Obama had its most vocal advocate in Donald Trump, who told Fox News in 2011, "He doesn't have a birth certificate. He may have one, but there's something on that, maybe religion, maybe it says he is a Muslim.... I don't know. Maybe he doesn't want that."[28] Unsurprisingly, Graham was a vocal supporter of Trump's candidacy for president, which earned him an invitation to offer a prayer at Trump's 2017 presidential inauguration.[29] The two men share a deep animosity toward Islam.

Government officials with similar views legitimize Islamophobia in speeches at churches and conferences hosted by Evangelical organizations. General William G. Boykin, who served as undersecretary of defense for intelligence, told the congregation at the First Baptist Church in Dayton, Florida, in 2003 that the enemy is not Osama bin Laden but rather "a spiritual enemy because we are a nation of believers.... We were founded on faith. And the enemy that comes against our nation is a spiritual enemy. His name is Satan."[30]

Boykin was also featured in videos and articles produced by a coalition of Evangelical and Pentecostal clergy leading the Oak Initiative. In an interview with the Evangelical organization, he stated:

> We need to realize that Islam itself is not simply a religion, it's a totalitarian way of life. It is a legal system, the law of Sharia; it's a financial system, it's a moral code, it's a political system, it's a military system. Islam should not be protected by the First Amendment, especially when one knows that those who obey the diktat of the Koran are duty bound to destroy our Constitution and to replace it with Sharia law.[31]

In another speech to the Good Shepherd Community Church in Sandy, Oregon, Boykin informed his audience, "Why do they hate us? The answer to that is because we're a Christian nation. We are hated because we are a nation of believers."[32] Boykin repeated the myths propagated by European and American Orientalists who believed Christianity was superior to Islam.

Boykin's message was amplified by James Dobson, an Evangelical leader with approximately 6.3 million followers, on his popular radio show, "Focus on the Family."[33] Dobson's fallacious claims that Muslims are under an obligation to replace the US Constitution with Sharia law fueled a movement seeking to exclude Muslims from religious accommodation. Tony Perkins, president of the Christian conservative Family Research Council and a member of the US Commission on International Religious Freedom, bluntly articulated the commonly held belief in 2015 among some within the Christian Right that "only 16 percent of Islam is a religion—the rest is a combination of military, judicial, economic, and political system. Christianity, by comparison, isn't a judicial or economic code—but a faith.... Sharia is not a religion in the context of the First Amendment."[34] According to this logic, banning mosques and targeting Muslims through surveillance, prosecution, and war do not contradict American ideals of religious freedom; rather, such actions keep America safe and preserve its White Judeo-Christian identity.

During the 2012 presidential campaign, Newt Gingrich warned his audience at the conservative American Enterprise Institute, "I believe Sharia is a mortal threat to the survival of freedom in the United States and in the world as we know it."[35] Gingrich also signed an anti-Sharia pledge, along with presidential candidates Michele Bachmann and Rick Santorum.[36] Five years later, Gingrich advocated for more surveillance of American mosques

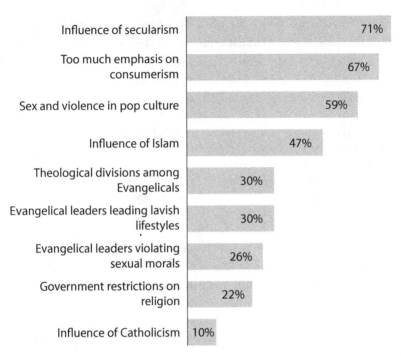

Influence of secularism	71%
Too much emphasis on consumerism	67%
Sex and violence in pop culture	59%
Influence of Islam	47%
Theological divisions among Evangelicals	30%
Evangelical leaders leading lavish lifestyles	30%
Evangelical leaders violating sexual morals	26%
Government restrictions on religion	22%
Influence of Catholicism	10%

FIGURE 8. Global survey of Evangelical Protestant Leaders on major threats to Evangelical Christianity (2011). Pew Research Forum.

after the terrorist attack in Nice, France. He warned viewers on Fox News in 2016, "Western civilization is in a war. We should frankly test every person here who is of a Muslim background, and if they believe in Sharia, they should be deported."[37]

Similar to the cottage industry of anti-Semitic and anti-Catholic literature in the early twentieth century, a surge in sales of religious fiction blended apocalypticism with anti-Muslim racism. Best-selling authors like Joel Richardson sold books entitled *Antichrist: Islam's Awaited Messiah* (2006), *The Islamic Antichrist: The Shocking Truth about the Nature of the Beast* (2009), and *Mideast Beast: The Case of the Islamic Antichrist* (2012). Another best-selling author, Hal Lindsay, published *The Everlasting Hatred: The Roots of Jihad* in 2002, in which he proclaims, "Islam represents the single greatest threat to the continued survival of the planet."[38] That same year, Mark Hitchcock published *War on Terror: Unfolding Bible Prophecy*, which claims that Islamic terrorism is a sign of the end times; Joel Rosenberg began *The Last Jihad* book series with Arab and Muslim terrorists as the primary

	Unfavorable	Favorable
Pentecostal Christians	8%	92%
Catholics	24%	76%
Jews	25%	75%
Orthodox Christians	26%	74%
Buddhists	65%	35%
Hindus	65%	35%
Muslims	67%	33%
Atheists	70%	30%

FIGURE 9. Global survey of Evangelical Protestant Leaders showing Evangelical views of religious groups (2011). Pew Research Forum.

antagonists. Notably, Rosenberg had worked for the right-wing radio host Rush Limbaugh, who frequently claimed that "Islam creates terrorism."[39]

Although rejected by liberal Christians, right-wing Evangelical leaders' Islamophobic rhetoric has fueled a demand for propaganda validating that Muslims in America are a national security threat.[40] Indeed, numerous surveys have found that American Evangelicals are significantly more likely to hold negative views of Islam and believe it has little if anything in common with Christianity.[41] The 2015 American Values Survey, for example, found that 73 percent of White Evangelical Protestants believe that Islam is incompatible with American values. This is ten percentage points higher than mainline White Protestants, at 63%; twelve points higher than Catholics, at 61%; and seventeen points higher than Black Protestants, at 55%, who hold unfavorable views of Islam.[42] These findings demonstrate that the sustained negative public discourse about Islam for nearly two decades has successfully shifted public opinion against Muslims.

THE RACIAL MUSLIM IN THE MEDIA

The Western media have also been instrumental in the social construction of the Racial Muslim. Before the September 11 attacks, terrorism carried out by Al-Qaeda was rarely covered by television news.[43] Meanwhile, coverage of conflicts in the Middle East in the 1990s tended to label the parties by ethnicity or nationality rather than as Muslim. All that changed after 2001. With the exception of the first six months, when Muslim and Arab Americans were frequently interviewed, media portrayals of these communities became increasingly negative with each passing year.[44] Muslim voices were noticeably absent, despite the spotlight on their religion.

As Evelyn Alsultany's work demonstrates, news coverage of terrorism lacked balance, resulting in the propagation of stereotypes that Muslims are suspect and Islam is incompatible with American values.[45] By 2007, there was ten times more coverage of conflicts and violence in Muslim-majority countries than of education, culture, or economic development in those same countries.[46] Coverage of the Middle East was almost exclusively through the lens of conflict, militancy, and political extremism.[47] In stark contrast, Jews and Christians were represented in the context of peaceful religious activities.[48]

Negative coverage of Islam continued to rise with every passing year. According to Media Tenor's analysis of Western media from 2007 to 2013, unfavorable coverage of Islam peaked in 2010.[49] By 2011, nearly 25 percent of stories about Muslims used the image of a militant, while only 0.1 percent presented images of ordinary Muslims.[50] In a 2015 report, Media Tenor analyzed over 2.6 million news stories in ten German, British, and US television shows from 2001 to 2014. Reporting about Islam focused on terrorists and armed groups in the Middle East and the West. The average daily lives of hundreds of millions of Muslims in the Middle East and North Africa were rarely portrayed.[51]

Also erased from media analysis was the relationship between state and non-state actors.[52] Few journalists explained to Americans the role of the United States in creating and arming the mujahideen in Afghanistan to fight the Soviets in the 1980s, many of whom later joined Al-Qaeda.[53] Rather than accurately portray Al-Qaeda and Osama bin Laden as the extremist fringe that they were, Western media stories made them out to be representatives of Muslims both abroad and in the United States.

Racial Double Standards on Religious Extremism

Double standards in media portrayals of Muslim extremists as compared to Christian extremists further evinces the racialization of Muslims.

Specifically, political violence by Christian extremists is attributed to the perpetrators' individual political beliefs, not to Christianity. For example, Paul Hill, who killed John Britton, a doctor who provided abortions, wrote in 1994, "I realized that using force to stop abortion is the same means that God has used to stop similar atrocities throughout history." This is a religious reference to a story in the Book of Esther about the Jews fighting the king of Persia in self-defense.[54] Hill's actions were praised by Michael Bray, a leader of the antiabortion group the Army of God. Bray assured his followers that Hill's actions were morally justified because he was defending innocent human life in accordance with biblical teachings. Despite the biblical justification for Hill's violence, Americans do not attribute Hill's terrorism to all Christians in the same way they associate terrorism by individual Muslims to all Muslims.[55]

Likewise, violence committed by members of the Christian Identity movement is not depicted as a Christian problem, even though they believe the Bible prescribes the moral and spiritual superiority of White Christians.[56] The American media does not describe the Army of God as representative of Christians the way Al-Qaeda or ISIS is portrayed as representing Muslims. Nor does the media connect the resurgence of the Ku Klux Klan since Obama's election with its Christian ideological roots. The public is not informed that the KKK's symbol, the Mystic Symbol of a Klansman, features a white cross with a red teardrop at the center, signifying the atonement and sacrifice of Jesus Christ. Dominion Theology, another growing movement aligned with sovereign citizens and other Alt-Right groups, asserts that America is a Christian nation.[57] These Christian White supremacists plan terrorist attacks against mosques, harass Muslims at armed protests outside of mosques, and support the anti-Sharia movement.

A convergence of anti-Black and anti-Muslim racism subsequent to Obama's election triggered a wave of violence by White Far-Right extremists. A study by the Combating Terrorism Center at West Point reports that 254 individuals were killed in 307 attacks by Far Right domestic groups from 2002 to 2011.[58] The Anti-Defamation League estimates that right-wing extremists—including White supremacists, sovereign citizens, and militia members—were responsible for 71 percent of the 387 deaths caused by violent extremism in the United States from 2008 to 2017.[59] A survey of law enforcement in 2014 found that 74 percent of respondents considered antigovernment extremism the number one violent threat in their jurisdiction, while only 39 percent considered Islamist extremism the top threat. Only 3 percent of law enforcement agencies identified the threat from "Islamist extremists" as severe.[60]

And yet few Americans have knowledge of right-wing domestic security threats, much less of their Christian ideological roots.[61] These right-wing groups, if covered at all in the media, are never described as Christian extremists.[62] Nor does the US government subject these extremist groups and their White sympathizers to the aggressive surveillance and sting operations imposed on Muslim communities. This explains in large part why a siege on the US Capitol on January 6, 2021, could be planned in plain sight on social media, notwithstanding two decades of official state policy of preventive counterterrorism.[63] And when right-wing violence is prosecuted, it is under criminal law, not antiterrorism statutes. Thus, the US Department of Justice's official lists of domestic terrorist incidents or designated domestic terrorist groups do not include right-wing extremists.[64]

Racializing Muslims as Terrorists

The media's focus on terrorism committed by Muslims was so intense that between 2006 and 2015, terrorism by Muslims was covered 350 percent more times than terrorism committed by non-Muslims in the United States.[65] This translates into an average of 15 print and online headlines per attack committed by non-Muslims, compared to 105 headlines for terrorist acts committed by Muslim extremists.[66] Put another way, Muslims perpetrated 12.5 percent of terrorist attacks in the United States but received a whopping 50 percent of the news coverage.

Christopher Bail's research explains why: anti-Muslim organizations' negative representations of Islam and Muslims have been effective in shaping public opinion.[67] The more anger and fear Islamophobes propagate, the more media coverage they receive.[68] The more leaders of anti-Muslim organizations warning of a domestic Muslim invasion become regular guests on mainstream television, the more Americans fear Islam and the more Muslims suffer discrimination and racial violence.

Rarely does the media cover the hundreds of press releases issued since 9/11 by American Muslim organizations and religious leaders condemning terrorism.[69] For example, few Americans are aware of the fatwa (Islamic legal opinion) issued in 2005 by the Fiqh Council of North America and signed by 145 Muslim organizations and mosques, condemning terrorism. Among the prominent organizations that endorsed the legal opinion were the Islamic Society of North America (ISNA), the Islamic Circle of North America (ICNA), the Muslim Public Affairs Council (MPAC), and the Council on American Islamic Relations (CAIR)—all of which have been wrongly accused of supporting terrorism by the Islamophobia industry and Republican members of Congress.[70]

Muslim organizations' measured explanations of the geopolitical origins of terrorism in the name of Islam fall on deaf ears.[71] On the few occasions when American Muslims have been invited to discuss Islam or the Middle East, they have been asked to defend their faith before a court of public opinion predisposed to be skeptical of Islam. Such efforts are futile so long as a Muslim's religiosity or disagreement with US foreign policy marks him as a security threat.

Television dramas further reinforce the association of Muslims with terrorism. Widely watched shows like *24* and *Sleeper Cell* portray Arabs and Muslims as intent on senseless terrorism against Americans. Despite inclusion of a few "good" Arab and Muslim characters playing the patriotic American in War on Terror movies, the enemy is frequently Muslim, and the motivating violent ideology is Islam.[72] Put another way, the characters portraying Religious Dissident Racial Muslims are the villains, Religious Racial Muslims are suspects, and Secular Racial Muslims are the "moderate Muslims" working with the US government.

Alsultany's analysis notes that although shows like *24* may signal that racism is wrong, the plots communicate to American audiences that torturing Muslims is necessary to protect the United States.[73] I argue that in order for the majority of Americans who believe in religious freedom to accept this narrative, Americans must first perceive Islam as a violent political ideology.[74] As such, profiling and targeting Muslims in counterterrorism efforts is not considered un-American or bigoted. To the contrary, it is viewed as smart national security. This divisive narrative is aggressively propagated by the Islamophobia industry and their Former Racial Muslim spokespersons.

THE ISLAMOPHOBIA INDUSTRY

A multimillion-dollar industry of organizations, pundits, and funders have successfully persuaded more than half of Americans that Islam is not eligible for religious freedom protections. A convergence of right-wing ideologues, journalists, filmmakers, lawyers, and wealthy donors has produced

TABLE I The top eight funders of Islamophobia

Funder	Clarion Project	Middle East Forum	David Horowitz Freedom Center	Center for Security Policy
Donors Capital Fund and Donors Trust	$18,403,600	$6,768,000	$177,000	$1,289,000
Scaife Foundations			$4,650,000	$3,425,000
Lynde and Harry Bradley Foundation		$430,000	$5,090,000	$1,020,000
William Rosenwald Family Fund, Middle Road Foundation, and Abstraction Fund	$25,000	$4,248,729	$54,750	$473,500
Russell Berrie Foundation		$273,016		
Fairbrook Foundation		$410,000	$789,500	$166,700
Newton D. and Rochelle F. Becker Foundation and Charitable Trust	$80,000	$464,000	$87,000	$405,000
Alan and Hope Winters Family Foundation				$271,075
Total	$18,508,600	$12,593,745	$10,848,250	$7,050,275

SOURCE: The eight largest donors to think tanks and organizations in the United States identified by the Center for American Progress as being anti-Islam and/or supporting policies discriminating against Muslims. Research based on the eight foundations' 990 forms filed with the US Internal Revenue Service from 2001 to 2012. *Fear Inc 2.0. Report* (2014), Center for American Progress.

an ongoing, national campaign to defame Islam and expel Muslims from the American political community. The Islamophobic narrative includes, but is not limited to, the following claims: mosques train terrorists, Muslim women are oppressed by their male family members, Muslims in political office are part of a conspiracy to Islamicize and invade the United States, Muslims who disagree with US Middle East policy support foreign terrorist groups, and Muslims practice *taqiyya* to lie about their illicit intentions to take over the United States.[75]

Purported experts on the Middle East and Islam publish reports, lobby Congress, and engage with mainstream media to promote the clash of civilizations narrative and reframe Islam as a violent political ideology.[76] For example, David Horowitz's Freedom Center intentionally featured Former Muslims and Arab Christian native informants such as Nonie Darwish,

CTSERF	Investigative Project on Terrorism	Society of Americans for National Existence	Jihad Watch	American Congress for Truth	American Islamic Forum for Democracy	Total
	$405,000					$27,042,60
$2,400,000						$10,475,000
						$6,540,000
$15,000	$86,000		$5,000		$45,000	$4,952,979
$2,736,000	$793,335					$3,802,351
	$25,000	$90,000	$253,250	$125,000		$1,859,450
$200,000	$100,000			$75,000		$1,411,000
	$75,000	$387,288		$8,697	$75,000	$817,060
$5,351,000	$1,484,335	$477,288	$258,250	$208,697	$120,000	$56,900,440

Wafa Sultan, and Bridgette Gabriel in its annual "Islamofascism Awareness Week" held at universities across the country.[77]

Although these individuals have long held anti-Muslim and anti-Arab beliefs that are informed by Orientalist and Zionist ideology, they were politically marginalized prior to 2001. Few reputable media outlets took them seriously. The September 11 attacks provided an opportune political moment for zealots to mainstream their racist ideology in the halls of government, churches, synagogues, and the media. And the rise of White nativism that culminated in the election of Donald Trump boosted Islamophobia to the top of the administration's policy priorities, as I discuss further in chapters 8 and 9.

Islamophobia is a lucrative business in American civil society. According to the Center for American Progress, a small circle of wealthy donors and foundations together contributed more than $56 million in the first decade after

9/11.[78] For instance, the Donors Capital Fund, managed by leaders of the conservative American Enterprise Institute and the Heritage Foundation, has donated more than $27 million to organizations focused on peddling anti-Muslim racism. The Scaife Foundations contributed over $10 million. Other conservative donors include the Russell Berrie Foundation, the Rosenwald Family Fund, the Abramson Family Foundation, the Fairbrook Foundation, the Lynde and Harry Bradley Foundation, and the Newton D. and Rochelle F. Becker Foundation.[79] This boost in funding contributed to the growth of Steven Emerson's Investigative Project on Terrorism and Counterterrorism and Security Educational Research Fund by more than 644 percent. Frank Gaffney's Center for Security Policy's budget grew by 253 percent.

Simultaneously, the September 11 attacks triggered interest in learning more about Islam, Muslims, and Muslim-majority countries. Christopher Bail's work shows how the Islamophobia industry increasingly dominated narratives about Islam and Muslims in the United States. Ten anti-Muslim organizations between 2001 and 2003 took the lead in propagating Islamophobic messages.[80] They leveraged their significant resources to create outsized access to the media, thereby manufacturing a steady stream of racist content. As the demand for information grew, so too did the number of these organizations. By 2006, the number of anti-Muslim organizations grew to sixteen, and by 2008 more than forty organizations peddled Islamophobia. With a burgeoning public following, the Islamophobia industry shaped public policy and government action affecting Muslims in America and US foreign policy in Muslim-majority countries.

Deploying Former Muslim and Christian Arab Women to Legitimize Islamophobia

To legitimize their Islamophobic narratives, anti-Muslim organizations strategically used Arab Christian women and Muslim women who converted to Christianity or atheism.[81] Ayaan Hirsi Ali, a Somali-born former member of the Dutch parliament, joined the American Enterprise Institute in 2007.[82] A Muslim-born convert to atheism, she became the darling of the Islamophobia industry. Hirsi Ali's autobiographical best-selling books, *Infidel* (2007), *Nomad* (2010), and *Heretic: Why Islam Needs a Reformation Now* (2015) regurgitated Orientalist tropes of Islam as a misogynistic religion, thereby justifying the need to save Muslim women as part of the War on Terror.[83] She validated First Lady Laura Bush's statements in a radio address on November

17, 2001: "The fight against terrorism is also a fight for the rights and dignity of women."[84] Curiously, Laura Bush's sudden interest in Muslim women's rights coincided with her husband's decision to invade Afghanistan.

Ayaan Hirsi Ali pays homage to Samuel P. Huntington's clash of civilizations theory in her assertion that Islam is incompatible with Western democratic values.[85] Her loathing of Islam, coupled with her claims of authenticity as a Former Muslim, makes her instrumental in political attacks on Muslim American organizations. Mirroring the animus of the Ku Klux Klan and the Know Nothing Party toward Jews and Catholics in the early twentieth century, the Islamophobia industry set its sights on destroying Muslim American civil society and quashing Muslims' political influence. Leaders of ISNA, CAIR, the North American Islamic Trust, and MPAC have all been subjected to well-financed defamation campaigns accusing them of supporting terrorism.[86] Being religious and challenging Islamophobia puts these Muslim leaders in the most targeted category: the Religious Dissident Racial Muslim.

Right-wing Christian conservatives' seemingly insatiable demand for Former Muslims' validation of anti-Muslim tropes prompted a genre of Islamophobia books. These books assert the same fallacious themes: (1) Islam is an inherently violent political ideology; (2) Muslims worship a false god who is not the same God worshipped by Christians and Jews; (3) Muslims are savages; and (4) Islam is irredeemably misogynist.

Some of the most widely read books are Nonie Darwish's *Now They Call Me Infidel: Why I Renounced Jihad for America, Israel, and the War on Terror* (2006), Wafa Sultan's *A God Who Hates: The Courageous Woman Who Inflamed the Muslim World Speaks Out Against the Evils of Islam* (2009), Reza Safa's reissued 1996 book, *Inside Islam: Exposing and Reaching the World of Islam*, and Mark A. Gabriel's *Culture Clash: Islam's War on America* and *Islam and Terrorism: What the Quran Really Teaches about Christianity, Violence and the Goals of the Islamic Jihad*.

In addition, two brothers, Former Muslims, Emir Fethi Caner and Ergun Caner, published *Unveiling Islam: An Insider's Look at Muslim Life and Beliefs*. They boldly proclaimed, "The [9/11] terrorists were not some fringe group that changed the Qur'an to suit political ends. They understood the Qur'an quite well and followed the teachings of jihad to the letter."[87] The book, which sold more than one hundred thousand copies, was cited by right-wing Christian leaders such as Jerry Vines to claim that Muhammad was a false prophet.

FIGURE 10. Members of Identity Europa, a White nationalist group, at a "March Against Sharia," organized by ACT for America in Orlando, Florida. Photo by Southern Poverty Law Center.

At the grassroots level, Brigitte Gabriel launched hundreds of local chapters of ACT for America across the country, which mobilize protests and media campaigns against mosques, Muslim American organizations, and Muslim American leaders.[88] Gabriel, a Lebanese American Christian woman, previously worked for the South Lebanon Army, which served as Israel's proxy in formerly occupied southern Lebanon.[89] Her association with right-wing Zionists merged with anti-Muslim Evangelical Christians to create ACT for America. Gabriel follows Gaffney's lead in lobbying for a ban on Sharia law in state courts, criminalizing CAIR, and admonishing Jews and Christians against engaging in interfaith dialogue with Muslims.

At an intelligence conference in Washington, DC, in 2006, Gabriel warned, "America and the West are doomed to failure in this war unless they stand up and identify the real enemy, Islam."[90] Gabriel went on to declare that every practicing Muslim is a radical Muslim.[91] The following year, she stated in a course at the Department of Defense's Joint Forces Staff College, "If a Muslim who has—who is—a practicing Muslim who believes the word of the Koran to be the world of Allah[,] ... this practicing Muslim, who believes in the teachings of the Koran, cannot be a loyal citizen of the United States of America."[92]

Spreading the conspiracy theory that an Islamic invasion of America was imminent, Gabriel declared in 2011 on CNN, "America has been infiltrated on all levels by radicals who wish to harm America. They have infiltrated us at the C.I.A., at the F.B.I., at the Pentagon, at the State Department. They are being radicalized in radical mosques in our cities and communities within the United States."[93] Gabriel's vitriolic attacks on Islam fill the pages of her widely read books, *Because They Hate: A Survivor of Islamic Terror Warns America* (2008), *They Must Be Stopped: Why We Must Defeat Radical Islam and How We Can Do It* (2010), and *Rise: In Defense of Judeo-Christian Values and Freedom* (2018)—all of which are promoted by the Islamophobia industry's national network.

By 2016, ACT for America's budget was $1 million and its 300,000 members across the country were propagating its Islamophobic propaganda. Local chapter leaders spread messages such as, "Islam is a supremacist, totalitarian political ideology masquerading as a religion. It's as dangerous as Nazism or communism and must be eradicated."[94] These toxic messages planted seeds of hatred across the country—targeting Muslim laypeople and intellectuals alike.

Production of Islamophobic Knowledge

The production of knowledge to discredit academics, civil society, and government officials who challenge the racialization of Muslims is a critical strategy of Islamophobes. The Middle East Forum (MEF), managed by Daniel Pipes and with a war chest of nearly $5 million, funds many Islamophobic organizations.[95] Borrowing from the McCarthyist playbook, the MEF has accused more than one hundred American academics of condoning terrorism, underestimating the threat of radical Islam, or being apologists for "radical Islam." Among MEF's targets are well-known Arab and Muslim professors, including Khaled Abou El Fadl, Nadia Abu Al-Haj, Lila Abu-Lughod, Hamid Dabashi, Rashid Khalili, Mahmood Mamdani, Joseph Massad, and Omid Safi.[96] MEF collaborates with conservative politicians to propagate the false idea that Muslims are infiltrating the US government and the White House as part of a secret plot to take over the country.[97] That MEF's revenue rose from $2 million in 2002 to more than $5 million in 2016 evinces the receptivity of Americans to its Islamophobic mission.[98]

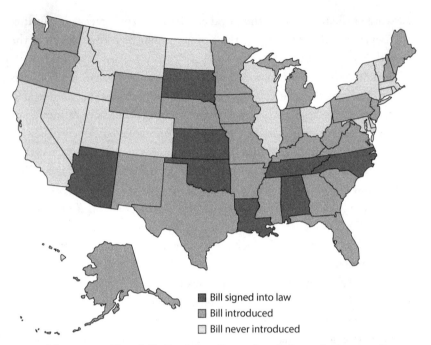

MAP 1. Mapping anti-Sharia bills. Fear Inc 2.0. Report (2014), Center for American Progress

Inside the DC Beltway, Gaffney and his Center for Security Policy are influential players in counterterrorism circles. Gaffney's work focuses on convincing the public and government officials that Sharia law is not a religious code but rather "a totalitarian ideology cloaked in religious garb."[99] Accordingly, the Center for Security Policy's 2010 report, *Shariah: The Threat to America*, called on states to pass anti-Sharia laws that would effectively prohibit Muslims from practicing their religion.[100] The report buttressed the national campaign led by David Yerushalmi, founder of the Society of Americans for National Existence (SANE), who drafted a template anti-Sharia bill introduced 216 times in at least forty-three states.[101] SANE warned Americans that a "creeping Sharia" would fully encroach into US courts such that Islamic law would eventually supersede the Constitution.[102]

This Islamophobic message resonated with numerous religious conservative groups.[103] Acting on their suspicion of Muslims, the American Public Policy Alliance and the American Center for Law and Justice provided legal counsel and lobbying to convince state politicians to pass the bills.[104] Concerned Women of America and the Florida Family Association mobilized their local communities to support the anti-Sharia bills in their state legislatures. These anti-Muslim efforts contributed to poll findings in 2012 that 30 percent of Americans believed Muslims sought to establish Sharia as the law of the land in the United States, a nearly 10 percent increase from 2011.[105] The anti-Sharia bills became law in at least seven states.[106]

To reassure Orthodox Jews and Catholics who view halacha and canon law, respectively, as protected by law, Gaffney argues that Sharia is comparable to Communism, Fascism, and Nazism—hence, it is not a protected religion. The Center for Security Policy stated in a 2015 report, "Over eighty percent of U.S. mosques have been shown to be shariah-adherent.... They are incubators of, at best, subversion and, at worst, violence and should be treated accordingly."[107] Gaffney thus propagates a racist narrative: Muslims are seditionists who seek to assault the US Constitution and American democracy, not religious minorities subject to religious freedom protections.[108] As I discuss in chapter 3, anti-Semitic and anti-Catholic American nativists propagated these same narratives a century earlier as justifications for deporting and banning Jewish and Catholic immigrants. History is repeating itself.

. . .

In the view of most Americans, the statement that their country oppresses religious minorities is not accurate. To the contrary, they pride themselves on the fact that religious freedom is privileged in law and society. However, what most Americans have not been taught in school or fail to recognize in the sustained Islamophobic coverage of the War on Terror is that the full panoply of religious freedom rights continues to be racially constrained. Thus, Muslims have been racialized by having their religion reframed as a violent political ideology. Just as enslaved Africans' religions (including Islam) were not considered legitimate on account of their imputed status as savages and inferiors, Muslims' religion is not really religion according to the post-9/11 Islamophobic narrative. Indeed, right-wing Evangelical leaders and right-wing politicians warned their tens of millions of followers that Muslims were a suspect race planning to invade the country by stealthily Islamicizing it.

Despite how ludicrous such claims may appear to be, they resonated with most Americans exposed to a daily diet of media coverage associating Muslims with terrorism, violence, and war. The more religious the Muslim, the more dangerous. And if the religious Muslim was also a political dissident opposed to the US war in Iraq or unconditional support of Israel, then he was the most lethal Religious Dissident Racial Muslim who deserved to be surveilled, deported, and prosecuted.

In 2008, by the end of the Bush administration, the Islamophobia industry had successfully infiltrated Republican politicians' approach to national security such that nearly half of Americans suspected Muslims as disloyal and prone to terrorism.[109] In turn, conservative politicians were granted license to officiate Islamophobia through rhetoric and public policies—the topic of the next chapter.

EIGHT

Officiating Islamophobia

Islam is a religion in which God requires you to send your son to die for him. Christianity is a faith in which God sends his son to die for you.

ATTORNEY GENERAL JOHN ASHCROFT *(2002)*

ISLAMOPHOBIA INFECTS AMERICAN POLITICS as elected officials propagate racist depictions of Muslims as presumptive security threats. No Muslim is immune from the effects of such racialization. Indeed, when in 2007 Keith Ellison, an African American Muslim, asked to use the Quran when he was sworn in as representative of the Fifth Congressional District of Minnesota, conservative politicians were outraged.

Congressman Virgil Goode of Virginia condemned the act as "a threat to the values and beliefs traditional to the United States" in an op-ed aptly titled, "Save Judeo-Christian Values."[1] In a letter to his constituents, Goode expressed his fears "that in the next century we will have many more Muslims in the United States if we do not adopt the strict immigration policies that I believe are necessary to preserve the values and beliefs traditional to the United States of America."[2] Dennis Prager, Bush's appointee to the Holocaust Museum Board and a conservative columnist, also disapproved of Ellison's actions because of his belief that the Bible is the repository of the nation's values.[3]

The message was clear: America is a White Judeo-Christian nation. The same nativist messages hurled at Al Smith in the early twentieth century— when he, a Catholic, ran for governor of New York and then president of the United States—are now directed at Muslim politicians. Just as Smith's Catholic faith put his national loyalty in question,[4] Keith Ellison, Ilhan Omar, and Rashida Tlaib—three Muslim representatives in Congress at the time of this writing—are frequently targeted by the contemporary version of the Know Nothings, the Islamophobes.[5]

155

CONGRESSIONAL HEARINGS ON
"HOMEGROWN TERRORISM"

Public scrutiny of Muslims in the United States became so intense that two congressional subcommittees held hearings in 2006 about the risk of the radicalization of Muslim Americans.[6] The Senate Committee on Homeland Security and Government Affairs, under the leadership of Joseph Lieberman and Susan Collins, invited anti-Muslim pundits to testify. Not by accident, no mainstream American Muslim organizations were invited to testify. Instead, leaders in the Islamophobia industry—Robert Emerson, Frank Gaffney, Robert Spencer, and Walid Pharis—warned the committee that American Muslims posed a serious threat of homegrown terrorism. Spencer, a conservative Catholic deacon, directs the blog *JihadWatch* and is the author of *The Politically Incorrect Guide to Islam (and the Crusades)* (2005) and *Religion of Peace? Why Christianity Is and Islam Isn't* (2007). His anti-Muslim crusade ironically mirrors the history of anti-Catholic prejudice in the United States. That these Islamophobes were invited to testify before Congress, despite their lack of objective evidence to prove their claims of radicalization among American Muslims, demonstrates the extent to which the racialization of Islam has become normalized in the halls of power.

In addition, law enforcement agencies have invited anti-Muslim organizations to train counterterrorism agents. Propaganda films like *The Third Jihad*, misrepresented as educational materials, have been shown to thousands of local and state officers.[7] One FBI training program described devout Muslims as those most likely to become terrorists.[8] Such federally funded training infects police departments across the country, contributing to the mass surveillance of Muslim communities and racialized counterterrorism enforcement.[9] Agents are taught that suspecting Muslims, particularly those who are devout and dissident, is not religious persecution; it is smart counterterrorism necessary to protect the nation.

That was the justification espoused by Congressman Peter King when he held two high-profile hearings in 2011, "The Extent of Radicalization in the American Muslim Community and that Community's Response" and "Homegrown Threat of Violent Islamic Extremist Terrorism."[10] As early as 2004, King proclaimed that most Muslim leaders are "enemies living amongst us." He alleged that 80 percent to 85 percent of mosques in the United States are run by Islamic fundamentalists, a thinly veiled accusation of terrorism.[11] The implication is obvious: mosques are not houses of worship under the purview of religious freedom protections. Rather, they are nefarious places that breed terrorists. Hence Religious Racial Muslims are legitimate targets of law enforcement scrutiny.

PEDDLING ISLAMOPHOBIA FOR VOTES

Anti-Muslim racial tropes were reinforced in the run-up to the 2008 presidential elections, when terrorism dominated media coverage and political discourse. Republican candidates promised to stop "radical Islamic extremism" and "violent radical jihadists."[12] Rudy Giuliani included angry-looking Muslim men and women in his campaign materials, promising to keep America safe from terrorism. Giuliani's adviser, former congressman King—the same person who held special congressional hearings on radical Islamic terrorism in 2011—told the media that there are too many mosques in the United States. John Deady, the co-chair of Giuliani's New Hampshire Veterans for Rudy group, stated what most Americans understood when they heard politicians use terms like *radical Muslim, jihadist,* or *Islamic extremism*: "I don't subscribe to the principle that there are good Muslims and bad Muslims. They're all Muslims [and we must] get rid of them."[13]

The Oklahoma lawmaker John Bennet went as far as declaring, "Islam is not even a religion; it is a political system that uses a deity to advance its agenda of global conquest."[14] He also required his Muslim constituents to answer a questionnaire asking if they beat their wives before he would meet with them.[15] Not coincidentally, Oklahoma had a public referendum in 2010 to amend the state constitution to prohibit any reference to Sharia in Oklahoma courts.[16] The "Save Our State Amendment" received the support of 70 percent of Oklahoma voters on election day after ACT for America, the Center for Security Policy, and the American Public Policy Alliance poured at least $60,000 into automated phone calls warning of the imminent threat of Sharia.[17]

Republican congressional candidates disseminated the conspiracy theory of an invasion by American Muslims. Congresspersons Michele Bachmann, Trent Franks, Tom Rooney, Louie Gohmert, and Lynn Westmoreland issued letters in 2012 to the inspectors general of the Departments of State, Defense, and Homeland Security, demanding that they investigate whether members of the Muslim Brotherhood worked in these agencies.[18] The letters, combined with the special congressional hearings on radical Islamic extremism between 2004 and 2011, were the contemporary version of McCarthy's Communist witch-hunt that targeted American Jews, among other leftists, in the mid-twentieth century.[19] This time, however, the enemy was an entire religion and its approximately six million followers in the United States.

Overt Islamophobia was more pervasive among Republican state politicians, particularly during the 2016 presidential elections.[20] In 2015, former Nebraska state senator Bill Kintner wanted to require Muslims to eat pork before they could enter the United States. In Rhode Island, Senator Elaine Morgan advocated placing Syrian refugees in a camp because Muslims seek "to murder, rape and decapitate anyone who is a non-Muslim." In 2016, Tennessee state representative Susan Lynn distributed one of the Islamophobia industry's propaganda films, *America's Mosques Exposed! Video Evidence They Are War Factories*, to her colleagues in the General Assembly. Four of Alabama's top elected officials, including the governor, a congressman, and a police chief, publicly denigrated Islam or Muslims.[21] And New Hampshire state lawmaker Kenneth Weyler argued that giving public benefits to "any person that practices Islam is aiding and abetting the enemy."

State and local politicians also attacked Muslims and Islam in their social media posts.[22] In 2016, Arkansas state senator Jason Rapert posted on Facebook, "Muslims wait for every opportunity to convert Americans to Islam or kill the infidels—that is what their holy book the Koran instructs them to do."[23] Fredy Burgos of Virginia's Republican State Central Committee tweeted that Islam is "a death cult organized by Satan."

Tennessee state senator Bill Ketron demonstrated his Islamophobia by inviting high profile anti-Muslim figures—such as the Dutch politician Geert Wilders, who stated that Islam is not a religion but rather "the ideology of a retarded culture"—to attend the 2016 Republican National Convention.[24] Wilders has compared the Quran to *Mein Kampf* and called for a ban on Muslim immigration to Europe, a common tactic used to strip Muslims of their status as a legally protected religious minority.[25]

Each time candidates and elected officials peddle such propaganda, anti-Muslim racism is legitimized among their constituents. Thus it should come as no surprise that in 2015, a Pew Research Center survey found that 46 percent of Americans believe Islam is more likely than other religions to encourage violence, and 49 percent report they are "very concerned" about the rise of Islamic extremism in the United States.[26]

Partisan political affiliation and religiosity determined the degree of suspicion of Muslims. Sixty percent of Republicans believed that "some" Muslims hold anti-American views, whereas 50 percent of Democrats believed "just a few" Muslims harbor anti-American sentiment. Likewise, only 37 percent of Republicans, compared to 57 percent of Democrats, report they would favor construction of a mosque in their neighborhood.[27] Despite their grievances against so-called secularists assaulting their religious freedom, White Evangelical Protestants were the least likely of all surveyed religious groups (26 percent) to say that few or none of the Muslims in the United States are anti-American.[28]

Anti-Muslim conspiracy theories permeated many congressional and state races in the 2017 and 2018 elections. A report by Muslim Advocates found at least eighty cases of anti-Muslim statements by candidates, with 64 percent of these candidates having previously held electoral or appointed office or receiving a presidential enforcement.[29] Thirty-three states ran campaigns using defamatory language against Muslims during the 2018 election season.

In a 2016 Pew Research study, when asked whether individuals or religions are to blame for violence committed in the name of religion, 22 percent of Americans reported that they believed that some religions promote violence. Islam was the most commonly referenced religion—by 14 percent of Americans—as having teachings that promote violence. Among Republicans, 39 percent believed that some religions encourage violence, and one-third identified Islam in particular as one of them.[30] These results evince the adverse impact of the Islamophobic discourse that permeates Republican and Evangelical Christian circles.

To a critical mass of Republican politicians, being Muslim is not a religious identity warranting religious freedom protections. Instead, there are only Racial Muslims who, like Blacks, Latinos, Native Americans, and other racial minorities, threaten White Judeo-Christian dominance. Meanwhile, self-described moderate Republicans accept Muslims on condition that they are secular and non-dissident.

CONVERGENCE OF ISLAMOPHOBIA
AND ANTI-BLACK RACISM

Racialization of Muslims has not occurred in a vacuum; rather, it has evolved in relation to other minorities. Hence when Barack Obama became a serious contender in the 2008 US presidential elections—the second African American man to do so after the Rev. Jesse Jackson—Islamophobia merged with anti-Black racism. White nationalists, both among the elite and among the grassroots, were distressed at the possibility of an African American becoming president of the United States. Because explicit anti-Black racism could ruin their careers, opponents had to find another way to attack presidential candidate Barack Obama. They exploited Americans' worst fears: a Muslim in the White House.

The strategy was launched in 2007, when Fox News aired a story claiming that Obama went to a "radical Muslim madrassa" when he was young.[31] The media emphasized his middle name, Hussein, and his Kenyan father's Muslim identity.[32] Sarah Palin, then Republican vice presidential candidate, accused Obama of "palling around with terrorists."[33] The concerted messaging was sufficiently successful that without any objective proof, 13 percent of Americans in 2008 believed Obama was secretly a Muslim. These numbers were even higher among Republicans, between 31 to 46 percent.[34]

Weeks before the 2008 presidential elections, a well-organized campaign by the Clarion Fund distributed 28 million copies of the propaganda film, *Obsession: Radical Islam's War Against the West*, to voters in swing states. *Obsession* was chock-full of images of Arabs and Muslims engaged in violence. And again, Islam was compared to Nazism.[35] The cover of the DVD declared, "The threat of radical Islam is the most important issue facing us today."[36] It was no coincidence that the timing of the campaign followed months of allegations that Obama is a Muslim. Although the Clarion Fund and its Islamophobic supporters ultimately failed to prevent Obama's election, labeling him a Muslim as a proxy for anti-Black racism demonstrated the extent to which Muslim identity was treated as a race.

The Islamophobia industry also misrepresented Obama's rhetoric and policies to bolster their claims of his secret Muslim identity. On June 4, 2009, Obama gave his first international speech in Cairo, Egypt, in which he stated, "I have come here to seek a new beginning between the United States and Muslims around the world, one based upon mutual interest and mutual respect, and one based upon the truth that America and Islam are not exclusive and need not be in competition."[37] Frank Gaffney, who would later serve as a campaign adviser to Donald J. Trump, condemned Obama as an apologist for Islamic extremism and an enabler of the establishment of Sharia in the United States. Gaffney stated, "For a man who now pridefully boasts of his intimate familiarity with Muslims and their faith, it raises troubling questions about his own religious beliefs."[38] By 2010, the number of Americans who believed Obama was a Muslim had increased to 50 percent.

And if that accusation did not stick, Republican leaders alleged that Obama was conducting a "war on religion" because of the Affordable Care Act's requirement that contraception and abortion services be made available to women.[39] The 2012 Republican presidential candidate Mitt Romney, who is Mormon, stated, "I think there is a desire to establish a religion in America known as secularism."[40] And Rick Santorum, who is Catholic, also emphasized religious freedom in his presidential campaign. He told a reporter, "To say that people of faith have no role in the public square? You bet that makes you throw up. What kind of country do we live in that says only people of non-faith can come into the public square and make their case?"[41] Such concerns with religious freedoms, however, did not extend to Muslims.

Despite his rhetorical commitment to religious pluralism, Obama went out of his way to prove he was not a Muslim. When two Muslim women wearing headscarves stood behind Obama during a televised speech, his aides asked them to move out of the camera's view to avoid the impression that Obama was associated with Muslims. Obama also declined many invitations to visit mosques, notwithstanding his visits to numerous churches and synagogues.[42] His first visit to a US mosque was not until his eighth and final year in office in February 2016.[43] In the end, the Obama administration did not go beyond lofty rhetoric to challenge the association of Muslims (and Arabs) with terrorism.[44] As a result, most Americans continued to hold unfavorable views of Muslims during his tenure.

Prior to Obama's candidacy for president, nearly half of Americans in 2005 reported the threat of radical Islamic terrorism as serious as the threat of Communism in the twentieth century.[45] In 2006, a USA Today / Gallup poll reported that 39 percent of Americans "felt at least some prejudice against Muslims" and 39 percent supported requiring Muslims, including US citizens, to carry special identification—a requirement imposed on Jews in Germany in the years preceding the Holocaust.[46] The same poll found that 51 percent of Americans believed Muslims are not loyal to the United States, and a quarter of Americans did not want a Muslim as a neighbor.[47]

By 2010, nearly half of Americans still believed Islam and American values were incompatible, according to a Public Religion Research Institute poll.[48] Suspicions of Muslims were grounded in beliefs that they were sympathetic to Al-Qaeda and other terrorist groups.

Moreover, 42 percent of Americans believed that an American Muslim's religion would influence their decision making in government jobs—the same suspicions leveled at Al Smith, John F. Kennedy, and other Catholics seeking elected office in the twentieth century. Twenty-eight percent of voters polled by *Time* magazine in 2010 (at the same time that 18 percent of Americans believed Obama was a Muslim) reported that Muslims should not be eligible to serve on the US Supreme Court, and nearly one-third believed Muslims should be barred from running for president.[49]

Negative public opinion of Muslims emboldened organizers of a national Islamophobia campaign in 2010 to stop the opening of the Cordoba Initiative interfaith community center in New York City that included a Muslim prayer space. The founders described the center as "a platform for multi-faith dialogue. It will strive to promote inter-community peace, tolerance and understanding locally in New York City, nationally in America, and globally."[50]

Among the hundreds of residents mobilized by the Islamophobia industry to oppose the so-called Ground Zero Mosque, one participant's statements during a public hearing are telling: "It shows such lack of respect to place a mosque so close to what we consider as a sacred space.... I'm ashamed that you could even be considering such a project after all that we have endured, and not just us New Yorkers but the entire country. We have suffered terribly. How can you authorize this when it is so painful for us?"[51] In other words, Muslims had no right to pray, much less to be near, the site where their supposedly violent ideology attacked the nation. Nor could Islam be a sacred religion as equally committed to peace as Christianity and Judaism.

Negative public opinion correlated with a lack of personal experiences and knowledge of Islam. Surveys show that respondents who know Muslims are less likely to hold unfavorable views than persons who have little knowledge of Islam or no interaction with Muslims.[52] Thus, the more a person interacts with Muslim neighbors, coworkers, classmates, roommates, and friends, the more favorable their views of Islam.[53] A 2015 Brookings Institution poll, for example, showed that Democrat respondents who did not know any Muslims reported 48 percent unfavorability, compared to 18 percent of Democrat respondents who knew some Muslims very well. Republican respondents who did not know any Muslims reported 78 percent unfavorability of Muslims, compared to 42 percent of Republicans who knew some Muslims very well.[54]

While the precise number of Muslims in America is unknown because the US Census does not collect data on religious affiliation, polls estimate a population of between four million and six million, no more than 3 percent of the population.[55] Muslim communities' attempts to civically engage locally

FIGURE 11. Protester holds a sign that states "A mosque at Ground Zero spits on the graves of 9/11 victims." Seth Wenig/AP Photo.

cannot undo the damage caused by the flood of political and media attacks on Islam. In 2017, after nearly two decades of interfaith dialogue and public engagement by Muslims, only 65 percent of Americans reported personally knowing a Muslim.[56] Though still too low to make a significant impact on national public opinion polls, interactions with Muslims have increased since 2011, when only 24 percent of Americans reported having occasionally talked with a Muslim in the past year.[57]

While polls illustrate the connection between Islamophobia and religious conservative political circles, they obscure the Islamophobia found in secular liberal circles. More tolerant of Muslims' political dissidence, American secular liberals frown on the religiosity of some Muslims. Liberals incorrectly assume that Religious Racial Muslims are misogynistic, homophobic, and autocratic. Their promotion of books such as *I am Malala: The Girl Who Stood Up for Education and Was Shot by the Taliban*[58] and *Reading Lolita in Tehran*[59] reflects American liberals' belief that the Muslim-majority world is backward and terrorism is primarily a Muslim problem. Devoid of context, liberals' analysis does not distinguish between the Taliban, Al-Qaeda, Al Shabaab, Saddam Hussein, and the two dozen Muslim-majority countries with diverse social, political, and economic circumstances. This phenomenon has prompted scholarship critiquing "liberal Islamophobia."[60] While liberals reject the "clash of civilizations" narrative, they support drone-killing programs, counter–violent extremism programs, and other practices within the War on Terror that collectively vilify and stigmatize Muslims.[61]

For more than fifteen years, Islamophobia and anti-Black racism nurtured the growing influence of White Christian nationalists within the Republican Party that would culminate in the election of Trump as president of the United States.[62]

ISLAMOPHOBIA UNDER TRUMP

Instead of abating with time, anti-Muslim racism has intensified. Indeed, Muslims serve as convenient scapegoats for Republican politicians eager to mobilize their right-wing base. Thus, it was no coincidence that Trump campaigned in 2015 and 2016 on an anti-Muslim and anti-immigrant platform. His advisers were unabashedly Islamophobic and White nationalist.

Steve Bannon, who advised Trump in the White House during the first six months of his presidency, repeatedly accused Muslims in America of secretly plotting to infiltrate the US government. Bannon believes the centuries-old crusades between the Christian West and Islam is ongoing.[63] He articulated these views in his 2017 proposal for the film, *Destroying the Great Satan: The Rise of Islamic Fascism in America*. Although the film was never produced, it demonstrates Bannon's long-standing belief that American Muslim civil society is plotting to turn America into an Islamic state.[64]

Lieutenant General Michael Flynn, another Trump campaign adviser, warned the public that Islam is a totalitarian ideology. A believer in the clash of civilizations theory, Flynn stated in a 2016 interview, "I don't believe all cultures are morally equivalent, and I think the West, and especially America, is far more civilized, far more ethical and moral, than the system our main enemies want to impose on us."[65] Flynn worked closely with leaders of the Islamophobia industry to frame Islam as a violent political ideology to their sizable constituency. For example, he spoke at an ACT for America event in San Antonio in the summer of 2016 at which he declared, "I don't see Islam as a religion. I see it as a political ideology.... [I]t will mask itself as a religion globally because, especially in the west, especially in the United States, because it can hide behind and protect itself behind what we call freedom of religion."[66]

Flynn reiterated his views in his 2016 book, *The Field of Fight: How to Win the Global War against Radical Islam and Its Allies*: "We're in a world war against a messianic mass movement of evil people, most of them inspired by a totalitarian ideology: Radical Islam."[67] Flynn's convictions ultimately earned him a place as a White House adviser in the Trump administration. Trump also appointed Mike Pompeo, first as CIA director and then as secretary of state, who stated in 2016 that a "practicing Muslim, who believes in the teachings of the Quran, cannot be a loyal citizen to the United States"— the implication being that only Secular Racial Muslims could be tolerated.[68]

Another staunch Islamophobe, Frank Gaffney, joined Trump's inner circle of campaign advisers. His influence can be found in Trump's presidential campaign speeches calling on the US government to "screen out any [immigrants] who have hostile attitudes towards our country or its principles—or who believe that Sharia law should supplant American law."[69] Trump went on to promise that "the support networks for Radical Islam in this country will be stripped out and removed one by one." "Radical Islam" is code for Religious Racial Muslims and Religious Dissident Racial Muslims, which I discuss further in chapter 9.[70]

Gaffney's influence extended into Trump's National Security Council when Fred Fleitz, a senior vice president at the Center for Security Policy, was tapped as a top adviser to John Bolton. Bolton served as Trump's national security adviser and US ambassador to the United Nations.[71] Under Fleitz's leadership, the Center for Security Policy brazenly argued for the denial of First Amendment rights to practicing American Muslims. Fleitz coauthored the 2015 report, "The Secure Freedom Strategy: A Plan for Victory over the Global Jihad Movement," which called for the revocation of citizenship of religious Muslims.[72] Notably, the Center for Security Policy was a vocal proponent of the myth that Islam is "as totalitarian a political program as ever were those of communism, fascism, National Socialism, or Japanese imperialism."[73] Again, the implication is that Muslims are not a religious minority deserving of religious freedom protections.

Himself a leading member of the Islamophobia industry, Bolton bolstered the echo chamber of anti-Muslim conspiracy theories through the Gatestone Institute.[74] Gatestone, an offshoot of the conservative Hudson Institute, was founded by the wealthy philanthropist Nina Rosenwald, heiress to the Sears Robuck empire who funds various anti-Muslim organizations.[75] Rosenwald served as a member of the national board of the American Israel Public Affairs Committee (AIPAC), further evincing the ties between right-wing

Zionists and the Islamophobia industry.[76] Gatestone published false stories of Muslim men gang raping European women and Muslims transforming the United Kingdom into an "Islamist Colony" and accused the Obama administration of having Muslim bias against Christians.[77]

Trump and his Islamophobic advisers fanned the flames of fear and hate of Muslims. At every opportunity during the 2016 presidential campaign, Trump validated Americans' suspicions of Muslims as disloyal, anti-American, and violent. His strategy was wildly successful, as more than 40 percent of his supporters believed that the word *violent* describes Muslims "extremely well," as compared to 10 percent of Democrats and 30 percent of Republicans.[78]

Likewise, a Brookings poll found that 61 percent of Americans had a generally unfavorable opinion of Islam in November 2015, as compared to 39 percent in October 2001 and 61 percent in August 2011.[79] That same poll found that 56 percent of Republicans believed "Islamic and Western religious and social traditions are incompatible with each other."[80] Another 2015 poll, by the American Values Survey, found that 70 percent of Republicans believed Islam is at odds with American values and the American way of life.[81]

By the end of 2016, 53 percent of Republicans believed almost all or about half of Muslims are anti-American.[82] Nearly half of all Americans believed that Islam is more likely than other religions to encourage violence.[83] These numbers emboldened conservative politicians and law enforcement to selectively target Muslims in national security practices, as shown in chapter 9. In the five years immediately following the September 11 attacks, "the threat of Islamic fundamentalism to the United States in the next ten years" was important or very important for 79 to 83 percent of Americans.[84]

Although perpetrators of anti-Muslim hate crimes and discrimination may support religious freedom, US government action and elected officials' rhetoric assures them that suspecting Muslims is not un-American because Muslims adhere to a political ideology, not a legitimate religion. Indeed, by 2018, approximately 50 percent of Americans believed that Islam is a false religion.[85]

The pollsters identified another trend—that Republicans and religious conservatives were more in favor of restricting American Muslims' civil liberties than were Democrats, Independents, or persons with moderate or low levels of religiosity.[86] As a result, when then-presidential candidate Trump declared his support for a "total and complete shutdown of Muslims entering the United States until our country's representatives can figure out what is going on," a whopping 81 percent of Republicans agreed with him.[87]

What came to be known as the "Muslim Ban," issued seven days after

FIGURE 12. Anti-Sharia protest in San Bernadino, California, in June 2017. Watchara Phomicinda, The Free-Press/SCNG.

Trump's inauguration, excluded all immigrants, nonimmigrants, and refugees from seven Muslim-majority countries, leaving thousands of people stranded at airports and disrupting hundreds of thousands of Muslims' lives.[88] Only contentious litigation forced Trump to narrow those prohibited from entering the country to certain categories of nonimmigrants from six Muslim-majority countries, which the US Supreme Court ultimately upheld as constitutional.[89] On the third anniversary of the Muslim Ban, Trump added more Muslim-majority countries, with minimal opposition from the American public.[90]

Although Trump's blatant Islamophobia drew condemnation from many Americans, including some Republicans, nearly half of people who identified as "strong Republicans" believed that being Christian was an essential trait of being American. For them, racializing Muslims is consistent with American patriotism.[91]

. . .

Each religious group is racialized in unique ways specific to international and domestic developments at a particular historical moment. Where the group fits into the Black-White racial paradigm, the group's immigration history, and the historical relationship between their religion and Protestantism all contribute to the racialization process. Moreover, members of the group experience racialization differently based on their willingness and ability to comport with Anglo-Protestant norms and support American mainstream politics. As a result, the material consequences of the racialization of immigrant Muslims differ based on an individual's religiosity, political dissident views, and secularization.

This prompts the question that runs throughout this book, Why is a religious group adversely racialized in the first place, as opposed to safeguarded by religious freedom norms? This chapter explains how the ideological expulsion of Islam from religion is integral to the social construction of the Racial Muslim. The media, politicians, and a well-funded Islamophobia industry position Islam as a national security threat within a global clash of civilizations.

As a consequence, Muslims are to be suspected, not protected. Mosques are treacherous places rather than sanctified houses of worship. Islamic practices such as prayer, hijab, fasting, the pilgrimage to Mecca, and zakat (charitable giving) are indicia of disloyalty, not piety. Once Islamic religious practices are viewed through the lens of security, religious freedom is no longer relevant to how the government and public treats Muslims. Securitization of the Racial Muslim becomes the lived reality of millions of people in the United States, which I turn to in the next chapter.

NINE

Criminalizing Muslim Identity

RACIALIZATION CRIMINALIZES MUSLIM IDENTITY. Presumptions that Muslims are more prone to terrorism inform US national security policies and practices. The consequent harms to Muslim communities range from direct employment discrimination, violent hate crimes, and denial of new mosque constructions to indirect chilling effects wherein surveillance and antiterrorism prosecutions cause Muslims to hide their religious identity or circumscribe how they practice their faith in public. Hence being Muslim in the post-9/11 era imposes forms of subordination not currently experienced by other religious minorities.

Some of the stereotypes of Jews, Catholics, and Mormons in the early twentieth century apply today to the Racial Muslim: disloyal, antidemocratic, and unfit for self-governance. The material consequences, however, differ, depending on the historical context and predominance of certain stereotypes associated with a particular faith community.

In the case of Racial Muslims, the US government interacts with Muslim communities exclusively through a security lens. A case in point is government-sponsored community outreach programs. Although described as initiatives to educate Muslims about the law and their rights, in practice the various agencies conducting such meetings across the country are tasked with countering radicalization, to which the Racial Muslim is presumed to be inherently susceptible.[1] Tellingly, no such community outreach is conducted in conservative Christian or right-wing White communities as a means of countering the rise of right-wing extremism by White males, notwithstanding the documented rise in White right-wing extremism and the unprecedented siege of the US Capitol on January 6, 2021.[2] Moreover, national security and immigration laws that are neutral on their face are selectively enforced against Muslims, particularly the Religious Dissident Racial Muslim and the Religious Racial Muslim.

As a result, Muslims are the primary targets of counterterrorism surveillance, investigations, and prosecutions.[3] They are singled out for heightened screening at airports and inclusion on terrorist watch lists. They are overpoliced through mass surveillance, material support to terrorism prosecutions, and countering violent extremism programs. And Muslims are tracked down in immigration enforcement aimed to root out potential terrorists.

The USA PATRIOT Act, the National Security Entry-Exit Registration System (NSEERS), and the Absconder Program are among the myriad national security laws and immigration initiatives granting the US government expansive authority in the securitization of Muslims.[4] Abroad, the US government kidnaps and tortures Muslims in secret rendition programs. It assassinates Muslims with drones and indefinitely detains Muslims at the Guantanamo Bay detention camp in Cuba. These authoritarian practices occur without concern for religious liberty, because the targets are perceived as a dangerous race.[5] Despite qualifiers that such practices are reserved only for "radical Muslims," all Muslims are potential targets of the post-9/11 counterterrorism regime.

Some degree of public approval is required for the government to engage in these racial projects against a religious minority. Otherwise, the government would be accused of eroding American religious freedom rights. Due in large part to a well-financed Islamophobia industry and negative media portrayals of Muslims, as described in chapters 7 and 8, public opinion of Muslims has remained low for nearly two decades. This trend will continue so long as a critical mass of Americans views Islam as a violent political ideology and Muslims as a collective security threat. With each passing year since 2001, polls have shown public opinion turning against Muslims. In stark contrast, pre-9/11 polls found that 64 percent of Americans were unable or unwilling to describe their view of Islam as favorable or unfavorable because they knew too little about the religion.[6] While consumers of the Islamophobia industry's propaganda were initially limited to right-wing White Christian nationalist and right-wing Zionist circles, as the demand for information about Islam and Muslims grew after 9/11, anti-Muslim narratives went mainstream.

Influenced by the constant flow of anti-Muslim discourse, some Americans believe they are patriotic when they vandalize mosques, shoot Muslims, harass Muslim coworkers, and demand that Muslims "go home" (to a foreign country). A little over half of Americans also support the govern-

FIGURE 13. Anti-Muslim graffiti defaces a shi'ite mosque at the Islamic Center of America January 23, 2007, in Dearborn, Michigan. Bill Pugliano.

ment's increasing surveillance of mosques and other places where Muslims gather. Likewise, they see profiling of Muslims in airports and counterterrorism sting operations as smart national security.[7]

THE RACIAL MUSLIM HIERARCHY

With capacity the primary restraint on government overreach, officials must prioritize which Muslims to target first. The criteria are religiosity and dissident politics. Thus, the Religious Dissident Racial Muslim represents everything the US government, whether controlled by Democrats or Republicans, deems inassimilable and is antithetical to American liberalism. Indeed, FBI agents have admitted that the radicalization model they are trained to follow "suggest[s] that Muslims harshly criticizing US foreign policy or sympathizing with radicalism are 'terrorists in waiting' ... who will eventually progress to violence."[8] Next in line are Religious Racial Muslims, whose religiosity the state views as a vulnerability to foreign terrorist recruitment, followed by the Secular Dissident Racial Muslim, whose vocal critiques of US policy threaten to expose the racist underpinnings of US national security practices. The Secular Racial Muslim stands the best chance of being tolerated by liberals and Christian conservatives as the model minority. And the Former Racial Muslim is the darling of the conservative and liberal Islamophobes.

Immigrant Muslims whose Islamic faith animates their principled opposition to America's support of Muslim dictators, occupation of Muslim lands, and Israeli occupation of Palestinians are precisely those who the US government wants to expel and ban from the country. Should they rise to power, as is the case with Representatives Rashida Tlaib and Ilhan Omar, they can more meaningfully challenge these long-standing American policies. For example, Omar and Tlaib refused to sign a US House resolution reaffirming support for a two-state solution because it failed to condemn annexation of Palestinian land in the West Bank, Israeli settlement expansion on Palestinian land, demolition of Palestinian housing in East Jerusalem, and deportation of human rights activists.[9] They also joined a group of progressive Democrats in May 2021 introducing a congressional resolution to halt weapons sales to Israel because of its human rights abuses of Palestinians—an unprecedented political move that feeds Islamophobic tropes that Muslims (and Arabs) are anti-Semitic when they challenge Israeli state practices.[10]

The government's second priority is Religious Racial Muslims who are either apolitical or hold mainstream political views. Even if one refrains from expressing dissident views, religiosity alone is sufficient to attract government scrutiny in the form of FBI investigations, requests for voluntary interviews, and antiterrorism prosecutions. Although the Religious Racial Muslim does not engage in politics opposing American foreign policy or challenge American liberalism, their lifestyle as practicing Muslims poses a threat to the assimilationist, Anglo-Protestant underpinnings of Islamophobia. For example, any Muslim associated with or sympathetic to Salafism, Wahabism, or the Muslim Brotherhood, even if they are not politically engaged in the United States, is labeled a radical Muslim. As a result, the US government scrutinizes their lives, social media accounts, and personal associations for evidence of illegal activity. Indeed, the Trump administration went so far as to call for the criminalization of the Muslim Brotherhood, which is the pretext needed for shutting down Muslim organizations led by Religious Dissident and Religious Racial Muslims.[11]

Less dangerous but still suspicious is the Secular Dissident Racial Muslim who does not practice Islam but fully exercises their constitutional rights to oppose American domestic and foreign policy. They defend the rights of Black and Brown bodies trapped in a cycle of poverty and mass incarceration

and decry unconditional US support for Israel, despite its systematic violations of Palestinian human rights. Secular Dissident Racial Muslims, consequently, experience surveillance and targeting because the combination of
dissent and immigrant status deems them inassimilable dangerous foreigners
undeserving of American citizenship.

The case of the Palestinian American community activist Rasmea Odeh
highlights the punitive consequences of being a Secular Dissident Racial
Muslim. For years, Odeh protested America's refusal to hold Israel account-
able for violating Palestinian human rights. She served as the associate director of the Arab American Action Network (AAAN) in Chicago, where she
established women's empowerment programs.[12] When AAAN employees
were targeted in FBI antiterrorism home raids in September 2010, the FBI
discovered Odeh's naturalized citizenship.[13]

Twenty years after she immigrated to the United States and ten years after
naturalizing as a US citizen, Odeh was prosecuted for failing to disclose a
1969 conviction in an Israeli military court on her immigration application—notwithstanding Odeh's claims that her confession was coerced under
torture with electroshock and instrument rape. Her torturers were Israeli
soldiers and Shin Bet secret police.[14] Odeh recanted her false confession during her military trial in Israel, to no avail.[15] Odeh's Muslim (and Palestinian)
identity combined with her political dissidence caused the US government
to transform an ordinary immigration violation into a high-profile terrorism
case. The US government successfully deported Odeh in 2017.[16] These are the
high stakes facing Racial Muslims who dare to dissent.

Those most likely to escape the harms of racialization are Muslims willing to pay what Lani Guinier and Gerald Torres call the racial bribe.[17] They
adopt lifestyles, associations, and anglicized names that signal they are secular and nondissident. Consistent with two centuries of coercive assimilationist ideology, the Secular Racial Muslim is palatable in the workplace, the
media, and the political system.

Liberal American elites point to the Secular Racial Muslim as proof that
they are not Islamophobes, even if they support national security and immigration policies disproportionately harming Muslims. Meanwhile, conservative American elites and Islamophobes prop up the Secular Racial Muslim
to show that they do not categorically reject all Muslims. Rather, only the
Religious and Religious Dissident Racial Muslims should be excluded or
deported. Toleration of the Secular Racial Muslim as a model minority is
the counterpoint to allegations of racial double standards in religious free-

dom norms. However, both liberals and conservatives support anti-Muslim immigration and national security government practices.

DETAINING, DEPORTING, AND BANNING MUSLIMS

Immigration law has long been a tool for enforcing White Protestant dominance in the United States. Whether excluding Asians, Jews, and Catholics in centuries past or Muslims and Latinos today, immigration officials possess significant discretion to determine who can be admitted, detained, and deported. To be sure, the domestic and international factors leading to the racialization of various groups differ across time and place. But racialization as a tool of subordination remains a constant feature of immigration law.

Thus, it is no surprise that the Bush administration's first call to action after the September 11 attacks was to round up all nationals of Muslim-majority countries. Arabs, whether Muslim or Christian, and any foreign national whose phenotype resembled that of the nineteen hijackers from Saudi Arabia, the United Arab Emirates, and Egypt were swept up in immigration raids. Within two months of the 9/11 attacks, over twelve hundred US citizens and foreign nationals were arrested and detained in the FBI's PENTTBOM investigation into the 9/11 attacks.[18] The majority of detainees were eventually deported for routine immigration violations as part of a broader multidecade policy to expel Muslims from the United States.[19]

Within a year of the September 11 attacks, Congress passed the USA PATRIOT Act of 2001, the Enhanced Border Security and Visa Entry Reform Act of 2002, and the Homeland Security Act of 2002.[20] Together, these laws facilitated enforcement of President Bush's Homeland Security Presidential Directive, "Combating Terrorism through Immigration Policies," issued on October 29, 2001.[21] The directive aimed to "aggressively to prevent aliens who engage in or support terrorist activity from entering the United States and to detain, prosecute, or deport any such aliens who are within the United States."[22]

Earlier that week, on October 25, Attorney General Ashcroft gave a speech to the US Conference of Mayors, announcing a counterterrorism policy that would effectively securitize all Muslims in the United States.

> Let the terrorists among us be warned: If you overstay your visa—even by one
> day—we will arrest you. If you violate a local law, you will be put in jail and

kept in custody as long as possible. We will use every available statute. We will seek every prosecutorial advantage.

We will use all our weapons within the law and under the Constitution to protect life and enhance security for America. In the war on terror, this Department of Justice will arrest and detain any suspected terrorist who has violated the law. Our single objective is to prevent terrorist attacks by taking suspected terrorists off the street.[23]

Immigration officials and prosecutors interpreted Ashcroft's declaration as a license to criminalize Muslims, starting with Religious Dissident Racial Muslims and followed by Religious Racial Muslims.

Toward that end, the government implemented a mandatory registration program on August 12, 2002. NSEERS required all nonimmigrant men over the age of sixteen from twenty-four Muslim-majority countries to register with the immigration service.[24] The program initiated mass fingerprinting for "higher-risk visiting aliens" at ports of entry, using "intelligence criteria reflecting patterns of terrorist organizations' activities."[25] These purportedly high-risk individuals would be required to "periodically confirm where they are living and what they are doing in the United States."[26] More than 80,000 Muslims and Arabs were registered under NSEERS. Knowing where these nonimmigrants were located facilitated the government's deportation of more than 13,000 of them on non-terrorism-related immigration violations.[27]

Concurrently with NSEERS, the US Department of Justice launched Operation Absconder to identify and deport thousands of Middle Eastern men.[28] The FBI targeted 8,000 men for interrogation about their knowledge of terrorism.[29] More than 1,000 Muslim immigrant men were arbitrarily arrested and abused.[30] The mandate from the top was clear: keep out and remove as many Muslims from the United States as possible. The same racial reasoning underpinned exclusionary immigration practices targeting Chinese, Japanese, Turks, and non-Protestant religions in the nineteenth and twentieth centuries. Meanwhile, the myriad preventive antiterrorism programs yielded a staggeringly small number of actual terrorists. Of the tens of thousands of Muslims detained in the years immediately after 9/11, fewer than ten were charged with crimes related to terrorism and none were charged with involvement in the 9/11 terrorist attacks.[31]

In 2003, as the US government prepared to invade Iraq, it launched Operation Liberty Shield as a multiagency initiative aimed at preventing domestic terrorist attacks. Then–Secretary of Homeland Security Tom Ridge announced a heightened terror alert level in a color-coded national terrorist threat index. Tens of thousands of federal, state, and local agents were deployed in a coordinated response team with the mandate to search for disgruntled Muslims opposed to the US military occupation of Iraq. All asylum seekers from thirty countries, most of whom were majority Muslim, were automatically detained, contrary to the standard practice of case-by-case determinations.[32] Travelers from Muslim-majority countries were also subjected to additional screening.

In the months leading up to the 2004 presidential elections, Operation Front Line targeted more than two thousand undocumented immigrants, three quarters of whom were from Muslim-majority countries, on national security grounds.[33] Operation Front Line was a partnership between the ICE National Security Investigations Unit and the FBI to identify and prevent potential terrorist activities in connection with the 2004 presidential election and 2005 inauguration.[34] The selection criteria were not individualized but rather based on the association of Islam with terrorism.[35] If these individuals had in fact planned terrorist plots, the government would have criminally prosecuted them. Instead, they deported them.

With the ultimate objective being to expel as many Muslims as legally permissible, these racialized immigration enforcement initiatives had little to do with securing the nation. Naturalization of Muslim immigrants was also delayed under the guise of national security checks. Specifically, DHS implemented a new covert program, the Controlled Application Review and Resolution Program (CARRP), in 2008. CARRP identifies applicants who should be considered a "national security concern" based on broad criteria that disproportionally affect Muslim applicants, resulting in the significant delay or denial of naturalization applications.[36] Terrorist watch lists, which grew from a few hundred before 9/11 to hundreds of thousands today, determine which applicants automatically are subject to CARRP. Absent legal requirements that the FBI show evidence of a listed individual's threat of engaging in terrorism, the terrorist watch lists are overinclusive of those with Muslim names. Moreover, removing oneself from a watch list is a lengthy process that is often futile.[37]

Another basis for being subject to CARRP is donating to Islamic charities. This is viewed as further evidence of Muslims' presumed disloyalty. But American Muslims' donations to Islamic charities are meant to provide humanitarian aid to civilians devastated by US sanctions against Iraq, Iran, Somalia, and other Muslim-majority countries. In other words, apparently neutral national security laws, policies, and discourses have become pretexts to silence Religious Dissident Muslims. A few months after the September 11 attacks, the federal government raided the homes and offices of numerous Muslim leaders and organizations. The targets were, not coincidentally, both religious and critical of American foreign policy. For example, the Holy Land Foundation (HLF), the largest American Muslim charity at the time, had raised millions of dollars for humanitarian aid in Bosnia, Palestine, and Iraq. HLF and its leadership, who were primarily of Palestinian national origin and devout Muslims, publicly rebuked US sanctions on Iraq as collective punishment of Iraqi civilians. They vocally opposed the Oslo agreement as a losing proposition for meaningful Palestinian self-determination.[38]

Two other Islamic charities shut down were Benevolence International and the Global Relief Fund. Both charities received millions of dollars from American Muslims donating their religiously mandated annual charitable donations, known as zakat. The funds supported Muslim children orphaned by the Serbian and Croatian Christians' massacre of Bosnians,[39] medical clinics in Palestine, and refugee camps in Muslim-majority Kosovo.[40] The assets of the three largest Muslim American charities were frozen within months of the September 11 attacks, notwithstanding the absence of any formal criminal charges, much less convictions.[41] Their status as organizations led by religious and dissident Muslims was enough to incur the full wrath of the state.

According to the American Civil Liberties Union (ACLU) of California, which represented numerous clients experiencing protracted delays in naturalization processes, CARRP effectively "treats religious practices, national origin, and innocuous associations and activities as national security concerns."[42] The ACLU's clients were either practicing Muslims, frequent visitors of Muslim majority countries, or donors to Islamic charities. These types of behaviors position them as Religious Dissident Racial or Religious Racial Muslims, both prioritized in the government's securitization of Muslims.

A recent use of immigration authority to exclude Muslims is the infamous "Muslim Ban." On January 29, 2017, President Donald J. Trump signed an executive order indefinitely halting admission of Syrian refugees and barring entry of all nationals from seven Muslim-majority countries for ninety days.[43] Citizens of Syria, Yemen, Iran, Iraq, Libya, Somalia, and Sudan were denied entry even if they were students, workers, or permanent residents who had lawfully lived in the United States for years.

Although few confirmed terrorists are nationals of these seven countries, all of their citizens were penalized.[44] Indeed, an affidavit signed by ten former national security, foreign policy, and intelligence officers in Democratic and Republican administrations stated that as of January 19, 2017 (when Trump was inaugurated as President), "there is no national security purpose" for a total bar of entry for aliens from the designated countries, an unprecedented and sweeping exclusion of a broad class of people.[45]

In response to litigation challenging the legality of the Muslim Ban, Trump issued a revised executive order in March that reiterated the national security justifications, removed some countries, and narrowed its application to exclude only nonimmigrants applying for a visa.[46] However, courts rejected the revised version because Trump's anti-Muslim statements during his presidential campaign, coupled with his advisers' admissions, demonstrated that his intent was not to protect the nation from security threats but rather to exclude Muslims from the United States.[47]

Courts cited Trump's statements during his presidential campaign in 2015 and 2016 when he revealed his deep suspicion of Muslims.[48] For instance, he stated that it is "hard to separate...who is who" between Muslims and terrorists.[49] Trump insisted that "hundreds of thousands of refugees from the Middle East" would attempt to "take over" and radicalize "our children."[50] He warned that Syrian refugees would "be a better, bigger, more horrible version than the legendary Trojan Horse."[51] When he talked about Muslims, Trump reiterated, "We have to have a ban...it's gotta be a ban."[52] In March 2016, Trump responded to a journalist asking him if he believed that "Islam is at war with the U.S.," by saying, "I think Islam hates us.... [T]here is a tremendous hatred and we have to be very vigilant and we have to be very careful and we can't allow people coming into this country who have this hatred of the United States and of people who are not Muslim."[53]

While liberal elites took issue with Trump's bald assertions, Muslims in the United States knew he was simply describing what Muslims had been experiencing for nearly two decades. Under the Bush, Obama, and Trump administrations, the government aggressively targeted Religious and Dissident Muslims—albeit to different degrees—in what was effectively a domestic war on Muslims.

THE DOMESTIC WAR ON MUSLIMS

As Americans watched thousands of compatriots in the Twin Towers perish in real time, the government promised to hunt down and kill the perpetrators. That pledge would soon translate into a systematic government campaign to collectively punish Muslims in the United States for decades to come.

The security state unleashed its heavy hand on Muslim communities nationwide. Mass surveillance became the norm as the FBI's counterterrorism budget tripled from $3.81 billion in 2001 to over $10 billion in 2017.[54] More than a third went toward counterterrorism operations, including thousands of paid informants and undercover agents infiltrating Muslim communities looking for terrorist plots.[55] If none could be found, then informants manufactured them.[56] Law enforcement scrutinized mosques, Muslim-owned businesses, and Muslim student groups in search of terrorist plots.

In the most aggressive mass surveillance program since 9/11, the New York Police Department (NYPD) established a web of informants who compiled dossiers on thousands of Muslims, designated mosques as potential terrorist organizations, recorded religious sermons, and surveilled congregations without reasonable suspicion of illegal activity.[57] A new Demographics Unit tasked with mapping Muslims in the Tri-State Area entailed plainclothes officers eavesdropping on political conversations in cafés where Muslims congregate.[58]

Undercover agents were predisposed to presume guilt, in part because of the Islamophobic training in police departments. NYPD officers, for example, received training by government-paid instructors who promoted the clash of civilizations narrative. Trainers warned officers that "Islam is a highly violent radical religion that mandates that all of the earth must be Muslim."[59]

Over 1,400 NYPD officers in 2010 watched *The Third Jihad*, the film funded by the Clarion Project—the same organization that sent 28 million copies of the propaganda film *Obsession: Radical Islam's War against the West* to voters in swing states during the 2008 presidential elections. *The Third Jihad* warned that only a "few Muslim leaders...can be trusted" and that Muslims are engaging in jihad "covertly throughout the West today."[60] The film shows images of Muslim terrorists shooting Christians and exploding car bombs, executed children covered in sheets, and "a doctored photograph show[ing] an Islamic flag flying over the White House," all while "ominous music" plays in the background. This law enforcement training, coupled with media coverage portraying Muslims as terrorists, produced a police force convinced that it was protecting the nation—and not engaging in racism or quashing religious freedom—when it targeted Muslims.

Reminiscent of the COINTELPRO playbook that subverted African American civil rights groups in the 1960s, including Black Muslims, the NYPD sent paid infiltrators into mosques, student associations, and Muslim communities, where they took photos, recorded license plate numbers, and kept notes of political conversations. One of the informants, paid $1,500 a month, stated in a court affidavit, "My NYPD boss Steve told me that the NYPD did not think the John Jay Muslim Student Association [MSA] was doing anything wrong, they just wanted to make sure."[61] Moreover, the informant admitted, "the members of the MSA were religious Muslims, and according to my NYPD boss Steve, the NYPD considers being a religious Muslim a terrorism indicator."[62]

Vulnerable Muslims were preyed upon in FBI sting operations across the country. According to the Center on National Security at Fordham University School of Law, approximately 60 percent of cases against Americans on ISIS-related charges have involved informants, as compared to 30 percent of all terrorism indictments since 9/11.[63] Likewise, more than thirty terrorism prosecutions between 2001 and 2010 involved informants.[64] These results are unsurprising in light of the FBI's widespread use of informants, estimated at 15,000 domestically as of 2008—reportedly ten times the number of informants active during the era of J. Edgar Hoover and COINTELPRO.[65]

These informants pose serious risks to Muslims' civil rights. In 2007, for instance, an informant, Mohamed Omar, lured three undocumented immigrant brothers from the former Yugoslavia into a conspiracy that he manufactured in Fort Dix, New Jersey. Then–Attorney General Chris Christie, eager for a high-profile antiterrorism case to launch his political career, argued the case on weak circumstantial evidence based on the defendants' opposition to the US war in Iraq, becoming more religious, going to a shooting range during a vacation in Pennsylvania, and watching videos by Al-Qaeda. Despite the informant's best efforts, he could not obtain even a verbal commitment by the brothers to engage in a violent act. Ultimately, Omar convinced the brothers to illegally purchase guns, which triggered multiple indictments, including antiterrorism charges. Omar walked away with $238,000 for spying, and the Muslim brothers are spending the rest of their lives in maximum security prisons.[66]

A year later, the FBI instructed one of its informants to manufacture a terrorist plot with congregants at the Islamic Center of Irvine in California. Their operation backfired when mosque leaders reported the informant to the FBI as a dangerous extremist. Craig Montielh, whose undercover name was Farouk Aziz, talked of jihad and claimed to have access to weapons. Instead of embracing extremist ideas, the leaders of the Islamic Center sought a restraining order barring him from returning to the mosque.[67] Only later did they discover Farouk Aziz was an informant who the FBI sent to entrap members of their congregation. These cases demonstrate that religious freedom norms safeguarding houses of worship from predatory law enforcement practices do not apply to mosques or their Muslim congregants.

Indeed, informant-led plots continued. In 2009, in Newburgh, New York, FBI informant Shahed Hussain lured four Muslim men—all of whom were African American converts and former convicts—into a fake terror attack on Jewish targets in the Bronx. Shahed Hussain offered the men $250,000, a free holiday, and expensive cars for help with the attack. The informant meticulously organized transporting the missile and bombs to the reconnaissance missions.[68] The defendants were so ill equipped to carry out the plot that they did not even have driver's licenses or own cars.[69]

The same informant had lured two other inept Muslim men in Albany, New York, six years earlier. In 2003, after befriending Mohammed Hossain, apparently to induce him into the plot, informant Hussain offered a loan for Mohammed's struggling pizzeria. The government's case relied on the informant's statement to the defendant that the money came from the sale of a missile launcher that would be used to kill a Pakistani diplomat in New York.[70] When the informant showed the defendant the missile launcher, the defendant questioned whether it was even legal to possess such a dangerous weapon.

Despite having no involvement in the purchase of the weapon or the fake plot, the defendant was arrested on charges of conspiring to aid a terrorist group, providing support for a weapon of mass destruction, money laundering, and supporting a foreign terrorist organization.[71] The taking and repayment of the loan was sufficient for a jury to convict the man of material support to terrorism. The association of Muslims with terrorism was so potent that mere accusations in a fake plot orchestrated by a government informant, without a defendant's direct involvement, tainted the jury's reasoning. The defendant's Muslim identity effectively criminalized him as a terrorist.

Unsurprisingly, news of mass surveillance and sting operations had a chilling effect on Muslim communities nationwide. They feared that attending mosques and associating with other Muslims could ensnare them in a government sting operation. Indeed, one of the plaintiffs who sued the NYPD for violating his constitutional rights, Syed Farhaj Hassan, admitted that he "has decreased his mosque attendance significantly since learning that the mosques he attends have been under surveillance by the NYPD."[72] Upon learning of the NYPD surveillance program, other Muslims also concluded that "the risk of subjecting oneself to being featured in a police file is reason enough to cease attending the mosque or praying with other Muslims."[73] Some altered their physical appearance by remaining clean shaven or not wearing a headscarf. Many Muslims were generally fearful of "being outspoken on political issues affecting Muslims in America." The message was clear: Religious and Religious Dissident Racial Muslims were the primary targets of what was effectively a domestic war on Muslims.

One of the intended objectives of the racialization process is making the stakes of practicing Islam high in terms of liberty and dignity. The FBI's counterterrorism mandate, thus, is informed by specious theories of radicalization associating Islamic practices with terrorist tendencies. Praying frequently at mosques, growing a beard, refraining from drinking alcohol, and criticism of the US war in Afghanistan or Iraq triggered FBI suspicion of terroristic plans. Thus, law enforcement attention is directed at Muslims with ideologies the government deems "radical"—the same reasoning that criminalized Black Muslim civil rights activists decades earlier. Only by secularization and assimilation into White Protestant norms, that is, by becoming a model Muslim minority, can a Muslim evade the heavy hand of the security state.

TARGETING THE RELIGIOUS DISSIDENT RACIAL MUSLIM

The archetypal "radical Muslim" is the Religious Dissident Racial Muslim, sometimes pejoratively referred to as a "political Islamist." A case in point is that of Professor Sami Al-Arian, who is a vocal Palestinian rights advocate and a devout Muslim. Al-Arian fell under the government's Arab (Palestinian) terrorist trope—later expanded to the Muslim terrorist trope (see chapter 6)—before 9/11. In 2003, the US Department of Justice accused Al-Arian of being the leader of a Palestinian jihadist group.[74] To support its case, prosecutors relied mainly on surveillance from the early 1990s, when Al-Arian expressed political views in support of Palestinian rights and opposed the Oslo Accords. The jury in the case acquitted Al-Arian on eight of the seventeen charges and hung on the remaining charges.

Deciding to forgo a retrial, the prosecution entered into a plea bargain with Al-Arian in which he pleaded guilty to a lesser charge and agreed to be deported.[75] Although Al-Arian was scheduled for release in April 2007, immigration authorities imprisoned him for an additional year and a half for "refusing to testify before a grand jury about a cluster of Muslim organizations in northern Virginia." In short, Al-Arian refused to assist the US government in prosecuting other Religious Dissident Racial Muslims. Following a successful habeas corpus petition, Al-Arian was released in September 2008, put under house arrest, and deported in 2015.[76] In expelling a Religious Dissident Racial Muslim, the government delivered a chilling warning to all Muslims: stay silent and assimilate.

The case of Al-Arian was one of a series of antiterrorism cases that morphed the Arab (Palestinian) terrorist trope into the Muslim terrorist trope, which began in earnest in the 1990s and solidified after 9/11. An illustration of this new trope is the Palestinian American Muhammad Salah. He was imprisoned, tortured, and coerced into a false confession by Israeli security forces that he was the leader of Hamas. As a result, Salah was designated in 1995 as a "specially designated terrorist" by the Office of Foreign Asset Control (OFAC) of the US Treasury Department in secret proceedings based on classified evidence.[77] He served a six-month prison sentence in Israel, after which, in 1997, he returned to the United States.

Despite the best efforts of FBI informants and undercover agents who spied on Salah, his family, and his friends, the US government's evidence was too flimsy to indict him. That all changed on September 11, 2001, when the government had the public's unconditional support to collectively punish Muslims. Salah was charged in 2004 with material support to terrorism and racketeering based on his humanitarian aid work with Palestinians in the 1990s.

Armed with expanded surveillance and investigatory powers granted by the USA PATRIOT Act, a public convinced that Muslims are presumptively terrorists, and a judiciary highly deferential in national security cases, the Bush administration aggressively targeted Religious Dissident Muslims. The judge in Salah's trial admitted into evidence his coerced confession to Israeli security forces, notwithstanding evidence of torture offered by the defense counsel.[78] After a three-month trial, the jury ultimately acquitted Salah on the terrorism charges but found him guilty of obstruction of justice charges related to a separate civil suit. Prosecutors sought a ten-year sentence, which the Chicago-area Muslim and Arab community challenged with more than six hundred letters of support. After a nearly two-decade ordeal, Salah served twenty-one months in jail. The same message to Muslims across the United States was reinforced: being religious and opposing US foreign policy in belief and action makes you a top priority in the US government's domestic war on Muslims.

The government used antiterrorism laws to make an example of another Religious Dissident Muslim, the Islamic cleric Ali Al-Tamimi. Al-Tamimi was a scientist, a well-known Islamic lecturer, and co-founder of the Center for Islamic Information and Education, which propagates conservative, literalist interpretations of Islam.[79] During one of his lectures in London in 1996, "Muslims and the Study of the Future," he expressed his belief that "we have the true source of knowledge, the Quran, and the Sunna, something which is inerrant. And therefore, because of that true source of knowledge, our ability to think and our ability to interpret is more correct than theirs." Three years later, at Purdue University, in a lecture titled "Islam: The Cure for Societal Ills," Al-Tamimi declared that "the United States is probably the best society known to humanity in terms of its justice.... But [its] problems... are insurmountable in my opinion because of the lack of the application of the sharia."[80]

Soon after 9/11, Al-Tamimi claimed the world was on the verge of an apocalyptic battle between Muslims and nonbelievers—ironically, a similar narrative propagated by right-wing Evangelical Christian Islamophobes.[81] He met with young Muslim men on September 16, 2001, and expressed his views that America was engaging in a war on Islam. Three of his followers later traveled to Pakistan and received military training but never went to Afghanistan to fight for the Taliban.[82] As a result, Al-Tamimi was charged with soliciting treason, among other charges. The lead federal prosecutor, Gordon Kromberg, called Al-Tamimi "a purveyor of hate and war" in court.[83] At a time when Islamophobia infected the media and political rhetoric, it was not hard to persuade the jury to convict Al-Tamimi on charges of conspiracy, attempting to aid the Taliban, soliciting treason, soliciting others to wage war against the United States, and aiding and abetting the use of firearms and explosives.[84] In retribution for his dissident politics informed by his religious beliefs, Al-Tamimi is serving life in prison.

The myriad antiterrorism prosecutions are the sharp edge of an expansive policing of Muslim's political and religious beliefs. A subtler but no less pernicious counterterrorism tool is the government's countering violent extremism program.

A common feature of the Islamophobia found in both secular liberal and religious conservative circles is the belief that Muslims are prone to "radicalization" more than any other religious group. These conclusions are based on the fallacy that because most terrorism is committed by Muslims globally, Muslims are more likely to commit terrorism. Completely overlooking the political, social, and economic factors causing instability in Muslim-majority countries, such as the US occupation of Iraq and Afghanistan and US support for brutal Muslim dictators, proponents of counter-radicalization focus exclusively on the perpetrators' religious identities. Whether the logic is that Islam is an illegitimate political ideology, as alleged by the religious conservatives, or that Islam is an illiberal religion in need of reformation, as alleged by the secular liberals, the outcome is the same anti-Muslim racial project: homegrown terrorism.

This label infused with the racial subtext of "Muslim domestic terrorists" fueled a cottage industry of counter-radicalization programs focused on Religious Dissident Racial Muslims and Religious Racial Muslims. The NYPD's influential counter-radicalization report stated outright that "radicalization in the West often starts with individuals who are frustrated with their lives or with the politics of their home governments" and that "Muslims in the U.S. are more resistant, but not immune to the radical message [of Salafi Islam]."[85] Typical signatures of homegrown terrorism include "giving up cigarettes, drinking, gambling and urban hip-hop gangster clothes, donning traditional Islamic clothing, growing a beard," and "becoming involved in social activism and community issues." Obama continued counter-radicalization policies targeting Muslims under the rubric "countering violent extremism" (CVE). To "break the radicalization cycle,"[86] the Obama administration promoted Religious and Secular Racial Muslims while simultaneously criminalizing Religious Dissident Muslims. The new CVE Interagency Task Force "coordinate[d] the development and dissemination of resources describing possible warning signs as well as steps families and friends can take if they believe someone close to them is becoming recruited or radicalized to violence."[87]

According to John Cohen, former undersecretary for intelligence and analysis and counterterrorism coordinator in the DHS: "In most cases, those radicalized to violence exhibit behaviors of concern that are observed by those who associate with that individual. This is why the United States law enforcement and homeland security officials have sought to develop and employ locally based prevention strategies designed to aid authorities in detecting those on the verge of ideologically motivated violence.... These programs have become known as 'countering violent extremism.'"[88] The so-called signs of radicalization include a combination of orthodox Islamic practices and political views disfavored by the US government. As a result, the government scrutinizes Religious Racial Muslims and Religious Dissident Racial Muslims, whose lifestyles and political beliefs trigger red flags in the purported radicalization stages: pre-radicalization, self-identification, indoctrination, and jihadization.[89]

That CVE programs focus exclusively on Muslim communities signals to the public that Muslims warrant collective suspicion and confirm international terrorists' narratives that America is at war with Islam.[90] The Trump administration made clear its exclusive focus on terrorism committed by Muslims when, in January 2017, the name of the CVE program was changed to "Countering Islamic Extremism."[91] Meanwhile, White supremacist violence has been growing at an alarming rate over the past decade, culminating in a right-wing insurgency on January 6, 2021, evincing that counterterrorism is more about anti-Muslim racism than national security.[92]

RACIAL VIOLENCE AGAINST MUSLIMS

Concurrent with the government's targeting of Muslims in national security enforcement is the public's violence against Muslims. The years 2015 and 2016 were the most violent for Muslims since 2001. Not coincidentally, anti-Muslim rhetoric by Republican presidential candidates reached a fever pitch during the same period, as discussed in chapter 7.[93] Reported hate crimes surged to 257 in 2015 and 307 in 2016, according to the Bridge Initiative at Georgetown University. That is nearly double the average 150 reported anti-Muslim hate crimes between 2002 and 2014. Among the incidents reported are twelve murders, thirty-four physical assaults, fifty-six acts of vandalism or destruction of property, nine cases of arson, and eight shootings or bombings.[94] When compared to an average of less than 30 hate crimes before the September 11 attacks, the salience of the Racial Muslim becomes even more glaring.[95]

A report by the Center for the Study of Hate and Extremism at California State University in San Bernardino found that anti-Muslim hate crimes increased 78 percent, from 110 in 2014 to 196 in 2015.[96] Similarly, Muslim Advocates reported that since the November 2015 Paris attacks, at least 100 hate crimes against Muslims in America have been reported.[97] Notably, these numbers do not reflect the entirety of anti-Muslim discrimination. The US Department of Justice Bureau of Statistics reports that only 44 percent of hate crimes are reported to the police, and in 2013, the bureau found that nearly two-thirds of all hate crimes were unreported.[98]

The following cases highlighted in Muslim Advocates' reports illustrate the physical danger caused by anti-Muslim racism: (1) two Muslim women pushing their children in strollers were attacked in Brooklyn by an assailant who spewed anti-Muslim slurs;[99] (2) the Islamic Center of Fort Pierce, Florida, was set on fire;[100] (3) a Muslim man was assaulted and beaten after leaving a mosque, resulting in five broken bones, a concussion, and fractured ribs;[101] (4) a delivery driver was brutally beaten by a passenger who called him a "Muslim a—hole" before pulling the driver to the ground, punching, and stomping on him;[102] (5) a Sikh temple was vandalized by a man who said he thought it was a mosque and affiliated with terrorists;[103] (6) a Muslim woman had hot liquid poured on her by another woman, who shouted, "F—ing Muslim trash";[104] (7) while a Muslim family was shopping for a home, a man in the neighborhood pointed a gun at them, saying they "should all die" because they are Muslim;[105] (8) an elderly Sikh man, mistaken for a Muslim, was stabbed to death while working at a convenience store;[106] and (9) a taxi driver—a thirty-eight-year-old Moroccan immigrant—was shot and injured by one of his passengers after being asked about his background.[107]

Racial violence continued throughout Trump's presidency. According to the Council on American Islamic Relations, anti-Muslim hate crimes increased by 15 percent in 2017, with 300 reported crimes as compared to 260 reported in 2016.[108] Anti-Muslim incidents were exponentially higher in 2017, at 2,599, compared to 1,409 in 2015. Examples of hate crimes committed during the first year of Trump's presidency include a man ripping off the headscarf of a fourteen-year-old outside a mall in Georgia, a Muslim couple subjected to racial slurs for weeks by their neighbor in Washington State, and arsonists bombing the Dar Al-Farooq Islamic Center in Indiana with an improvised explosive device.

Indeed, Trump's anti-Muslim statements were cited by White nationalists when harassing Muslims. A female Muslim airline employee wearing a headscarf was assailed by a man at JFK who shouted, "Are you [expletive] sleeping? Are you praying? What are you doing?," before kicking her in the leg.

He also shouted, ""F— Islam, f— ISIS, Trump is here now. He will get rid of all of you. You can ask Germany, Belgium, and France about these kinds of people. You will see what happens."[109] In Texas, an intoxicated man verbally attacked a Muslim family, screaming, "You're a f— Muslim, motherf—," and "Donald Trump will stop you."[110]

Bullying of Muslim students also surged. In 2010, a study in northern Virginia found that 80 percent of Muslim youth were subjected to taunts and harassment at school.[111] In 2014, a survey of Muslim children in the third through twelfth grades in Maryland found that nearly one-third "said they had experienced insults or abuse at least once because of their faith."[112] That same year, a statewide survey of more than six hundred Muslim American students ages eleven through eighteen in California found that 55 percent of respondents reported being bullied or discriminated against, twice the number of students nationally who reported the same.[113] In addition, 29 percent of Muslim female students who wore a headscarf experienced offensive touching or pulling off of their hijab. Another report by the Southern Poverty Law Center in 2019 found that of the more than two hundred anti-Muslim hate incidents in schools reported by educators and the media, most involved associating Muslim students with terrorism.[114]

. . .

The deployment of state power to surveil, investigate, prosecute, and deport immigrant Muslims works in concert with an influential and well-funded Islamophobia industry to produce systemic anti-Muslim racism. Aggressive propaganda campaigns defaming Islam, Muslim leaders, and Muslim organizations enable selective, racialized national security enforcement to occur with negligible public opposition. Indeed, it was not until Trump's 2017 Muslim Ban that a critical mass of Americans realized the extent to which Islamophobia had infected the political system at the highest levels.

Nevertheless, the War on Terror was understood and accepted by the public as a war on Muslims. Although the Alt-Right movement inspires right-wing White extremists to kill, vandalize, and attack Muslims, Latinos, and African Americans; the government and the public refuse to acknowledge the danger these extremists pose to society. Shielded by White and Christian privilege, right-wing terrorists are treated as individual wrongdoers. Their targeting of an entire faith group is not perceived as contradicting American religious freedom norms.[115]

The explanation to this paradox, I argue, lies in the racialization of Muslims from a people of faith to a savage, uncivilized, and suspect race. Islam is reframed as a political ideology founded by an imposter prophet. Even for those Americans who acknowledge that Islam is a religion, Muslims remain collectively threatening to America's Judeo-Christian national identity, just as Judaism, Catholicism, and Mormonism had previously threatened America's Protestant national identity. Consistent with the social identity theory of in-group and out-group phenomena, Muslims are in the out-group—if not for their religion, then for their racialized identity.[116]

As chapters 1 through 5 show, what Muslims are experiencing today is a continuation of a long history of exclusion against groups of people racialized as inferior on account of religious beliefs deemed inconsistent with America's ethnocultural White Christian identity. This begs the question whether racialization is American Muslims' fate. That is, will Muslims be permanently racialized, joining Blacks and Native Americans? Will they become honorary Whites, alongside Asians and White-presenting Latinos? Or will Muslims attempt to become White, similar to Jews, Catholics, and Mormons, by advocating for a shift to an Abrahamic national identity? And if entrance into Whiteness is available and desirable for some Muslims, what is the price of deracialization for them as well as for faiths outside the Abrahamic tradition? What racial bribe will Muslims have to pay to avoid subordination?[117]

The final chapter explores these provocative questions as America's diverse Muslim population wrestles with racism, xenophobia, and Islamophobia at a time of seismic demographic change in the United States.[118]

TEN

The Future of the Racial Muslim and Religious Freedom in America

> May the children of the stock of Abraham who dwell in this land continue to merit and enjoy the good will of the other inhabitants—while every one shall sit in safety under his own vine and fig tree and there shall be none to make him afraid.
>
> GEORGE WASHINGTON,
> *Letter to the Jews of Newport (1790)*

BEFORE THE ASH AND DEBRIS SETTLED from the attacks on the World Trade Center, American flags were raised across the country. On cars and lapels, in front of homes and businesses, the Stars and Stripes symbolized resilience and unity after a national trauma. Under intense scrutiny in their towns, Muslims also displayed the American flag in their windows and in Islamic schools and mosques.[1] "Proud to Be American" posters were displayed in Muslim-owned businesses across the country.[2] Not only were Muslims seeking to prove their loyalty, but they also hoped the flag would protect them from assault and vandalism.

Previously living relatively apolitical lives, many immigrant Muslims suddenly felt an urgency to become civically engaged.[3] Some spearheaded public relations campaigns to salvage the sullied image of Islam.[4] Others went so far as to join the US military to serve in Afghanistan and Iraq.[5] And nearly every American Muslim organization repeatedly condemned the September 11 attacks and terrorism ad nauseam. Their condemnations, both after the September 11 attacks and each time terrorism occurred in a Western country, fell on deaf ears.[6] Every Muslim would be suspect until and unless each could individually prove loyalty to the United States.

For over two centuries, immigrants from throughout the world have come to the United States seeking work, education, wealth, and protection from persecution.[7] Their ability to successfully pursue the so-called American dream of wealth, liberty, and the pursuit of happiness, however, depends in large part on where they fit in America's racial-religious hierarchy. The closer a group is to White Christian identity, as defined at a particular historical moment, the more socioeconomic and legal privileges they enjoy. Simultaneously, the further they can distance their identities from Blacks, the higher new immigrants and their progeny move up the racial-religious hierarchy in a White supremacist society.[8]

As they confront rising Islamophobia, immigrant Muslims face a choice: accept the "racial bribe" and seek mobility toward Whiteness, or engage in cross-racial alliances to end systemic racism grounded in White Judeo-Christian supremacy. As Guinier and Torres explain, "The racial bribe is a strategy that invites specific racial or ethnic groups to advance within the existing black-white racial hierarchy by becoming 'white.'" It expands who can fit into Whiteness based on four goals: "(1) to defuse the previously marginalized group's oppositional agenda, (2) to offer incentives that discourage the group from affiliating with black people, (3) to secure high status for individual group members within existing hierarchies, and (4) to make the social position of 'whiteness' appear more racially or ethnically diverse."[9]

Twenty years after the Racial Muslim became a fixture in American race politics, some Muslims are willing to pay the racial bribe, while others reject it outright. For those who realize that their racialization is built on centuries of religious oppression and racism against African Americans and Native Americans, later extended to other immigrants excluded from Whiteness, their quest for equality attempts to destroy the racial-religious hierarchy from its roots. Other Muslims who view prejudice as a temporal anomaly or an individual prejudice hold fast to the colorblind discourse of American meritocracy, equality, and religious freedom. In other words, this too shall pass because the problems are circumstantial, not systemic.

Should immigrant Muslims choose the path of assimilation and accommodation, then anti-Islamophobia campaigns will focus on expanding American national identity from Judeo-Christian to Abrahamic. Like other immigrants before them, some Muslims will be merely following the "American dream" of seeking Whiteness with all the attendant privileges, all the while excluding Blacks, Native Americans, and other groups that have been permanently racialized as non-White.[10] These Muslims hope that one day, they too will be socially accepted as part of the American mainstream, as are Jews and Catholics today. Indeed, by 1987, the renowned sociologist Seymour Martin Lipset reported that American public opinion viewed Jews as "just as honest, just as unobjectionable as neighbors and co-workers, and just as supportable for high public office as white Catholics and mainline Protestants.... Their energy and achievements are viewed with admiration.... Jews have arrived."[11] However, some Jews were and are still viewed as outsiders, Orthodox Jews in particular. Likewise, not all Muslims will be permitted entrance into Whiteness should America adopt an Abrahamic national identity. Phenotype, religiosity, and political dissidence will likely remain litmus tests.

If Muslims seek to merely shift American national identity from Judeo-Christian to Abrahamic without uprooting the racial-religious hierarchy, the Racial Muslim will be a temporary way station for some descendants of immigrant Muslims who phenotypically present as White and can assimilate into Anglo-Protestant normativity. Meanwhile, African American Muslims will always be Black regardless of identity performance, levels of religiosity, or political views.

Similar to the pre-9/11 era, immigrant Muslims will experience segmented assimilation, wherein some will enter the mainstream (i.e., Whiteness) while others will be permanently excluded.[12] Rather than assimilation outcomes arising primarily from high levels of education, income, and wealth (as is the case for most immigrants), levels of religiosity and political dissent will shape the Racial Muslims' existence. As such, some White-presenting immigrant Muslims will regain their pre-9/11 socially White status, while other immigrant Muslims and all African American Muslims will permanently remain Racial Muslims.

The experiences of Jews and Catholics after World War II, as I describe in chapter 4, demonstrate that assimilation for Muslims is likely to entail the secularization and Protestantization of Islamic practices.[13] Thus the first to be accepted into America's newfound Abrahamic national identity (should it actually occur) will be the White-presenting Secular Racial Muslims. White-presenting Religious Muslims who Protestanize how they practice will also fit in the Abrahamic faith tradition, making them either White or honorary White. The least likely to be accepted into an Abrahamic national identity is the Religious Dissident Muslim, whose Orthodox lifestyle, combined with staunch opposition to US government policy in Muslim-majority countries, clashes with Anglo-Protestant assimilationist pressures and the national ideology of empire. Even a White-presenting phenotype is insufficient for the Religious Dissident Muslim to gain full acceptance into the national identity.[14]

Because colorism undergirds American racism, phenotype (skin color in particular) will still bar some Muslims from the privileges of first-class citizenship, regardless of their secularization or assimilation. Immigrant Muslims, from the Middle East and North Africa, for example, will fall somewhere below White within the racial-religious hierarchy. However, non-White-presenting South Asian and Middle Eastern Muslims may become honorary Whites, depending on their accommodation of evolving social constructions of Whiteness and the prospective Abrahamic national identity. Meanwhile, African American Muslims and African immigrant Muslims will remain Black within a racial-religious hierarchy constrained by a deeply entrenched Black-White paradigm. The consequence is that only some immigrant Muslims will attain the full panoply of religious freedom rights, among other civil rights attendant to Whiteness—depending on how they practice Islam, their political beliefs, and their skin color.

This chapter unpacks these admittedly provocative predictions by looking at the various ways immigrant Muslims have attempted to counter Islamophobia since 9/11, ranging from antiracism advocacy that confronts the racial-religious hierarchy to liberal, colorblind, interfaith, political projects that emphasize an Abrahamic common identity while glossing over anti-Black racism. America's four to eight million Muslims have diverse perspectives, phenotypes, classes, and degrees of religiosity that affect their myriad responses to discrimination.[15]

A NEW RACIAL PROJECT: ABRAHAMIC NATIONAL IDENTITY IN A LIBERAL COLORBLIND PARADIGM

Since their arrival in large numbers after 1965, immigrant Muslims have been negotiating their place in the racial-religious hierarchy. When anti-Arab racism began merging with anti-Muslim racism after the 1979 Iranian Revolution, some Muslim communities responded by reaching out to their White Christian and Jewish neighbors. Concerned that their religion was being unfairly vilified based on geopolitical conflicts in the Middle East, Muslims sought to educate the American public that Islam is a peaceful religion that shares common values with "the People of the Book," a Quranic phrase referring exclusively to Christians and Jews.[16]

With Abraham in common, Muslims emphasize the historical relationship of the three monotheistic faiths.[17] In Judaism, Abraham is the first Jew who faithfully followed God's commandments. For Christians, Abraham is "the father of all that believe" and an exemplar of faith, according to the apostle Paul. In Islam, Abraham is the archetype of complete submission to God for his willingness to sacrifice his son, Ishmael. Notably, Muslims believe that Abraham was a Muslim prophet and that "the people who are worthiest of Abraham are those who followed him, together with this Prophet [Muhammad] and the believers."[18]

While theological differences abound between Judaism, Christianity, and Islam as to what Abraham represents and who he is, the patriarch serves as a unifying figure in contemporary civic discourse.[19] Partly in response to the first Intifada in the Arab-Israeli conflict, in the 1990s, a genre of Abrahamic books began calling for peace among the three religions. *The Abraham Connection: A Jew, Christian, and Muslim in Dialogue*, published in 1994, for example, describes interfaith discussions between David Gordis, George Grose, and Muzammil Siddiqi about the significance of Abraham in the three faiths.[20] The dialogues were hosted by the Academy for Judaic, Christian, and Islamic Studies, an institute affiliated with the University of California, Los Angeles, and devoted to comparative studies of the three Abrahamic religions.[21]

After 9/11, the Abrahamic political project became more urgent. American Muslim organizations needed to make Islam a major religion of the United States to counteract propaganda that indicted Muslims as dangerous outsiders.[22] Some leaders, such as Imam Feisal Abdul Rauf, support assimilation through development of a new American Muslim identity that both understands Islam and engages in interfaith projects.[23] Conservative Christians and Jews are thus assured that the Religious Racial Muslim is not a dissident (on domestic race issues or US policy on Israel, for example) but rather a deeply spiritual person who keeps his faith a private matter in accordance with Western liberal norms.[24] The emphasis on an Abrahamic religious identity, thus, has become a strategy for deracializing and depoliticizing Muslims.

To that end, Muslims have participated, and in some cases helped start, initiatives such as the Interfaith Conference of Metropolitan Washington, the North American Interfaith Network, the Interfaith Network of New York, and the Shoulder to Shoulder Campaign.[25] What have come to be known as Abrahamic dialogues take many forms, with the most widely publicized being the Abraham Salon. An institute created by Bruce Feiler, author of *Abraham: A Journey to the Heart of Three Faiths*, the Abraham Salons provide free online tool kits for grassroots discussion groups held around the country in private homes.[26] The discussions revolve around excerpts from the Torah, the New Testament, and the Quran that examine the character of Abraham as a uniting theme among the three monotheistic faiths. That thousands of these tool kits have been downloaded across the country demonstrates the salience of the colorblind interfaith narrative.

Numerous similar initiatives have sprung up across the country, such as the Little Rock Daughters of Abraham Book Club,[27] the Children of Abraham Institute at the University of Virginia,[28] the Lubar Institute for the Study of Abrahamic Religions at the University of Wisconsin,[29] the Tent of Abraham, Hagar, and Sarah hosted by the Shalom Center,[30] and the Community of Living Traditions at Stony Point Center.[31] Leaders of the three faiths have engaged in interfaith projects emphasizing their common values as monotheists. Their motives include concerns with interreligious conflicts in the Middle East, Islamophobia and anti-Semitism in the West, and the secularization of American society. In contrast to right-wing religious conservative Christians, who hold fast to their belief that secular liberalism and Islam are interconnected threats,[32] centrist religious conservative Christians and Jews are finding partners in Religious Racial Muslims in the broader culture wars, wherein they believe that monotheistic religions are under attack by the burgeoning civil religion of secularism.[33]

Contemporary initiatives to find common ground among Christians, Jews, and Muslims mirror efforts by Jews, Catholics, and Protestants in the first half of the twentieth century to combat anti-Semitism and anti-Catholicism. Reminiscent of the National Conference of Christians and Jews, established in the 1920s, as shown in chapter 4, a group of eight Muslim, six Jewish, and eight Christian scholar-leaders met in 2007 to discuss how they could unite their faith communities.[34] Sponsored by the United States Institute of Peace (USIP) and the Churches' Center for Theology and Public Policy, the conference in New York addressed how the three religions' sacred scriptures supported an "Abrahamic Just Peacemaking" model to prevent war. Their interfaith debate culminated in the 2008 USIP report, "Abrahamic Alternatives to War: Jewish, Christian and Muslim Perspectives on Just Peacemaking," which concluded that "the scriptures and traditions of these three faiths contain a great deal of insight about the means to create sustainable, peaceful societies."[35] That said, some on the Christian Right reject interfaith projects because they believe the nation's ideological foe, Islam, can never be accepted into the national fold.[36]

Grassroots efforts emphasizing the Abrahamic tradition are buttressed by government rhetoric when politically expedient. In 1979, for example, at the signing of the Camp David Accords between Egyptian president

Anwar El Sadat and Israeli prime minister Menachem Begin, President Jimmy Carter stated, "Let us now lay aside war. Let us reward all the children of Abraham who hunger for a comprehensive peace in the Middle East. Let us now enjoy the adventure of becoming human, fully neighbors, even brothers and sisters."[37] Twenty years later, President George W. Bush's first inaugural speech (nine months before 9/11) explicitly referred to American Muslims: "Church and charity, synagogue and mosque lend our communities their humanity, and they will have an honored place in our plans and in our laws."[38] Yet Bush's national security practices targeting Muslims directly contradicted his acknowledgment of Muslims' religious freedom rights and allusion to a common Abrahamic tradition.

As Barack Obama prepared to run for the presidency, he gave a speech in 2006 on faith and politics, wherein he too emphasized the similarities between Christians, Jews, and Muslims in the United States. In declaring his Christian faith, Obama stated, "I submitted myself to His will, and dedicated myself to discovering His truth. That's a path that has been shared by millions upon millions of Americans—Evangelicals, Catholics, Protestants, Jews, and Muslims alike."[39] In the same speech, however, Obama noted the ongoing transition in America's identity as it relates to religion: "Our law is by definition a codification of morality, much of it grounded in the Judeo-Christian tradition,"[40] and yet "we are no longer just a Christian nation; we are also a Jewish nation, a Muslim nation, a Buddhist nation, a Hindu nation, and a nation of nonbelievers."[41] Such statements would attract the wrath of the Evangelical Christian Right and Islamophobes, who believed Obama was simultaneously a secret Muslim and a liberal secularist.[42]

In the international context, US officials frequently reference the Abrahamic tradition when speaking to Muslim audiences or in speeches about the Middle East. Obama selected the Muslim-majority country Egypt to give his first major speech abroad in 2009, in which he intentionally referenced the "children of Abraham" to call for peace in the Holy Land between Jews, Christians, and Muslims.[43] Obama noted that "the rituals of Hajj and Eid-ul-Adha both serve as reminders of the shared Abrahamic roots of three of the world's major religions."

Ten years later, in 2019, Mike Pence, vice president under Trump, invoked the Abrahamic tradition in his speech at the Ministerial to Promote a Future of Peace and Security in the Middle East in Warsaw, Poland. In his address to foreign diplomats, Pence declared, "Jews, Christians, and Muslims—more than half the population of the Earth and nearly all the people of the

Middle East—claim Abraham as their forefather in faith. And so he is. And as we gather at this historic conference, I believe, on that foundation of that Abrahamic tradition, we can find a firm foundation for a brighter future for all the peoples and all the faiths of the Middle East."[44]

Domestically, however, the Trump administration's rhetoric and infamous Muslim Ban treated Muslims as a suspect race. Likewise, Obama's national security policies were grounded in the logic that racialized Muslims are inherently violent national security threats. Whether disguised in liberals' neutral-sounding labels such as "countering violent extremism" or conservatives' explicit focus on combating "Islamic extremism," racialization of Muslims is bipartisan. The result is a co-optation of religious tolerance, under the guise of an Abrahamic tradition, in pursuit of racial projects at home and empire building abroad. Put another way, government officials' reference to an Abrahamic national identity has been used as a cover for continued anti-Muslim national security practices rather than a basis for deracializing Muslim identity.

And yet some Muslim Americans are among the biggest proponents, even if unwittingly, of the Abrahamic racial-religious project. They believe that interfaith politics will mitigate anti-Muslim racism.[45] Through the discourse of religious inclusion and pluralism, Muslim leaders ally with Jewish and Christian leaders to defend against an anti-Muslim backlash.[46] As Sunaina Maira's ethnographic work demonstrates, interfaith programs have become "a sanctioned site of public engagement for Muslim American youth," including on college campuses.[47] For example, Islam Awareness Week (which began before 9/11) is now the signature annual event hosted by Muslim Student Associations across the country seeking to persuade fellow students that Islam is a religion of peace with the same moral principles as Christianity and Judaism.[48]

Muslims also encourage their neighbors and government officials to visit their mosques as part of "open house" interfaith initiatives.[49] The largest Muslim American organization, the Islamic Society of North America (ISNA), led national campaigns encouraging mosques across the country to engage in interfaith outreach.[50] Evoking religious pluralism, American Muslim organizations aim to debunk Americans' perceptions that Islam's purported illiberalism makes Muslims hostile to people of other faiths. Toward that end, ISNA plays a leading role in the Shoulder to Shoulder Campaign, which is a coalition of thirty-two national Jewish and Christian organizations created in 2010 for the stated purpose of countering discrimination and violence against Muslims.[51] The campaign has organized inter-faith solidarity rallies in person and online in response to right-wing armed protests at mosques and the anti-Sharia movement across the country.[52]

The national and state chapters of the Council on American Islamic Relations also lead interfaith activities in the hope of changing the hearts and minds of their Jewish and Christian neighbors.[53] Under the Bush administration, Muslim American organizations across the country engaged in the federal government's faith-based initiatives as another means of proving they were model minorities and "good Muslims."[54] In 2003, the National Conference on Interfaith Youth Work held its first annual meeting in Chicago, where the interfaith leader Eboo Patel promoted transnational networks of interfaith youth. Patel's religious pluralism agenda was couched in Islamic discourse that God intentionally created people of different colors and religions to get to know each other.[55] Through mosque open houses, interfaith dialogues, and community service for non-Muslim communities, Muslims are seeking to prove their faith is consistent with the Judeo-Christian tradition.

While well intentioned, the post-9/11 interfaith movement does not address systemic racism or the economic inequities of a neoliberal, individualistic society. Instead, participant Muslim groups accept American liberalism's treatment of prejudice as an individual problem, solved through education and interfaith engagement. The Sisterhood of Salaam Shalom, for example, gathers Muslim and Jewish women annually to discuss how to talk to friends whose views of Islam are shaped by media portrayals of Muslims as terrorists.[56] The Islamic Networks Group (ING) boasts that its educational presentations and interfaith panels decrease stereotypes of Islam as promoting terrorism among participants.[57] The reasoning goes that if only Christian and Jews met a Muslim, attended a Ramadan *iftar* (the meal at the end of the daily fast), and visited a mosque, then they would understand that Islam is a religion of peace and Muslims are not terrorists.

Although this may be true at an individual level, and indeed polls show that knowing a Muslim mitigates prejudice, interfaith projects are not addressing the broader structural forces that produce government systems of oppression, including the social construction of the Racial Muslim through national security, immigration, and foreign policy.[58] In fact, it is quite the opposite: the emphasis on Muslims' belonging as members of an Abrahamic tradition co-opts Muslims into the racial-religious hierarchy as model minorities. A certain way of practicing Islam and a certain type of Muslim, specifically, one that is not a dissident or "too religious" by mainstream Protestant standards, make for the palatable Muslim under the interfaith paradigm. Religious Dissident and Secular Dissident Racial Muslims, meanwhile, are marginalized, and the underlying causes of anti-Muslim racism remain unchanged.

The political marginalization of dissident Muslims is on full display on the issue of Palestinian human rights. Muslims engaged in interfaith activities are loathe to criticize Israeli state practices that treat Palestinians (both Muslim and Christian) in the occupied West Bank and Gaza as colonial subjects, lest they offend their Jewish partners. Indeed, some Muslims have gone to the extent of joining the Muslim Leadership Initiative (MLI) at the Shalom Hartman Institute in Jerusalem, which provides Muslim participants an immersive experience engaging with Jewish scholars and educators about their religious lives and relationship to Israel.[59] While a seemingly benign interfaith project, the MLI has been criticized by Religious Dissident Racial Muslims as a form of "faithwashing." As journalist Sana Saeed puts it, "what *washing* the occupation and apartheid clean actually is: to sanitize the narrative in which the oppressor becomes the oppressed or, at the very least, a *relatable* oppressor."[60]

Toward that end, the MLI hosts (mostly) South Asian Muslim anti-Islamophobia activists who know little about the historical connections between right-wing Zionism, Islamophobia, and anti-Arab racism. They are coopted into lending moral legitimacy to the Israeli occupation of nearly five million Palestinians. This marginalizes activists within Muslim American communities who warn of the relationships between some American Zionist organizations and the post-9/11 Islamophobia industry documented in the Center for American Progress's report *Fear Inc.: The Roots of the Islamophobia Network in America*.[61] Disconnecting anti-Palestinian racism from Islamophobia also overlooks how the anti-Arab terrorist trope (personified as a Palestinian before 9/11) is the conceptual foundation on which the post-9/11 Muslim terrorist trope is built, as I discuss in chapter 6. Ultimately, Dissident Religious and Dissident Racial Muslims argue that the failure to understand the full extent of the structural forces that subordinate Muslim communities in the US, some of which overlap with the subordination of other communities of color, contributes toward the failure to confront anti-Muslim racism as a systemic and institutionalized problem.

Another derivative of the liberal interfaith agenda is the Muslim-led effort to counter violent extremism in Muslim communities. Seeking to prove to religious conservatives in their coalitions (and the US government) their willingness to confront terrorism by Muslims, organizations such as the Muslim Public Affairs Council (MPAC) launched grassroots campaigns such as Safe Spaces. This program worked with imams, counselors, and Muslim parents to train them how to recognize signs of radicalization in their families and communities.[62] Similarly, another Muslim organization, Muflehun, hosts programs to prevent violent extremism through prevention, intervention, and reintegration of Muslim youth deemed to hold extremist ideas.[63] Voices Against Radicalism was launched in 2014 by Project Nur, a student-led interfaith initiative to condemn terrorism, sponsored by the American Islamic Congress.[64] Under the auspices of constructive community intervention that protects youth from criminalization, these strategies incorporate cooperation with law enforcement. As a result, Muslims are deputized to do the work of antiterrorism agencies in government-funded programs misrepresented as community engagement.[65]

These CVE programs signal to the government and the American public that Religious Racial Muslims can be "good Muslims" if they accept US national security policies and practices. This entails, among other things, acceding that Religious Dissident Racial Muslims should be the primary targets of counterterrorism because they are the quintessential "bad Muslims."

But not all Muslims accept the colorblind Abrahamic interfaith approach.[66] Some, in particular the more than half of American Muslims who came of age after 9/11, see Islamophobia as a derivative of anti-Black, anti–Native American, anti-Asian, and anti-Latino racism.[67] For this younger generation of Muslims, emphasizing an Abrahamic national identity as a means of combating Islamophobia merely rearranges the racial-religious hierarchy to exclude people who believe in polytheism, atheism, or pantheism—and continues to penalize Secular Dissident and Religious Dissident Muslims.[68] This new generation's progressive politics prompts them to reject their parents' pursuit of Whiteness or honorary White status.

CHALLENGING THE RACIAL MUSLIM CONSTRUCT THROUGH ANTIRACISM ADVOCACY

Achieving the American dream of middle-class status and US citizenship signifies success for most immigrant Muslims. So long as their children do not abandon their Islamic faith, the first generation accepts some degree of acculturation to Anglo-Protestant norms in language, dress, and lifestyle as the price for educational and economic opportunities.[69] To the extent that these immigrants engage in politics, it tends to be limited to getting out the vote and not challenging mainstream politics.[70]

However, not all immigrants experience the same outcomes from Americanization. In what sociologists call *segmented assimilation*, some immigrant Muslims experience upward social mobility toward White middle-class status, while others experience chronic poverty in racially segregated American cities.[71] Parental human capital in the form of educational achievement, English-language fluency, and occupation in combination affects whether the first generation of American Muslim immigrants economically and socially assimilate upward or downward.[72] Racial identity also plays a key role in where a person falls in segmented assimilation. An immigrant who can pass as White is more likely to evade the anti-Muslim discrimination that impedes social and economic mobility.

Fall from Whiteness

Prior to the September 11 attacks, Middle Eastern Muslims presumed, if not outright emphasized, that their legal status as Whites granted them social Whiteness.[73] Middle-class and upper-middle-class South Asian Muslim communities, who are not legally White, rarely identified as racial minorities whose politics aligned with historically subordinated African Americans, Native Americans, and Latinos.[74] Instead, many sought honorary Whiteness or model minority status to secure their middle- and upper-middle-class status and its attendant privileges.[75] The aftermath of the September 11 attacks abruptly interrupted the upward trajectory of some Muslims, as well as revealed that not all first-generation Muslim Americans experience the same degree of social mobility.

For many Middle Eastern and South Asian Muslims, their fall from (honorary) Whiteness resulted in unprecedented rates of racial discrimination at work, at school, and in interactions with law enforcement. For others who found middle-class status elusive prior to 9/11, such as the darker-skinned Yemeni Americans in Queens and Black Somali Americans in Minneapolis, the post-9/11 era merged anti-Black racism with anti-Muslim racism. Young Somali men, for example, confront a perilous combination of poverty, overpolicing, xenophobia, and hate crimes.[76]

As Islamophobia intensified after 9/11, so too did White nationalism. Mirroring the rise of White nativism in the early twentieth century that afflicted Jews and Catholics, recent demographic changes coupled with a gradual increase of racial minorities in elected office have triggered collective angst among conservative White Americans. Due in large part to President Donald J. Trump's nativist policy agenda, White supremacists previously on the fringes of conservative politics were mainstreamed, triggering a resurgence of anti-Semitic, Islamophobic, and xenophobic discourse. An ecosystem of White nationalist organizations known as the Alt-Right is now playing the role of the Ku Klux Klan in the 1920s and 1930s. Tellingly, the Alt-Right frequently invokes Christian identity in its warnings that America is under threat by Jews, Mexicans, African Americans, and Muslim savages.[77] Other groups, such as the Army of God, the Creativity Movement, and Christian Identity groups, explicitly cite Christian theology to justify their hate, intolerance of, and violence against racial minorities.[78]

Despite this rise in right-wing extremism, national security resources have focused exclusively on Muslim communities. And young, progressive Muslims are taking note. They are joining dissident movements that view the American government as an imperialistic and racist power. For them, get out the vote campaigns grounded in a neoliberal colorblind paradigm fail to address the structural causes socially constructing and oppressing the Racial Muslim.[79] The interfaith approach falls short by dealing only with the symptoms of anti-Muslim racism. These young Muslim progressives critique how Religious and Secular Racial Muslims attempt to prove they are loyal and peaceful rather than upend the White Christian supremacist structures causing broader structural racism that harms Muslims.

Religious Dissident and Secular Dissident Racial Muslims are allying and learning from African American (Muslim and non-Muslim) civil rights activists in combating anti-Muslim racism.[80] As Hisham Aidi and Sylvia Chan-Malik's work shows, Islam is becoming a unifying, antihegemonic force that blends Arab, Islamic, Black, and Hispanic elements, galvanizing working-class people and people of color into a countercultural Muslim American identity.[81] Similar to the Black nationalist movements, in which African American Muslims played a leading role, racial otherness is being deployed as a mark of resistance in combating Islamophobia.[82] Indeed, many immigrant Muslim Americans look to African American Muslims for leadership and guidance on how to fight systemic racism both through advocacy and artistic expression.[83] In the case of Muslim women, some have chosen to wear the headscarf as a symbol of defiance and rebuke to intolerance of Islam, including gendered Islamophobia that stereotypes Muslim women as passive and submissive.[84]

Attaching a heightened sense of racial identification to their Muslim identity, young American Muslims reject advice, primarily from elder immigrants, that they deal with Islamophobia by reminding Americans that Iranians, Arabs, and other Middle Easterners are legally White.[85] Even if they were to follow such advice, claims of Whiteness would fall on deaf ears given the entrenchment of the Racial Muslim construct. Thus, younger members of immigrant Muslim communities who previously identified primarily as Arab, Pakistani, Afghan, or Indian American now embrace a (racialized) Muslim American identity.[86]

Confronting Anti-Black Racism

As immigrant Muslims work more with African American Muslims, they are forced to confront anti-Black racism within their communities. Immigrant Muslims are affected by the anti-Black racism that is prevalent in their Middle Eastern and South Asian countries of origin, which causes some to distance themselves socially from African American Muslims. Moreover, Arab Muslims view themselves as more authentically Muslim because the Quran is in Arabic and was revealed to the Prophet Muhammad in Saudi Arabia.[87] Therefore, African American Muslim leaders are not seen as credible sources of religious authority.[88]

Although deeply entrenched in immigrant Muslim life, intracommunity racial biases are increasingly becoming part of a broader conversation about systemic racism. The Muslim Anti-Racism Coalition (MuslimARC), based in Detroit, started in 2014 and includes the elimination of intra-Muslim anti-Black racism, along with internalized racism and institutionalized racism, as a programmatic goal.[89] MuslimARC's mission is inspired by a Quranic verse interpreted by Muslims as Islam's antidiscrimination mandate: "O mankind, indeed We have created you from male and female and made you peoples and tribes that you may know one another. Indeed, the most noble of you in the sight of Allah is the most righteous of you. Indeed, Allah is Knowing and Acquainted."

Margari Hill, executive director of MuslimARC, explains, "[This verse] is dear to many Muslims, including our family at MuslimARC. It is a perfect example of Islam's egalitarian spirit, highlighting that we all came from the same family. Regardless of racial or national identity, what matters is your consciousness of God. We felt that the verse would allow Muslims of all stripes to discuss what it means to them."[90]

Toward that end, MuslimARC's 2014 Twitter campaign #DroptheAWord sought to eliminate the use of *Abeed* (meaning "slave" or "servant" in Arabic), which is commonly used in the Middle East to refer to sub-Saharan African people.[91] Some immigrant Muslims from the Middle East continued this practice in the United States by referring to African American Muslims by the same term.[92] MuslimARC also called on Muslims in the United States to sign the #SacredPledge and make the following commitment: "Reflect: I will develop a racial self awareness. I will check my own racial biases and internalized oppression. I will be aware of overt and subtle forms of racism. I will interrupt harmful behaviors."[93]

Another effective cross-racial Muslim initiative, based in Chicago, is the Inner City Muslim Action Network (IMAN), which brings together people of various races, both Muslim and non-Muslim, to work on racial justice issues in inner city communities. "Take It to the Streets," for example, is a festival intentionally held in the inner city that incorporates art, spirituality, and urban creativity to inspire social change for people of color.[94]

Taken together, these myriad initiatives led by immigrant Muslims and African Americans in their twenties and thirties is pushing Muslim communities to adopt a cross-racial approach to combating Islamophobia.

A Race-Conscious Approach to Islamophobia

Race consciousness characterizes Religious Dissident and Secular Dissident Racial Muslims' political activism. Rejecting the liberal colorblind model of civil rights, a strategy of engaged resistance to racism has become the animating theme of their cross-racial alliances.[95] Defiant in their refusal to hide their religious identity and political beliefs, Dissident Racial Muslims (many of whom are US born) work with other racial minority groups to identify structural racism and imperial violence as the common cause of Islamophobia, anti-Black racism, homophobia, and anti-Latinx xenophobia.[96]

They tie their opposition to the US occupation of Iraq, drone attacks in Pakistan and Afghanistan, and denial of Palestinian human rights abroad to mass incarceration of African Americans and criminalization of Latinx immigrants at home. In stark contrast to interfaith colorblind spaces where Muslims cannot criticize Israel's treatment of the Palestinians for fear of being called anti-Semitic by their Jewish partners, the antiracism spaces (which also include progressive Jewish partners) connect criticism of US empire in Muslim-majority countries and the government's unconditional support of Israel's rights-infringing practices against Palestinians with domestic racism.[97]

The varied responses of Muslims to Islamophobia bring to light a tension between a race-neutral individual rights–based approach and a race-conscious systemic approach. Race-conscious advocacy operates on the premise that the same root causes produce different forms of subordination of racial minorities, including the Racial Muslim. Its proponents understand that one cannot effectively combat anti-Muslim racism without also tackling anti-Black and anti-Latinx racism. Nor can one meaningfully challenge systems of oppression without including all groups harmed by such systems, albeit in different ways.

In contrast, the race-neutral approach emphasizes multiculturalism, religious pluralism, and individual responsibility. In what some scholars call *Islamophilia*, American Muslims seek to prove they are a modern, liberal, and safe religious minority that fits into a diverse and pluralistic society.[98] As a result, colorblind approaches propagate an assimilationist narrative that avoids alienating the political mainstream and exonerates neoconservatives whose foreign policy generates anti-Muslim racism.[99] Symbolic patriotism, interfaith activities, and race-neutral civil rights advocacy feed Islamophilia's need to point to Religious and Secular Racial Muslims as the "good Muslim."

Erik Love's work on Muslim organizational advocacy illustrates the "decidedly race-neutral strategy" adopted by a significant number of Muslim, Arab, and South Asian American organizations and "professional Muslims" called on by the media to answer broad questions about Islam.[100] Muslim American organizations attempt to refute the claim that Islam is incompatible with American values, thereby accepting Islamophobia's racialized frame.[101] Instead of confronting the racial-religious hierarchy that imposes on Muslims the burden of proving that their religion is not violent, antidemocratic, or illiberal, these mainstream Muslim organizations accommodate it.

After the election of Trump, when White nationalism became normalized, more Muslim American organizations began to talk openly about systemic racism. The Institute for Social Policy and Understanding's "2017 Muslims at a Crossroads Poll" found that 66 percent of Muslims support the Black Lives Matter movement, as compared to 58 percent of Jews and 39 percent of Catholics and Protestants.[102] Muslims increasingly connected the oppression arising from a border wall in Mexico with the Muslim ban through the #NoBanNoWall movement and acknowledged the intersectionality of gender and race in the #MeToo movement.

On the issue of prison reform, the Coalition for Civil Freedoms (CCF) advocates on behalf of Muslim victims of political trials under the guise of counterterrorism. Recognizing that the same mass incarceration system that has been herding African Americans into prisons since Reconstruction is now ensnaring Religious Dissident Racial Muslim men, CCF educates its Muslim constituents about anti-Black racism. For example, in a November 2020 webinar titled "Prisoner Lives Matter—Unseen Suffering Behind the Prison Walls," CCF highlighted the parallels between African Americans and Muslim political prisoners after 9/11.[103] That CCF is headed by Leena Al-Arian, daughter of the former political prisoner Sami Al-Arian, signifies a political awakening among the new generation of immigrant Muslim communities directly harmed by the War on Terror.

These developments contribute to what the scholars Junaid Rana and Sohail Daulatzai describe as "the Muslim Left and a broader movement of a Muslim International seek[ing] to differentiate itself from the logics and intellectual formation of Islamophobia and instead name anti-Muslim racism as an operative and generative logic of white supremacy."[104] Religious Dissident and Secular Dissident Racial Muslims who join these movements understand they cannot end the racialization of national security laws without also ending the racialization of criminal law that disproportionately harms African Americans.[105] Nor can they stop the abuse of immigration laws to ban and deport Muslims without connecting them to the abuse of Central American migrants at the US-Mexico border.

A noteworthy outcome of Muslims' increasing cross-racial coalitions is the election of the first two immigrant Muslims to the US Congress in 2018— both of whom are women. Representative Ilhan Omar from Minnesota and Representative Rashida Tlaib from Michigan campaigned as progressive Democrats with a race-conscious agenda. Tlaib is a first-generation American of Palestinian descent, and Omar is a naturalized American of Somali descent. Their life experiences as dissident Palestinian and Somali Americans (the most targeted Racial Muslims in the US counterterrorism regime), respectively, give them a profound understanding of how the intersection of race and religion extends structural racism against African Americans, Native Americans, and other racial minorities to Muslims in the post-9/11 era. Accordingly, Representative Omar explicitly states on her official website: "The criminal justice system has been built to criminalize people of color and Indigenous people, disproportionately sending them to prison for minor offenses and entrapping them in a vicious cycle of incarceration. If we are going to dismantle systemic racism in our country, we must radically transform our approach to criminal justice and invest in restorative justice practices."[106]

Omar's focus on systemic racism extends to the racialization of Muslims in counterterrorism. "Programs like Countering Violent Extremism (CVE) and the Black Identity Extremism program," she states, "function to monitor and criminalize black immigrants and African-Americans, especially black Muslims. They are based on a model of racial profiling and meant to incite fear and the suppression of black organizers and activists." Omar's dissident politics, Somali heritage, and headscarf mark her as a Religious Dissident Racial Muslim.

Rashida Tlaib's anti-Muslim racism work and vocal support of the Boycott, Divestment, Sanctions (BDS) movement and Palestinian human rights generally also mark her as a Dissident Racial Muslim.[107] Prior to running for Congress, Tlaib played a leading role in campaigns to combat anti-Arab and anti-Muslim bigotry.[108] She managed the national Take On Hate campaign, a grassroots effort "that inspires a positive perception of Arab and Muslim Americans (including refugees), systemic policy changes at the national and local levels, and builds greater capacity for this community as a whole."[109] Since being elected to Congress, Tlaib has not backed down from her support for BDS, which calls for an economic boycott of Israel as a "central form of civil resistance to Israeli occupation, colonialism and apartheid."[110] As a Palestinian who vocally defends a people stereotyped as terrorists before and after 9/11, Tlaib has attracted the ire of conservative Islamophobes and right-wing Zionists.[111] Indeed, the attacks on Tlaib reveal that the Arab (Palestinian) terrorist trope still lurks in the shadow of the Racial Muslim.[112]

That both women were elected to political office offers some hope for the future of American race politics. As dissidents who embrace their Muslim, Palestinian, and African identities, Tlaib's and Omar's leadership is emboldening Muslim Americans, particularly younger generations, to tackle Islamophobia through an antiracism and cross-racial approach.[113] Muslim American civil rights organizations that previously avoided framing their advocacy as antiracism work are now calling Islamophobia a form of racism.[114] And nearly two decades after 9/11, Islamophobia is now explicitly named in Democratic politicians' and mainstream civil rights groups' anti-racism agendas.

. . .

In the two decades following the worst terrorist attack on US soil, America's diverse immigrant Muslim communities have politically evolved, by necessity. Integral to that process has been the recognition that the liberal, colorblind paradigm perpetuates the structures that undergird Islamophobia on a systemic scale. Initiatives to expand national identity from Judeo-Christian to Abrahamic, mirroring those of Jews and Catholics a century earlier to expand it from Protestant to Judeo-Christian, merely expand the racial boundaries of religious freedom—rather than de-racialize such freedoms altogether. And while interfaith activities emphasizing religious commonalities between Muslims, Christians, and Jews continue to animate Muslims' civic engagement, the younger generation of Muslims who came of age after 2001 are increasingly adopting an antiracism approach to defending their civil and human rights. As such, their advocacy takes place within cross-racial coalitions to combat racism against African Americans, Latinx, immigrant, Jewish, LGBTQ, and other minority communities. Rather than seeking to expand Whiteness to include them, these young Muslim leaders embrace their Racial Muslim identity.

Conclusion

IT TOOK THE ELECTION of a White nationalist to the White House and nearly two decades of systematic discrimination against Muslims for Islamophobia to finally be recognized as part of America's "race problem."[1] For years, American liberals misguidedly believed that anti-Muslim racism was merely a temporary backlash after 9/11. To them, eroding the civil liberties of Muslims was a small (and worthwhile) price to pay for securing the nation.

Religious conservatives, meanwhile, only became bolder and more aggressive in their attempts to expel, exclude, and prosecute Muslims—notwithstanding their own grievances over alleged violations of religious rights.[2] Each time a Muslim conducted a terrorist attack anywhere in the world, even in places where wars had been started by the United States, both conservatives and liberals ratcheted up state practices criminalizing Muslim identity.

As I have demonstrated in this book, racial difference is not neutral.[3] Nor is it stable. Rather, race is a dialectic process of construction that creates an "other" who is inferior.[4] Meanwhile, what constitutes "White" changes over time to secure Eurocentric Christian power. As legal scholar Cheryl Harris highlights, "The possessors of whiteness were granted the legal right to exclude others from the privileges inhering in whiteness."[5] Consequently, each wave of new immigrants attempted to escape subordination by claiming inclusion in Whiteness and supporting exclusion of Blacks, Asians, Native Americans, and Mexicans.

But race is not the only category of difference that contributes to social hierarchies. Religion is also an unstable and fluid differentiating category insofar as it interacts with race to affect "other" certain groups and in turn justify their subordinate status and unequal treatment.[6] In other words, religion works to racialize groups. Racial meanings arising out of religious beliefs evolve based on the social, political, and economic influences of the time.[7] Depending on the interests of the White Christian majority, the US government has used religion to justify enslavement of Africans, settlement of Native Americans' lands, exclusionary immigration laws, criminalization of Blacks, and securitization of immigrant Muslims.

Less than one hundred years ago, Jewish immigrants from Eastern Europe and Catholic immigrants from Southern Europe and Ireland faced the indignities of second-class citizenship—in large part due to their religious identities. They were barred from applying to high-status jobs, living in affluent White neighborhoods, and attending elite schools.[8] Mainstream American society stereotyped Jews as greedy, dishonest, duplicitous, and loyal only to so-called World Jewry. Meanwhile, Catholics were stereotyped as superstitious, slavish, and blindly loyal to the pope in Rome over the United States, their nation of citizenship. Political conflicts in immigrants' countries of origin attracted suspicions that these new immigrant communities were disloyal. Even Mormons, who were US born and of Anglo-Saxon origin, were excluded from American national identity because Protestants deemed their prophet, Joseph Smith, a heretic. Mormons' practice of polygamy and intermarriage with Native Americans made them a cultural and security threat to the state. As I discuss in chapter 3, each of these three religious groups, despite their legal White status, suffered systemic forms of violence and discrimination by the state and the public in a country that proclaims to be a bastion of religious freedom.

While immigrant Muslims' experiences mirror those of Jewish, Catholic, and Mormon communities a century earlier, they differ in important ways. The four million to six million Muslims in the United States possess an unprecedented diversity of ancestry, skin color, phenotypes, and pathways of arrival to the United States. Nearly a third of Muslims are African Americans, whose ancestors arrived on slave ships starting in the seventeenth century. The remaining 70 percent immigrated to the United States from over seventy-five different countries.[9] Sixty percent of Muslims are born abroad, and another 20 percent are US-born children of immigrants who arrived in the United States after 1965. Their relatively recent arrival, coupled with their demographic diversity, poses challenges for a unified resistance to Islamophobia, as well as the internalization of anti-Black racism within immigrant Muslim communities.

In addition to White Protestant supremacy and xenophobia that racialized Jews, Catholics and Mormons, Orientalism and American empire uniquely racialize immigrant Muslims. As I discuss in chapters 5 and 6, long-standing Christian theological depictions of Islam as an evil ideology and Muhammad as a false prophet give fodder to right-wing religious conservatives in the post-9/11 era. Timeless European Orientalist depictions of Mahometans and Turks as uncivilized and despotic are imputed to Muslims to justify their detention, prosecution, and deportation. Because US hegemonic interests in Muslim-majority countries require the dehumanization and vilification of the native populations, empire building abroad animates anti-Muslim racism at home.

Hence the Racial Muslim has been under social construction for more than a century. Whether he was the barbaric Turk categorized as Asian in naturalization laws, the Black Muslim militant challenging White supremacy, the Arab nationalist suspected of being a Communist, or the Palestinian terrorist prioritized as a security threat, the Racial Muslim serves the state's and the elites' political interests.

Today, the Racial Muslim is a terrorist, permanently foreign, uncivilized, and presumptively disloyal. Tomorrow, the Racial Muslim may be a model minority or an honorary White utilized to further US geopolitical interests abroad and culture wars at home. As the United States experiences an unprecedented demographic shift wherein Whites will no longer be the majority race, the majoritarian political system may give way to a minority-controlled nation. In the alternative, Whiteness may be socially reconstructed around an Abrahamic national identity that encompasses groups not currently within its ambit—including a subset of Muslims—to retain White dominance. Or the United States may finally enter an era where no one racial religious group is overrepresented in the halls of power that house the political and economic elites.

Whatever the future of the Racial Muslim may hold, this book demonstrates that being Muslim currently circumscribes access to the privileges of first-class citizenship, including the panoply of religious freedom rights. Despite advances in civil rights law, race continues to function as a master category that determines how resources, dignity, and rights are distributed in the United States. As a result, the lessons taught in school of "liberty and justice for all" have been elusive for tens of millions of racial minorities in the United States.

For the past two decades, Muslims have faced the brunt of that reality. Their experiences evince what African Americans and Native Americans already know: religious freedom is not, nor has it ever been, equally available to all faith communities in the United States.[10] Only when we face this reality can we as a nation move forward and transform our aspirations for religious freedom and racial equality into practice.

For it is the freedom and willingness to examine and eradicate racialized double standards that distinguishes America from other nations.

NOTES

FOREWORD

1. Said, *Covering Islam*, 136.
2. www.nationalreview.com/coulter/coulter091301.shtml.

INTRODUCTION

1. Matt Apuzzo and Adam Goldman, "Documents: NYPD Gathered Intelligence on 250-Plus Mosques, Student Groups in Terrorist Hunt," Associated Press, Sept. 6, 2011, www.pulitzer.org/files/2012/investigative_reporting/ap/nypd3.pdf.
2. Title VI of the Civil Rights Act of 1964, 42 U.S.C. § 2000d, et seq.
3. *Washington v. Davis*, 426 U.S. 229 (1976).
4. Title VI of the Civil Rights Act of 1964, 42 U.S.C. § 2000d, et seq. (emphasis added).
5. Gillum, *Muslims in a Post-9/11 America*, 19; Marzouki, *Islam: An American Religion*, 69.
6. Bulliet, *The Case for Islamo-Christian Civilization*, 44–45.
7. "U.S. Muslims Concerned about Their Place in Society, but Continue to Believe in the American Dream," *Pew Research Center*, July 26, 2017. https://www.pewforum.org/2017/07/26/how-the-u-s-general-public-views-muslims-and-islam/.
8. Marzouki, *Islam: An American Religion*, 189.
9. Haddad, Smith, and Esposito, *Religion and Immigration*; Kumar, *Islamophobia and the Politics of Empire*; Maira, *The 9/11 Generation*, 15. See also Samhan, "Not Quite White"; Gualtieri, "Becoming 'White'"; Gualtieri, *Between Arab and White*; Cainkar, "Fluid Terror Threat"; Cainkar and Selod, "Review of Race Scholarship and the War on Terror"; Selod and Embrick, "Racialization and Muslims."

10. Jamal and Naber, *Race and Arab Americans before and after 9/11*; Bayoumi, *How Does It Feel to Be a Problem?*; Naber, *Arab America: Gender, Cultural Politics and Activism*.

11. Wenger, *Religious Freedom*, 1; Love, *Islamophobia and Racism in America*.

12. Ajrouch and Jamal, "Assimilating to a White Identity"; Jamal and Naber, *Race and Arab Americans before and after 9/11*.

13. Jacobson and Wadsworth, *Faith and Race in American Political Life*, 4; Hill Fletcher, *The Sin of White Supremacy*, 5.

14. Rana, "The Story of Islamophobia," 148; Bayoumi, "Racing Religion," 267; Daulatzai and Rana, *With Stones in Our Hands*; Ibrahim, "The Origins of Muslim Racialization in U.S. Law," 121; Daulatzai, *Black Star, Crescent Moon*; Kalmar, "Race by Grace," 482.

15. Joshi, "The Racialization of Religion in the United States," 214. For an explanation of the process by which Jews and Catholics became whitened through assimilation and intermarriage with Anglo-Americans, see Alba and Nee, *Remaking the American Mainstream*, 285.

16. Beydoun, "Islamophobia: Toward a Legal Definition and Framework," 108; Gottschalk and Greenberg, *Islamophobia: Making Muslims the Enemy*; Garner and Selod, "The Racialization of Muslims."

17. Moore, "Muslims in the American Legal System," 146.

18. Young, *Justice and the Politics of Difference*; Alba and Nee, *Remaking the American Mainstream*, 32; Tamimi, "Islam, Arabs, and Ethnicity."

19. Mamdani, *Good Muslim, Bad Muslim*.

20. Aziz, "Coercive Assimilationism," 1.

21. Gordon, *Assimilation in American Life*, 87; Cheah, *Race and Religion in American Buddhism*, 3–4; Alba and Nee, *Remaking the American Mainstream*, 281; Tehranian, *White Washed*, 54.

22. Examples of high-profile Muslims who have fallen prey to this pernicious racial construction are Dr. Sami Al Arian, Nihad Awad, Hatem Bazian, Imam Khaled Latif, Linda Sarsour, Imam Dawud Walid, Imam Omar Suleiman, Margari Aziza, and Dalia Mogahed. Sheehi, *Islamophobia: The Ideological Campaign against Muslims*, 116–21.

23. Shams, "Visibility as Resistance by Muslim Americans in a Surveillance and Security Atmosphere," 87, 94; Norris, "Explaining the Emergence of Entrapment in Post-9/11 Terrorism Investigations," 467, 471 (documenting the common belief among FBI agents that Muslims who harshly criticize US foreign policy or sympathize with radicalism are "terrorists in waiting").

24. Examples of this Racial Muslim are Imam Faisal Abdul Rauf, Daisy Khan, Imam Mohamed Magid, Muqtader Khan, Rabia Chaudry, and Wajahat Ali—all of whom have worked with the government on community outreach, countering violent extremism, or interfaith activities.

25. Qureshi and Sells, *The New Crusades*, 91–95; Haddad, *Becoming American?*, 71; Sheehi, *Islamophobia: The Ideological Campaign against Muslims*, 132–71; Bail, *Terrified*, 30; Geller, "Obama Administration and UN Announce Global Police

Force to Fight 'Extremism' in US," *Breitbart*, Oct. 2, 2015, https://www.breitbart
.com/politics/2015/10/02/obama-administration-and-un-announce-global-police
-force-to-fight-extremism-in-u-s/.

26. Lawyers, advocates, and academics such as Ramzi Kassem, Baher Azmy, Wadie Said (the son of Edward Said), Joseph Massad, Rashid Khalidi, Deepa Kumar, Jasbir Puar, and Faiza Patel fall into this category.

27. *Salaita v. Kennedy*, 118 F. Supp. 3d 1068 (N.D. Ill. 2015); Nagra and Power, "Taking Trauma Seriously: Torture Orgs File Amicus Brief in Support of Rasmeah Odeh." *CCRJustice*, July 2, 2015, https://ccrjustice.org/home/blog/2015 /07/02/taking-trauma-seriously-torture-orgs-file-amicus-brief-support-rasmea -odeh; Asraa Mustufa, "Rasmea Odeh: Deported But Not Defeated," *Colorlines*, Oct. 1, 2018, www.colorlines.com/articles/rasmea-odeh-deported-not-defeated.

28. Selod, *Forever Suspect*, 86–87; Dabashi, *Brown Skins, White Masks.*

29. Dabashi, *Brown Skins, White Masks.*

30. Sheehi, *Islamophobia: The Ideological Campaign against Muslims*, 90–110; Marzouki, *Islam: An American Religion*, 108–9.

31. Sarkar, *Why Does the West Need to Save Muslim Women?*, 95.

32. Sheehi, *Islamophobia: The Ideological Campaign against Muslims*, 91–92, 176; Alsultany, *Arabs and Muslims in the Media*, 84; Rascoff, "Establishing Official Islam?," 125, 181; Asifa Quraishi-Landes, "5 Myths about Sharia Law Debunked by a Law Professor," *Dallas News*, July 19, 2016, http://www.dallasnews.com/opinion /commentary/2016/07/19/asifa-quraishi-landes-5-myths-shariah-law.

33. Gordon, *Assimilation in American Life*, 89, 221; Omi and Winant, "Concept of Race," 77; Barkan, "Race, Religion, and Nationality in American Society," 59.

34. Omi and Winant, "Concept of Race," 43; Gordon, *Assimilation in American Life*, 127; Painter, *The History of White People*, 185.

35. Gordon, *Assimilation in American Life*, 137.

36. Kidd, *American Christians and Islam*, xi–xii.

37. Feener, *Islam in World Cultures*, 286–87.

38. Kidd, *American Christians and Islam*, 19.

39. Spellberg, *Thomas Jefferson's Quran.*

40. Spellberg, *Thomas Jefferson's Quran*, 25; Curtis, "The Study of American Muslims."

41. Curtis, *Muslims in America*, 76; Hammer and Safi, "Introduction: American Islam, Muslim Americans, and the American Experience."

42. Lyons, *Islam through Western Eyes*, 125.

43. Gottschalk and Greenberg, *Islamophobia: Making Muslims the Enemy*, 147.

44. Little, *American Orientalism*, 44.

45. Little, *American Orientalism*, 269.

46. Chomsky, *The Fateful Triangle.*

47. Jeremy M. Sharp, "U.S. Foreign Assistance to the Middle East: Historical Background, Recent Trends, and the FY2011 Request," *Congressional Research Service*, 2010: RL 32260, https://fas.org/sgp/crs/mideast/RL32260.pdf.

48. Gottschalk and Greenberg, *Islamophobia: Making Muslims the Enemy*, 82.

49. Friedman, *Spider's Web*.

50. Kumar, *Islamophobia and the Politics of Empire*, 141–42; Ernst, *Introduction to Islamophobia in America*.

51. Merritt Kennedy, "N.J. Town Must Pay Islamic Group $3.25 Million to Settle Discrimination Lawsuit," *NPR*, May 30, 2017, www.npr.org/sections/thetwo-way/2017/05/30/530766018/n-j-town-must-pay-islamic-group-3-25-million-to-settle-discrimination-lawsuit; "Anti-Muslim Activities in the United States," *New America*, www.newamerica.org/in-depth/anti-muslim-activity/.

52. Asma T. Uddin, "The Latest Attack on Islam: It's Not a Religion," *New York Times*, Sept. 26, 2018, www.nytimes.com/2018/09/26/opinion/islamophobia-muslim-religion-politics.html; Uddin, *When Islam Is Not a Religion*.

53. Renteln, "A Psychohistorical Analysis of the Japanese American Internment," 618, 620.

54. Omi and Winant, *Racial Formation in the United States*, 125–27.

55. Kumar, *Islamophobia and the Politics of Empire*; Noah Feldman, "How Different Is Obama Than Bush on Terrorism," *Foreign Policy*, Sept. 3, 2010, https://foreignpolicy.com/2010/09/03/how-different-is-obama-from-bush-on-terrorism/; Michael Hirsh, "How Obama's National Security Strategy Is Like Bush's," *Newsweek*, May 26, 2010, www.newsweek.com/how-obamas-national-security-strategy-bushs-214072.

56. Aziz, "A Muslim Registry," 101.

57. "The Campaign to Take On Hate," www.takeonhate.org/; www.emgage usa.org/; Muslim Anti-Racism Collaborative (MuslimARC), www.muslimarc .org/; "Linda Sarsour, Women's March," https://womensmarch.com/national-team/linda-sarsour.

58. The Muslim population is projected to surpass Jews in 2050 at 2.1% of the US population, as compared to 1.4% of Jews. "The Future of World Religions: Population Growth Projections 2010–2050," *Pew Research Center*, Apr. 2, 2015. www.pewforum.org/2015/04/02/religious-projections-2010-2050/. Ewing, *Being and Belonging*, 3.

59. Haddad, *Not Quite American?*, 2–3.

60. Jamal and Albana, "Demographics, Political Participation, and Representation," 99–100; Leonard, "Organizing Communities," 173; Feener, *Islam in World Cultures*, 288–89.

61. "Demographic Portrait of Muslims in America," *Pew Research Center*, July 26, 2017, www.pewforum.org/2017/07/26/demographic-portrait-of-muslim-americans/.

62. Jamal and Albana, "Demographics, Political Participation, and Representation," 99–100.

63. Curtis, *The Columbia Sourcebook of Muslims in the United States*, 264–67.

64. One study found that 11 percent of Muslims in 2007 identified as Republican. "Republicans Account for a Small but Steady Share of U.S. Muslims,"

Pew Research Center, Nov. 6, 2018, www.pewresearch.org/fact-tank/2018/11/06
/republicans-account-for-a-small-but-steady-share-of-u-s-muslims/.

65. Ali, "Learning in the Shadow of the War on Terror."

66. Chan-Malik, "Cultural and Literary Production of Muslim America";
Curtis, *Islam in Black America*; Abdullah, "American Muslims in the Contemporary World."

67. Edward E. Curtis IV, "Black History, Islam, and the Future of Humanities."

68. Alexander, *The New Jim Crow*; Gilmore, *Golden Gulag*.

69. In an empirical study of 113 Muslims subject to government surveillance and counterterrorism enforcement, "a disproportionate focus on men (83%) was noteworthy in contrast to women (11%), and unknown 5%, demonstrating that indeed Muslim men are subjected to broad stereotypes that assume that their gender and religion are legitimate, identifiable precursor factors in potentially committing violent acts and engaging in terrorist activities." Alimahomed-Wilson, "When the FBI Knocks."

70. "Women and Violent Radicalization," Centre for the Prevention of Radicalization Leading to Violence, Oct. 2016, www.csf.gouv.qc.ca/wp-content/uploads/radicalisation_recherche_anglais.pdf; Erin Marie Saltman and Melanie Smith, "'Till Martyrdom Do Us Part': Gender and the ISIS Phenomenon," Institute for Strategic Dialogue, 2015, https://icsr.info/wp-content/uploads/2015/06/ICSR-Report-%E2%80%98Till-Martyrdom-Do-Us-Part%E2%80%99-Gender-and-the-ISIS-Phenomenon.pdf; Anita Perešin, "Fatal Attraction: Western Muslimas and ISIS," *Perspectives on Terrorism* 9 (2015), www.jstor.org/stable/26297379.

71. Aziz, "From the Oppressed to the Terrorist"; Hammer, "Studying American Muslim Women."

72. Aziz, "From the Oppressed to the Terrorist," 191; "Coercive Assimilationism," 1.

73. Schildkraut, "The More Things Change"; Jacobson and Wadsworth, *Faith and Race in American Political Life*, 12; Rich, "Performing Racial and Ethnic Identity," 1134.

74. Bonilla-Silva, "Rethinking Racism," 465, 466.

75. Bonilla-Silva, "Rethinking Racism," 469; Feagin, *The White Racial Frame*, 10–11.

76. Alba and Nee, *Remaking the American Mainstream*, 31.

77. Fields, "Ideology and Race in American History."

78. Feagin, *The White Racial Frame*, 34; Alba and Nee, *Remaking the American Mainstream*, 32.

79. Bonilla-Silva, "Rethinking Racism," 475.

80. Bonilla-Silva, "Rethinking Racism," 470; Johnson, *The Myth of Ham in Nineteenth-Century American Christianity*, 25.

81. Bonilla-Silva, "Rethinking Racism," 465–66.

82. Omi and Winant, *Racial Formations in the United States*, 4; Jennings, *The Christian Imagination*, 290; Cook, *The Least of These: Race, Law, and Reli-*

gion in American Culture, 122; Meer, "Racialization and Religion," 387–89; Rana, "The Story of Islamophobia"; Joshi, "The Racialization of Religion in the United States," 212–16; Ibrahim, "The Origins of Muslim Racialization in U.S. Law," 19; Jacobson and Wadsworth, *Faith and Race in American Political Life*, 9; Blumenfeld, Joshi, and Fairchild, *Investigating Christian Privilege and Religious Oppression in the United States*, 51; Kang, "Trojan Horses of Race."

83. Johnson, *The Myth of Ham in Nineteenth-Century American Christianity*.

84. Miles, *Racism*, 75; Barot and Bird, "Racialization."

85. Dunn, Klocker, and Salabay, "Contemporary Racism and Islamaphobia in Australia," 564, 567.

86. McCloud, "American Muslim Women and U.S. Society"; Cainkar, "Hijab as a Human Right: Hegemonic Femininity and Gender Policing."

87. Mahamdallie, "Islamophobia: The Othering of Europe's Muslims"; Elver, "Racializing Islam before and after 9/11," 119, 174; Rana, "The Story of Islamophobia," 148–61; Khan and Ecklund, "Attitudes toward Muslim Americans Post-9/11."

88. Runneymede Trust, *Islamophobia: A Challenge for Us All*.

89. Taras, "Islamophobia Never Stands Still," 417, 418.

90. Daulatzai and Rana, *With Stones in Our Hands*, xvii–xviii.

91. Kumar, *Islamophobia and the Politics of Empire*; Love, *Islamophobia and Racism in America*; Wajahat Ali, Eli Clifton, Matthew Duss, Lee Fang, Scott Keyes, and Faiz Shakir, "FEAR, Inc.: The Roots of the Islamophobia Network in America," *American Progress*, Aug. 26, 2011, www.americanprogress.org/issues/religion/reports/2011/08/26/10165/fear-inc/.

92. Herberg, *Protestant–Catholic–Jew*. US Rep. Virgil Goode of Virginia stated his opposition to newly elected Rep. Keith Ellison's use of Thomas Jefferson's copy of the Quran for his swearing-in ceremony: "We are leaving ourselves vulnerable to infiltration by those who want to mold the United States into the image of their religion, rather than working within the Judeo-Christian principles that have made us a beacon of freedom-loving persons around the world." Curtis, *Muslims in America*, 106–7. See also Mazur, "Religion, Race, and the American Constitutional Order,", 40–41.

93. Bonilla-Silva, "Rethinking Racism," 470.

94. Harris, "Whiteness as Property," 1707.

95. Haney Lopez, *Merge Left*.

CHAPTER 1. WHEN AMERICAN RACISM QUASHES
RELIGIOUS FREEDOM

1. Green, *Inventing a Christian America*; Wenger, *Religious Freedom*; Daniel Cox et al., "What It Means to Be American: Attitudes towards Increasing Diversity in America Ten Years after 9/11," Public Religion Research Institute, Sept. 6,

2011, www.prri.org/research/what-it-means-to-be-american/ (finding that "88% of Americans agree that America is founded on the idea of religious freedom for everyone, including religious groups that are unpopular").

2. Maghbouleh, *The Limits of Whiteness*.

3. Aziz, "A Muslim Registry," 779, 824 (listing Trump's various Islamophobic comments).

4. McElwee and Cohen, "The Secret to Trump's Success"; Hurd, *Beyond Religious Freedom*; Wadsworth, "Ambivalent Miracles."

5. Joshi, "The Racialization of Hinduism, Islam, and Sikhism in the United States," 215; Gordon, "Race, National Identity, and the Changing Circumstances of Jewish Immigrants in the United States"; Blumenfeld, "Christian Privilege and the Promotion of 'Secular' and Not-So 'Secular' Mainline Christianity in Public Schooling and in the Larger Society," 195, 197; Kerstetter, *God's Country, Uncle Sam's Land*.

6. Green, *Inventing a Christian America*, 60; Jacobson and Wadsworth, *Faith and Race in American Political Life*, 45; Gordon, *Assimilation in American Life*, 87.

7. Green, *Inventing a Christian America*, 59; Jacobson and Wadsworth, *Faith and Race in American Political Life*, 45.

8. Johnson, *The Myth of Ham in Nineteenth-Century American Christianity*, 14–15.

9. Omi and Winant, "Concept of Race," 4.

10. Corrigan and Neal, *Religious Intolerance in America*, 7; Haddad, Smith, and Esposito, *Religion and Immigration*, 1–17; Wenger, *Religious Freedom*, 196.

11. Corrigan and Neal, *Religious Intolerance in America*, 25, 99; Joshi, "The Racialization of Religion in the United States," 37; Green, *Inventing a Christian America*, 52; Wenger, *Religious Freedom*, 1–13.

12. Schildkraut, "The More Things Change..."; Julie Zauzmer, "You Have to Be Christian to Truly Be American? Many People in the U.S. Say So," *Washington Post*, Feb. 1, 2017, www.washingtonpost.com/news/acts-of-faith/wp/2017/02 /01/you-have-to-be-christian-to-truly-be-american-people-in-the-us-are-far-more -likely-to-say-so/?utm_term=.07de557202f1.

13. Harris, "Whiteness as Property," 1707.

14. Painter, *The History of White People*, 108.

15. Omi and Winant, "Concept of Race: Biological Reality or Social Construction?," 75–76; Corrigan and Neal, *Religious Intolerance in America*, 4; Green, *Inventing a Christian America*, 15.

16. Hutchison, *Religious Pluralism in America*, 30–43 (noting the tolerance of religious diversity within Protestantism but opposition to Catholics and other non-Protestants in the early American period).

17. Haney Lopez, *White by Law*, 104.

18. Gordon, "Race, National Identity, and the Changing Circumstances of Jewish Immigrants in the United States," 97; Ewing, *Being and Belonging*, 16; Joshi, "The Racialization of Hinduism, Islam, and Sikhism in the United

States," 212; Ajrouch and Jamal, "Assimilating to a White Identity," 860; Jamal and Naber, *Race and Arab Americans before and after 9/11*.

19. Green, *Inventing a Christian America*, 140.

20. McConnell, "The Problem of Singling Out Religion," 427 (noting the influence of Locke on the drafting of the US Constitution); Hill Fletcher, *The Sin of White Supremacy*, 14; but see Green, "The Separation of Church and State in the United States," 7; Dwight, "The Duty of Americans, at the Present Crisis (1798)."

21. McConnell, "The Problem of Singling Out Religion," 422.

22. Jacobson and Wadsworth, *Faith and Race in American Political Life*, 6, 17; Green, *Inventing a Christian America*, 49; Blumenfeld, "Christian Privilege and the Promotion of 'Secular' and Not-So 'Secular' Mainline Christianity in Public Schooling and in the Larger Society," 197; Hutchison, *Religious Pluralism in America*, 30–43.

23. Hutchison, *Religious Pluralism in America*; Rob Boston, "Christianizing the Constitution?," Americans United for the Separation of Church and State, Oct. 2001, www.au.org/church-state/october-2001-church-state/featured/christianizing-the-constitution.

24. Green, "The Separation of Church and State in the United States," 7.

25. Tocqueville, *Democracy in America*, 326–27.

26. Gordon, *Assimilation in American Life: The Role of Race, Religion, and National Origin*, 81; Jennings, *The Christian Imagination*, 290; see also Cook, *The Least of These: Race, Law, and Religion in American Culture*, 122; Johnson, *The Myth of Ham in Nineteenth-Century American Christianity*, 19.

27. Painter, *The History of White People*, 34.

28. Omi and Winant, *Racial Formation in the United States*, 473; Gomez, *Manifest Destinies*, 58–59.

29. Omi and Winant, *Racial Formation in the United States*, 106, 109.

30. Bonilla-Silva, "Rethinking Racism," 465.

31. Miles, *Racism*.

32. Johnson, *The Myth of Ham in Nineteenth-Century American Christianity*, 19–20.

33. Cheah, *Race and Religion in American Buddhism*, 129.

34. Blumenfeld, Joshi, and Fairchild, *Investigating Christian Privilege and Religious Oppression in the United States*, 38; Feagin, *The White Racial Frame*, 41.

35. Noll, *God and Race in American Politics*, 24–26.

36. Green, *Inventing a Christian America*, 228; Smith, "Religion and Ethnicity in America," 1163 (noting that Puritans adopted an ethnoreligious identity as English Puritans); Wenger, *Religious Freedom*, 6.

37. Blumenfeld, Joshi, and Fairchild, *Investigating Christian Privilege and Religious Oppression in the United States*, 39–40; Fletcher, *The Sin of White Supremacy*, 5.

38. Omi and Winant, *Racial Formation in the United States*.

39. Gordon, *Assimilation in American Life: The Role of Race, Religion, and*

National Origin, 72–73; Painter, *The History of White People*, 185; Marzouki, *Islam: An American Religion*, 24–25.

40. Bellah, "Civil Religion in America"; Williams, "Civil Religion and the Cultural Politics of National Identity in Obama's America," 239.

41. "The 'Jesus Day' Proclamation Official Memorandum," State of Texas, Office of the Governor, Mar. 17, 2000, www.pbs.org/wgbh/pages/frontline/shows /jesus/readings/jesusdaymemo.html.

42. Cesari, *Muslims in the West after 9/11*, 76.

43. Wenger, *Religious Freedom*, 9; Gomez, *Manifest Destinies*, 96.

44. Feener, *Islam in World Cultures*, 284.

45. Jacobson and Wadsworth, *Faith and Race in American Political Life*, 17; Rana, "The Racial Infrastructure of the Terror-Industrial Complex."

46. Love, *Islamophobia and Racism in America*, 42.

47. Gordon, *Assimilation in American Life: The Role of Race, Religion, and National Origin*, 87; Cheah, *Race and Religion in American Buddhism*, 3–4; see also Blumenfeld, Joshi, and Fairchild, *Investigating Christian Privilege and Religious Oppression in the United States*, 45; Friedlander, *Sojourners and Settlers*.

48. Spellberg, *Thomas Jefferson's Quran*, 25; Daulatzai and Rana, *With Stones in our Hands*, xiv.

49. Lisa Argyle, Ian Gray, Matti Nelimarkka, and Rochelle Terman, "Cultural Threats and Islamophobia in American News Media," paper presented at NCAPSA American Politics Workshop, June 6, 2018, 1.

50. Kalkan, Layman, and Uslaner, "'Bands of Others'?"

51. Hafez, "Comparing Anti-Semitism and Islamophobia," 27.

CHAPTER 2. THE COLOR OF RELIGION

Epigraph: International Religious Freedom Act, 22 U.S.C.A. § 6401(a)(1) (2016).

1. US Constitution, Amendment I; Civil Rights Act of 1964 § 7, 42 U.S.C. § 2000e et seq (1964); McConnell, "The Problem of Singling Out Religion," 453.

2. Selod and Embrick, "Racialization and Muslims," 646, https://doi.org/10 .1111/soc4.12057; Tebbe, *Religion and Equality Law*, xi–xxiv.

3. Jacobson and Wadsworth, *Faith and Race in American Political Life*, 5; Feagin, *The White Racial Frame*, 93–94.

4. Wenger, *Religious Freedom*, 20; Schildkraut, *Americanism in the 21st Century*, 66; Hutchison, *Religious Pluralism in America*, 30–43.

5. Sha'ban, *Islam and Arabs in Early American Thought*, 1–2.

6. Ibrahim, "The Origins of Muslim Racialization in U.S. Law," 129; Green, *Inventing a Christian America*, 20.

7. Sha'ban, *Islam and Arabs in Early American Thought*, 1–2, 12–13; Hill Fletcher, *The Sin of White Supremacy*, 50.

8. Hill Fletcher, *The Sin of White Supremacy*, 6.

9. Corrigan and Neal, *Religious Intolerance in America*, 102; Blumenfeld, "Christian Privilege and the Promotion of 'Secular' and Not-So 'Secular' Mainline Christianity in Public Schooling and in the Larger Society," 198; Wenger, *Religious Freedom*, 5.

10. Corrigan and Neal, *Religious Intolerance in America*, 25; Haddad, Smith, and Esposito, *Religion and Immigration*, 17.

11. Jacobson and Wadsworth, *Faith and Race in American Political Life*, 16; Hutchison, *Religious Pluralism in America*, 21–22 (noting that of the 3,200 congregations in 1780, nearly 600 were non–English speaking and over 300 were Quaker meetings).

12. Green, *Inventing a Christian America*, 130; Jacobson and Wadsworth, *Faith and Race in American Political Life*, 5–6; Gomez, *Manifest Destinies*, 86.

13. Melville, *White-Jacket*, 151; Green, *Inventing a Christian America*, 59, 60.

14. Omi and Winant, "Concept of Race," 110; Gottschalk and Greenberg, *Islamophobia: Making Muslims the Enemy*, 97; Paddison, *American Heathens*, 1–2. Similar to the Spaniards who settled Central and South America, the Puritans referred to Native Americans as savages, infidels, heathens, and barbarians. Feagin, *The White Racial Frame*, 43; Gomez, *Manifest Destinies*, 50; Wenger, *Religious Freedom*, 9.

15. Hernandez, "Indigenous Identity and Story," 61, 62.

16. Hill Fletcher, *The Sin of White Supremacy*, 50 (quoting Governor Harvey).

17. Robert C. Winthrop, "Governor Winthrop's Journal: June Meeting, 1872," 233, 239. Quotation from Genesis 1:28, King James Version.

18. Hernandez, "Indigenous Identity and Story," 62–63; Soni, *Freedom from Subordination*, 37; Mazur, "Religion, Race, and the American Constitutional Order," 42 (noting that Native Americans' religious liberty cases have largely failed before the Supreme Court); *Johnson v. McIntosh*, 21 U.S. 543, 572–73 (1823); Corrigan and Neal, *Religious Intolerance in America*, 130, 131; Wenger, *Religious Freedom*, 9.

19. Wenger, *Religious Freedom*, 4; Paddison, *American Heathens*, 3.

20. *Johnson v. McIntosh*, 21 U.S. 543, 572–73 (1823).

21. "Third Charter of Virginia (1612)," Thomas Jefferson Papers at the Library of Congress, vol. 8, Virginia Records Manuscripts, 1606–1737, http://hdl.loc.gov/loc.mss/mtj.mtjbib026587.

22. "A Declaration of Proposals of the Lord Proprietor of Carolina, Aug. 25–Sept. 4, 1663," in *The Federal and State Constitutions Colonial Charters, and Other Organic Laws of the States, Territories, and Colonies Now or Heretofore Forming the United States of America* (1909), edited by Francis Newton Thorpe, http://avalon.law.yale.edu/17th_century/nc02.asp.

23. Jacobson, *Whiteness of a Different Color*, 23.

24. Cremin, *American Education*, 10.

25. Jacobson, *Whiteness of a Different Color*, 32, 33; Brodkin, *How Jews Became White Folks and What That Says about Race in America*, 178; Gomez, *Manifest Destinies*, 58, 59; Esposito and Kalin, *Islamophobia: The Challenge of Pluralism in the*

21st Century, 110 (describing how the spread of Christianity as a civilizing imperial project animated European colonialism in Muslim-majority countries).

26. Soni, *Freedom from Subordination*, 37; Wenger, *Religious Freedom*, 112, 113; Johnson, *The Myth of Ham in Nineteenth-Century American Christianity*, 5–6.

27. Blumenfeld, "Christian Privilege and the Promotion of 'Secular' and Not-So 'Secular' Mainline Christianity in Public Schooling and in the Larger Society," 198; Young, "Indian Removal and Land Allotment," 31.

28. Young, "Indian Removal and Land Allotment," 31; Kumar, *Islamophobia and the Politics of Empire*, 30.

29. Corrigan and Neal, *Religious Intolerance in America*, 140.

30. Corrigan and Neal, *Religious Intolerance in America*, 127; Gomez, *Manifest Destinies*, 50.

31. Wood, "It Wasn't an Accident."

32. Andrew K. Frank, "Five Civilized Tribes," in *Encyclopedia of Oklahoma*, www.okhistory.org/publications/enc/entry.php?entry=FI011. The same association between conversion to Christianity and being civilized applied in the nineteenth century when New Mexico was seeking statehood. Gomez, *Manifest Destinies*, 96; Young, "Indian Removal and Land Allotment," 31–45.

33. Boaz, "Practices 'Odious Among the Northern and Western Nations of Europe.'"

34. Soni, *Freedom from Subordination*, 38; Wenger, *Religious Freedom*, 109.

35. Wenger, *Religious Freedom*, 101 (citing Pawnee Chiefs to the Honorable Cato Sells, Aug. 18, BIA Central Classified Files, 1907–1939, Series B: Indian Customs, Pawnee, Records of the Bureau of Indian Affairs, Record Group 75, National Archives and Records Administration, Washington, DC).

36. Wenger, *Religious Freedom*, 101.

37. Irwin, "Freedom, Law, and Prophecy," 35–36; "Any Indian who shall engage in the sun dance, scalp dance, or war dance, or any similar feast, so called, shall be guilty of an offense" (quoting Thomas J. Morgan, commissioner of the Bureau of Indian Affairs in 1892, in his "Rules for Indian Court" criminalizing Native American religious practices).

38. Wenger, *Religious Freedom*, 105.

39. Wenger, *Religious Freedom*, 121; see generally Peyote Hearings, Subcomm. of the Comm. on Indian Affairs of the House of Rep. on H.R. 2614 (1918), https://archive.org/details/cu31924097625895/page/n5.

40. Peyote Hearings, Subcomm. of the Comm. on Indian Affairs of the House of Rep. on H.R. 2614, 149 (1918), https://archive.org/details/cu31924097625895/page/n5 (quoting Fred Lookout, Chief of the Osage Tribe of Indians in Pawhuska, OK).

41. Wenger, *Religious Freedom*, 125.

42. Wenger, *Religious Freedom*, 122, 123.

43. American Indian Religious Freedom Act of 1978, P. L. No. 95-341, 42 U.S.C.A. § 1996; Theodore B. Olson, "Peyote Exemption for Native American Church: Memorandum Opinion for the Chief Counsel, Drug Enforcement

Administration," Office of Legal Counsel, December 22, 1981, https://www.jus
tice.gov/olc/opinion/peyote-exemption-native-american-church; McConnell,
"Free Exercise Revisionism and the Smith Decision."

44. Johnson, *The Myth of Ham in Nineteenth-Century American Christianity*, 11.

45. Blumenfeld, "Christian Privilege and the Promotion of 'Secular' and Not-So 'Secular' Mainline Christianity in Public Schooling and in the Larger Society," 195–210; Finkelman, "The Crime of Color"; Joshi, "The Racialization of Religion in the United States," 213; Painter, *The History of White People*, 195; Wenger, *Religious Freedom*, 9.

46. Hill Fletcher, *The Sin of White Supremacy*, 11; Johnson, *The Myth of Ham in Nineteenth-Century American Christianity*, 4; Omi and Winant, "Concept of Race," 3.

47. Johnson, *The Myth of Ham in Nineteenth-Century American Christianity*, 5.

48. Johnson, *The Myth of Ham in Nineteenth-Century American Christianity*, 31.

49. Harvey, "A Servant of Servants Shall He Be," 13, 18–19; Hill Fletcher, *The Sin of White Supremacy*, 10–11.

50. Hill Fletcher, *The Sin of White Supremacy*, 11; Johnson, *The Myth of Ham in Nineteenth-Century American Christianity*, 14–15.

51. Blumenfeld, Joshi, and Fairchild, *Investigating Christian Privilege and Religious Oppression in the United States*, 39; Feagin, *The White Racial Frame*, 39; Harvey, "A Servant of Servants Shall He Be," 15; Disney, "Associations between Humanitarianism, Othering, and Religious Affiliation," 60, 61; Selod and Embrick, "Racialization and Muslims," 646.

52. "An Act for the Better Ordering and Governing of Negroes and Slaves," in *Statutes at Large of South Carolina, 1712*, edited by David McCord, vol. 7, 1840, 352; Higginbotham, *In the Matter of Color*, 200; Feagin, *The White Racial Frame*, 46.

53. Tehranian, *Whitewashed*.

54. Joshi, "The Racialization of Religion in America," 212.

55. Blumenfeld, Joshi, and Fairchild, *Investigating Christian Privilege and Religious Oppression in the United States*, 8; Blumenfeld, "Christian Privilege and the Promotion of 'Secular' and Not-So 'Secular' Mainline Christianity in Public Schooling and in the Larger Society," 195–210; Harvey, "A Servant of Servants Shall He Be," 20; Feagin, *The White Racial Frame*, 54.

56. "Virginia Slave Laws," *Statutes at Large; Being a Collection of All the Laws of Virginia, 1667*, edited by William Waller Hening, vol. 11, 1823, 260, www
.swarthmore.edu/SocSci/bdorsey1/41docs/24-sla.html; Tehranian, *White Washed*, 30 (citing Higginbotham, *In the Matter of Color*, 36–37).

57. South Carolina acts relating to slavery, *An Act for the Better Ordering of Slaves*, No. 5T, Section II (stating "no slave shall be free by becoming a christian"), https://archive.org/stream/statutesatlargeoo7edit/statutesatlargeoo7edit_djvu.txt.

58. Turner, "African Muslim Slaves and Islam in Antebellum America."

59. Gottschalk and Greenberg, *Islamophobia: Making Muslims the Enemy*, 22–23.

60. Rana, "The Story of Islamophobia"; Blumenfeld, Joshi, and Fairchild, *Investigating Christian Privilege and Religious Oppression in the United States*, 50; Jacobson and Wadsworth, *Faith and Race in American Political Life*, 42; Wenger, *Religious Freedom*, 8.

61. Qureshi and Sells, *The New Crusades*, 90–119.

62. Wenger, *Religious Freedom*, 6, 9.

63. Harvey, "A Servant of Servants Shall He Be," 15–16.

64. "Truth, Facts and Democracy: The Partisan Divide on Political Values Grows Even Wider," *Pew Research Center*, Oct. 5, 2017, www.people-press.org /2017/10/05/4-race-immigration-and-discrimination.

65. Alba and Nee, *Remaking the American Mainstream*, 103.

66. Roediger, *Working toward Whiteness*, 11; Gordon, "Race, National Identity, and the Changing Circumstances of Jewish Immigrants in the United States," 87 (noting that in 1776, Jews accounted for only 0.1 percent of the population at 1,000 to 2,500, and by 1880, they were 0.5 percent of the population at over 2 million).

67. Roediger, *Working toward Whiteness*, 146.

68. Joshi, "The Racialization of Religion in the United States," 213; Hutchison, *Religious Pluralism in America*, 111–14.

69. Gordon, *The Second Coming of the KKK*, 2.

70. Corrigan and Neal, *Religious Intolerance in America*, 70; Wenger, *Religious Freedom*, 165; Feingold, *The Jewish People in America*, 3.

71. Corrigan and Neal, *Religious Intolerance in America*, 12.

72. Schultz, *Tri-Faith America*, 15, 21; Marable, *Malcolm X*, 21.

73. Gordon, *The Second Coming of the KKK*, 201.

74. Gordon, *The Second Coming of the KKK*, 88.

75. Wadsworth, "The Racial Demons That Help Explain Evangelical Support for Trump."

76. Brodkin, *How Jews Became White Folks*, 56 (stating 23 million immigrants arrived in the United States after 1880).

77. Naff, *Becoming American*, 119–20; Jacobson, *Whiteness of a Different Color*, 43; Naff, "The Early Arab Immigrant Experience."

78. Blumenfeld, "Christian Privilege in the United States," 10.

79. Schultz, *Tri-Faith America*, 18; Brodkin, *How Jews Became White Folks*, 25; Jacobson and Wadsworth, *Faith and Race in American Political Life*, 82.

80. Jacobson and Wadsworth, *Faith and Race in American Political Life*, 54–55, 58.

81. Schultz, *Tri-Faith America*, 18.

82. Painter, *The History of White People*, 250–51.

83. Jacobson and Wadsworth, *Faith and Race in American Political Life*, 82; Painter, *The History of White People*, 210.

84. Blumenfeld, Joshi, and Fairchild, *Investigating Christian Privilege and*

Religious Oppression in the United States, 11; Nick Miroff, "Family Ties Drive U.S. Immigration: Why Trump Wants to Break the 'Chains,'" *Washington Post,* Jan. 2, 2017, www.washingtonpost.com/world/national-security/how-chain-migration -became-a-target-in-trumps-immigration-agenda/2018/01/02/dd30e034-efdb-11e7 -90ed-77167c6861f2_story.html?utm_term=.5da4a78e4ef9.

85. Brodkin, *How Jews Became White Folks,* 29; Gordon, "Race, National Identity, and the Changing Circumstances of Jewish Immigrants in the United States," 90, 91; Gualtieri, *Between Arab and White,* 54; Roediger, *Working toward Whiteness,* 68.

86. Feagin, *The White Racial Frame,* 83 (quoting then–vice president elect Calvin Coolidge's "Whose Country Is This?," *Good Housekeeping Magazine,* Feb. 1921).

87. Roediger, *Working toward Whiteness,* 7.

88. Jacobson and Wadsworth, *Faith and Race in American Political Life,* 79; Smith, *Race, Nationality, and Reality.*

89. Jacobson and Wadsworth, *Faith and Race in American Political Life,* 96–97.

90. Tehranian, *Whitewashed,* 20–21.

91. Tehranian, *Whitewashed,* 28.

92. Painter, *The History of White People,* 286.

93. Gordon, "Race, National Identity, and the Changing Circumstances of Jewish Immigrants in the United States," 82; Roediger, *Working toward Whiteness,* 141; Bjorck, *A Little Olive Leaf.*

94. Brodkin, *How Jews Became White Folks,* 29.

95. Painter, *The History of White People,* 288 (notably, Turks and Greeks were ranked just above the foreign-born average).

96. Cubberley, Ellwood. *Changing Conceptions of Education,* 1909.

97. Jacobson and Wadsworth, *Faith and Race in American Political Life,* 84.

98. *Dillingham Commission's Report on Immigration,* 1911; Roediger, *Working toward Whiteness,* 16.

99. *Dictionary of Race or Peoples,* Dillingham Commission's Report on Immigration, 1911, https://archive.org/details/reportsimmigrato2croxgoog/page/n7.

100. "Immigration Restriction League Report," *Dillingham Commission,* 1910.

101. Jacobson and Wadsworth, *Faith and Race in American Political Life,* 8–9.

102. Tehranian, *Whitewashed,* 24–25.

103. Feingold, *The Jewish People in America,* 26–27.

104. National Origins Act of 1924; Naff, *Becoming American,* 123.

105. Blumenfeld, Joshi, and Fairchild, *Investigating Christian Privilege and Religious Oppression in the United States,* 11; Wenger, *Religious Freedom,* 21.

106. Gordon, *The Second Coming of the KKK,* 195.

107. Blumenfeld, Joshi, and Fairchild, *Investigating Christian Privilege and Religious Oppression in the United States,* 11; Takao Ozawa v. U.S., 260 U.S. 178 (1922) (denying a Japanese immigrant the right to be a naturalized citizen because he was not Caucasian).

108. Kidd, *American Christians and Islam*, 18; 1924 Immigration Act.

109. Feingold, *The Jewish People in America*, 26–29.

110. Roediger, *Working toward Whiteness*, 145.

111. Painter, *The History of White People*, 384; Curtis, *Muslims in America*.

112. Michael Lipka, "Muslims and Islam: Key Findings in the U.S. and around the World," Pew Research Center, Aug. 9, 2017, www.pewresearch.org/fact-tank /2017/08/09/muslims-and-islam-key-findings-in-the-u-s-and-around-the-world/.

CHAPTER 3. RACIALIZATION OF JEWS, CATHOLICS, AND MORMONS IN THE TWENTIETH CENTURY

1. Gordon, "Race, National Identity, and the Changing Circumstances of Jewish Immigrants in the United States," 80; Jacobson, *Whiteness of a Different Color*, 68.

2. Schultz, *Tri-Faith America*, 9–10; Gordon, *Assimilation in American Life*, 91–92; Jacobson and Wadsworth, "Introduction," in *Faith and Race in American Political Life*, 15.

3. Levine, "Matthew, Mark, and Luke," 91; Corrigan and Neal, *Religious Intolerance in America*, 149; Roediger, *Working toward Whiteness*, 32–33.

4. Jacobson, *Whiteness of a Different Color*, 28; Kidd, *American Christians and Islam*, 78.

5. Levine, "Matthew, Mark, and Luke," 91; Corrigan and Neal, *Religious Intolerance in America*, 149.

6. Corrigan and Neal, *Religious Intolerance in America*, 23, 149.

7. Leiner, *The End of Barbary Terror*, 28; letter from George Washington to the Hebrew Congregation at Newport, Aug. 18, 1790, https://founders.archives .gov/documents/Washington/05-06-02-0135.

8. "From Haven to Home: 350 Years of Jewish Life in America," Library of Congress, www.loc.gov/exhibits/haventohome/haven-century.html; Goldstein, *The Price of Whiteness*.

9. Goldstein, *The Price of Whiteness*, 12; Pegelow, "'German Jews,' 'National Jews,' 'Jewish Volk' or 'Racial Jews'?," 195.

10. Corrigan and Neal, *Religious Intolerance in America*, 149; Wenger, *Religious Freedom*, 149.

11. Goldstein, *The Price of Whiteness*, 31.

12. Blumenfeld, "Christian Privilege and the Promotion of 'Secular' and Not-So 'Secular' Mainline Christianity in Public Schooling and in the Larger Society."

13. Goldstein, *The Price of Whiteness*, 12.

14. Goldstein, *The Price of Whiteness*, 102–3.

15. Goldstein, "Contesting the Categories," 79.

16. Goldstein, *The Price of Whiteness*, 108–9.

17. Selod and Embrick, "Racialization and Muslims," 646–47; Fredrickson,

Racism: A Short History, 19; Blumenfeld, Joshi, and Fairchild, *Investigating Christian Privilege and Religious Oppression in the United States*, 39–40.

18. Jacobson, *Whiteness of a Different Color*, 65; Goldstein, *The Price of Whiteness*, 35.

19. Goldstein, *The Price of Whiteness*, 41–42.

20. Haddad, Smith, and Esposito, *Religion and Immigration*, 106, 107; Hutchison, *Religious Pluralism in America*, 113–14.

21. "From Haven to Home"; Gordon, "Race, National Identity, and the Changing Circumstances of Jewish Immigrants in the United States," 83, 84; Selod and Embrick, "Racialization and Muslims," 646–47; Painter, *The History of White People*, 310; Gordon, *Assimilation in American Life*, 241; Schultz, *Tri-Faith America*, 9–10.

22. A century later, the US Supreme Court acknowledged Jews were racialized when the 1866 Civil Rights Act was passed. *Shaare Tafila Congregation v. Cobb*, 481 U.S. 615, 617 (4th Cir. 1987).

23. Samuel Huntington, "The Hispanic Challenge"; Schultz, *Tri-Faith America*, 122; Gottschalk and Greenberg, *Islamophobia: Making Muslims the Enemy*.

24. Wenger, *Religious Freedom*, 148; Jones, "Sound the Tocsin of Alarm."

25. Wenger, *Religious Freedom*, 148, 149; Goldstein, *The Price of Whiteness*, 41–42.

26. Huntington, *The Clash of Civilizations*.

27. Taras, "'Islamophobia Never Stands Still,'" 425.

28. Schultz, *Tri-Faith America*, 24; Gordon, *Assimilation in American Life,* 5.

29. Schneiderman, "The Jews of the United States," 24; Goldstein, *The Price of Whiteness*, 36.

30. Feingold, *The Jewish People in America*, 8–9; Henry Ford, "The International Jew: The World's Foremost Problem."

31. Corrigan and Neal, *Religious Intolerance in America*, 162.

32. Goldstein, *The Price of Whiteness*, 47.

33. Schultz, *Tri-Faith America*, 27.

34. Prashad, "How the Hindus Became Jews," 595.

35. Painter, *The History of White People*, 210; Brodkin, *How Jews Became White Folks and What That Says about Race in America*, 26.

36. Holmes, "Whitecapping," 244; Painter, *The History of White People*, 240.

37. Corrigan and Neal, *Religious Intolerance in America*, 162.

38. David Grubin, "The Jewish Americans: Anti-Semitism in America," PBS, January 2008, www.pbs.org/jewishamericans/jewish_life/anti-semitism.html.

39. Gualtieri, *Between Arab and White*, 77, 131.

40. Roediger, *Working toward Whiteness*, 106; Wenger, *Religious Freedom*, 149.

41. The lynching of Leo Frank prompted the establishment of the Anti-Defamation League. Gualtieri, *Between Arab and White*, 131; Schultz, *Tri-Faith America*, 122.

42. Schultz, *Tri-Faith America*, 92–93.

43. Cowan, "Theologizing Race," 115–16; Feingold, *The Jewish People in America*, 2.

44. Ford, "The International Jew"; Cowan, "Theologizing Race," 115–16; Painter, *The History of White People*, 326.

45. Roediger, *Working toward Whiteness*, 49.

46. Daniel Green and Frank Newport, "American Public Opinion and the Holocaust," *Gallup*, Apr. 23, 2018, https://news.gallup.com/opinion/polling-matters/232949/american-public-opinion-holocaust.aspx; Schultz, *Tri-Faith America*, 122.

47. "U.S. Muslims Concerned about Their Place in Society, but Continue to Believe in the American Dream," Pew Research Center, July 26, 2017, www.pewforum.org/2017/07/26/how-the-u-s-general-public-views-muslims-and-islam/.

48. Schultz, *Tri-Faith America*, 24.

49. Corrigan and Neal, *Religious Intolerance in America*, 149.

50. Feingold, *The Jewish People in America*, 3.

51. Gordon, *Assimilation in American Life*, 175–77; Roediger, *Working toward Whiteness*, 94.

52. Feingold, *The Jewish People in America*, 150.

53. Haddad, Smith, and Esposito, *Religion and Immigration*, 109; Goldstein, *The Price of Whiteness*, 13–14.

54. Feingold, *The Jewish People in America*, 19.

55. Diana B. Turk, "College Students in the United States," in *Jewish Women: A Comprehensive Historical Encyclopedia*, Jewish Women's Archive, Feb. 27, 2009, https://jwa.org/encyclopedia/article/college-students-in-united-states.

56. "Anti-Semitism in the U.S.: Harvard's Jewish Problem," Jewish Virtual Library, www.jewishvirtuallibrary.org/harvard-s-jewish-problem; Feingold, *The Jewish People in America*, 16; Brodkin, *How Jews Became White Folks and What That Says about Race in America*, 31.

57. "May Jews Go to College?," *The Nation* 114 (1922): 708; Schultz, *Tri-Faith America*, 143.

58. Feingold, *The Jewish People in America*, 22–23.

59. Green, *Inventing a Christian America*, 64; Corrigan and Neal, *Religious Intolerance in America*, 50.

60. Wenger, *Religious Freedom*, 5–6.

61. Deuteronomy 25:19; I Samuel 15:3.

62. Corrigan and Neal, *Religious Intolerance in America*, 19.

63. Green, *Inventing a Christian America*, 32; Figueroa, "Quakerism and Racialism in Early Twentieth-Century U.S. Politics."

64. Green, *Inventing a Christian America*, 79.

65. Wenger, *Religious Freedom*, 16–17.

66. An estimated 25,000 Catholics lived in Maryland. Spellberg, *Thomas Jefferson's Quran*, 175; "Proceedings and Acts of the General Assembly of Maryland, *Archives of Maryland 1704–1706*, edited by William Hand Browne, vol. 26, 1906,

340–41, https://msa.maryland.gov/megafile/msa/speccol/sc2900/sc2908/000001/000026/html/index.html; Painter, *The History of White People*, 133; Fisher, *Communion of Immigrants*; Corrigan and Neal, *Religious Intolerance in America*, 5; Blumenfeld, "Christian Privilege and the Promotion of 'Secular' and Not-So 'Secular' Mainline Christianity in Public Schooling and in the Larger Society," 197.

67. Corrigan and Neal, *Religious Intolerance in America*, 149.

68. Gordon, "Race, National Identity, and the Changing Circumstances of Jewish Immigrants in the United States," 81; Yang, "Race, Religion, and Cultural Identity," 119, 124.

69. "An Act passed the 12th of September, 1693, for settling a Ministry and raising a Maintenance for them in the City of New-York, County of Richmond, Westchester and Queens County," Evans Early American Imprint Collection, https://quod.lib.umich.edu/e/evans/N29507.0001.001/1:1?rgn=div1;view=fulltext; Green, *Inventing a Christian America*, 36.

70. Corrigan and Neal, *Religious Intolerance in America*, 50.

71. Noll, *God and Race in American Politics*, 25.

72. In the 1790 US Census, Catholics comprised only one percent of the population, estimated at 35,000 people. Gordon, *Assimilation in American Life*, 196; Stein, *Communities of Dissent*, 9.

73. Green, *Inventing a Christian America*, 185; Feagin, *The White Racial Frame*, 34.

74. *Cantwell v. Connecticut*, 310 U.S. 296 (1940); *Everson v. Board of Education*, 330 U.S. 1 (1947).

75. Green, *Inventing a Christian America*, 56.

76. North Carolina Constitution of 1776, Provision XXXII, http://avalon.law.yale.edu/18th_century/nc07.asp.

77. South Carolina Constitution of 1778, Provision XII, http://avalon.law.yale.edu/18th_century/sc02.asp.

78. New Jersey Constitution of 1776, Provision XIX, http://avalon.law.yale.edu/18th_century/nj15.asp.

79. Corrigan and Neal, *Religious Intolerance in America*, 149.

80. Painter, *The History of White People*, 134; Williams, "The Right of the People Shall Not Be Violated," 1.

81. Duncan, *Citizens or Papists?*, 181; "Reports of the Proceedings and Debates of the New York Constitutional Convention," 1821, 679–80, https://nysl.ptfs.com/data/Library1/118314.pdf.

82. Archie P. Jones, "Remaining Early States' History of Religious Freedom and Disestablishment: South Carolina, New Jersey, Delaware, Pennsylvania, Maryland, Georgia, Rhode Island," *Constituting America*, https://constitutingamerica.org/remaining-early-states-history-religious-freedom-disestablishment-sc-nj-de-pa-md-ga-ri-archie-p-jones/; Corrigan and Neal, *Religious Intolerance in America*, 37.

83. Fisher, *Communion of Immigrants*, 71; Gordon, *Assimilation in American Life*, 96–97.

84. "The American Protestant vindicator, and defender of civil and religious liberty against the inroads of popery," American Society for the Promotion of the Principles of the Reformation, New York, 1836–39, https://chroniclingamerica.loc.gov/lccn/sn92060570/; Painter, *The History of White People*, 137.

85. Morse, *Foreign Conspiracy Against the Liberties of the United States.*

86. Froude, "Romanism and the Irish Race."

87. Strong, *Our Country.*

88. Wenger, *Religious Freedom*, 21.

89. Hutchison, *Religious Pluralism in America*, 139.

90. Kidd, *American Christians and Islam*, 36.

91. Kidd, "Is It Worse to Follow Mahomet Than the Devil?"

92. Reeve, *Religion of a Different Color*, 39–40; Schultz, *Tri-Faith America*, 19.

93. Fisher, *Communion of Immigrants*, 73.

94. Fisher, *Communion of Immigrants*, 44, 51.

95. Gordon, *Assimilation in American Life*, 197; Fisher, *Communion of Immigrants*, ix.

96. Loring, *Report of the Committee, Relating to the Destruction of the Ursuline Convent, August 11, 1834.*

97. Zachary M. Schrag, "Nativist Riots of 1844," *Encyclopedia of Greater Philadelphia*, 2013, https://philadelphiaencyclopedia.org/archive/nativist-riots-of-1844/; Corrigan and Neal, *Religious Intolerance in America*, 51.

98. Corrigan and Neal, *Religious Intolerance in America*, 51.

99. Corrigan and Neal, *Religious Intolerance in America*, 63.

100. Jacobson, *Whiteness of a Different Color*, 41–42.

101. Fisher, *Communion of Immigrants*, 82–83; Wenger, *Religious Freedom*, 26.

102. Schultz, *Tri-Faith America*, 87; Fisher, *Communion of Immigrants*, 95.

103. Gordon, "'Free' Religion and 'Captive' Schools"; *Sherrard v. Jefferson County Bd. of Educ.*, 171 S.W.2d 963 (Ky. 1943); *Borden v. La. State Bd. of Educ.*, 123 So. 655 (La. 1929): *Bd. of Educ. v. Wheat*, 199 A. 628 (Md. 1938); *Chance v. Miss. State Textbook Rating & Purchasing Bd.*, 200 So. 706 (Miss. 1941); *Judd v. Bd. of Educ. of Union Free Sch. Dist. No. 2*, 15 N.E.2d 576 (N.Y. 1938); *Gurnev v. Ferguson*, 122 P.2d 1002 (Okla. 1941); *Mitchell v. Consol. Sch. Dist. No. 201.*, 135 P.2d 79 (Wash. 1943). But see *Everson v. Board of Education*, 330 U.S. 1 (1947) (upholding the constitutionality of a New Jersey statute allocating taxpayer funds to bus children to religious schools); Jones, *The End of White Christian America*, 12, 32–34.

104. Macedo, *Diversity and Distrust*, 130.

105. Corrigan and Neal, *Religious Intolerance in America*, 69.

106. Macedo, *Diversity and Distrust*, 130.

107. Schultz, *Tri-Faith America*, 19–20.

108. Schultz, *Tri-Faith America*, 9–10.

109. Gordon, *Assimilation in American Life*, 152–53.

110. Gordon, *Assimilation in American Life*, 53.

111. Wenger, *Religious Freedom*, 175.

112. Gordon, *Assimilation in American Life*, 93.

113. Corrigan and Neal, *Religious Intolerance in America*, 52.

114. The Secret Oath of the American Protective Association, Oct. 31, 1893, 103–4, http://historymatters.gmu.edu/d/5351/; Gordon, *Assimilation in American Life*, 27.

115. Gordon, *Assimilation in American Life*, 27.

116. Jacobson, *Whiteness of a Different Color*, 70; Haddad, Smith, and Esposito, *Religion and Immigration*, 36.

117. Painter, *The History of White People*, 148.

118. Gordon, *Assimilation in American Life*, 196.

119. John F. Kennedy, Speech to Greater Houston Ministerial Association, Sept. 12, 1960, www.npr.org/templates/story/story.php?storyId=16920600; Peter Braestrup, "Protestant Unit Wary on Kennedy; Statement by Peal Group Sees Vatican Pressure on Democratic Nominee," *New York Times*, Sept. 8, 1960.

120. Corrigan and Neal, *Religious Intolerance in America*, 52, 71.

121. Curtis, *The Bloomsbury Reader on Islam in the West*, 168; Bail, *Terrified*, 101; Thomas, *Scapegoating Islam*, 110; Qureshi and Sells, *The New Crusades*, 101–2; Gordon, *The Second Coming of the KKK*, 149; Pipes, "The Muslims are Coming!," 28.

122. Corrigan and Neal, *Religious Intolerance in America*, 70.

123. Hutchison, *Religious Pluralism in America*, 48–50; Haddad, *Becoming American?*, 78.

124. Jacobson, *Whiteness of a Different Color*, 70.

125. Fisher, *Communion of Immigrants*, 47; Jacobson, *Whiteness of a Different Color*, 4–5. Tehranian, *Whitewashed*, 21–23; Stovall, *White Freedom*, 151–52.

126. Emerson, *Selected Essays, Lectures and Poems*, 284; Painter, *The History of White People*, 141; Roediger, *Working toward Whiteness*, 133.

127. Painter, *The History of White People*, 138.

128. Corrigan and Neal, *Religious Intolerance in America*, 54.

129. Kessner and Caroli, *Today's Immigrants, Their Stories*, 149; Fisher, *Communion of Immigrants*, 45.

130. Fisher, *Communion of Immigrants*, 47.

131. Reeve, *Religion of a Different Color*, 18–19.

132. Corrigan and Neal, *Religious Intolerance in America*, 73, 126.

133. Prentiss, "'Loathsome unto Thy People,'" 128.

134. Corrigan and Neal, *Religious Intolerance in America*, 79, 183.

135. Davis, "Some Themes of Counter-Subversion."

136. Corrigan and Neal, *Religious Intolerance in America*, 74.

137. Blair, "Haun's Mill Massacre," 577; Hutchison, *Religious Pluralism in America*, 52–53.

138. Hill, "Carthage Conspiracy Reconsidered."

139. Corrigan and Neal, *Religious Intolerance in America*, 75.

140. Reeve, *Religion of a Different Color*, 25–26.

141. Reeve, *Religion of a Different Color*, 15.

142. Reeve, *Religion of a Different Color*, 34–35.

143. Corrigan and Neal, *Religious Intolerance in America*, 77.

144. Reeve, *Religion of a Different Color*, 229.

145. Corrigan and Neal, *Religious Intolerance in America*, 79.

146. Reeve, *Religion of a Different Color*, 230.

147. Fluhman, "An 'American Mahomet,'" 32, 43.

148. Corrigan and Neal, *Religious Intolerance in America*, 91; Philpott, "Islam: The World's Largest Cult?," *Evangelical Times,* Feb. 2002, www.evangelical-times .org/27331/islam-the-worlds-largest-cult-2/; Randy Kleine, "Islam the Ultimate Political Cult," *Cincinnati.com*, Mar. 22, 2017, www.cincinnati.com/story/news /local/milford/2017/03/22/column-islam-ultimate-political-cult/99210446/; Olivier Roy, "Islam and the Cult of Death," *Open Magazine,* Mar. 31, 2017, www .openthemagazine.com/article/cover-story/islam-and-the-cult-of-death.

149. *Reynolds v. U.S.*, 98 U.S. 145 (1878).

150. Reeve, *Religion of a Different Color*, 231.

151. Kidd, *American Christians and Islam*, 26.

152. Caleb Lyon, *Congressional Globe* (33–1), May 4, 1854, 1100–1101; Reeve, *Religion of a Different Color*, 224.

153. *Reynolds v. United States*, 98 U.S. 145, 164 (1878).

154. Corrigan and Neal, *Religious Intolerance in America*, 79.

155. Feagin, *The White Racial Frame*, 79.

156. *Chae Chin Ping v. US*, 130 U.S. 581 (1889).

157. Alba and Nee, *Remaking the American Mainstream*, 44.

158. Blumenfeld, Joshi, and Fairchild, *Investigating Christian Privilege and Religious Oppression in the United States*, 51; Jacobson and Wadsworth, "Introduction," in *Faith and Race in American Political Life*, 6–7; Kim, "The Racial Triangulation of Asian Americans," 105, 110; Paddison, *American Heathens*, 8.

159. 39th Cong., 1st sess. 2766, *Congressional Globe*, 1866 (quoting William Higby); Jacobson and Wadsworth, "Introduction," in *Faith and Race in American Political Life*, 7; Paddison, *American Heathens*, 3–4.

160. *Butte Bystander* (Montana), Feb. 11, 1893; Swartout, "From Kwangtung to the Big Sky," 78.

161. Hon. Edward R. Meade, "The Chinese Question," address to annual meeting of the Social Science Association of America, Saratoga, NY, Sept. 7, 1887, https://immigrationhistory.org/item/scott-act.

162. Speech of Hon. A. A. Sargent of California, in the Senate of the United States, Mar. 7, 1878, https://oac.cdlib.org/ark:/13030/hb387002gk/?brand=oac4; Hill Fletcher, *The Sin of White Supremacy*, 1.

163. Chinese Exclusion Act of 1882.

164. *Fong Yue Ting v. United States*, 149 U.S. 698 (1893).

165. The Magnuson Act of 1943, signed by President Franklin D. Roosevelt, repealed the Chinese Exclusion Act.

166. Joo, "Presumed Disloyal," 1, 28 (citing *People v. Brady*, 40 Cal. 198 [1870]); *People v. George Hall*, 4 Cal. 399 [1854]).

167. *Plessy v. Ferguson*, 163 U.S. 537 (1896) (dissenting, Justice Harlan); *In re Ah Yup*, 1 Fed. Cas. 223 (1878).

168. Singh, "'Everything I'm Not Made Me Everything I Am,'" 54, 65.

169. California Alien Land Law Act of 1913; Immigration Act of 1917; Cheng, *Citizens of Asian America*, 26.

170. Koshy, "Morphing Race into Ethnicity," 169.

171. Ama, "American Buddhism during World War II Imprisonment," in *Oxford Research Encyclopedias,* Aug. 2018, https://oxfordre.com/religion/view/10.1093/acrefore/9780199340378.001.0001/acrefore-9780199340378-e-593#acrefore-9780199340378-e-593-bibliography-0001; Corrigan and Neal, *Religious Intolerance in America*, 3.

172. Joo, "Presumed Disloyal," 20–21.

173. DeWitt, Testimony before House Naval Affairs Committee April 1943, https://text-message.blogs.archives.gov/2013/11/22/a-slaps-a-slap-general-john-l-dewitt-and-four-little-words/; "A More Perfect Union: Japanese and the U.S. Constitution," Smithsonian National Museum of American History, https://amhistory.si.edu/perfectunion/non-flash/removal_process.html.

174. Joo, "Presumed Disloyal," 20, 21; Blumenfeld, "Christian Privilege and the Promotion of 'Secular' and Not-So 'Secular' Mainline Christianity in Public Schooling and in the Larger Society," 195–210; Cheng, *Citizens of Asian America*, 6; Feagin, *The White Racial Frame*, 111, 112.

175. Corrigan and Neal, *Religious Intolerance in America*, 3.

176. Bonilla-Silva, *Racism without Racists*, 470; Mazur, *The Americanization of Religious Minorities*, 39–40; Roediger, *Working toward Whiteness*, 241.

177. Kim, "The Racial Triangulation of Asian Americans," 105, 107.

178. Cheah, *Race and Religion in American Buddhism*, 84.

179. Cheng, *Citizens of Asian America*, 4, 5.

180. Cheah, *Race and Religion in American Buddhism*, 86; Hsu, *The Good Immigrants*.

181. Gordon, *Assimilation in American Life*, 101–2.

182. Painter, *The History of White People*, 301.

183. Blumenfeld, Joshi, and Fairchild, *Investigating Christian Privilege and Religious Oppression in the United States*, 40.

184. Joshi, "The Racialization of Religion in America," 211. See also Joshi, *White Christian Privilege*; Martinez, Hernandez, and Pena, "Latino Religion and Its Political Consequences."

185. Gottschalk and Greenberg, *Islamophobia: Making Muslims the Enemy*, 94.

CHAPTER 4. FROM PROTESTANT TO JUDEO-CHRISTIAN NATIONAL IDENTITY

1. Jacobson, *Whiteness of a Different Color*, 10.
2. Spellberg, *Thomas Jefferson's Quran*.
3. Harris, "Whiteness as Property," 1707.
4. Roediger, *Working toward Whiteness*, 13.
5. Jacobson, *Whiteness of a Different Color*, 8, 9; Cheah, *Race and Religion in American Buddhism*, 10; Gordon, *The Second Coming of the KKK*, 27.
6. Gordon, "Race, National Identity, and the Changing Circumstances of Jewish Immigrants in the United States," 97; Schultz, *Tri-Faith America*, 7.
7. Koshy, "Morphing Race into Ethnicity"; Alba, *Ethnic Identity*.
8. Alba and Nee, *Remaking the American Mainstream*, 101.
9. Feagin, *The White Racial Frame*, 117; Wenger, *Religious Freedom*, 12–13; Bonilla-Silva, "Rethinking Racism," 902–3; Omi and Winant, *Racial Formation in the United States*, 46.
10. Gans, "Toward a Reconciliation of 'Assimilation' and 'Pluralism,'" 877 (noting the difference between acculturation and assimilation, wherein the former occurs more quickly than the latter); Omi and Winant, *Racial Formation in the United States*, 22; Gomez, *Manifest Destinies*, 2–3.
11. Bonilla-Silva, "Rethinking Racism," 902–3.
12. Massad, *Islam in Liberalism*.
13. Brodkin, *How Jews Became White Folks and What That Says about Race in America*, 37; Conzen et al., "The Invention of Ethnicity," 13; Roediger, *Working toward Whiteness*, 53.
14. Tehranian, *Whitewashed*, 40. But see Nathan Glazer's work acknowledging that assimilation is not linear because later generations may return to their ethnic roots based on nostalgia or ideology.
15. Jacobson and Wadsworth, *Faith and Race in American Political Life*, 14–15.
16. Roediger, *Working toward Whiteness*, 68.
17. Gordon, *Assimilation in American Life*, 142; Barkan, "Race, Religion, and Nationality in American Society," 46.
18. Goldstein, *The Price of Whiteness*, 90–91.
19. James Baldwin and William Buckley, "Debate: Has the American Dream Been Achieved at the Expense of the American Negro?," Cambridge Union, Feb. 18, 1965, www.youtube.com/watch?v=VOCZOHQ7fCE.
20. Tehranian, *Whitewashed*, 46–47.
21. Brodkin, *How Jews Became White Folks and What That Says about Race in America*, 72; Gomez, *Manifest Destinies*, 45, 100–101; Tehranian, *Whitewashed*, 20–23.
22. Jacobson, *Whiteness of a Different Color*, 12; Gordon, *Assimilation in American Life*, 32, 33 (quoting E. B. Tylor, *Primitive Culture* [1871]); Roediger, *Working toward Whiteness*, 69; Goldstein, *The Price of Whiteness*, 1–7.

23. Alba and Nee, *Remaking the American Mainstream*.

24. Cheah, *Race and Religion in American Buddhism*, 9, 10.

25. Park and Burgess, *Introduction to the Science of Sociology*, 735.

26. Park, *Race and Culture*, 150.

27. Roediger, *Working toward Whiteness*, 53.

28. Gordon, *Assimilation in American Life*, 72. All migrants from Europe were granted legally White status, although they were not treated as White socially. Roediger, *Working toward Whiteness*, 61.

29. Gordon, *Assimilation in American Life*, 72.

30. Barkan, "Race, Religion, and Nationality in American Society," 47–48.

31. Barkan, "Race, Religion, and Nationality in American Society," 59.

32. Alba and Nee, *Remaking the American Mainstream*.

33. Gordon, *Assimilation in American Life*, 158.

34. Gordon, *Assimilation in American Life*, 145.

35. Feagin, *The White Racial Frame*, xi, 10–11; Omi and Winant, *Racial Formation in the United States*, 22.

36. Jung, "The Racial Unconscious of Assimilation Theory," 384.

37. Feagin, *The White Racial Frame*, 10.

38. Omi and Winant, *Racial Formation in the United States*, 39, 40.

39. Shapiro, *A Time for Healing*, 254.

40. Cheah, *Race and Religion in American Buddhism*, 80.

41. Roediger, *Working toward Whiteness*, 20; Gans, "Toward a Reconciliation of 'Assimilation' and 'Pluralism,'" 877.

42. Roediger, *Working toward Whiteness*, 22; Gordon, *The Second Coming of the KKK*, 50 (noting that Jews were referred to as a race and an ethnicity during the 1920s).

43. Roediger, *Working toward Whiteness*, 52.

44. Feagin, *The White Racial Frame*, 93, 94.

45. Satzewich, "Whiteness Limited," 271, 278.

46. Gordon, *Assimilation in American Life*, 77, 78.

47. Qureshi and Sells, *The New Crusades*, 173; Goldstein, *The Price of Whiteness*, 2–3.

48. Goldstein, *The Price of Whiteness*, 52–55.

49. Omi and Winant, *Racial Formation in the United States*, 29; Gomez, *Manifest Destinies*, 2, 3; Alba and Nee, *Remaking the American Mainstream*, 11–13.

50. Jacobson, *Whiteness of a Different Color*, 110–11.

51. Susan K. Brown and Frank D. Bean, "Assimilation Models, Old and New: Explaining a Long-Term Process," Migration Policy Institute, Oct. 1, 2006, www.migrationpolicy.org/article/assimilation-models-old-and-new-explaining-long-term-process; Jacobson, *Whiteness of a Different Color*, 10, 11; Feagin, *The White Racial Frame*, 80, 81.

52. Jung, "The Racial Unconscious of Assimilation Theory."

53. "A Poor Parallel," *Modern View St. Louis* 22 (May 4, 1906): 2; Goldstein, *The Price of Whiteness*, 55–57.

54. Goldstein, *The Price of Whiteness*, 58, 63.

55. Dollinger, *Black Power, Jewish Politics*.

56. Omi and Winant, *Racial Formation in the United States*, 22.

57. Tehranian, *Whitewashed*, 160.

58. Stovall, *White Freedom*, 108.

59. "The New Orleans Affair," *New York Times*, Mar. 16, 1891, https://timesmachine.nytimes.com/timesmachine/1891/03/16/103299119.pdf; Roediger, *Working toward Whiteness*, 52.

60. "Italy's Claim for Lynching: Louisiana's Reply Causes the Government to Apologize," *New York Times*, Aug. 28, 1896, 9, https://timesmachine.nytimes.com/timesmachine/1896/08/29/103387206.html?pageNumber=9; Roediger, *Working toward Whiteness*, 67.

61. "The Convention," *Times-Democrat*, Mar. 22, 1898; Roediger, *Working toward Whiteness*, 47; Stovall, *White Freedom*, 180.

62. Roediger, *Working toward Whiteness*, 46; Tehranian, *Whitewashed*, 24.

63. Roediger, *Working toward Whiteness*, 47 (citing Indictments, Appearance Bonds, and Court Summons, 1908–1920, Tangipahoa Parish Clerk of Court Office, Amite City, LA; Charter Book No. 1, pp. 81–93, 135–41, Tangipahoa Parish Clerk of Court Office; *Hammond Vindicator*, Aug. 6, 1937; Senate Documents, 61st Cong., 2nd sess., vol. 84, p. 268).

64. Tehranian, *Whitewashed*, 24.

65. Roediger, *Working toward Whiteness*, 67.

66. Feagin, *The White Racial Frame*, 196.

67. Roediger, *Working toward Whiteness*, 136–37; Shapiro, *A Time for Healing*, 54.

68. Roediger, *Working toward Whiteness*, 196 (noting a 1969 Current Population Survey that found a little over half of the respondents didn't know when asked of their national origin).

69. Roediger, *Working toward Whiteness*, 25; Tehranian, *White Washed*, 20.

70. Smith, "Religion and Ethnicity in America," 1155–56; Bonilla-Silva, "Rethinking Racism," 902–3.

71. Peek, "Becoming Muslim," 218; Roediger, *Working toward Whiteness*, 29.

72. Smith, "Religion and Ethnicity in America," 1169; Prentiss, "Introduction," *Religion and the Creation of Race and Ethnicity*.

73. Hammond, *Religion and Personal Autonomy*, 7–8.

74. Goldstein, *The Price of Whiteness*, 88–89.

75. Goldstein, *The Price of Whiteness*, 94–95; Louis D. Brandeis, "The Jewish Problem: How to Solve It," speech to the Conference of Eastern Council of reform Rabbis, Apr. 25, 1915, https://louisville.edu/law/library/special-collections/the-louis-d.-brandeis-collection/the-jewish-problem-how-to-solve-it-by-louis-d.-brandeis.

76. Conzen et al., "The Invention of Ethnicity," 4–5.

77. Alba, *Ethnic Identity*, 82–83; Roediger, *Working toward Whiteness*, 20.

78. Campbell J. Gibson and Emily Lennon, "Historical Census Statistics

on the Foreign-Born Population of the United States: 1850–1990," US Census Bureau, www.census.gov/population/www/documentation/twps0029/twps0029 .html (the 2.2 million foreign-born population in 1850 comprised 9.7 percent of the total population); Stovall, *White Freedom*, 176–77.

79. Barry, *The Catholic Church and German Americans*, 4–7; Hutchison, *Religious Pluralism in America*, 25–27.

80. Barry, *The Catholic Church and German Americans*, 4–7.

81. Barry, *The Catholic Church and German Americans*, 8–10.

82. Barry, *The Catholic Church and German Americans*, 184–85.

83. Stovall, *White Freedom*, 83–84.

84. Bakalian and Bozorgmehr, *Backlash 9/11*, 34–35.

85. Bakalian and Bozorgmehr, *Backlash 9/11*, 34, 35.

86. *The German Catholics in the United States of America*, 36, Records of the American Catholic Historical Society of Philadelphia, 305–58 (1924); Bakalian and Bozorgmehr, *Backlash 9/11*, 35, 36.

87. Bakalian and Bozorgmehr, *Backlash 9/11*, 34, 35; Aziz, "A Muslim Registry," 779, 824.

88. "German Enemy of U.S. Hanged By Mob: Robert P. Prager Taken from Jail and Strung Up to Tree by 300 Men and Boys after Officers Are Overpowered," *St. Louis Globe-Democrat*, Apr. 5, 1918, https://web.viu.ca/davies/h324war /prager.lynching.1918.htm; Bakalian and Bozorgmehr, *Backlash 9/11*, 34, 35; Steve Nagy, "German immigrant in Collinsville was the first lynched on US soil during WWI," *Miami Herald*, Apr. 17, 2018, 5:10 PM, www.miamiherald.com/news /local/article209158554.html. See also John J. Dunphy, "The Lynching of Robert Prager: A World War I Hate Crime," *Medium*, Nov. 17, 2018, https://medium .com/@johnjdunphy/the-lynching-of-robert-prager-a-world-war-i-hate-crime -11b7a5e567a.

89. Bakalian and Bozorgmehr, *Backlash 9/11*, 34, 35.

90. Bakalian and Bozorgmehr, *Backlash 9/11*, 56.

91. Haddad, Smith, and Esposito, *Religion and Immigration*, 33.

92. Gordon, *Assimilation in American Life*, 135.

93. Painter, *The History of White People*, 318.

94. Omi and Winant, *Racial Formation in the United States*, 43; Alba and Foner, *Strangers No More*.

95. Brodkin, *How Jews Became White Folks and What That Says about Race in America*, 65; Barkan, "Race, Religion, and Nationality in American Society," 59.

96. Conzen et al., "The Invention of Ethnicity," 14.

97. Barkan, "Race, Religion, and Nationality in American Society," 66; Bonilla-Silva, "Rethinking Racism," 902, 903.

98. Johnson, *The Myth of Ham in Nineteenth-Century American Christianity*, 5–6.

99. Wenger, *Religious Freedom*, 194, 198, 204.

100. Wenger, *Religious Freedom*, 196.

101. Wenger, *Religious Freedom*, 200, 201.

102. Wenger, *Religious Freedom*, 195; Julie Moreau, "129 anti-LGBTQ state bills were introduced in 2017, new report says," *NBC News,* Jan. 12, 2018, www .nbcnews.com/feature/nbc-out/129-anti-lgbtq-state-bills-were-introduced -2017-new-report-n837076; "End the Use of Religion to Discriminate," American Civil Liberties Union, www.aclu.org/issues/religious-liberty/using-religion -discriminate/end-use-religion-discriminate.

103. Wenger, *Religious Freedom*, 192.

104. Roediger, *Working toward Whiteness*, 30, 119, 230. Susan Koshy's work examines how Chinese Americans engaged in the same racial distancing from Blacks in the South by affirming the practice of segregation as part of their unsuccessful attempts to place their children in the White schools. See Koshy, "Morphing Race into Ethnicity," 175.

105. Roediger, *Working toward Whiteness*, 223, 224, 225.

106. Glazer and Moynihan, *Beyond the Melting Pot.*

107. Cheah, *Race and Religion in American Buddhism*, 10.

108. Roediger, *Working toward Whiteness*, 136; Blumenfeld, "Christian Privilege in the United States," 202.

109. Silk, "The Abrahamic Religions as a Modern Concept."

110. Wenger, *Religious Freedom*, 175.

111. Hutchison, *Religious Pluralism in America*, 196; Feingold, *The Jewish People in America*, 122–23.

112. Schultz, *Tri-Faith America*, 50, 51.

113. Wenger, *Religious Freedom*, 145.

114. Hutchison, *Religious Pluralism in America*, 123–26.

115. Goldstein, *The Price of Whiteness*, 90.

116. "U.S. Presidential Elections: Jewish Voting Record (1916–present)," Jewish Virtual Library, www.jewishvirtuallibrary.org/jewish-voting-record-in-u-s -presidential-elections; Feingold, *The Jewish People in America*, 198.

117. Gordon, "Race, National Identity, and the Changing Circumstances of Jewish Immigrants in the United States," 93, 94.

118. Wenger, *Religious Freedom*, 168, 173.

119. Brodkin, *How Jews Became White Folks and What That Says about Race in America*, 37.

120. *Good News Club v. Milford Central School*, 533 U.S. 98; *Lee v. Weisman*, 505 U.S. 577; Schultz, *Tri-Faith America*, 11.

121. *U.S. v. Carolene Products Co.*, 304 U.S. 144, 152n4 (1938) (describing the heightened scrutiny applied in situations where the law or statute conflicts with Bill of Rights protections and when regulations impact "discrete and insular minorities," creating a new role for the federal courts to protect individual rights).

122. Shapiro, *A Time for Healing*, 5n8; Worrell, "Signifying the Jew" (citing Paul Massing and A. R. L. Gurland et. al. "Anti-Semitism among American Labor," Institute of Social Research of Columbia University [1944–45], https://doi .org/10.1016/S0278-1204(08)00006-6).

123. Gordon, "Race, National Identity, and the Changing Circumstances of

Jewish Immigrants in the United States," 92; Cheng, *Citizens of Asian America*, 45.

124. James, *Why Negroes Should Oppose the War*, www.marxists.org/archive /james-clr/works/1939/xx/war.htm; Jacobson, *Whiteness of a Different Color*, 111.

125. Roediger, *Working toward Whiteness*, 25, 26; Gordon, "Race, National Identity, and the Changing Circumstances of Jewish Immigrants in the United States," 91, 92.

126. Wenger, *Religious Freedom*, 179; Shapiro, *A Time for Healing*, 53.

127. Goldstein, *The Price of Whiteness*, 17; Gordon, "Race, National Identity, and the Changing Circumstances of Jewish Immigrants in the United States," 91–92; Painter, *The History of White People*, 357; Johnson, *The Myth of Ham in Nineteenth-Century American Christianity*, 14–15.

128. Schultz, *Tri-Faith America*, 50, 72–73.

129. Wenger, *Religious Freedom*, 172; Straus, *Religious Liberty and Democracy Writings and Addresses*; Feingold, *The Jewish People in America*, 249.

130. Bulliet, *The Case for Islamo-Christian Civilization*, 6–7.

131. Feingold, *The Jewish People in America*, 220–34.

132. Wenger, *Religious Freedom*, 186; Gordon, *The Second Coming of the KKK*, 199, 200; Shapiro, *A Time for Healing*, 16.

133. Herberg, *Protestant–Catholic–Jew*; Ghanea Bassiri, *A History of Islam in America*, 63–64.

134. Stein, "Some Reflections on Will Herberg's Insights and Oversights."

135. Fisher, *Communion of Immigrants*, 124. Herberg, *Protestant–Catholic–Jew*, 74–81; Mazur, "Religion, Race, and the American Constitutional Order"; Haddad, Smith, and Esposito, *Religion and Immigration*, 5; Hutchison, *Religious Pluralism in America*, 201–4.

136. Haddad, Smith, and Esposito, *Religion and Immigration*, 5.

137. Albert L. Winseman, "Religion 'Very Important' to Most Americans," *Gallup*, Dec. 20, 2005, news.gallup.com/poll/20539/religion-very-important-most -americans.aspx (describing Gallup polls from 1952 and 1957); Schultz, *Tri-Faith America*, 74.

138. Schultz, *Tri-Faith America*, 74–75.

139. Feingold, *The Jewish People in America*, 98–99.

140. Shapiro, *A Time for Healing*, 190.

141. Shapiro, *A Time for Healing*, 190; Kaplan, *American Reform Judaism*, 82.

142. Gordon, "Race, National Identity, and the Changing Circumstances of Jewish Immigrants in the United States," 96.

143. Feingold, *The Jewish People in America*, 93–94.

144. Gordon, *Assimilation in American Life*, 193, 194; Feingold, *The Jewish People in America*, 88.

145. Feingold, *The Jewish People in America*, 103.

146. Shapiro, *A Time for Healing*, 168.

147. Neusner, "Jew and Judaist, Ethnic and Religious," 93; Alba and Nee,

Remaking the American Mainstream, 92 (noting that according to the 1990 US Census, half of Jews married since 1985 married partners of a different religion).

148. Shapiro, *A Time for Healing*, 233; Feingold, *The Jewish People in America*, xvi.

149. Kaplan, *American Reform Judaism*, 24–25.

150. Roediger, *Working toward Whiteness*, 196 (citing a November 1969 Current Population Survey).

151. Alba and Nee, *Remaking the American Mainstream*, 91.

152. Feingold, *The Jewish People in America*, 143–44.

153. Brodkin, *How Jews Became White Folks and What That Says about Race in America*, 40–41.

154. Feingold, *The Jewish People in America*, 140–41, 220.

155. Feingold, *The Jewish People in America*, 127–28.

156. Brodkin, *How Jews Became White Folks and What That Says about Race in America*, 40–41.

157. Schultz, *Tri-Faith America*, 202, 203; Haddad, Smith, and Esposito, *Religion and Immigration*, 109.

158. Feingold, *The Jewish People in America*, 145.

159. Shapiro, *A Time for Healing*, xv.

160. Shapiro, *A Time for Healing*, 39–40.

161. Shapiro, *A Time for Healing*, 39–40.

162. Shapiro, *A Time for Healing*, 18.

163. Schultz, *Tri-Faith America*, 202, 203. In a 1981 poll, three quarters of Americans stated they would vote for a qualified Jew for president. See Shapiro, *A Time for Healing*, 39–40.

164. Painter, *The History of White People*, 383.

165. Gordon, *Assimilation in American Life*, 196.

166. Peel and Donnelly, "The 1928 Campaign, an Analysis," 456–57; Roediger, *Working toward Whiteness*, 152, 153.

167. Airhart and Lamberts Bendroth, *Faith Traditions and the Family*, 55n10 ("By 1957, 45 percent of the population in the northeastern states, and 37.8 percent of the population in all large urban areas, identified themselves as Catholic"); Cunningham, *An Introduction to Catholicism*, 22; Finke and Stark, *The Churching of America*, 13–16; Fisher, *Communion of Immigrants*, 125.

168. Schultz, *Tri-Faith America*, 202, 203.

169. Cheng, *Citizens of Asian America*, 62–63.

170. Shapiro, *A Time for Healing*, 52.

171. Gordon, "Race, National Identity, and the Changing Circumstances of Jewish Immigrants in the United States," 95; Feingold, *The Jewish People in America*, 93.

172. Schultz, *Tri-Faith America*, 202, 203.

173. Roediger, *Working toward Whiteness*, 152, 153 (noting that by then, more than seventy percent of foreign-born immigrants were U.S. citizens).

174. Fletcher Knebel, "Democratic Forecast: A Catholic in 1960," *LOOK*, Mar. 3, 1959; Fisher, *Communion of Immigrants*, 132–33.

175. Gordon, "Race, National Identity, and the Changing Circumstances of Jewish Immigrants in the United States," 94.

176. Bellah, "Civil Religion in America."

177. Gordon, "Race, National Identity, and the Changing Circumstances of Jewish Immigrants in the United States," 94–95.

178. Schultz, *Tri-Faith America*, 193.

179. Roediger, *Working toward Whiteness*, 137.

180. "An Appeal to the Conscience of the American People," *National Conference on Religion and Race*, Jan. 17, 1963, www.senate.gov/artandhistory/history /resources/pdf/CivilRightsFilibuster_MaidenSpeechTedKennedy.pdf; Schultz, *Tri-Faith America* 183, 184.

181. Cheng, *Citizens of Asian America*, 63, 173.

182. Maira, *The 9/11 Generation*, 91.

183. "Records of the President's Committee on Civil Rights Record Group 220," Harry S. Truman Presidential Library & Museum, www.trumanlibrary .org/hstpaper/pccr.htm; Dudziak, *Cold War Civil Rights*; Gergel, *Unexampled Courage*.

184. Cheng, *Citizens of Asian America*, 192.

185. Brief for the United States as Amicus Curiae, *Brown v. Board of Educ.*, 347 U.S. 483 (1954); Jacobson, *Whiteness of a Different Color*, 113.

186. Civil Rights Act of 1964 § 7, 42 U.S.C. § 2000e et seq (1964).

187. Lyndon B. Johnson, "Radio and Television Address at the Signing of the 1964 Civil Rights Act," www.blackpast.org/1964-lyndon-b-johnson-radio-and -television-address-signing-1964-civil-rights-act.

188. Cheng, *Citizens of Asian America*, 6, 7; "An act to repeal the Chinese Exclusion Acts, to establish quotas, and for other purposes," 78th Congress, H.R. 3070. Dec. 17, 1943, www.loc.gov/law/help/statutes-at-large/78th-congress/session -1/c78s1ch344.pdf.

189. Cheng, *Citizens of Asian America*, 176. "An act to revise the laws relating to immigration, naturalization, and nationality; and for other purposes (Immigration and Nationality Act)," H.R. 5678, June 27, 1952, www.govinfo.gov/content /pkg/STATUTE-66/pdf/STATUTE-66-Pg163.pdf.

190. Cheng, *Citizens of Asian America*, 125.

191. Theoharis, *Abuse of Power*.

192. Feingold, *The Jewish People in America*, 220–24.

193. Freedland, *Witch Hunt in Hollywood*; Feingold, *The Jewish People in America*, 6–7.

194. Shapiro, *A Time for Healing*, 35–36; "Execution of the Rosenbergs: 'Enemies of Democracy,'" *The Guardian*, June 20, 1953, www.theguardian.com/world /1953/jun/20/usa.fromthearchive.

195. Shapiro, *American Reform Judaism*, 38.

196. Cole, *Enemy Aliens*.

197. Cheah, *Race and Religion in American Buddhism*, 134.

198. Cheng, *Citizens of Asian America*, 16.

199. Bell, "*Brown v. Board of Education* and the Interest-Convergence Dilemma," 518; Bell, "Brown v. Board of Education and the Interest-Convergence Dilemma," 93.

200. Ghanea Bassiri, *A History of Islam in America*, 55; Rana, "The Story of Islamophobia," 148.

CHAPTER 5. SOCIAL CONSTRUCTION OF THE RACIAL MUSLIM

1. Moore, *Al-Mughtaribun*, 35 (quoting the first US ambassador to Persia supporting immigration restrictions: "As for the Asiatic races, however brilliant they may be in certain directions, they have never had any clear notion of self-government, as understood by many Caucasian people of northern Europe, a matter of blood rather than education in its origin"); Ewing, *Being and Belonging*, 16.

2. Bulliet, *The Case for Islamo-Christian Civilization*, 6.

3. Joshi, "The Racialization of Hinduism, Islam, and Sikhism in the United States," 212; Ghanea, "Religion, Equality, and Non-Discrimination."

4. Hickman, "Globalization and the Gods, or the Political Theology of 'Race,'" 153; Feener, *Islam in World Cultures*; Kumar, *Islamophobia and the Politics of Empire*, 38.

5. Kidd, *American Christians and Islam*, 15; Said, *Covering Islam*, 8, 157; Esposito and Kalin, *Islamophobia: The Challenge of Pluralism in the Twenty-First Century*, 175; Sha'ban, *Islam and Arabs in Early American Thought*, 42.

6. Thomas, *Scapegoating Islam*, 2; Lyons, *Islam through Western Eyes*, 133–35.

7. Mastnak, "Western Hostility toward Muslims."

8. Mastnak, "Western Hostility toward Muslims," 32–33.

9. Love, *Islamophobia and Racism in America*, 39; Gottschalk and Greenberg, *Islamophobia: Making Muslims the Enemy*, 22–23.

10. Mastnak, "Western Hostility toward Muslims," 35.

11. Little, *American Orientalism*, 12.

12. Said, *Orientalism*; Cheah, *Race and Religion in American Buddhism*, 3, 21.

13. Esposito and Kalin, *Islamophobia: The Challenge of Pluralism in the Twenty-First Century*, 145–46; Kumar, *Islamophobia and the Politics of Empire*, 34–35.

14. Selod and Embrick, "Racialization and Muslims," 646. Orientalism also undergirded eugenics, which legitimated White supremacy in the United States. Esposito and Kalin, *Islamophobia: The Challenge of Pluralism in the Twenty-First Century*, 145–46.

15. Love, *Islamophobia and Racism in America*, 40; Said, *Orientalism*.

16. George W. Bush, speech presented to the American Legion National

Convention, Salt Lake City, UT, Aug. 31, 2006, https://georgewbush-whitehouse
.archives.gov/news/releases/2006/08/20060831-1.html; Kumar, *Islamophobia and
the Politics of Empire*, 113; Peek, *Behind the Backlash.*

17. Massad, *Islam in Liberalism*, 49–51.

18. Spellberg, *Thomas Jefferson's Quran*, 27.

19. Said, *Covering Islam*, 30; Sha'ban, *Islam and Arabs in Early American
Thought*, 27–28.

20. Esposito and Kalin, *Islamophobia: The Challenge of Pluralism in the
Twenty-First Century*, 176.

21. Mastnak, "Western Hostility toward Muslims," 38.

22. Thomas, *Scapegoating Islam*, 3; Esposito and Kalin, *Islamophobia: The
Challenge of Pluralism in the Twenty-First Century*, 176; John Foxe, *Acts and Monuments of These Latter and Perillous Dayes*, ed. Harold J. Chadwick.

23. Prideaux, *The True Nature of Imposture Displayed in the Life of Mahomet*,
27–28; Kidd, *American Christians and Islam*, 8–9.

24. Thomas, *Scapegoating Islam*, 3; Gottschalk and Greenberg, *Islamophobia:
Making Muslims the Enemy*, 79; Spellberg, *Thomas Jefferson's Quran*, 18–19.

25. Spellberg, *Thomas Jefferson's Quran*, 14–15.

26. Said, *Covering Islam*, 15; Thomas, *Scapegoating Islam*, 3.

27. Antonius, *The Arab Awakening*, 35–45.

28. Kidd, *American Christians and Islam*, 36.

29. Kidd, *American Christians and Islam*, 9; Carney and Stuckey, "The World
as the American Frontier," 165; Love, *Islamophobia and Racism in America*, 40.

30. Kidd, *American Christians and Islam*, 6 (citing Jonathan Edwards, *A History of the Work of Redemption* [New York, 1816]).

31. Green, *Inventing a Christian America*, 213.

32. Little, *American Orientalism*, 12.

33. Kidd, *American Christians and Islam*, 18; Kumar, *Islamophobia and the
Politics of Empire*, 15–16.

34. Haddad, *Becoming American?*, 41; Sha'ban, *Islam and Arabs in Early American Thought*, ix.

35. Spellberg, *Thomas Jefferson's Quran*, 25.

36. Henry Jessup, a Presbyterian missionary in Syria, held strong negative
views of Islam. Kidd, *American Christians and Islam*, 48; Feener, *Islam in World
Cultures*, 286.

37. Sha'ban, *Islam and Arabs in Early American Thought*, 84.

38. Leiner, *The End of Barbary Terror*, 8; Esposito and Kalin, *Islamophobia: The
Challenge of Pluralism in the Twenty-First Century*, 110.

39. Spellberg, *Thomas Jefferson's Quran*, 132–33, 216.

40. Leiner, *The End of Barbary Terror*, 1–2, 13.

41. Sha'ban, *Islam and Arabs in Early American Thought*, 76–77.

42. Leiner, *The End of Barbary Terror*, 17.

43. Kidd, *American Christians and Islam*, 21.

44. Everett and Bingham, *Slaves in Barbary*; Rowson, *Slaves in Algiers*; Sha'ban, *Islam and Arabs in Early American Thought*, 76–77.

45. More than 100 Barbary captivity editions were published between 1798 and 1817 in the United States. Leiner, *The End of Barbary Terror*, 18; Thomas, *Scapegoating Islam*, 13.

46. Thomas, *Scapegoating Islam*, 4. Tellingly, the image of Christian slavery was used by abolitionists in opposing Black slavery in the United States. Kidd, *American Christians and Islam*, 36; Stovall, *White Freedom*, 51.

47. There were failed efforts of abolitionists to use White slavery in the Barbary states to call for the end of Black slavery in America. Leiner, *The End of Barbary Terror*, 175.

48. "The Early Muslim Presence and Its Significance," in Marable and Aidi, eds., *Black Routes to Islam*, 8.

49. Kidd, *American Christians and Islam*, 6. *The Sheik* (1921) portrayed stereotypes of the savage Arab. See also Jacobson, *Whiteness of a Different Color*, 5.

50. Forrell, "Luther and the War against the Turks," 264; Spellberg, *Thomas Jefferson's Quran*, 15.

51. Kidd, *American Christians and Islam*, 8.

52. Jessup, *The Mohammedan Missionary Problem*.

53. Spellberg, *Thomas Jefferson's Quran*, 5–6.

54. Spellberg, *Thomas Jefferson's Quran*, 119–22, 230.

55. Papers of Thomas Jefferson, 1:548; Spellberg, *Thomas Jefferson's Quran*, 237–38.

56. Daouf, *Servants of Allah*.

57. Kidd, *American Christians and Islam*, 19; Said, *Covering Islam*, 42.

58. Guir, *The Life of Mahomet*; Gottschalk and Greenberg, *Islamophobia: Making Muslims the Enemy*, 19–20; Sha'ban, *Islam and Arabs in Early American Thought*, 33.

59. Twain, *The Innocents Abroad*.

60. Irving, *Mahomet and His Successors & Spanish Legends*; Little, *American Orientalism*, 13.

61. Esposito and Kalin, *Islamophobia: The Challenge of Pluralism in the Twenty-First Century*, 154–55.

62. Gottschalk and Greenberg, *Islamophobia: Making Muslims the Enemy*, 36; Shaheen, *Reel Bad Arabs*.

63. Esposito and Kalin, *Islamophobia: The Challenge of Pluralism in the Twenty-First Century*, 156–57; Selod, "Criminalization of Muslim American Men in the United States."

64. Thomas, *Scapegoating Islam*, vii–x. The number of Syrians in the United States in 1908 was estimated to be between 100,000 and 150,000. Naff, *Becoming American*, 108. The Syrian population, which was predominantly Christian, was so small that it did not attract any national attention, in contrast to the large number of Jewish and Catholic immigrants from Southern and Eastern Europe. Naff, *Becoming American*, 248.

65. Naturalization Act of 1790, Sess. II, Chap. 3; 1 Stat 103. 1st Cong., Mar. 26, 1790.

66. Asultany, *Arabs and Muslims in the Media*, 9.

67. Some historians estimate that between 27,000 and 36,000 Muslims emigrated from the Ottoman Empire to the United States between 1860 and 1914, while others estimate closer to 60,000. Thomas, *Scapegoating Islam*, 15. Ottoman conscription laws placed restrictions on Muslim subjects from emigrating. Bakalian and Bozorgmehr, *Backlash 9/11*, 72.

68. Little, *American Orientalism*, 10.

69. Comparisons have been made between Arab Bedouins and Native Americans in writings by American travelers to the Middle East in the nineteenth century. Sha'ban, *Islam and Arabs in Early American Thought*, 187–89.

70. Kahera, "Muslim Spaces and Mosque Architecture," 229–30.

71. Kahera, "Muslim Spaces and Mosque Architecture," 229–30; Curtis, *Muslims in America*, 54.

72. Howell, "Laying the Groundwork for American Muslim Histories," 45.

73. Howell, "Laying the Groundwork for American Muslim Histories," 47.

74. Naff, *Becoming American*, 2; Gualtieri, *Between Arab and White*, 47; Orfalea, *The Arab Americans*.

75. Naff, *Becoming American*, 13.

76. Gualtieri, *Between Arab and White*, 50; Hitti, *The Syrians in America*.

77. Ewing, *Being and Belonging*, 109–11.

78. Naff, *Becoming American*, 199; Haddad, *Becoming American?*, 3–4.

79. Naff, *Becoming American*, 85, 112.

80. Curtis, *Muslims in America*, 50; Haddad, *Not Quite American?*, 3–4.

81. Naff, *Becoming American*, 110; Haddad, *Becoming American?*, 3.

82. Naff, *Becoming American*, 15.

83. Naff, *Becoming American*, 15.

84. Gualtieri, *Between Arab and White*, 151.

85. Gualtieri, *Between Arab and White*, 52; Bawardi, *The Making of Arab Americans*.

86. Naturalization Act of 1790 Sess. II, Chap. 3; 1 Stat 103. 1st Cong., Mar. 26, 1790; Naff, *Becoming American*, 252.

87. The 1930 U.S. Census reported over fifty percent of the foreign-born Syrians were naturalized U.S. citizens, the same percentage as southern Italians. Gualtieri, *Between Arab and White*, 80; Naff, *Becoming American*, 253.

88. Naff, *Becoming American*, 254.

89. Samhan, "Not Quite White."

90. Gordon, "Race, National Identity, and the Changing Circumstances of Jewish Immigrants in the United States," 82–83.

91. Gualtieri, *Between Arab and White*, 52–53.

92. Naff, *Becoming American*, 252.

93. Gordon, "Race, National Identity, and the Changing Circumstances of

Jewish Immigrants in the United States," 89; Koshy, "Morphing Race into Ethnicity," 164.

94. Courts accepted a Syrian applicant's status as a White free person within
the meaning of Rev. St. § 2169 because "fair or dark complexion should not
be allowed to control, provided the person seeking naturalization comes within
the classification of the white or Caucasian race, and [District Judge Newman]
consider[s] the Syrians as belonging to what we recognize, and what the world
recognizes, as the white race." *In re Najour*, 174 F. 735 (N.D. Ga. 1909). But later,
they rejected the Whiteness of a Syrian applicant and found that "the meaning of
free white persons is to be such as would have naturally been given to it when used
in the first naturalization act of 1790[,]...such persons as were in 1790 known
as white Europeans." *Ex parte Shahid*, 205 F. 812, 814 (E.D. S.C. 1913). Gordon,
"Race, National Identity, and the Changing Circumstances of Jewish Immigrants
in the United States," 82–83 (citing Haney Lopez, *White by Law*).

95. Ten of the fifty-three naturalization hearings during this era involved
a petitioner from the "Arab World." Beydoun, "Between Muslim and White,"
29. Joseph R. Haiek, Dept. of Justice Affirms Arab Race in 1909, in *Arab
American Almanac* (News Circle Publ'g House, 6th ed., 2010) (1972), www
.arabamericanhistory.org/archives/dept-of-justice-affirms-arab-race-in-1909/;
Gordon, "Race, National Identity, and the Changing Circumstances of Jewish
Immigrants in the United States," 88.

96. Thomas, *Scapegoating Islam*, 18; 1891 Immigration Act, Sess. II, Chap. 551;
26 Stat. 1084. 51st Cong. (Mar. 3, 1891).

97. Gualtieri, *Between Arab and White*, 59.

98. *In re Ellis*, 179 Fed. 1003 (1910).

99. Gualtieri, *Between Arab and White*, 63.

100. *Ellis*, 1004; Gualtieri, *Between Arab and White*, 65; *Takao Ozawa v.
United States*, 260 U.S. 178 (1922).

101. *Ellis*, 1003.

102. *In re Mudarri*, 176 F. 465 (D.C. Mass. 1910); *Najour*, 735; Gualtieri,
Between Arab and White, 51.

103. *Najour*, 735.

104. *Mudarri*, 466.

105. According to the 1910 U.S. Census, "eastern Mediterranean" included
Syrians, Palestinians, Turks, and Armenians. 1917 Immigration Law, 39 Stat. 874,
http://library.uwb.edu/Static/USimmigration/39%20stat%20874.pdf; Moore,
"Muslims in the American Legal System," 143; Naff, *Becoming American*, 253.

106. The Supreme Court of the United States affirmed that the applicant, a
high-caste Hindu, was not considered White within the meaning of Section 2169,
Revised Statutes (Comp. St. § 4358) and therefore found that he was ineligible for
naturalization. *U.S. v. Bhagat Singh Thind*, 43 S.Ct. 338 (1923); Moore, "Muslims
in the American Legal System," 145.

107. The Immigration Act of 1917 banned a list of undesirables from entering
the country. Gualtieri, "Becoming 'White.'"

108. Although courts in the early 1900s rejected government claims that one had to be of European descent to be a free White person eligible to naturalized, they acknowledged the legal bases for the claim. *Ellis*, 1002, 1003; *Dow v. United States*, 226 F. 145 (1915).

109. *Shahid*, 814.

110. *Dow,* 148; Gualtieri, *Between Arab and White*, 61.

111. Naff, *Becoming American*, 257; *Takao Ozawa v. United States*, 260 U.S. 178 (1922).

112. Gualtieri, *Between Arab and White*, 66.

113. *Bhagat Singh Thind*, 338; Tehranian, *Whitewashed*, 43–45.

114. Chinese Exclusion Repeal Act, P. L. No. 78-199, 57 Stat. 600 (1943); Luce-Celler Act of 1946, P. L. no. 483 (1946); Moore, "Muslims in the American Legal System," 145.

115. Gualtieri, *Between Arab and White*, 132.

116. Halaby, H. E. "SYRIAN CITIZENSHIP; Says Syrians Should Not Be Classed among Mongolians," *New York Times,* Oct. 15, 1909.

117. Naff, *Becoming American*, 252.

118. Gualtieri, *Between Arab and White*, 57n73.

119. "Mob in Florida Lynches White Man; Wife Slain," *New York Evening World,* May 17, 1929; 71 Cong. Rec. 2502 (1929) (statement of Sen. Theodore Burton condemning Sen. Reed's disparaging remarks about Syrians); Gualtieri, *Between Arab and White*, 4.

120. Gualtieri, *Between Arab and White*, 72, 132; Roediger, *Working toward Whiteness*, 119.

121. *In re Halladjian*, 174 F. 834, 838–39 (1909)

122. Gordon, "Race, National Identity, and the Changing Circumstances of Jewish Immigrants in the United States," 85 (citing NARA, RG 85, entry 26, box 1572, file 19783/43, pt. 1).

123. *Halladjian*, 840–41; Love, *Islamophobia and Racism in America*, 40.

124. *United States v. Cartozian*, 6 F.2d 919, 920 (D.C. Or. 1925).

125. Tehranian, *White Washed*, 52–53.

126. *In re Ahmed Hassan*, 48 F.Supp. 843 (1942).

127. *Hassan*, 845.

128. *Ex parte Mohriez*, 54 F.Supp. 941, 942-43 (1944) (citing the official publication of the Immigration and Naturalization Service, *Monthly Review* 1 [Oct. 1943]: 12–16).

129. *Mohriez*, 943.

130. *Mohriez*, 943.

131. Little, *American Orientalism*, 47–48.

132. Qureshi and Sells, *The New Crusades*, 57–58; Gottschalk and Greenberg, *Islamophobia: Making Muslims the Enemy*, 38.

133. "The Great Migration," HISTORY.com, Mar. 4, 2010, www.history.com /topics/black-history/great-migration.

134. Johnson, *The Myth of Ham in Nineteenth-Century American Christianity*, 23.

135. Daouf, *Servants of Allah*, 278–80.

136. Beydoun, "Antebellum Islam," 141.

137. Feener, *Islam in World Cultures*, 289.

138. Daouf, *Servants of Allah*, 21.

139. Daouf, *Servants of Allah*, 43.

140. Daouf, *Servants of Allah*, 26.

141. Daouf, *Servants of Allah*, 30–32.

142. Daouf, *Servants of Allah*, 161.

143. Daouf, *Servants of Allah*, 87.

144. Alford, Prince among Slaves, 119.

145. Daouf, *Servants of Allah*, 132; Marable and Hishaam, "The Early Muslim Presence and Its Significance," in *Black Routes to Islam*, 6.

146. Alford, *Prince among Slaves*, 126.

147. Daouf, *Servants of Allah*, 251.

148. Daouf, *Servants of Allah*, 253.

149. Daouf, *Servants of Allah*, 257.

150. Curtis, *Muslims in America,* 93; McCloud, *African American Islam.*

151. Howell, "Laying the Groundwork for American Muslim Histories," 45–64, 52–53.

152. Moustafa Bayoumi, "East of the Sun (West of the Moon)," in *Black Routes to Islam*, ed. Marable and Aidi, 70–73.

153. Marable, *Malcolm X*, 84.

154. Bowen, Patrick Denis, *The African-American Islamic Renaissance and the Rise of the Nation of Islam*, 250–53, University of Denver, 2013, https://digital commons.du.edu/etd/963; Curtis, *Black Muslim Religion in the Nation of Islam.*

155. Curtis, *Muslims in America,* 32. Hansford, "Jailing a Rainbow"; Justin Hansford, "Marcus Garvey's Message and Why a Pardon for Him Matters," *Huffington Post*, Dec. 23, 2016, www.huffpost.com/entry/marcus-garveys-message -and-why-a-pardon-for-him-matters_b_585c68f4e4b068764965bba1.

156. Marable, *Malcolm X*, 83.

157. Kidd, *American Christians and Islam*, 97; Sherman Jackson, "Black Orientalism: Its Genesis, Aims, and Significance for American Islam," in Marable and Aidi, eds., *Black Routes to Islam*, 33–47.

158. Marable, *Malcolm X*, 82.

159. Feener, *Islam in World Cultures*, 292.

160. Marable, *Malcolm X*, 82.

161. Kidd, *American Christians and Islam*, 100–101; Howell, "Laying the Groundwork for American Muslim Histories," 54.

162. Howell, "Laying the Groundwork for American Muslim Histories," 55; Abdullah, "American Muslims in the Contemporary World," 74.

163. Kidd, *American Christians and Islam*, 97, 105; Paden, "Political Advocacy through Religious Organization? The Evolving Role of the Nation of Islam."

164. Marable, *Malcolm X*, 123.

165. Abdul Khabeer, *Muslim Cool*, 52–53.

166. Marable, *Malcolm X*, 100.

167. Marable, *Malcolm X*, 224.

168. Marable, *Malcolm X*, 251–52.

169. Kidd, *American Christians and Islam*, 118; Abdul Khabeer, *Muslim Cool*, 25.

170. Curtis, *Muslims in America*, 15–16.

171. Edward E. Curtis, IV, "Islamism and Its African American Muslim Critics," in Marable and Aidi, eds., *Black Routes to Islam*, 49–68.

172. Curtis, IV, "Islamism and Its African American Muslim Critics," 90. A 730-page FBI report included a catalog of all African American Muslim organizations despite the FBI's failure to find any evidence of collusion between African American Muslim groups and Japanese agents. Thomas, *Scapegoating Islam*, 20.

173. "Black Militants," in *Civil Rights in a Northern City: Philadelphia*, digitized archive, *Temple University Libraries*, http://northerncity.library.temple.edu/exhibits/show/civil-rights-in-a-northern-cit/people-and-places/black-militants; "God in America," *PBS*, www.pbs.org/godinamerica/people/malcolm-x.html.

174. Marable, *Malcolm X*, 422–24.

175. Thomas, *Scapegoating Islam*, 24; COINTELPRO Report: Black Extremist, https://vault.fbi.gov/cointel-pro/cointel-pro-black-extremists/cointelpro-black-extremists-part-01-of/view.

176. Thomas, *Scapegoating Islam*, 23.

177. Thomas, *Scapegoating Islam*, 24.

178. Gottschalk and Greenberg, *Islamophobia: Making Muslims the Enemy*, 101.

179. Thomas, *Scapegoating Islam*, 22.

180. Curtis, *Muslims in America*, 37; *Clay v. United States*, 403 U.S. 698 (1971).

181. Love, *Islamophobia and Racism in America*, 40; Bulliet, *The Case for Islamo-Christian Civilization*, 30–31.

182. Haddad and Smith, "Introduction," xi; Nacos and Torres-Reyna, *Fueling Our Fears*, 42–43; Bassiouni, *The Civil Rights of Arab-Americans: The Special Measures*.

CHAPTER 6. AMERICAN ORIENTALISM AND THE ARAB
TERRORIST TROPE

1. Thomas, *Scapegoating Islam*, vii–x.

2. "Political Reforms in Persia: Minister Pearson to the Secretary of State," in *Papers Relating to the Foreign Relations of the United States*, vol. 2 (Washington, D.C.: Government Printing Office, 1909), 1217.

3. Love, *Islamophobia and Racism in America*, 42.

4. Ewing, *Being and Belonging*, 110–11; Zarrugh, "Racialized Political Shock."

5. James J. Zogby, "Washington Watch: Balfour, the Shame and Dangers of Ignoring Arab Opinion and Rights," Arab American Institute, Nov. 4, 2017, www .aaiusa.org/balfour_the_shame_and_dangers_of_ignoring_arab_opinion_and _rights; King-Crane Commission Report, 1919, https://ecf.org.il/issues/issue/1367.

6. Lansing, *The Peace Negotiations*, 97–98; Alsultany, *Arabs and Muslims in the Media*, 101–2.

7. Little, *American Orientalism*, 150.

8. Said, *Covering Islam*, 28–29; McAlister, *Epic Encounters*.

9. Said, *Covering Islam*, 28.

10. Love, *Islamophobia and Racism in America*, 41.

11. Thomas, *Scapegoating Islam*, vii–x.

12. Said, *Covering Islam*, 112.

13. Feener, *Islam in World Cultures*, 286–87; Joshi, "The Racialization of Religion in the United States," 46.

14. Haddad and Smith, "Introduction," in *Religion and Immigration*, xi; Said, *Orientalism*; Little, *American Orientalism*, 35; Al-Qazzaz, "Images of the Arab in American Social Science Textbooks"; McAlister, *Epic Encounters*.

15. Love, *Islamophobia and Racism in America*, 42; Little, *American Orientalism*, 15; Barlow, *Evaluation of Secondary-Level Textbooks for Coverage of the Middle East and North Africa*.

16. Qureshi and Sells, *The New Crusades*, 101–2.

17. "Britain and France Conclude Sykes-Picot Agreement," *History*, www .history.com/this-day-in-history/britain-and-france-conclude-sykes-picot -agreement

18. Franklin Foer, "Selling Land to Jews," *Slate*, May 18, 1997, https://slate .com/news-and-politics/1997/05/selling-land-to-jews.html; Charles Glass, "The Mandate Years: Colonialism and the Creation of Israel," *The Guardian*, May 31, 2001, www.theguardian.com/books/2001/may/31/londonreviewofbookks?.

19. Said, *The Question of Palestine*, 116–18.

20. "British White Paper of 1939," Avalon Project: Documents in Law, History, and Diplomacy at Yale Law School, https://avalon.law.yale.edu/20th _century/brwh1939.asp; Feingold, *The Jewish People in America*, 174, 228.

21. Feingold, *The Jewish People in America*, 100–115.

22. Said, *The Question of Palestine*; Feingold, *The Jewish People in America*, 185–86, 244–45.

23. Little, *American Orientalism*, 23.

24. Little, *American Orientalism*, 87; Gottschalk and Greenberg, *Islamophobia: Making Muslims the Enemy*, 40–41.

25. Shapiro, *A Time for Healing*.

26. Shapiro, *A Time for Healing*, 28.

27. "Jewish Population in the United States, Nationally," Jewish Virtual Library, www.jewishvirtuallibrary.org/jewish-population-in-the-united-states -nationally; Little, *American Orientalism*, 81.

28. Shapiro, *A Time for Healing*, 211.

29. Richard H. Curtiss, "Truman Adviser Recalls May 14, 1948 U.S. Decision to Recognize Israel," *Washington Report on Middle East Affairs,* May–June 1991, 17; Little, *American Orientalism,* 81.

30. Said and Hitchens, *Blaming the Victims,* 5–6; Said, et. al., "A Profile of the Palestinian People."

31. Little, *American Orientalism,* 9; Qureshi and Sells, *The New Crusades,* 116.

32. Little, *American Orientalism,* 24.

33. Haddad, *Becoming American?,* 1–16.

34. Alsultany, *Arabs and Muslims in the Media,* 8; Sha'ban, *Islam and Arabs in Early American Thought,* 196–98.

35. David Friedman, "Spirit of Camp David at Emmy Awards; Holocaust Wins 8 Emmys," *Jewish Telegraphic Agency,* Sept. 20, 1978, www.jta.org/1978/09 /20/archive/spirit-of-camp-david-at-emmy-awards-holocaust-wins-8-emmys.

36. "Sophie's Choice—Awards," *IMDB,* www.imdb.com/title/tt0084707 /awards.

37. Sha'ban, *Islam and Arabs in Early American Thought,* viii–x.

38. Kidd, *American Christians and Islam,* 72; Salaita, *Anti-Arab Racism in the United States,* 169.

39. Esposito and Kalin, *Islamophobia: The Challenge of Pluralism in the 21st Century,* 110; Feagin, *The White Racial Frame,* 26–27.

40. Kidd, *American Christians and Islam,* 72.

41. Bail, *Terrified,* 22.

42. Salaita, *Holy Land in Transit;* Salaita, *Anti-Arab Racism in the United States,* 2006; Little, *American Orientalism,* 4.

43. Little, *American Orientalism,* 30–31.

44. Little, *American Orientalism,* 127.

45. Haddad, *Becoming American?,* 41.

46. Little, *American Orientalism,* 11; Treaty of Versailles, Article 22, https:// avalon.law.yale.edu/imt/parti.asp.

47. "CIA Report SR-13: Arab World," Office of Privacy Coordination, CIA, Sept. 27, 1949, https://www.cia.gov/readingroom/docs/1953-12-01.pdf.

48. Little, *American Orientalism,* 27; Massad, *Islam in Liberalism,* 97.

49. "Memorandum of Discussion at the 410th Meeting of the National Security Council, Washington, June 18, 1959," Office of the Historian, United States Department of State, https://history.state.gov/historicaldocuments/frus1958 -60v16/d36.

50. Little, *American Orientalism,* 131, 180.

51. Khalidi, *The Hundred Years' War on Palestine,* 102–6.

52. Khalidi, *The Hundred Years' War on Palestine,* 144.

53. Khalidi, *The Hundred Years' War on Palestine,* 168; Gottschalk and Greenberg, *Islamophobia: Making Muslims the Enemy,* 112.

54. Little, *American Orientalism,* 168; Gottschalk and Greenberg, *Islamophobia: Making Muslims the Enemy,* 112.

55. Massad, *Islam in Liberalism,* 77

56. Bulliet, *The Case for Islamo-Christian Civilization*, 99–101.

57. Massad, *Islam in Liberalism*, 81.

58. Kumar, *Islamophobia and the Politics of Empire*, 64.

59. Kumar, *Islamophobia and the Politics of Empire*, 67–71.

60. Gottschalk and Greenberg, *Islamophobia: Making Muslims the Enemy*, 101.

61. "Oil Take-over Pact Announced by Iraq," *New York Times*, Mar. 1, 1973, www.nytimes.com/1973/03/01/archives/oil-takeover-pact-announced-by-iraq-iraq-oil-nationalization-pact.html.

62. Little, *American Orientalism*, 314.

63. Little, *American Orientalism*; Gottschalk and Greenberg, *Islamophobia: Making Muslims the Enemy*, 42.

64. Salaita, *Anti-Arab Racism*, 44.

65. Khalidi, *The Hundred Years' War on Palestine*, 8–14.

66. Maira, *The 9/11 Generation*, 137.

67. Little, *American Orientalism*, 25, 32.

68. Gualtieri, *Between Arab and White*, 170; Haddad, *Becoming American?*, 92–93; Maira, *The 9/11 Generation*, 136–37; Pennock, *The Rise of the Arab American Left*, 1–79.

69. Thomas, *Scapegoating Islam*; Stockton, "Ethnic Archetypes and the Arab Image."

70. Gottschalk and Greenberg, *Islamophobia: Making Muslims the Enemy*, 122.

71. Feagin, *The White Racial Frame*, 157.

72. Haddad, *Becoming American?*, 18–19; Pennock, *The Rise of the Arab American Left*, 143–53.

73. Pennock, *The Rise of the Arab American Left*, 147–48; Griggs, "Fattah Islamic Party in North America."

74. Haddad, *Becoming American?*, 18–19; Pennock, *The Rise of the Arab American Left*, 149.

75. Love, *Islamophobia and Racism in America*, 86; Little, *American Orientalism*, 223; Zarnowitz and Moore, "The Recession and Recovery of 1973–1976"; Gottschalk and Greenberg, *Islamophobia: Making Muslims the Enemy*, 118; Abraham, "Anti-Arab Racism and Violence in the United States," 155–214.

76. Haddad, *Becoming American?*, 92–93; Bail, *Terrified*, 21.

77. Pennock, *The Rise of the Arab American Left*, 154 (citing "Arabs, Jews Wage War on the Propaganda Front," *Chicago Tribune*, July 27, 1975).

78. Alsultany, *Arabs and Muslims in the Media*, 90–91; Ghareeb, "Split Vision: The Portrayal of Arabs in the American Media"; Joseph, "Against the Grain of the Nation—The Arab."

79. Stampnitzky, *Disciplining Terror*, 67; Marzouki, *Islam*, 51.

80. Stampnitzky, *Disciplining Terror*, 27, 66.

81. Despite its increasing usage, however, *terrorism* is ill defined. No universal definition exists to consistently organize international counterterrorism around political, rational, and moral grounds. The New York Times Index, the British Humanities Index, and the London Times Index did not include terrorism as

a major category before 1972. Stampnitzky, *Disciplining Terror*, 25; Aziz, "The Authoritarianization of U.S. Counterterrorism," 1573.

82. Stampnitzky, *Disciplining Terror*, 31.

83. Said, *Covering Islam*, 150.

84. Stampnitzky, *Disciplining Terror*, 46 (finding that "of the 1,796 individuals presenting at conferences on terrorism between 1972 and 2001, eighty-four percent of them made only one appearance").

85. Kumar, *Islamophobia and the Politics of Empire*, 120–21; Netanyahu, *International Terrorism*.

86. Stampnitzky, *Disciplining Terror*, 114, 116.

87. Stampnitzky, *Disciplining Terror*, 88, 91.

88. Love, *Islamophobia and Racism in America*, 99.

89. Love, *Islamophobia and Racism in America*, 99; Moore, "A Closer Look at Anti-Terrorism Law."

90. Haddad, *Becoming American?*, 24, 72; Feldman, *A Shadow over Palestine*.

91. McCarran-Walter Act, 66 Stat. 163, 82nd Cong. (1952).

92. "Judge Throws Out Charges in 'Los Angeles Eight' Case," Center for Constitutional Rights, Oct. 23, 2007, https://ccrjustice.org/home/press-center /press-releases/judge-throws-out-charges-los-angeles-eight-case.

93. Said, *Covering Islam*, 149; Marzouki, *Islam*, 51; Akram and Johnson, "Race and Civil Rights Pre-September 11, 2001."

94. Gottschalk and Greenberg, *Islamophobia: Making Muslims the Enemy*, 133; Fahmy, "The Green Scare Is Not McCarthyism 2.0."

95. Stampnitzky, *Disciplining Terror*, 184.

96. Abdullah, "American Muslims in the Contemporary World," 66; Maghbouleh, *The Limits of Whiteness*, 26.

97. Abdo, "Days of Rage in Tehran."

98. Little, *American Orientalism*, 144.

99. Feener, *Islam in World Cultures*, 287–88; Maghbouleh, *The Limits of Whiteness*, 27–30.

100. Nacos and Torres-Reyna, *Fueling Our Fears*, 6; Stephen Kinzer, "Thirty-Five Years after Iranian Hostage Crisis, Aftershocks Remain," *Boston Globe*, Nov. 4, 2011, https://www.bostonglobe.com/opinion/2014/11/04/thirty-five-years-after -iranian-hostage-crisis-aftershocks-remain/VIEKSajEUvSmDQICGF8R7K /story.html.

101. Said, *Covering Islam*, 85, 112.

102. "Militant Islam: The Historic Whirlwind," *New York Times Sunday Magazine*, Jan. 6, 1980; Casanova, "Cosmopolitanism, the Clash of Civilizations and Multiple Modernities," 256.

103. Gottschalk and Greenberg, *Islamophobia: Making Muslims the Enemy*, 124–25; Maghbouleh, *The Limits of Whiteness*.

104. Exec. Order No. 12170, 44 Fed. Reg. 65729 (Nov. 14, 1979).

105. Bail, *Terrified*, 24.

106. Charles R. Babcock, "U.S. Admits 5,000 Iranians Who Feared Religious

Persecution," *Washington Post*, Mar. 14, 1980, www.washingtonpost.com/archive /politics/1980/03/14/us-admits-5000-iranians-who-feared-religious-persecution /73696322-beda-4c06-af6c-97521b5bb2e5/?utm_term=.e0f1e71f35a3.

107. Maghbouleh, *The Limits of Whiteness*, 28–29.

108. Tehranian, *Whitewashed*, 122.

109. Falwell, *Listen America!*

110. Robertson, *The New World Order*.

111. Marzouki, *Islam*, 200; Kumar, *Islamophobia and the Politics of Empire*, 118–21.

112. Maira, *The 9/11 Generation*, 150–51.

113. The United States arranged to provide the mujahideen with the weapons and training and the Saudis provided the funding and operations bases. Qureshi and Sells, *The New Crusades*, 103; Little, *American Orientalism*, 227.

114. Lisa Leff, "World Still Dangerous, Quayle Tells Midshipmen," *Washington Post*, May 31, 1990, www.washingtonpost.com/archive/local/1990/05/31/world -still-dangerous-quayle-tells-midshipmen/2fa0f152-cfb2-4917-9351-2c46641ce82b /?utm_term=.cf15f5b39933.

115. Little, *American Orientalism*, 311.

116. Stampnitzky, *Disciplining Terror*, 159; Thomas, *Scapegoating Islam*, 30; Little, *American Orientalism*, 313.

117. Thomas, *Scapegoating Islam*, 30; Little, *American Orientalism*, 254.

118. Little, *American Orientalism*, 73.

119. George H. W. Bush, "Remarks at the Annual Convention of the National Religious Broadcasters," Jan. 27, 1992, https://www.govinfo.gov/content/pkg/PPP -1992-book1/html/PPP-1992-book1-doc-pg151.htm.

120. Stampintzky, *Disciplining Terror*, 141.

121. Bernard Lewis, "The Roots of Muslim Rage," *The Atlantic*, Sept. 1990, www.theatlantic.com/magazine/archive/1990/09/the-roots-of-muslim-rage /304643/.

122. Casanova, "Cosmopolitanism, the Clash of Civilizations and Multiple Modernities," 260.

123. Qureshi and Sells, *The New Crusades*, 99–100.

124. Lewis, *What Went Wrong?*

125. Lewis, *The Crisis of Islam*.

126. Massad, *Islam in Liberalism*, 56.

127. Huntington, *The Clash of Civilizations*.

128. Casanova, "Cosmopolitanism, the Clash of Civilizations and Multiple Modernities," 258; Stampintzky, *Disciplining Terror*, 141; Daniel Pipes, "The Politics of Muslim Anti-Semitism," *Commentary*, August 1981, http://www .danielpipes.org/161/the-politics-of-muslim-anti-semitism; Bulliet, *The Case for Islamo-Christian Civilization*; Daniel Pipes, "Imagine a Palestinian State: A Nightmare for the Arabs and for Israel," Apr. 25, 1988, www.danielpipes.org/180 /imagine-a-palestinian-state-a-nightmare-for-the-arabs.

129. Casanova, "Cosmopolitanism, the Clash of Civilizations and Multiple Modernities," 268; Massad, *Islam in Liberalism*, 49.

130. Massad, *Islam in Liberalism*, 47; Qureshi and Sells, *The New Crusades*, 101–2; Huntington, 258.

131. Saeed, "The American Muslim Paradox," 40.

132. Morey, *The Islamic Invasion*.

133. Wagner, *How Islam Plans to Change the World*.

134. Mathews, *Young Islam on Trek*.

135. Bulliet, *The Case for Islamo-Christian Civilization*, 2.

136. "Task Force on Terrorism & Unconventional Warfare," *New Islamist International*, Feb. 1, 1993, https://fas.org/irp/congress/1993_rpt/house_repub _report.html.

137. Judith Miller, "The Challenge of Radical Islam."

138. Daniel Pipes, "There Are No Moderates: Dealing with Fundamentalist Islam"; Stampnitzky, *Disciplining Terror*, 142.

139. Pipes, "The Muslims Are Coming! The Muslims Are Coming!"

140. "Middle East Forum," *Middle East Quarterly*, https://www.meforum.org /middle-east-quarterly/.

141. Bail, *Terrified*, 30; Nacos and Torres-Reyna, *Fueling Our Fears*, 1.

142. Said, *Covering Islam*, 8–9.

143. Emerson, dir., "Terrorists Among Us."

144. Said, *Covering Islam*, 77.

145. Bail, *Terrified*, 31.

146. Ali et al, "Fear, Inc," 27–50.

147. Gregg, *The Middle East*, 13.

148. Saliba, "Resisting Invisibility."

CHAPTER 7. FIGHTING TERRORISM, NOT RELIGION

1. Lyons, *Islam through Western Eyes*, 3–4; Sheehi, *Islamophobia: The Ideological Campaign against Muslims*, 68; Massad, *Islam in Liberalism*, 55; Salaita, *Anti-Arab Racism in the United States*, 9.

2. George W. Bush, Press Release, White House, Office of the Press Secretary, Sept. 17, 2001, https://georgewbush-whitehouse.archives.gov/news/releases /2001/09/20010917-11.html.

3. Kidd, *American Christians and Islam*, 147; George W. Bush, "Remarks by the President in Honor of Eid Al-Fitr," Dec. 17, 2001, https://georgewbush -whitehouse.archives.gov/infocus/ramadan/islam.html.

4. George W. Bush, "State of the Union Address," Jan. 29, 2002, https:// georgewbush-whitehouse.archives.gov/news/releases/2002/01/20020129-11.html.

5. George W. Bush, "Graduation Speech at West Point," June 1, 2002, https:// georgewbush-whitehouse.archives.gov/news/releases/2002/06/20020601-3.html.

6. Lyons, *Islam through Western Eyes*, 154, 12.

7. "The National Security Strategy of the United States of America," Mar. 2006, www.state.gov/documents/organization/64884.pdf.

8. Esposito and Kalin, *Islamophobia: The Challenge of Pluralism in the 21st Century*, 32.

9. Aziz, "The Authoritarianization of U.S. Counterterrorism," 1573.

10. Michael Schulson, "Why Do So Many Americans Believe That Islam Is a Political Ideology, Not a Religion?," *Washington Post*, Feb. 3, 2017, https://www.washingtonpost.com/news/acts-of-faith/wp/2017/02/03/why-do-so-many-americans-believe-that-islam-is-a-political-ideology-not-a-religion/?utm_term=.3ed83009ce80.

11. Brief for United States of America as Amicus Curiae, *James Estes, et al., v. Rutherford County Regional Planning Commission, and the Rutherford County Board of Commissioners, et al.*, www.justice.gov/crt/spec_topics/religiousdiscrimination/rutherford_amicus_brief.pdf; Christian Grantham, "U.S. Attorneys Make Presence Known in Murfreesboro Mosque Trial," *Murfreesboro Post* (TN), Oct. 22, 2010; "Zelenik Issues Statement on Proposed Islamic Center," *Murfreesboro Post* (TN), June 24, 2010.

12. Christian Grantham, "Murfreesboro Mosque Opponents Appear in Chancery Court," *Murfreesboro Post* (TN), Sept. 27, 2010, www.murfreesboropost.com/news/murfreesboro-mosque-opponents-appear-in-chancery-court/article_1ad791ff-d868-50e6-a7fb-c04396bd3848.html.

13. *United States v. Rutherford Cnty. Tenn.*, LEXIS 99710 3-4 (M.D. Tenn. 2012).

14. Amicus curiae brief for *James Estes, et al.*

15. Michael Lipka and Conrad Hackett, "Why Muslims Are the World's Fastest Growing Religious Group," Pew Research Center, Apr. 6, 2017, www.pewresearch.org/fact-tank/2017/04/06/why-muslims-are-the-worlds-fastest-growing-religious-group/.

16. Cimino, "No God in Common," 162.

17. Haddad, *Becoming American?*, 79; Tomas Dixon, "Youth with a Mission Calls for Reconciliation," *Charisma Magazine*, Sept. 2002.

18. Associated Press, "Threats and Responses; Muhammad a Terrorist to Falwell," *New York Times*, Oct. 4, 2002, www.nytimes.com/2002/10/04/us/threats-and-responses-muhammad-a-terrorist-to-falwell.html.

19. Tara Isabella Burton, "Understanding the Christian Broadcasting Network, the Force Behind the Latest Pro-Trump TV Newscast," *Vox*, Aug. 5, 2017, www.vox.com/identities/2017/8/5/16091740/christian-broadcasting-network-cbn-pat-robertson-trump.

20. Elaihu Salpeter, "Rev. Vines Called Mohammed a Demon-Possessed Pedophile," *Haaretz*, July 17, 2002, www.haaretz.com/1.5208211.

21. Graham and Vines, *Why Islam Is a Threat to America and the West*.

22. Nicholas D. Kristof, "Giving God a Break," *New York Times*, June 10, 2003, www.nytimes.com/2003/06/10/opinion/giving-god-a-break.html

23. Brian Tashman, "Pat Robertson: Islam Is a Dangerous Infection That Must Be Eliminated," *Right Wing Watch*, April 7, 2016, https://www.rightwingwatch .org/post/pat-robertson-islam-is-a-dangerous-infection-that-must-be-eliminated.

24. David Belt, "How U.S. Social Conservatives Created Political Unity in Islam Fearmongering," *Fuller Magazine*, Fuller Studio/Fuller Theological Seminary, 2016, https://fullerstudio.fuller.edu/u-s-social-conservatives-created -political-unity-islam-fearmongering; Cimino, "No God in Common," 163.

25. *WORLD*, https://world.wng.org/about; https://world.wng.org/2002/12 /speaking_frankly.

26. Ruth Gledhill and Franklin Graham, "'Islam Is a Religion of War,'" *Christian Today*, Dec. 6, 2014, www.christiantoday.com/article/franklin-graham -islam-is-a-religion-of-war/43986.htm.

27. "Franklin Graham Says This One Thing Will Lead to Christian Perse- cution in America," *Charisma News*, Mar. 2, 2015, www.charismanews.com/us /48552-franklin-graham-says-this-one-thing-will-lead-to-christian-persecution-in -america.

28. Chris Moody and Kristen Holmes, "Donald Trump's History of Suggest- ing Obama Is a Muslim," CNN, Sept. 18, 2015, www.cnn.com/2015/09/18/politics /trump-obama-muslim-birther/index.html.

29. Tim Funk, "In Prayer, Franklin Graham Sees Rain at Inauguration as Good Omen for Trump," *Charlotte Observer*, Jan. 20, 2017, www.charlotteobserver .com/living/religion/article127687134.html.

30. Gottschalk and Greenberg, *Islamophobia: Making Muslims the Enemy*, 13.

31. John V. Morehead, "Evangelical Credibility and Religious Pluralism," *Qideas*, http://qideas.org/articles/evangelical-credibility-and-religious-pluralism.

32. Lyons, *Islam through Western Eyes*, 9–10.

33. Belt, "How U.S. Social Conservatives Created Political Unity in Islam Fearmongering," 215.

34. Miranda Blue Perkins, "'Only 16 Percent of Islam Is a Religion' So Immi- gration Ban Not a 'Religious Test on Muslims,'" *Right Wing Watch*, Dec. 10, 2015, www.rightwingwatch.org/post/perkins-only-16-percent-of-islam-is-a-religion-so -immigration-ban-not-a-religious-test-on-muslims/; US Commission on Interna- tional Religious Freedom, Tony Perkins, USCIRF, www.uscirf.gov/about-uscirf /tony-perkins-commissioner.

35. Scott Shane, "In Islamic Law, Gingrich Sees a Mortal Threat to U.S.," *New York Times*, Dec. 21, 2011, www.nytimes.com/2011/12/22/us/politics/in-shariah -gingrich-sees-mortal-threat-to-us.html.

36. Bail, *Terrified*, 102.

37. Alan Rappeport, "Newt Gingrich Echoes Donald Trump with Remarks on Muslims and Terrorism," *New York Times*, July 15, 2016.

38. Lindsay, *The Everlasting Hatred*, 10.

39. Robert Kraychik, "Limbaugh: Islam Creates Terrorism," *Daily Wire*, Jan. 31, 2017, www.dailywire.com/news/13022/limbaugh-islam-creates-terrorism-robert -kraychik; "Elections in Israel: Israeli Perspective with Joel Rosenberg," *Wash-

ington Post, Jan. 29, 2003, https://web.archive.org/web/20090328231946/http:// discuss.washingtonpost.com/wp-srv/zforum/03/sp_world_rosenberg012903.htm.

40. Participants in a study "who reported that Muslims were incompatible with Western ways" were nearly 1.4 times more likely to identify as Christian. Disney, "Associations Between Humanitarianism, Othering, and Religious Affiliation," 68.

41. Cimino, "No God in Common," 162–63; Nacos and Torres-Reyna, *Fueling Our Fears*, 66.

42. Betsy Cooper, Daniel Cox, Rachel Lienesch, and Robert P. Jones, "PhD, Anxiety, Nostalgia, and Mistrust: Findings from the 2015 American Values Survey," PRRI, Nov. 17, 2015, www.prri.org/research/survey-anxiety-nostalgia-and -mistrust-findings-from-the-2015-american-values-survey/.

43. Media Tenor International, "Openness for Dialogue Reached a New Low," *Annual Dialogue Report*, 2015, http://us.mediatenor.com/images/library /reports/ADR_2015_LR_WEB_PREVIEW.pdf.

44. Alsultany, *Arabs and Muslims in the Media*.

45. Nacos and Torres-Reyna, *Fueling Our Fears*, 26–28.

46. Esposito and Kalin, *Islamophobia: The Challenge of Pluralism in the 21st Century*, 14.

47. Media Tenor, "Openness for Dialogue Reached a New Low," *Annual Dialogue Report*, 9.

48. Esposito and Kalin, *Islamophobia: The Challenge of Pluralism in the 21st Century*, 14.

49. Media Tenor, "Coverage of American Muslims Gets Worse," http://us.media tenor.com/en/library/speeches/260/coverage-of-american-muslims-gets-worse.

50. *A New Era for Arab-Western Relations—Media Analysis*.

51. Media Tenor, "Openness for Dialogue Reached a New Low," 4, 6.

52. Alsultany, *Arabs and Muslims in the Media*, 108.

53. Khatab, *Understanding Islamic Fundamentalism*, 85–105.

54. Corrigan and Neal, *Religious Intolerance in America*, 248.

55. Alsultany, *Arabs and Muslims in the Media*, 106; Cohen and Connon, *Living in the Crosshairs*, 77, 80, 238.

56. Daryl Johnson, "Hate in God's Name," Southern Poverty Law Center, Sept. 25, 2017, www.splcenter.org/20170925/hate-god%E2%80%99s-name; Sara Kamali, *Homegrown Hate*, 50–53.

57. Johnson, "Hate in God's Name."

58. Arie Perliger, "Challengers from the Sidelines: Understanding America's Violent Far-Right," Combating Terrorism Center at West Point, 2013, https:// ctc.usma.edu/challengers-from-the-sidelines-understanding-americas-violent-far -right/.

59. "Murder and Extremism in the United States in 2017: An ADL Center on Extremism Report," Anti-Defamation League, Jan. 17, 2018, www.adl.org/media /10827/download.

60. Charles Kurzman and David Schanzer, "Law Enforcement Assessment of

the Violent Extremism Threat," Duke Triangle Center on Terrorism and Homeland Security, June 25, 2015, https://sites.duke.edu/tcths/files/2013/06/Kurzman _Schanzer_Law_Enforcement_Assessment_of_the_Violent_Extremist_Threat _final.pdf.

61. Johnson, "Hate in God's Name."

62. Joshi, "The Racialization of Religion in the United States," 46.

63. Adam Goldman, "FBI Report Is Said to Have Warned of Plans for Violence at the Capitol," *New York Times*, January 12, 2021, https://www.nytimes .com/live/2021/01/12/us/capitol-riot-trump. (Note that the report was issued just one day before the siege, in stark contrast to the multi-year sting operations targeting Muslims who post ISIS or Al-Qaeda extremist content on the internet).

64. Gillum, *Muslims in a Post-9/11 America*, 29.

65. Kearns, Betus, and Lemieux, "Why Do Some Terrorist Attacks Receive More Media Attention than Others?"

66. Kearns, Betus, and Lemieux, "Why Do Some Terrorist Attacks Receive More Media Attention than Others?"

67. Bail, *Terrified*, 61.

68. Bail, *Terrified*, 61.

69. Thomas, *Scapegoating Islam*, 155.

70. Jason DeRose, "U.S. Muslim Scholars Issue Edict against Terrorism," *NPR*, July 28, 2005, www.npr.org/templates/story/story.php?storyId=4775588.

71. Bail, *Terrified*, 56.

72. Alsultany, *Arabs and Muslims in the Media*, 31; Shaheen, *Reel Bad Arabs*.

73. Alsultany, *Arabs and Muslims in the Media*, 40.

74. "Americans Evaluate the Balance between Security and Civil Liberties," AP-NORC Center for Public Affairs Research, www.apnorc.org/projects/Pages /HTML%20Reports/americans-evaluate-the-balance-between-security-and-civil -liberties1222-4187.aspx.

75. *Taqiyyah* is defined as "the practice of concealing one's belief and foregoing ordinary religious duties when under threat of death or injury. Derived from the Arabic word *waqa* ('to shield oneself'), *taqiyyah* defies easy translation." Matt Stefon, "Taqiyyah," *Encyclopaedia Britannica*, www.britannica.com/topic /taqiyyah.

76. The most commonly cited purported terrorism experts by conservative politicians are Daniel Pipes, Frank Gaffney, Steven Emerson, David Horowitz, Sebastian Gorka, and John Bolton.

77. Isabel Macdonald and Steve Rendall, "Islamofascism Awareness Week: Anti-Muslim Smearcasting on Campus," *CommonDreams.org*, Oct. 14, 2008, www.commondreams.org/views/2008/10/14/islamofascism-awareness-week -anti-muslim-smearcasting-campus; Sheehi, *Islamophobia: The Ideological Campaign against Muslims*, 94; Nonie Darwish, Islamophobia Network, https:// islamophobianetwork.com/echo-chamber/nonie-darwish/.

78. Wajahat Ali, Eli Clifton, Matthew Duss, Lee Fang, Scott Keyes, and Faiz

Shakir, "FEAR, Inc.: The Roots of the Islamophobia Network in America," *American Progress*, Aug. 26, 2011, www.americanprogress.org/issues/religion/reports /2011/08/26/10165/fear-inc/; Matthew Duss, Yasmine Taeb, Ken Gude, and Ken Sofer, "FEAR, Inc. 2: The Islamophobia Network's Efforts to Manufacture Hate in America," *American Progress*, Feb. 11, 2015, www.americanprogress.org/issues /religion/reports/2015/02/11/106394/fear-inc-2-0/.

79. Bail, *Terrified*, 74–75.

80. Bail, *Terrified*, 74–75.

81. Sheehi, *Islamophobia: The Ideological Campaign against Muslims*, 91.

82. "Ayaan Hirsi Ali," C-SPAN, https://www.c-span.org/person/?ayaanhirsiali.

83. Massad, *Islam in Liberalism*; Kumar, *Islamophobia and the Politics of Empire*, 44–47.

84. Laura Bush, Radio address by Mrs. Bush, White House, Nov. 17, 2001.

85. Ayaan Hirsi Ali, "How to Win the Clash of Civilizations," *Wall Street Journal*, August 18, 2020, https://www.wsj.com/articles/SB10001424052748703426004575338471355710184.

86. Bail, *Terrified*, 92–93.

87. Caner and Caner, *Unveiling Islam*, 184.

88. "Act America," Southern Poverty Law Center, www.splcenter.org/fighting -hate/extremist-files/group/act-america.

89. Sheehi, *Islamophobia: The Ideological Campaign against Muslims*, 91.

90. Syndicated News, "Islam's March against the West," AINA, Feb. 2, 2006, www.aina.org/news/20060219174802.htm.

91. Belt, "How U.S. Social Conservatives Created Political Unity in Islam Fearmongering," 212.

92. "The Denationalization of American Muslims," *The Atlantic*, May 19, 2017; "Women against Islam," Southern Poverty Law Center, June 10, 2015, www .splcenter.org/fighting-hate/intelligence-report/2015/women-against-islam.

93. "In the Arena," CNN, Mar. 8, 2011, www.cnn.com/TRANSCRIPTS/11 March03/08/ita.01.html.

94. "Women against Islam."

95. Form 990 Middle East Forum 2016 (reporting total assets of $4,367,310; Form 990 Middle East Forum 2015 (reporting total assets of $4,324,625); Form 990 Middle East Forum 2014 (reporting total assets of $4,126,021). https://projects .propublica.org/nonprofits/organizations/237749796.

96. "Campus Watch: Professors to Avoid," *Middle East Forum*, www.meforum .org/campus-watch/campus-resources/professors-to-avoid.

97. Bail, *Terrified*, 49.

98. Form 990 Middle East Forum 2002 (reporting $2,136,592 in revenue); Form 990 Middle East Forum 2016 (reporting total assets of $4,367,310). https:// projects.propublica.org/nonprofits/organizations/237749796 and https://projects .propublica.org/nonprofits/display_990/237749796/2003_10_EO%2F23-7749796 _990_200212.

99. "The Denationalization of American Muslims," *The Atlantic*, May 19, 2017.

100. Peter Beinart, "A Radical Pick for the National Security Council," *The Atlantic*, June 1, 2018, www.theatlantic.com/ideas/archive/2018/06/the-report-on -global-jihad-co-authored-by-a-senior-nsc-official/561680/; Faiza Patel and Rachel Levinson-Waldman, "The Islamophobic Administration," Brennan Center for Justice, Apr. 19, 2017; "US Civil Rights Groups Decry 'Anti-Muslim' Bill in Idaho," *Al-Jazeera*, Feb. 28, 2018, www.aljazeera.com/news/2018/02/civil-rights -groups-decry-anti-muslim-bill-idaho-180228132324284.html; "New Database Exposes Anti-Muslim Legislation across the US," Haas Institute, Apr. 25, 2018, https://haasinstitute.berkeley.edu/new-database-exposes-anti-muslim-legislation -across-us.

101. Spellberg, *Thomas Jefferson's Quran*, 294–96; Swathi Shanmugasunda-ram, "Anti-Sharia Law Bills in the United States," Southern Poverty Law Center, Feb. 5, 2018, www.splcenter.org/hatewatch/2018/02/05/anti-sharia-law-bills -united-states; "New Database Exposes Anti-Muslim Legislation across the US."

102. Bail, *Terrified*, 100.

103. Marzouki, *Islam: An American Religion*, 123–24; Elsadig Elsheikh, Basima Sisemore, and Natalia Ramirez Lee, "Legalizing Othering," Haas Institute, Sept. 2017, https://haasinstitute.berkeley.edu/sites/default/files/haas _institute_legalizing_othering_the_united_states_of_islamophobia.pdf.

104. Marzouki, *Islam: An American Religion*, 110–11.

105. Robert P. Jones et al., "The 2012 American Values Survey: How Catholics and the Religiously Unaffiliated Will Shape the 2012 Election and Beyond," Oct. 23, 2012.

106. States implementing Sharia bans include Alabama, Arizona, Kansas, Louisiana, North Carolina, South Dakota, and Tennessee. Liz Farmer, "Alabama Joins Wave of States Banning Foreign Laws," Governing.com, Nov. 4, 2014, www .governing.com/topics/elections/gov-alabama-foreign-law-courts-amendment .html; "Anti-Sharia Legislation," Arab American Institute, 2015, www.aaiusa.org /anti_sharia_legislation.

107. Boykin et al., *The Secure Freedom Strategy*.

108. Beinart; Southern Poverty Law Center, Roundup of anti-Muslim events and activities: 7/18/2018, www.splcenter.org/hatewatch/2018/07/18/roundup-anti -muslim-events-and-activities-7182018; Philip Bump, "Meet Frank Gaffney, the Anti-Muslim Gadfly Reportedly Advising Donald Trump's Transition Team," *Washington Post*, Nov. 16, 2016.

109. "U.S. Muslims Concerned about Their Place in Society, but Continue to Believe in the American Dream," Pew Research Center, July 26, 2017, www .pewforum.org/2017/07/26/findings-from-pew-research-centers-2017-survey-of -us-muslims/; "How the US General Public Views Muslims and Islam," Pew Research Center, July 26, 2017, www.pewforum.org/2017/07/26/how-the-u-s -general-public-views-muslims-and-islam/.

CHAPTER 8. OFFICIATING ISLAMOPHOBIA

Epigraph: Thomas, "Ashcroft Invokes Religion in US War on Terrorism," *Washington Post*, Feb. 20, 2002.

1. Virgil Goode, "Save Judeo-Christian Values," *USA Today*, Jan. 2, 2007.

2. "Lawmaker Won't Apologize for 'Islamophobic' Letter,'" *CNN*, Dec. 21, 2006, www.cnn.com/2006/POLITICS/12/20/lawmaker.koran/.

3. Spellberg, *Thomas Jefferson's Quran*, 285.

4. Lichtman, *Prejudice and the Old Politics*.

5. Veronica Stracqualrusi, "Pelosi Admonishes Trump for Using 9/11 Video to Criticize Ilhan Omar," *CNN.com* (April 13, 2019), https://edition.cnn.com/2019/04/13/politics/nancy-pelosi-ilhan-omar-trump-9-11/index.html; Emily Stewart, "The Attacks on Ilhan Omar Reveal a Disturbing Truth about Racism in America," *Vox.com*, Dec. 4, 2019, https://www.vox.com/policy-and-politics/2019/12/4/20995589/ilhan-omar-racism-attacks-twitter-danielle-stella-minnesota; David Smith, Michael McGowan, Christopher Knaus, and Nick Evershed, "Revealed: Ilhan Omar and Rashida Tlaib Targeted in Far-Right Fake News Operation," *The Guardian*, Dec. 5, 2019, https://www.theguardian.com/technology/2019/dec/05/ilhan-omar-rashida-tlaib-targeted-far-right-fake-news-operation-facebook.

6. Bail, *Terrified*, 96.

7. Bail, *Terrified*, 106.

8. Love, *Islamophobia and Racism in America*, 105.

9. Selod, *Forever Suspect*.

10. "Hearing on 'The Extent of Radicalization in the American Muslim Community and That Community's Response," US Government House Committee on Homeland Security, Mar. 10, 2011, https://www.c-span.org/video/?298377-1/radicalization-us-muslim-community-congressional-panel&event=298377&playEvent; Maira, *The 9/11 Generation* (citing "Report on Hate Crimes and Discrimination Against Arab Americans," American-Arab Anti-Discrimination Committee, 39).

11. Jamal and Albana, "Demographics, Political Participation, and Representation," 107.

12. Esposito and Kalin, *Islamophobia: The Challenge of Pluralism in the 21st Century*, 135.

13. James Ridgeway, "Giuliani Campaign's Muslim Fallout," *The Guardian*, Dec. 31, 2007, https://www.theguardian.com/world/deadlineusa/2007/dec/31/giulianicampaignsmuslimfall.

14. Eugene Volokh, "Islam is not even a religion; it is a social, political system that uses a deity to advance its agenda of global conquest," *Washington Post*, September 22, 2014, https://www.washingtonpost.com/news/volokh-conspiracy/wp/2014/09/22/islam-is-not-even-a-religion-it-is-a-social-political-system-that-uses-a-deity-to-advance-its-agenda-of-global-conquest.

15. Justin Juozapavicius, "Oklahoma lawmaker asks Muslims: 'Do you beat

your wife?,'" *Associated Press*, March 4, 2017, https://apnews.com/article/581f82ec
9d994c7088cd6e6594334881.

16. Mark Schlachtenhaufen, "Sharia Law, Courts Likely on 2010 Ballot,"
Edmond (OK) Sun, June 4, 2010, www.edmondsun.com/news/local_news/sharia
-law-courts-likely-on-ballot/article_a9028340-24bd-5675-9b2a-9c62650e3cae
.html; "Federal Judge Strikes Down Oklahoma's Anti-Shariah Amendment,"
Southern Poverty Law Center, Aug. 19, 2013, www.splcenter.org/hatewatch
/2013/08/19/federal-judge-strikes-down-oklahoma%E2%80%99s-anti-shariah
-amendment.

17. Bail, *Terrified*, 101; "Oklahoma International and Sharia Law, State Question 755," Ballotpedia, 2010, https://ballotpedia.org/Oklahoma_International
_and_Sharia_Law,_State_Question_755_(2010).

18. Office of United States Congressman Louie Gohmert, "House Members
Seek National Security Answers from Inspectors General," Press Releases, June
14, 2012, https://gohmert.house.gov/news/documentsingle.aspx?DocumentID=
299623.

19. Shapiro, *A Time for Healing*, 34–36.

20. Brian Levin and John David Reitzal, "Hate Crimes: Rise in US Cities and
Counties in Time of Division and Foreign Interference," Center for the Study of
Hate and Extremism, May 2018, https://www.csusb.edu/sites/default/files/2018
%20Hate%20Final%20Report%205-14.pdf.

21. Hala Allam and Talal Ansari, "State and Local Republican Officials Have
Been Bashing Muslims. We Counted." *Buzzfeed*, Apr. 10, 2018, https://www
.buzzfeednews.com/article/hannahallam/trump-republicans-bashing-muslims
-without-repercussions.

22. Allam and Ansari, "State and Local Republican Officials Have Been
Bashing Muslims."

23. "Priming the Pump: The Dangerous Political Environment," Council on
American Islamic Relations, Oct. 21, 2017, www.islamophobia.org/reports/196
-civil-rights-report-2017-priming-the-pump.html.

24. Allam and Ansari, "State and Local Republican Officials Have Been
Bashing Muslims."

25. Ian Traynor, "'I don't hate Muslims. I hate Islam,' says Holland's Rising Political Star," *The Guardian*, Feb. 16, 2008, www.theguardian.com/world
/2008/feb/17/netherlands.islam; "Steve King Tweet Backing Geert Wilders Sparks
Social Media Backlash," *BBC News*, Mar. 13, 2017, www.bbc.com/news/world-us
-canada-39250251.

26. "Republicans Prefer Blunt Talk about Islamic Extremism, Democrats
Favor Caution," Pew Research Center, Feb. 3, 2016, www.pewforum.org/2016
/02/03/republicans-prefer-blunt-talk-about-islamic-extremism-democrats-favor
-caution/.

27. Marzouki, *Islam: An American Religion*, 104.

28. "Republicans Prefer Blunt Talk about Islamic Extremism, Democrats
Favor Caution."

29. Muslim Advocates, "Running on Hate: 2018 Pre-Election Report," www
.muslimadvocates.org/running-on-hate/.

30. "Republicans Prefer Blunt Talk about Islamic Extremism, Democrats
Favor Caution."

31. Gottschalk and Greenberg, *Islamophobia: Making Muslims the Enemy*, 144.

32. Sheehi, *Islamopohobia: The Ideological Campaign against Muslims*, 199.

33. Gottschalk and Greenberg, *Islamophobia: Making Muslims the Enemy*, 144.

34. Spellberg, *Thomas Jefferson's Quran*, 291.

35. Bail, *Terrified*, 83.

36. Esposito and Kalin, *Islamophobia: The Challenge of Pluralism in the 21st
Century*, 83.

37. "Remarks by the President at Cairo University," White House Office of
the Press Secretary, June 4, 2009, https://obamawhitehouse.archives.gov/the-press
-office/remarks-president-cairo-university-6-04-09.

38. Frank Gaffney Jr., "Deciphering Obama in Cairo," Center for Security
Policy, June 5, 2009, www.centerforsecuritypolicy.org/2009/06/05/deciphering
-obama-in-cairo-2/.

39. Marzouki, *Islam: An American Religion*, 189.

40. Mitt Romney, Speech to supporters in Milwaukee, Wisconsin, Apr. 2,
2012, www.rawstory.com/2012/04/romney-obama-wants-to-establish-a-religion
-called-secularism/.

41. Rick Santorum, "This Week" interview, *ABC News*, Feb. 2012, https://
abcnews.go.com/Politics/week-transcript-rick-santorum/story?id=15785514.

42. Andrea Elliot, "White House Quietly Courts Muslims in US," *New York
Times*, Apr. 18, 2010, www.nytimes.com/2010/04/19/us/politics/19muslim.html;
Sarah Wheaton, "Obama Camp Apologizes to Muslim Women," *New York
Times*, June 18, 2008, https://thecaucus.blogs.nytimes.com/2008/06/18/obama
-camp-apologizes-to-muslim-women/; Ben Smith, "Muslims Barred from Picture at Obama Event," *Politico*, June 18, 2008, www.politico.com/story/2008/06
/muslims-barred-from-picture-at-obama-event-011168.

43. "In Photos: President Obama Visits a Mosque in Baltimore," The White
House President Barack Obama Archives, Feb. 4, 2016, https://obamawhitehouse
.archives.gov/blog/2016/02/04/photos-president-obama-visits-mosque-baltimore.

44. "Remarks by the President at Islamic Society of Baltimore," White House
Office of the Press Secretary, Feb. 3, 2016, https://obamawhitehouse.archives.gov
/the-press-office/2016/02/03/remarks-president-islamic-society-baltimore.

45. Nacos and Torres-Reyna, *Fueling Our Fears*, 69.

46. Saad, "Anti-Muslim Sentiments Fairly Commonplace"; "Timeline
of Events," United States Holocaust Memorial Museum, www.ushmm.org
/learn/timeline-of-events/1933-1938/reich-ministry-of-the-interior-invalidates-all
-german-passports-held-by-jew.

47. Saad, "Anti-Muslim Sentiments Fairly Commonplace."

48. "[In 2015], a majority (56%) of Americans agree that the values of Islam are
at odds with American values and way of life, while roughly four in ten (41%) dis-

agree. In 2011, Americans were divided in their views of Islam (47% agreed, 48% disagreed)." Betsy Cooper, Daniel Cox, Rachel Lienesch, and Robert P. Jones, "Anxiety, Nostalgia, and Mistrust: Findings from the 2015 American Values Survey," Public Religion Research Institute, Nov. 15, 2015, www.prri.org/research/survey-anxiety-nostalgia-and-mistrust-findings-from-the-2015-american-values-survey/.

49. Jamal and Albana, "Demographics, Political Participation, and Representation"; "Anti-Muslim Sentiments Fairly Commonplace."

50. "Frequently Asked Questions," Cordoba Initiative, www.cordobainitiative.org/?q=content/frequently-asked-questions.

51. Marzouki, *Islam: An American Religion*, 76–77n24.

52. In one survey, 61 percent of respondents who knew about Islam had more favorable attitudes toward Muslim Americans. Nacos and Torres-Reyna, *Fueling Our Fears*, 56, 60. Polls show limited contact of non-Muslim Americans with Muslims before 9/11. See "American Muslim Voters: A Demographic Profile and Survey of Attitudes," Council on American-Islamic Relations (CAIR), http://www.cair.com/pdf/American_Muslim_Voter_Survey_2006.pdf.

53. Saeed, "The American Muslim Paradox," 44.

54. Shibley Telhami, "What Americans Really Think about Muslims and Islam," Brookings Institution, Dec. 9, 2015, www.brookings.edu/blog/markaz/2015/12/09/what-americans-really-think-about-muslims-and-islam/.

55. Approximately 2.35 million Muslims lived in the United States in 2007. "Muslim Americans: Middle Class and Mostly Mainstream," Pew Research Center, May 22, 2007, www.pewresearch.org/2007/05/22/muslim-americans-middle-class-and-mostly-mainstream/.

56. "American Attitudes towards Arabs and Muslims," Arab American Institute, Dec. 5, 2017, https://d3n8a8pro7vhmx.cloudfront.net/aai/pages/13564/attachments/original/1512430036/Poll_Release.pdf?1512430036; "US Muslims Concerned about Their Place in Society, but Continue to Believe in the American Dream," Pew Research Center, July 26, 2017, www.pewresearch.org/wp-content/uploads/sites/7/2017/07/US-MUSLIMS-FULL-REPORT.pdf.

57. Daniel Cox, E. J. Dionne, William A. Galston, and Robert P. Jones, "What It Means to Be an American: Attitudes in an Increasingly Diverse America Ten Years after 9/11," Brookings Institution, Sept. 6, 2011, www.brookings.edu/research/what-it-means-to-be-an-american-attitudes-in-an-increasingly-diverse-america-ten-years-after-911/.

58. Yousafzai, *I Am Malala*.

59. Nafisi, *Reading Lolita in Tehran*.

60. Jews against Anti-Muslim Racism, "What Is Liberal Islamophobia," https://jaamr.com/islamophobia/what-is-liberal-islamophobia/.

61. Kumar, *Islamophobia and the Politics of Empire*.

62. "Growing Number of Americans Say Obama Is a Muslim," Pew Research Center, 2010, www.pewforum.org/2010/08/18/growing-number-of-americans-say-obama-is-a-muslim/.

63. Uri Friedman, "Donald Trump and the Coming War on 'Radical Islam,'" *The Atlantic*, Nov. 29, 2016, www.theatlantic.com/international/archive/2016/11/trump-radical-islam/508331/.

64. Mattea Gold, "Bannon Film Outline Warned US Could Turn into 'Islamic States of America,'" *Washington Post*, Feb. 3, 2017, www.washingtonpost.com/politics/bannon-film-outline-warned-us-could-turn-into-islamic-states-of-america/2017/02/03/f73832f4-e8be-11e6-b82f-687d6e6a3e7c_story.html?utm_term=.6ee1783baee5; Patel, *Out of Many Faiths*, 55.

65. Mariam Khan, "Donald Trump National Security Adviser Mike Flynn Has Called Islam 'a Cancer,'" ABC News, Nov. 18, 2016, https://abcnews.go.com/Politics/donald-trump-national-security-adviser-mike-flynn-called/story?id=43575658; Flynn and Ledeen, *The Field of Fight*, 9.

66. Peter Beinart, "The Denationalization of American Muslims," *The Atlantic*, May 19, 2017, www.theatlantic.com/politics/archive/2017/03/frank-gaffney-donald-trump-and-the-denationalization-of-american-muslims/519954/.

67. Flynn and Ledeen, *The Field of Fight*, 9.

68. "New Database Exposes Anti-Muslim Legislation across the US," Haas Institute, Apr. 25, 2018, https://haasinstitute.berkeley.edu/new-database-exposes-anti-muslim-legislation-across-us.

69. President Donald Trump speech on immigration and terrorism policy in Youngstown, OH, Aug. 15, 2016, http://time.com/4453110/donald trump national-security-immigration-terrorism-speech/.

70. Mahmood, "Secularism, Hermeneutics, and Empire," 232.

71. Peter Beinart, "Fred Fleitz and the Radicalization of the National Security Council," *The Atlantic*, June 1, 2018, https://www.theatlantic.com/ideas/archive/2018/06/the-report-on-global-jihad-co-authored-by-a-senior-nsc-official/561680/.

72. Boykin et al., *The Secure Freedom Strategy*.

73. William J. Boykin, *Shariah: The Threat to America: An Exercise in Competitive Analysis*, Center for Security Policy, October 7, 2010.

74. Eli Clifton, "Dershowitz Received $120K from Anti-Muslim Gatestone Institute," *Lobelog.com*, Nov. 15, 2018, https://lobelog.com/dershowitz-received-120k-from-anti-muslim-gatestone-institute/.

75. Right Web, The Gatestone Institute, Jan. 13, 2015, https://rightweb.irc-online.org/profile/gatestone_institute/.

76. Marzouki, *Islam: An American Religion*, 66, 92.

77. Biography of Nina Rosenwald, Gatestone Institute, https://www.gatestoneinstitute.org/biography/Nina+Rosenwald.

78. McElwee and Cohen, "The Secret to Trump's Success."

79. Telhami, "What Americans Really Think about Muslims and Islam."

80. Telhami, "What Americans Really Think about Muslims and Islam."

81. Cooper et al., "Anxiety, Nostalgia, and Mistrust: Findings from the 2015 American Values Survey," 179.

82. "US Muslims Concerned about Their Place in Society, but Continue to Believe in the American Dream."

83. Gillum, *Muslims in a Post-9/11 America*.

84. Nacos and Torres-Reyna, *Fueling Our Fears*, 69.

85. John Sides and Dalia Mogahed, "Muslims in America: Public Perceptions in the Trump Era, Figure 3," Voter Study Group, June 2018, www.voterstudygroup.org/publication/muslims-in-america.

86. "Conservative Republicans are the only major ideological, demographic or religious group in which a majority (57%) says Muslims in this country should be subject to greater scrutiny than those in other religious groups." "Views of Government's Handling of Terrorism Fall to Post-9/11 Low," Pew Research Center, Dec. 15, 2015, www.people-press.org/2015/12/15/views-of-governments-handling-of-terrorism-fall-to-post-911-low/.

87. Love, *Islamophobia and Racism in America*, 20.

88. "Exec. Order No. 13769: Executive Order Protecting the Nation from Foreign Terrorist Entry into the United States," White House, Jan. 27, 2017, www.whitehouse.gov/presidential-actions/executive-order-protecting-nation-foreign-terrorist-entry-united-states-2/.

89. Aziz, "A Muslim Registry," 779; *Trump v. Hawaii*, 585 US (2018).

90. "Proclamation on Improving Enhanced Vetting Capabilities and Processes for Detecting Attempted Entry," White House, Jan. 31, 2020, www.whitehouse.gov/presidential-actions/proclamation-improving-enhanced-vetting-capabilities-processes-detecting-attempted-entry/.

91. Caleb Elfenbein and Peter Hanson, "What Does It Mean to Be a 'Real' American?," *Washington Post*, Jan. 3, 2019, www.washingtonpost.com/outlook/2019/01/03/what-does-it-mean-be-real-american/?utm_term=.330f311e7826.

CHAPTER 9. CRIMINALIZING MUSLIM IDENTITY

1. Aziz, "Policing Terrorists in the Community," 147.

2. Kamali, *Homegrown Hate,* 39–78; National Public Radio, "Capitol Insurrection Updates," https://www.npr.org/sections/insurrection-at-the-capitol.

3. Aziz, "Caught in a Preventive Dragnet: Selective Counterterrorism in a Post-9/11 America"; Aziz and Beydoun, "Fear of a Black and Brown Internet"; Cainkar, *Homeland Insecurity*.

4. Aziz, "A Muslim Registry," 101; Bakalian and Bozorgmehr, *Backlash 9/11*, 246; Eggen and Thompson, "U.S. Seeks Thousands of Fugitive Deportees," *Washington Post*, Jan. 8, 2002, www.washingtonpost.com/archive/politics/2002/01/08/us-seeks-thousands-of-fugitive-deportees/9938c817-337d-4b57-97b2-5a3c50deeb82/?utm_term=.0c828c36471d.

5. "17 Years Later, Guantánamo Prison Remains a Threat to Human Rights," Amnesty International, USA, Jan. 10, 2019, www.amnesty.org/en/latest

/news/2019/01/usa-17-years-later-guantanamo-prison-remains-a-threat-to-human
-rights/; Naureen Shah, "A Year in Drones: The Secrets Exposed, Promises Made
and Ugly Realities That Remain," Amnesty International, www.amnestyusa.org
/the-year-in-drones-the-secrets-exposed-promises-made-and-ugly-realities-that
-remain/; "Guantanamo by the Numbers," American Civil Liberties Union, www
.aclu.org/issues/national-security/detention/guantanamo-numbers; Aziz, "The
Authoritarianization of U.S. Counterterrorism," 1573.

6. Nacos and Torres-Reyna, *Fueling Our Fears*, 59; Wuthnow, *All in Sync*.

7. John Sides and Dalia Mogahed, "Muslims in America Public Perceptions in
the Trump Era: Figure 3," Voter Study Group, June 2018, www.voterstudygroup
.org/publication/muslims-in-america.

8. Norris, "Explaining the Emergence of Entrapment in Post-9/11 Terrorism
Investigations," 467, 471.

9. Michael Arria, "Omar, Tlaib, Ocasio-Cortez, and Pressley only Dems to
oppose Israel resolution that omits all mentions of occupation," *Mondoweiss*, Dec.
6, 2019, https://mondoweiss.net/2019/12/omar-tlaib-ocasio-cortez-and-pressley
-only-dems-to-oppose-israel-resolution-that-omits-all-mentions-of-occupation/.

10. H.J.Res.49—Providing for Congressional Disapproval of the Proposed
Direct Commercial Sale to Israel of Certain Weaponry and Munitions, 117th
Congress (2021–2022), https://www.congress.gov/bill/117th-congress/house-joint
-resolution/49/text?q=%7B%22search%22%3A%5B%22israel+arms+sale%22%5D
%7D&r=2&s=2; Jacqueline Alemany and Karoun Demirjian, "Sen. Bernie Sanders to Introduce Resolution on Disapproval on $735 Million U.S. Arms Sale to
Israel," *Washington Post*, May 20, 2021, https://www.washingtonpost.com/politics
/2021/05/20/sen-bernie-sanders-introduce-resolution-disapproval-735-million-us
-arms-sale-israel/.

11. Rebecca Ballhaus, Courtney McBride, and Jared Malsin, "Trump Administration Seeks to Designate Muslim Brotherhood as Terrorist Organization," *Wall
Street Journal*, Apr. 30, 2019, www.wsj.com/articles/trump-administration-seeks
-to-designate-muslim-brotherhood-as-terrorist-organization-11556631257; Arsalan
Iftikhar, "Calling the Muslim Brotherhood a Terrorist Group Would Make All
Muslims Scapegoats," *Washington Post*, May 6, 2019, www.washingtonpost.com
/outlook/2019/05/06/calling-muslim-brotherhood-terrorist-group-would-make
-all-muslims-scapegoats/?utm_term=.530210c60ff5.

12. Ali Abunimah, "Rasmea Odeh Unbowed as Judge Passes Sentence," Electronic Intifada, Aug. 17, 2017, https://electronicintifada.net/blogs/ali-abunimah
/rasmea-odeh-unbowed-judge-passes-sentence.

13. Brief for Appellant, 55, in *United States of America v. Rasmieh Yusef Odeh*,
815 F.3d 968 (6th Cir. 2016) (No. 15-1331).

14. Maureen Clare Murphy, "Rasmea Odeh Seeks Reversal of Immigration
Fraud Conviction," *Electronic Intifada*, June 11, 2015, https://electronicintifada
.net/blogs/maureen-clare-murphy/rasmea-odeh-seeks-reversal-immigration-fraud
-conviction; Brief for Appellant, 8; Mark Mondalek, "The Campaign against

Rasmea Odeh," *Jacobin*, Oct. 13, 2015, www.jacobinmag.com/2015/10/rasmea-odeh-palestine-israel-midwest-23-bds-fbi/.

15. Charlotte Silver, "Will Rasmea Odeh Go to Prison Because of a Confession Obtained Through Torture?," *The Nation*, Nov. 4, 2014, www.thenation.com/article/will-rasmeah-odeh-go-prison-because-confession-obtained-through-torture/.

16. Teresa Crawford, "Palestinian Activist Deported to Jordan from Chicago," *Chicago Tribune*, Sept. 19, 2017, www.chicagotribune.com/news/breaking/ct-palestinian-activist-deported-chicago-20170919-story.html.

17. Guinier and Torres, *The Miner's Canary*, 224–25.

18. "The September 11 Detainees: A Review of Treatment of Aliens Held on Immigration Charges in Connection with the Investigation of the September 11 Attacks," U.S. Department of Justice, Office of the Inspector General, 2003, 1, https://oig.justice.gov/special/0306/full.pdf.

19. Philip Heymann, "Muslims in America after 9/11: The Legal Situation," Nov. 30, 2006, https://sites.fas.harvard.edu/~ces/conferences/muslims/Heymann.pdf; Wong, "The USA Patriot Act."

20. Uniting and Strengthening America by Providing Appropriate Tools Required to Intercept and Obstruct Terrorism Act of 2001, Pub. L. No. 107-056, 2001; Enhanced Border Security and Visa Entry Reform Act of 2001, Pub. L. No. 107-173, 2001; Homeland Security Act of 2002, Pub. L. No. 107-296, 116 Stat. 2135 (2002).

21. "Homeland Security Presidential Directive 2: Combating Terrorism through Immigration Policies," Administration of George W. Bush, Oct. 29, 2001, https://fas.org/irp/offdocs/nspd/hspd-2.htm.

22. Homeland Security Presidential Directive-2: Combating Terrorism Through Immigration Policies adopted on October 30, 2001, https://www.legislationline.org/documents/action/popup/id/6070.

23. John Ashcroft, "Remarks Before the United States Conference of Mayors," Oct. 25, 2001, www.justice.gov/archive/ag/speeches/2001/agcrisisremarks1025.htm.

24. "Registration and Monitoring of Certain Nonimmigrants," *Federal Register* 67 (Aug. 12, 2002): 52584, 52589. Codified at 8 C.F.R. pts. 214, 264.

25. "Attorney General Ashcroft Announces Implementation of the First Phase of the National Security Entry-Exit Registration System," U.S. Department of Justice, Aug. 12, 2002, www.justice.gov/archive/opa/pr/2002/August/02_ag_466.htm.

26. "Attorney General Ashcroft."

27. Mishra, "Religion and Race," 239.

28. Tehranian, *Whitewashed*, 125.

29. Curtis, *Muslims in America: A Short History*, 100.

30. *Ashcroft v. Iqbal*, 556 U.S. 662 (2009); Panagopoulos, "Trends: Arab and Muslim Americans and Islam in the Aftermath of 9/11."

31. Cole, "The New McCarthyism," 24–26.

32. "Operation Liberty Shield," FEMA, Mar. 18, 2003, www.fema.gov/news -release/2003/03/17/operation-liberty-shield; Gerry J. Gilmore, "Ridge Launches 'Operation Liberty Shield' as War Footing Steps Up," Department of Defense, Mar. 18, 2003, https://archive.defense.gov/news/newsarticle.aspx?id=29280.

33. U.S. Immigration and Customs Enforcement, *ICE Immigration Enforcement Strategy and Highlights*, Jan. 2006, https://www.hsdl.org/?view&did =462257; "ICE Targets Immigrants from Muslim Majority Countries Prior to 2004 Presidential Election," press release, Am.-Arab Anti-Discrimination Comm. and Yale Law School, Oct. 31, 2008.

34. "Detailed Information on the Immigration and Customs Enforcement: Office of Investigations Assessment," ExpectMore.gov, https://obamawhitehouse .archives.gov/sites/default/files/omb/assets/omb/expectmore/detail/10002388 .2004.html; *Lowenstein v. Dept. of Homeland Sec*, 09-2225-cv (2d Cir. 2010), https://www.courtlistener.com/opinion/179606/lowenstein-v-dept-of-homeland -sec/; "ICE Targets Immigrants from Muslim Majority Countries Prior to 2004 Presidential Election."

35. Thomas, *Scapegoating Islam*, 38–39.

36. Gillum, *Muslims in a Post-9/11 America*, 72–73.

37. "The Progress and Pitfalls of the Terrorist Watch List," Field Hearing of the Committee on Homeland Security, 110th Cong., 2007, 10, www.govinfo .gov/content/pkg/CHRG-110hhrg48979/html/CHRG-110hhrg48979.htm; Sahar F. Aziz, "Court Recognizes Reputational Harm to Muslims on Terrorist Watchlist," American Constitution Society Expert Forum: Law and Policy Analysis, Sept. 16, 2019, www.acslaw.org/expertforum/court-recognizes-reputational-harm -to-muslims-on-terrorist-watchlist/.

38. Jason Trahan, "Stakes High in Holy Land Trial," Dallas News, July 16, 2007, http://freedomarchives.org/pipermail/ppnews_freedomarchives.org/2007 -July/001301.html.

39. Aziz, "The Laws on Providing Material Support to Terrorist Organizations," 45, 48.

40. Bakalian and Bozorgmehr, *Backlash 9/11*, 163–64.

41. Aziz, "The Laws on Providing Material Support to Terrorist Organizations," 52.

42. "Muslims Need Not Apply: How USCIS Secretly Mandates the Discriminatory Delay and Denial of Citizenship and Immigration Benefits to Aspiring Americans," American Civil Liberties Union of Southern California, Aug. 2013, 2, www.aclusocal.org/sites/default/files/carrp-muslims-need-not-apply-aclu-socal -report.pdf.

43. "Full Executive Order Text: Trump's Action Limiting Refugees into the U.S.," *New York Times*, Jan. 27, 2017, www.nytimes.com/2017/01/27/us/politics /refugee-muslim-executive-order-trump.html.

44. Volpp, "The Citizen and the Terrorist," 1581; Alex Nowrasteh, "Where Do Terrorists Come From? Not the Nations Named in Trump Ban," *Newsweek*, Jan.

31, 2017, http://bit.ly/2kWoddx; Aziz, "Policing Terrorists," 194; Gotanda, "Comparative Racialization," 1689, 1692.

45. Corrected Brief of Former National Security Officials as Amici Curiae in Support of Plaintiff-Appellees and Against a Stay Pending Appeal, IRAP, 857 F.3d 554 (No. 17-1351). See also Brief of Amici Curiae Former National Security Officials in Opposition to the Applications for a Stay, *Trump v. Int'l Refugee Assistance Project* (IRAP), 137 S. Ct. 2080 (2017) (Nos. 16-1436 [16A1190]).

46. *Washington v. Trump*, 847 F.3d 1151, 1151 (9th Cir. 2017); Order Granting Motion for Temporary Restraining Order, Hawai'i v. Trump, 1119; *IRAP v. Trump*, 539.

47. *IRAP v. Trump*, 557.

48. Jenna Johnson and Abigail Hauslohner, "'I Think Islam Hates Us': A Timeline of Trump's Comments about Islam and Muslims," *Washington Post*, May 20, 2017, www.washingtonpost.com/news/post-politics/wp/2017/05/20/i-think-islam-hates-us-a-timeline-of-trumps-comments-about-islam-and-muslims.

49. "Anderson Cooper 360°," CNN, Mar. 9, 2016, http://cnn.it/2jJmaEC.

50. "Donald Trump Remarks in Manchester, New Hampshire," *C-SPAN*, June 13, 2016, http://cs.pn/2k7bHGq.

51. Emily Schultheis, "Donald Trump Warns Refugees Could be 'Trojan Horse' for U.S.," *CBS News*, June 13, 2016, www.cbsnews.com/news/donald-trump-warns-refugees-could-be-trojan-horse-for-u-s.

52. "Presidential Candidate Donald Trump Town Hall Meeting in Londonderry, New Hampshire," C-SPAN, Feb. 8, 2016, http://cs.pn/2kY4fiT.

53. "Anderson Cooper 360°: Trump One-on-One," *CNN*, Mar. 9, 2016, www.cnn.com/2016/03/09/politics/donald-trump-islam-hates-us/index.html; *Ali v. Trump*, 241 F. Supp. 3d 1147, 1149 (W.D. Wash. 2017) (documenting anti-Muslim statements by Trump as presidential candidate and US president).

54. "The FBI: Protecting the Homeland in the 21st Century," 9/11 Review Commission, Mar. 2015, www.hsdl.org/?abstract&did=763412; "Audit of the Federal Bureau of Investigation Annual Financial Statements Fiscal Year 2017," Office of the Inspector General, US Department of Justice, Dec. 2017, https://oig.justice.gov/reports/2017/a1807.pdf.

55. "Budget and Performance Summary," US Department of Justice, 2009, www.justice.gov/archives/jmd/2009-budget-and-performance-summary-federal-bureau-investigation-fbi.

56. Caroline Simon, "The FBI Is 'Manufacturing Terrorism Cases' on a Greater Scale than Ever Before," *Business Insider,* Jun. 9, 2016, www.businessinsider.com/fbi-is-manufacturing-terrorism-cases-2016-6.

57. Matt Apuzzo and Adam Goldman, "After Spying on Muslims, New York Police Agree to Greater Oversight," *New York Times*, Mar. 6, 2017; Apuzzo and Goldman, "Documents Show NY Police Watched Devout Muslims," *San Diego Union-Tribune*, Sept. 6, 2011, https://www.sandiegouniontribune.com/sdut-documents-show-ny-police-watched-devout-muslims-2011sep06-story.html.

58. Apuzzo and Goldman, "After Spying on Muslims, New York Police Agree

to Greater Oversight"; Apuzzo and Goldman, "Documents Show NY Police Watched Devout Muslims."

59. Meg Stalcup and Joshua Craze, "How We Train Our Cops to Fear Islam," *Washington Monthly*, Mar.–Apr. 2011, 20, 21, https://washington monthly.com/magazine/marchapril-2011/how-we-train-our-cops-to-fear -islam/; "Joint Statement on Meeting with FBI Director Robert Muel- ler," Press Release, Arab American Anti-Discrimination Committee, Feb. 15, 2012, www.adc.org/media/press-releases/2012/february-2012/joint-statement -onmeeting-with-fbi-director-robert-mueller/.

60. Michael Powell, "In Police Training, a Dark Film on U.S. Muslims," *New York Times*, Jan. 24, 2012, www.nytimes.com/2012/01/24/nyregion/in-police -training-a-dark-film-on-us-muslims.

61. Apuzzo and Goldman, "After Spying on Muslims, New York Police Agree to Greater Oversight."

62. "Court Filing Seeks to End NYPD Surveillance of Muslim Community," New York Civil Liberties Union, Feb. 4, 2013, www.nyclu.org/en/press-releases /court-filing-seeks-end-nypd-surveillance-muslim-community.

63. Eric Lichtblau, "F.B.I. Steps Up Use of Stings in ISIS Cases," *New York Times*, June 7, 2016, www.nytimes.com/2016/06/08/us/fbi-isis-terrorism-stings .html.

64. William Glaberson, "Newburgh Terrorism Case May Establish a Line for Entrapment," *New York Times*, June 15, 2010, www.nytimes.com/2010/06/16 /nyregion/16terror.html.

65. Cora Currier and Murtaza Hussain, "Letter Details FBI Plan for Secretive Anti-Radicalization Committees," *The Intercept*, Apr. 28, 2016, https://theintercept.com/2016/04/28/letter-details-fbiplan-for-secretive-anti -radicalization-committees/.

66. Murtaza Hussain and Razan Ghalayini, "The Real Story Behind the Fort Dix Five Terror Plot," *The Intercept*, June 25, 2015, https://theintercept.com/2015 /06/25/fort-dix-five-terror-plot-the-real-story/.

67. Paul Harris, "The Ex-FBI Informant with a Change of Heart: 'There is no real hunt. It's fixed,'" *The Guardian*, Mar. 20, 2012, www.theguardian.com/world /2012/mar/20/fbi-informant.

68. Paul Harris, "Newburgh Four: Poor, Black, and Jailed under FBI 'Entrap- ment' Tactics," *The Guardian*, Dec. 12, 2011, www.theguardian.com/world/2011 /dec/12/newburgh-four-fbi-entrapment-terror.

69. Glaberson, "Newburgh Terrorism Case May Establish a Line for Entrapment."

70. Michael Wilson, "Jury Convicts 2 Albany Men in Missile Sting," *New York Times*, Oct. 11, 2006, https://www.nytimes.com/2006/10/11/nyregion/11plot .html.

71. Anjali Kamat and Jacquie Soohen, "Entrapment or Foiling Terror? FBI's Reliance on Paid Informants Raises Questions about Validity of Terrorism Cases,"

DemocracyNow!, Oct. 6, 2010, www.democracynow.org/2010/10/6/entrapment-or
-foilingterrorfbis-reliance.

72. Mark Toor, "Muslim Group Sues NYPD: Say New Jersey Surveillance
Amounts to Illegal Profiling," *The Chief*, June 15, 2012, https://thechiefleader
.com/news/news_of_the_week/say-new-jersey-surveillance-amounts-to-illegal
-profiling/article_f37fd79e-b1a9-11e1-984c-0019bb30f31a.html.

73. Diala Shamas and Nermeen Arastu, "Mapping Muslims: NYPD Spying
and Its Impact on American Muslims," March 14, 2013, 14, https://www.aljazeera
.com/opinions/2013/3/14/mapping-surveillance-and-its-impact-on-american
-muslims.

74. Jennifer Steinhauer, "Palestinian to Be Imprisoned before Deportation,"
New York Times, May 1, 2006, www.nytimes.com/2006/05/01/us/01cnd-islamic
.html?_r-1&oref-slogin.

75. "Sami Al-Arian Released after 5.5 Years in Prison," *DemocracyNow!*, Sept.
3, 2008, www.democracynow.org/2008/9/3/samialarianreleasedafter-five.

76. Murtaza Hussain and Glenn Greenwald, "Exclusive Interview: Sami Al-
Arian, Professor Who Defeated Controversial Terrorism Charges Is Deported
from U.S.," *The Intercept*, Feb. 5, 2015, https://theintercept.com/2015/02/05/sami
-al-arian-charged-terrorism-never-convicted-deported-today-u-s/.

77. Deutsch and Thompson, "Secrets and Lies," 51.

78. Deutsch and Thompson, "Secrets and Lies," 44–45.

79. Milton Viorst, "The Education of Ali Al-Timimi," *The Atlantic*, June
2006, www.theatlantic.com/magazine/archive/2006/06/the-education-of-ali-al
-timimi/304884/.

80. Milton Viorst, "The Education of Ali Al-Timimi."

81. "Judge Tosses Terror Case Convictions, Orders Prisoner Freed," *U.S.
News*, July 19, 2018, www.usnews.com/news/best-states/virginia/articles/2018-07
-19/judge-tosses-terror-case-convictions-orders-prisoner-freed.

82. Terry Frieden, "Muslim cleric Convicted," CNN, Apr. 26, 2005, www.cnn
.com/2005/LAW/04/26/cleric.trial/.

83. Eric Lichtblau, "Scholar Is Given Life Sentence in 'Virginia Jihad' Case,"
New York Times, July 14, 2005, www.nytimes.com/2005/07/14/us/scholar-is-given
-life-sentence-in-virginia-jihad-case.html.

84. Lichtblau, "Scholar Is Given Life Sentence."

85. Mitchell D. Silber and Arvin Bhatt, "Radicalization in the West: The
Homegrown Threat," N.Y.C. Police Department, 2007, 21, www.nypdshield.org
/public/Site Files/documents/NYPD Report-RadicalizationintheWest.pdf.

86. Carpenter, Levitt, and Jacobson, "Confronting the Ideology of Radical
Extremism," 301.

87. Aziz, "Policing Terrorists," 147.

88. Cohen, "The Next Generation of Government CVE Strategies at Home,"
124.

89. Kundnani, *The Muslims Are Coming!*, 83–84.

90. Aziz, "Policing Terrorists"; Aziz, "Caught in a Preventive Dragnet," 429.

91. Julia Edwards Ainsley et al., "Exclusive: Trump to Focus Counter-Extremism Program Solely on Islam—Sources," *Reuters*, Feb. 2, 2017, www.reuters.com /article/us-usa-trumpextremists-program-exclusiv-idUSKBN15G5VO.

92. Bill Morlin, "Study Shows Two-Thirds of U.S. Terrorism Tied to Right-Wing Extremists," Southern Poverty Law Center, Sept. 12, 2018, www.splcenter .org/hatewatch/2018/09/12/study-shows-two-thirds-us-terrorism-tied-righ t-wing-extremists; "Murder and Extremism in the United States in 2018," Anti-Defamation League, Jan. 2019, www.adl.org/media/12480/download.

93. "Two Decades of Prejudice: FBI Hate Crime Statistics," Bridge Initiative, Georgetown University, July 8, 2015, https://bridge.georgetown.edu/research/two -decades-of-prejudice-fbi-hate-crime-statistics/; "Anti-Muslim Incidents since Sept. 11, 2001," Southern Poverty Law Center, Mar. 29, 2011, www.splcenter.org /news/2011/03/29/anti-muslim-incidents-sept-11-2001.

94. Engy Abdelkader, "When Islamophobia Turns Violent: The 2016 U.S. Presidential Elections," Bridge Initiative, Georgetown University, May 2, 2016, 1–2, 11.

95. Bridge Initiative Team, "Two Decades of Prejudice: FBI Hate Crime Statistics," Bridge Initiative, Georgetown University, July 8, 2015, https://bridge .georgetown.edu/research/two-decades-of-prejudice-fbi-hate-crime-statistics/.

96. Brian Levin, "Special Status Report: Hate Crime in the United States," Center for the Study of Hate and Extremism, California State University, San Bernardino, 2016, 6, https://big.assets.huffingtonpost.com /SPECIALSTATUSREPORTv5.pdf.

97. "Map: Recent Incidents of Anti-Muslim Hate Crimes," *Muslim Advocates*, www.muslimadvocates.org/map-anti-muslim-hate-crimes/.

98. "Nearly Two-Thirds of Hate Crimes Went Unreported to Police in Recent Years," Bureau of Justice Statistics, Mar. 21, 2013, https://www.ojp.gov/sites/g /files/xychuk241/files/archives/pressreleases/2013/ojppr032113.pdf.

99. Lauren del Valle, "2 Muslim Women, Babies Attacked in Alleged Hate Crime in New York," CNN, Sept. 10, 2016, www.cnn.com/2016/09/10/us /brooklyn-muslim-women-attacked/.

100. Lindsey Bever, "Arrest Made in Arson at Orlando Gunman's Mosque, Authorities Say," *Washington Post*, Sept. 14, 2016, www.washingtonpost.com/news /acts-of-faith/wp/2016/09/12/arson-suspected-in-fireat-florida-mosque-attended -by-pulse-shooter-omar-mateen/.

101. Laurel Raymond, "Assault of Muslim Man in NYC Comes amid Rising Islamophobia Nationwide," *ThinkProgress*, June 6, 2016, http://thinkprogress.org /justice/2016/06/06/3785049/muslim-manattackedqueens/.

102. Rocco Parascandola, "Bronx Livery Driver Repeatedly Punched in the Face by Passenger Who Called Him 'Muslim Driver A—hole,'" *New York Daily News*, May 25, 2016, www.nydailynews.com/newyork/bronx-livery-driver -punched-called-muslim-driver-a-hole-article-1.2648669.

103. Ajay Ghosh, "Hate Crime Charged against Pittman for Spokane Gurd-

wara Vandalism," *Universal News Network*, Mar. 15, 2016, http://theunn.com/2016/03/hate-crime-charged-against-pittman-for-spokane-gurdwara-vandalism/.

104. Steve Birr, "Police Release Video of Assault on Muslim Woman Outside DC Starbucks," *Daily Caller*, May 3, 2016, http://dailycaller.com/2016/05/03/police-release-video-of-assault-onmuslim-woman-outside-dc-starbucks/.

105. Kevin Killeen, "Update: Affton Man Charged with Anti-Muslim Hate Crime," CBS St. Louis, Feb. 29, 2016, http://stlouis.cbslocal.com/2016/02/29/muslims-wait-for-bob-mcculloch-to-file-charges/.

106. Charles Lam, "Sikh Man Stabbed to Death in Robbery of Central California Convenience Store," *NBC News*, Jan. 5, 2016, www.nbcnews.com/news/asian-america/sikh-man-stabbed-deathrobberycentral-california-convenience-store-n490786.

107. Dan Majors, "Muslim Taxi Driver Shot on Thanksgiving in Hazelwood Calls Attack a Hate Crime," *Pittsburgh Post Gazette*, Nov. 28, 2015, www.post-gazette.com/local/city/2015/11/29/Muslimtaxi-driver-shot-on-Thanksgiving-in-Pittsburgh-calls-attack-a-hate-crime/stories/201511290154.

108. "Targeted: 2018 Civil Rights Report," Council on American Islamic Relations, 2008, 11, www.islamophobia.org/reports/224-2018-civil-rights-report-targeted.html.

109. "JFK Flier Attacks Worker: 'Trump Will Get Rid of All of You,'" NBC New York, Jan. 26, 2017, www.nbcnewyork.com/news/local/muslim-employee-hijab-delta-sky-lounge-kicked-harassed-flyer-shouts-trump-is-here-now/244264/.

110. "Waterford Man Swears at Family, Yells 'Trump Will Stop You' in Drunk Tirade at Texas Beach," *FOX 61*, May 11, 2017, http:// fox61.com/2017/05/10/waterford-man-arrested-for-racist-tiradein-texas/.

111. "Protecting the Civil Rights of Muslim Americans," Hearing Before the Subcomm. on the Constitution, Civil Rights and Human Rights of the S. Comm. on the Judiciary, 112th Cong., 2011, 15; Nguyen, *A Curriculum of Fear.*

112. Donna St. George, "During a School Year of Terrorist Attacks, Muslim Students Report Bullying," *Washington Post*, June 14, 2016, http://wapo.st/1UitKUB?tid=ss_mail.

113. "Mislabeled: The Impact of School Bullying and Discrimination on California Muslim Students," Council on American-Islamic Relations, 2015, 4, https://youthlaw.org/publication/mislabeled-impact-school-bullying-discrimination-california-muslim-students/.

114. "Hate at School," Southern Poverty Law Center, 2019, /www.splcenter.org/sites/default/files/tt_2019_hate_at_school_report_final_0.pdf.

115. Cohen and Connon, *Living in the Crosshairs*, 77, 80, 238.

116. Schildkraut, "The More Things Change...," 515, 517.

117. Guinier and Torres, *The Miner's Canary*, 224–25.

118. Jeffrey S. Passel and D'Vera Cohn, "U.S. Population Projections: 2005–2050," Pew Research Center, Feb. 11, 2008, www.pewresearch.org/hispanic/2008/02/11/us-population-projections-2005-2050/.

CHAPTER 10. THE FUTURE OF THE RACIAL MUSLIM
AND RELIGIOUS FREEDOM IN AMERICA

Epigraph: George Washington, "Letter to the Jews of Newport," in *The Papers of George Washington, Digital Edition*, ed. Theodore J. Crackel (Charlottesville: University of Virginia Press, Rotunda, 2007), http://rotunda.upress.virginia.edu /pgwde/search-Preo6d132.

1. Ewing, *Being and Belonging*, 29.
2. Tehranian, *Whitewashed*, 83; Bakalian and Bozorgmehr, *Backlash 9/11*, 15.
3. Al-Arian and Knjawa, "The Perils of American Muslim Politics," 20.
4. Bakalian and Bozorgmehr, *Backlash 9/11*, 196–97.
5. Dave Philipps, "Muslims in the Military: The Few, the Proud, the Welcome," *New York Times*, Aug. 2, 2016, www.nytimes.com/2016/08/03/us/muslims -us-military.html; Muslim Marine, www.muslimmarine.org/; Thomas Gibbons-Neff, "For Muslims in the U.S. Military, a Different U.S. than the One They Swore to Defend," *Washington Post*, Dec. 9, 2015, www.washingtonpost.com/news /checkpoint/wp/2015/12/09/for-muslims-in-the-u-s-military-a-different-u-s-than -the-one-they-swore-to-defend/?noredirect=on&utm_term=.4f1e155c3a05; Alexandra Marks, "One Muslim's Decision to Join the US Army," *Christian Science Monitor*, Mar. 28, 2007, www.csmonitor.com/2007/0328/p01s02-usmi.html; Ruth Nasrullah, "4 Muslim Vets on Life in the Military," *Religion News Service*, Aug. 19, 2016, https://religionnews.com/2016/08/19/4-muslim-vets-on-life-in-the-military/; "Khizr Khan's Speech to the 2016 Democratic National Convention," *ABC News*, Aug 1, 2016, https://abcnews.go.com/Politics/full-text-khizr-khans-speech-2016 -democratic-national/story?id=41043609.
6. Bakalian and Bozorgmehr, *Backlash 9/11*, 186.
7. Gordon, *Assimilation in American Life*, 55–56.
8. Jacobson, *Whiteness of a Different Color*, 76; Kang, "Trojan Horses of Race."
9. Guinier and Torres, *The Miner's Canary*, 224–25.
10. Selod, *Forever Suspect*, 126. For analysis of how Chinese Americans sought to prove their loyalty, see Cheng, *Citizens of Asian America*.
11. Lipset, "Blacks and Jews, How Much Bias?," 57–58.
12. Maghbouleh, *The Limits of Whiteness*.
13. Kalkan, Layman, and Uslaner, "'Bands of Others'? Attitudes toward Muslims in Contemporary American Society"; Patel, *Out of Many Faiths*, 19.
14. Hasidism lacks the privilege of Whiteness. Sylvia Rodriguez, "Tourism, Whiteness, and the Vanishing Anglo Paper," paper presented at the conference Seeing and Being Seen: Tourism in the American West, Center for the American West, Boulder, CO, May 2, 1997, 12, 15; Barbara Demick, "Raids in New Jersey Town Target Ultra-Orthodox Jews Accused of Welfare Fraud; 'What Is Going on Here?,'" *Los Angeles Times*, Sept. 23, 2017, www.latimes.com/nation/la -na-new-jersey-orthodox-20170923-story.html; Joseph Berger, "Uneasy Welcome as Ultra-Orthodox Jews Extend beyond New York," *New York Times*, Aug. 2,

2017, www.nytimes.com/2017/08/02/nyregion/ultra-orthodox-jews-hasidim-new
-jersey.html; John Feffer, interview with Arthur Waskow, Institute for Policy
Studies, Apr. 4, 2011, https://ips-dc.org/interview_with_arthur_waskow/.

15. Cesari, *Muslims in the West after 9/11*, 45; Ewing, *Being and Belonging*,
4; Maira, *The 9/11 Generation*, 16; Ghanea Bassiri, "Religious Normativity and
Praxis among American Muslims."

16. Silk, "The Abrahamic Religions as a Modern Concept," 71.

17. Silk, "The Abrahamic Religions as a Modern Concept," 77.

18. Jon D. Levenson, "The Idea of Abrahamic Religions: A Qualified Dissent," *The Jewish Review of Books* (Spring 2010), https://jewishreviewofbooks.com
/articles/244/the-idea-of-abrahamic-religions-a-qualified-dissent; Quran, 3:68.

19. Ulrich Rosenhagen, "One Abraham or Three?," *Christian Century* 33 (Dec.
9, 2015); Peter L. Berger, "Judeo-Christian or Abrahamic?," *American Interest*,
Dec. 23, 2015, www.the-american-interest.com/2015/12/23/judeo-christian-or
-abrahamic/.

20. Gordis, Grose, Siddiqi, and Hubbard, *The Abraham Connection*.

21. Founded in 1977, the Academy for Judaic, Christian, and Islamic Studies
"promote[s] greater understanding of the interrelations and commonality among
the three monotheistic religions stemming from a common religious heritage,"
http://afjcis.org/.

22. Bakalian and Bozorgmehr, *Backlash 9/11*, 243–44; Cimino, "No God in
Common," 171.

23. Rauf, *Moving the Mountain*.

24. Marzouki, *Islam: An American Religion*, 23–25.

25. Bakalian and Bozorgmehr, *Backlash 9/11*, 230; Osborne, "Shoulder to
Shoulder with American Muslims."

26. Jane Lampman, "Abrahamic Faiths Crack the Door to Deeper Dialogue,"
Christian Science Monitor, June 19, 2003, www.csmonitor.com/2003/0619/p17s01
-lire.html.

27. This book group began in 2012. See www.trinitylittlerock.org/adults
/interfaith-book-group.

28. This book group began in 2001. See http://abraham.lib.virginia.edu/.

29. This book group ran from 2005 to 2016. See https://lubar.wisc.edu/.

30. This book group began in 2004. See https://theshalomcenter.org/content
/tent-abraham-hagar-and-sarah-multireligious-call-peacemaking.

31. This book group began in 2008. See https://stonypointcenter.org
/multifaith-community.

32. Ben Shapiro, "Why the Left Protects Islam," *Investor's Business Daily*,
July 26, 2017, www.investors.com/politics/columnists/ben-shapiro-why-the-left
-protects-islam/.

33. Peter Beinart, "Breaking Faith," *The Atlantic*, Apr. 2017, www.theatlantic
.com/magazine/archive/2017/04/breaking-faith/517785/; Hunter, "The Culture
War and the Sacred/Secular Divide"; David Belt, "How U.S. Social Conservatives
Created Political Unity in Islam Fearmongering," *Fuller Magazine*, Fuller Stu-

dio/Fuller Theological Seminary, 2016, https://fullerstudio.fuller.edu/u-s-social
-conservatives-created-political-unity-islam-fearmongering.

34. Susan Thistlethwaite and Glen Stassen, "Abrahamic Alternatives to War: Jewish, Christian, and Muslim Perspectives on Just Peacemaking," U.S. Institute of Peace, Oct. 1, 2008, www.usip.org/publications/2008/10/abrahamic -alternatives-war-jewish-christian-and-muslim-perspectives-just.

35. Thistlethwaite and Stassen, "Abrahamic Alternatives to War."

36. Silk, "The Abrahamic Religions as a Modern Concept," 83; Jacobson, "The Stranger Among Us."

37. President Jimmy Carter, remarks at the Signing of the Peace Treaty between Egypt and Israel, Mar. 26, 1979, www.historyplace.com/specials /calendar/docs-pix/mar-carter-cdavid.htm.

38. President George W. Bush, Inaugural Address, Jan. 20, 2001, https:// georgewbush-whitehouse.archives.gov/news/inaugural-address.html.

39. Barack Obama, Keynote Speech on Faith and Politics at the Sojourners/ Call to Renewal "Building a Covenant for a New America," Washington, D.C., June 26, 2006, https://sojo.net/articles/transcript-obamas-2006-sojournerscall -renewal-address-faith-and-politics.

40. Obama, Keynote Speech on Faith and Politics.

41. Obama, Keynote Speech on Faith and Politics.

42. Andrew Kaczynski, Chris Massie, and Nathan McDermott, "Republican Congressional Candidate Called Obama a Secret Terrorist-Supporting Muslim," CNN, Sept. 12, 2018, www.cnn.com/2018/09/11/politics/kfile-donnelly/index .html.

43. Remarks by President Barack Obama at Cairo University, June 4, 2009, https://obamawhitehouse.archives.gov/the-press-office/remarks-president-cairo -university-6-04-09.

44. Remarks by Vice President Pence at the Warsaw Ministerial Working Luncheon, Feb. 18, 2019, www.whitehouse.gov/briefings-statements/remarks-vice -president-pence-warsaw-ministerial-working-luncheon-warsaw-poland/.

45. Saeed, "The American Muslim Paradox," 47–48; Cimino, "No God in Common," 172.

46. Bakalian and Bozorgmehr, Backlash 9/11, 2.

47. Maira, The 9/11 Generation; Maira, Missing: Youth, Citizenship, and Empire After 9/11.

48. A Google search of "Islam Awareness Week" brings up several pages of such events hosted by Muslim Student Associations across the United States.

49. Feener, Islam in World Cultures, 284; Hicks, "Religious Pluralism, Secularism, and Interfaith Endeavors," 157.

50. Hicks, "Religious Pluralism, Secularism, and Interfaith Endeavors," 158; Saeed, "The American Muslim Paradox," 47.

51. Osborne, "Shoulder to Shoulder with American Muslims."

52. Shoulder to Shoulder Campaign, www.shouldertoshouldercampaign.org.

53. Maira, The 9/11 Generation, 96.

54. Maira, *The 9/11 Generation*, 106.

55. Curtis, *Muslims in America*, 115; "Eboo Patel on the Importance of Religious Pluralism," "This American Moment," *NPR*, Oct. 2, 2008, www.npr.org /templates/story/story.php?storyId=95286690; Quran, 49:13 ("O mankind, indeed We have created you from male and female and made you peoples and tribes that you may know one another").

56. Laurie Goodstein, "Both Feeling Threatened, American Muslims and Jews Join Hands," *New York Times*, Dec. 5, 2016, www.nytimes.com/2016/12/05 /us/muslim-jewish-alliance-after-trump.html.

57. Maha Elgenaidi, "Fewer Americans View Muslims Favorably, But the Door Is Wide Open to Better Understanding," *HuffPost Religion*, July 31, 2014; Maha Elgenaidi, "Coming in from the Cold: Pew Survey Reveals Continuing Icy Attitudes toward Muslims," *HuffPost Religion*, July 17, 2014, www.huffpost.com /entry/pew-survey-reveals-continuing-icy-attitudes-toward-muslims_b_5596562; Balaji and Millstein, "Beyond Curry and Caliphs," 293.

58. Dalia Mogahed and Azka Mahmoud, "American Muslim Poll 2019: Predicting and Preventing Islamophobia, The Institute for Social Policy and Understanding," May 1, 2019, https://www.ispu.org/american-muslim-poll-2019 -predicting-and-preventing-islamophobia/.

59. Homayra Ziad, "Why I Left the Muslim Leadership Initiative," *Muslim-Matters.org*, June 6, 2018, https://muslimmatters.org/2018/06/06/why-i-left-the -muslim-leadership-initiative/.

60. Sana Saeed, "An Interfaith Trojan Horse: Faithwashing Apartheid and Occupation," *The Islamic Monthly*, July 1, 2014, https://www.theislamicmonthly .com/an-interfaith-trojan-horse-faithwashing-apartheid-and-occupation/ (emphasis in original).

61. Wajahat Ali, Eli Clifton, Matthew Duss, Lee Fang, Scott Keyes, and Faiz Shakir, "Fear, Inc.," The Center for American Progress, Aug. 26, 2011, https:// www.americanprogress.org/issues/religion/reports/2011/08/26/10165/fear-inc/; Matthew Duss, Yasmine Taeb, Ken Gude, and Ken Sofer, "Fear, Inc. 2.0," The Center for American Progress, Feb. 11, 2015, https://www.americanprogress.org /issues/religion/reports/2015/02/11/106394/fear-inc-2-0/; Sana Saeed, "An Interfaith Trojan Horse: Faithwashing Apartheid and Occupation," *The Islamic Monthly*, July 1, 2014, https://www.theislamicmonthly.com/an-interfaith-trojan -horse-faithwashing-apartheid-and-occupation/.

62. "Safe Spaces: An Updated Toolkit for Empowering Communities and Addressing Ideological Violence," MPAC, www.mpac.org/safespaces/files/MPAC -Safe-Spaces.pdf; Thomas, *Scapegoating Islam, 156*.

63. Muflehun, http://muflehun.org/ourwork/.

64. Thomas, *Scapegoating Islam*, 156.

65. Aziz, "Policing Terrorists," 147.

66. Muslims voted overwhelmingly Republican in the 1990s. Jamal and Albana, "Demographics, Political Participation, and Representation," 106; This trend shifted; in 2007, 11 percent of Muslims identified as Republican. "Republi-

cans Account for a Small but Steady Share of U.S. Muslims," Pew Research Center, Nov. 6, 2018, www.pewresearch.org/fact-tank/2018/11/06/republicans-account-for-a-small-but-steady-share-of-u-s-muslims/.

67. Jeff Diamant and Claire Gecewicz, "5 Facts about Muslim Millennials in the U.S.," Pew Research Center, Oct. 26, 2017, www.pewresearch.org/fact-tank/2017/10/26/5-facts-about-muslim-millennials-us/; Paden, Behind the Backlash.

68. Levenson, "The Idea of Abrahamic Religions."

69. Haddad, *Becoming American?*, 36.

70. Jamal and Albana, "Demographics, Political Participation, and Representation," 102; Leonard, "Organizing Communities," 173.

71. Warner, "The Role of Religion in the Process of Segmented Assimilation," 102–3.

72. Warner, "The Role of Religion in the Process of Segmented Assimilation," 105; Grewal, *Islam Is a Foreign Country*.

73. Warner, "The Role of Religion in the Process of Segmented Assimilation," 108.

74. For an examination of working-class South Asian communities' interactions with race, see Bald, *Bengali Harlem and the Lost Histories of South Asian America*.

75. Love, *Islamophobia and Racism in America*, 158–59.

76. Beydoun, "Between Indigence, Islamophobia, and Erasure," 1463; Mauleon, "Black Twice."

77. Daryl Johnson, "Hate in God's Name," Southern Poverty Law Center, Sept. 25, 2017, www.splcenter.org/20170925/hate-god%E2%80%99s-name.

78. Corrigan and Neal, *Religious Intolerance in America*, 255; Kamali, *Homegrown Hate*, 42–64, 187–93.

79. Maira, *The 9/11 Generation*, 87. Forty-five percent of Muslim Millennials believe Americans are friendly toward Muslim Americans, as compared to 65 percent of other generations of Muslim Americans. Diamant and Gecewicz, "5 Facts about Muslim Millennials in the U.S."; Rana, *Terrifying Muslims*.

80. Khabeer, *Muslim Cool*, 224–25; Maira, *The 9/11 Generation*, 12; Maghbouleh, *The Limits of Whiteness*, 106–7.

81. Aidi, *Rebel Music*; Chan-Malik, *Becoming Muslim*.

82. Gualtieri, *Between Arab and White*, 188.

83. Chan-Malik, "Cultural and Literary Production of Muslim America," 295; Jackson, *Islam and the Blackamerican*.

84. Ewing, *Being and Belonging*, 94–95; Aziz, *From the Oppressed to the Terrorist*; Karim, *American Muslim Women*.

85. Maghbouleh, *The Limits of Whiteness*, 11, 53; Ewing, *Being and Belonging*, 38.

86. Salaita, *Anti-Arab Racism in the United States*, 96; Bakalian and Bozorgmehr, *Backlash 9/11*, 178–79; Jamal and Naber, *Race and Arab Americans before and after 9/11*.

87. Esposito and Kalin, *Islamophobia: The Challenge of Pluralism in the 21st Century*, 97.

88. Abdul Khabeer, *Muslim Cool*, 14–15; Sherman, *Islam and the Blackamerican*.

89. Muslim Anti-Racism Collaborative, http://www.muslimarc.org/about.

90. Shazia K. Farook, "A Critical Verse in the Quran: Interview with the Muslim Anti-Racism Collaborative," *AltMuslimah*, Apr. 3, 2014, www.altmuslimah.com/2014/04/a_critical_verse_in_the_quran_interview_with_the_muslim_anti_racism_collabo/.

91. Ahmed Ali Akbar, "21 Kick-Ass Muslims Who Changed the Narrative in 2014," *Buzzfeed*, Dec. 16, 2014, www.buzzfeed.com/ahmedaliakbar/kick-ass-muslims-of-2014.

92. "New Online Campaign Urges American Muslims to 'Drop the A-Word,'" *Al Arabiya News*, Feb. 27, 2014, http://english.alarabiya.net/en/life-style/art-and-culture/2014/02/27/New-online-campaign-urges-American-Muslims-to-drop-the-A-word-.html.

93. "The Sacred Pledge," Muslim Anti-Racism Collaborative, https://pledge.muslimarc.org.

94. Takin' It to the Streets, http://streets2016.com/about/.

95. Leonard, "Organizing Communities," 187; Lopez, *Merge Left*.

96. A central finding in a study conducted in 2013 was that "U.S.-born Muslims tend to hold relatively more critical feelings toward government than immigrant Muslims." Gillum, *Muslims in a Post-9/11 America*, 10, 16; Maira, *The 9/11 Generation*, 119.

97. Maira, *The 9/11 Generation*, 100; Jewish Voice for Peace, https://jewishvoiceforpeace.org/.

98. Nazia Kazi, "The Struggle for Recognition: Muslim American Spokesmanship in the Age of Islamophobia," CUNY Academic Works, 2014, https://academicworks.cuny.edu/cgi/gc_etds/436; Shryock, *Islamophobia/Islamophilia*.

99. Sheehi, "Duplicity and Fear toward a Race and Class Critique of Islamophobia," 36–38.

100. Love, *Islamophobia and Racism in America*, 149; "Rabia Chaudry on the American Muslim Identity," Hollings Center for International Dialogue, Sept. 2, 2015, https://hollingscenter.org/rabia-chaudry-on-american-muslim-identity/.

101. Shams, "Visibility as Resistance by Muslim Americans in a Surveillance and Security Atmosphere."

102. "American Muslim Poll 2017: Muslims at the Crossroad," Institute for Social Policy and Understanding, June 2017, www.ispu.org/wp-content/uploads/2017/06/AMP-2017-Key-Findings.pdf.

103. Coalition for Civil Freedoms. "Prisoner Lives Matter—Unseen Suffering Behind the Prison Walls," *News Digest* 9, no. 704, Friday, Nov. 13, 2020, https://mailchi.mp/396bc4482eb2/news-digest-1113-only-one-prosecutor-has-ever-been-jailed-for-misconduct-leading-to-a-wrongful-conviction?fbclid=IwAR1hW_fsltgo8Pgl5LUK-O8JJfDZLFk2KB55NWeBXXH22zhO9KB_ygSD_go.

104. Daulatzai and Rana, *With Stones in Our Hands*, xvii–xviii.

105. Love, *Islamophobia and Racism in America*, 172.

106. Ilhan Omar, "Criminal Justice," www.ilhanomar.com/criminal-justice.

107. Sheryl Gay Stolberg, "From Celebrated to Vilified, House's Muslim Women Absorb Blows over Israel," *New York Times*, Feb. 1, 2019, www.nytimes .com/2019/02/01/us/politics/ilhan-omar-rashida-tlaib-israel.html.

108. Erin Kelly, "Six Things about Rashida Tlaib, Who Will Likely Become First Muslim Woman in Congress," *USA Today*, Aug. 8, 2018, www.usatoday .com/story/news/politics/2018/08/08/rashida-tlaib-michigan-democrat-muslim -woman-congress/933253002/.

109. "Rashida Tlaib to Speak at Carlow University in Pennsylvania," Take On Hate, Apr. 4, 2016, www.takeonhate.org/take_on_hate_s_rashida_tlaib_to _speak_at_carlow_university_in_pennsylvania.

110. "Palestinian BDS National Committee," BDS Movement, https:// bdsmovement.net/bnc.

111. Stolberg, "From Celebrated to Vilified, House's Muslim Women Absorb Blows over Israel"; Josh Marshall, "The Attacks on Rashida Tlaib Are Dishonest and Disgraceful," *Talking Points Memo*, May 13, 2019, https://talkingpointsmemo .com/edblog/the-attacks-on-rashida-tlaib-are-dishonest-and-disgraceful.

112. Brendan Cole, "Fox News Host Compares Rashida Tlaib to Terrorist Organization: 'She Has a Hamas Agenda,'" *Newsweek*, July 30, 2019, https://www .newsweek.com/rashida-tlaib-hegseth-fox-democrats-hamas-1451652

113. "Muslims in America: Immigrants and Those Born in U.S. See Life Differently in Many Ways," *Pew Forum*, Apr. 17, 2018, www.pewforum.org/essay /muslims-in-america-immigrants-and-those-born-in-u-s-see-life-differently-in -many-ways/.

114. "Total and Complete Shutdown," Muslim Advocates, Apr. 2018, https://muslimadvocates.org/wp-content/uploads/2019/06/Total-and-Complete -Shutdown_Report.pdf.

CONCLUSION

1. West, *Race Matters*.

2. Todd Green, "Confronting Christian Islamophobia," Berkeley Center for Religion, Peace and World Affairs at Georgetown University, May 24, 2021, https://berkleycenter.georgetown.edu/responses/confronting-christian -islamophobia; Gregory A. Smith, "Most White Evangelicals Approve of Trump Travel Prohibition and Express Concerns About Extremism," Pew Research Center, Feb. 27, 2017, https://www.pewresearch.org/fact-tank/2017/02/27/most-white -evangelicals-approve-of-trump-travel-prohibition-and-express-concerns-about -extremism/; Tom Gjelten, "How the Fight for Religious Freedom Has Fallen Victim to the Culture Wars," National Public Radio, May 23, 2019.

3. Joshi, "The Racialization of Religion in the United States," 38.

4. Mishra, "Religion and Race," 232; Painter, *The History of White People*, 391; Bonilla-Silva, "Rethinking Racism," 465, 470; Feagin, *The White Racial Frame*, 115.

5. Harris, "Whiteness as Property," 1736.

6. Omi and Winant, "Concept of Race," 16; Joshi, "The Racialization of Hinduism, Islam, and Sikhism in the United States," 222.

7. Painter, *The History of White People*, 256; Blumenfeld, "Christian Privilege and the Promotion of 'Secular' and Not-So 'Secular' Mainline Christianity in Public Schooling and in the Larger Society."

8. Green, *Inventing a Christian America*, 1.

9. "Muslims in America: Immigrants and Those Born in U.S. See Life Differently in Many Ways," Pew Forum, Apr. 17, 2018, https://www.pewforum.org/essay/muslims-in-america-immigrants-and-those-born-in-u-s-see-life-differently-in-many-ways/.

10. Robert P. Jones, *White Too Long: The Legacy of White Supremacy in American Christianity*.

BIBLIOGRAPHY

Abdo, Geneive. "Days of Rage in Tehran." *Middle East Policy Journal* 4 (1999). www.epc.org/journal/9910_abdo.html.

Abdul Khabeer, Suad. *Muslim Cool: Race, Religion, and Hip Hop in the United States*. New York: NYU Press, 2017.

Abdullah, Zain. "American Muslims in the Contemporary World: 1965 to the Present." In *The Cambridge Companion to American Islam*, edited by Juliane Hammer and Omid Safi, 65–82. Cambridge: Cambridge University Press, 2013.

Abraham, Nabeel. "Anti-Arab Racism and Violence in the United States." In *The Development of Arab-American Identity*, edited by Ernest McCarus, 155–214. Ann Arbor: University of Michigan Press, 1994.

Aidi, Hishaam. *Rebel Music: Race, Empire, and the New Muslim Youth Culture*. New York: Vintage Books, 2014.

Airhart, Phyllis D., and Margaret Lamberts Bendroth, eds. *Faith Traditions and the Family*. Louisville: Westminster John Knox Press, 1996.

Ajrouch, Kristine J., and Amaney Jamal. "Assimilating to a White Identity: The Case of Arab Americans." *International Migration Review* 41 (2007): 860–79.

Akram, Susan, and Kevin Johnson. "Race and Civil Rights Pre-September 11, 2001: The Targeting of Arabs and Muslims." In *Civil Rights in Peril: The Targeting of Arabs and Muslims*, edited by Elaine C. Hagopian. Chicago: Haymarket, 2014.

Al-Arian, Abdullah, and Hafsa Knjawa. "The Perils of American Muslim Politics." In *With Stones in Our Hands: Writings on Muslims, Racism and Empire*, edited by Sohail Daulatzai and Junaid Rana. Minneapolis: University of Minnesota Press, 2018.

Alba, Richard D. *Ethnic Identity: The Transformation of White America*. New Haven: Yale University Press, 1990.

Alba, Richard, and Nancy Foner. *Strangers No More: Immigration and the Challenges of Integration in North America and Western Europe*. Princeton: Princeton University Press, 2015.

Alba, Richard D., and Victor Nee. *Remaking the American Mainstream: Assimilation and Contemporary Immigration*. Cambridge, MA: Harvard University Press, 2005.

Alemany, Jacqueline, and Karoun Demirjian. "Sen. Bernie Sanders to Introduce Resolution on Disapproval on $735 Million U.S. Arms Sale to Israel." *Washington Post*, May 20, 2021. https://www.washingtonpost.com/politics/2021/05/20/sen-bernie-sanders-introduce-resolution-disapproval-735-million-us-arms-sale-israel.

Alexander, Michelle. *The New Jim Crow: Mass Incarceration in the Age of Colorblindness*. New York: New Press, 2010.

Alford, Terry. *Prince among Slaves: The True Story of an African Prince Sold into Slavery in the American South*. Oxford University Press 2007.

Ali, Arshad Imtiaz. "Learning in the Shadow of the War on Terror toward a Pedagogy of Muslim Indignation." In *With Stones in Our Hands: Writings on Muslims, Racism and Empire*, edited by Sohail Daulatzai and Junaid Rana, 247–54. Minneapolis: University of Minnesota Press, 2018.

Ali, Wajahat, Eli Clifton, Matthew Duss, Lee Fang, Scott Keyes, and Faiz Shakir. *Fear, Inc.: The Roots of the Islamophobia Network in America*. Center for American Progress, 2011. http://www.americanprogress.org/issues/2011/08/pdf/islamophobia.pdf.

Alimahomed-Wilson, Sabrina. "When the FBI Knocks: Racialized State Surveillance of Muslims." *Critical Sociology* 45 (2018): 871–87.

Alsultany, Evelyn. *Arabs and Muslims in the Media: Race and Representation after 9/11*. New York: NYU Press, 2012.

Antonius, George. *The Arab Awakening: The Story of the Arab National Movement*. Shelby Township: International Book Centre, 1939. Reprint, 1985.

Apuzzo, Matt, and Adam Goldman. "Documents: NYPD Gathered Intelligence on 250-Plus Mosques, Student Groups in Terrorist Hunt." Associated Press, Sept. 6, 2011. www.pulitzer.org/files/2012/investigative_reporting/ap/nypd3.pdf.

Aziz, Sahar F. "The Authoritarianization of U.S. Counterterrorism." *Washington & Lee Law Review* 75 (2018): 1573–635.

———. "Caught in a Preventive Dragnet: Selective Counterterrorism in a Post-9/11 America." 47 Gonz. L. Rev. 429 (2011/2012).

———. "Coercive Assimilationism: The Perils of Muslim Women's Identity Performance in the Workplace." *Michigan Journal of Race and Law* 20 (2014): 1–64.

———. "From the Oppressed to the Terrorist: Muslim-American Women in the Crosshairs of Intersectionality." 9 *Hastings Race and Poverty Law Journal* 191 (2012): 191–263.

———. "The Laws on Providing Material Support to Terrorist Organizations: The Erosion of Constitutional Rights or a Legitimate Tool for Preventing Terrorism?" *Texas Civil Rights and Liberties Journal* 9 (2003): 45–92.

————. "A Muslim Registry: The Precursor to Internment?" *Brigham Young University Law Review* 4, no. 4 (2018): 779–838.

————. "Policing Terrorists in the Community." *Harvard National Security Law Journal* 5 (2014): 147–224.

Aziz, Sahar F., and Khaled A. Beydoun. "Fear of a Black and Brown Internet: Policing Online Activism." *Boston University Law Review* 100 (2020): 1153–93.

Bail, Christopher A. *Terrified: How Anti-Muslim Fringe Organizations Became Mainstream.* Princeton: Princeton University Press, 2015.

Bakalian, Anny, and Medhi Bozorgmehr. *Backlash 9/11: Middle Eastern and Muslim Americans Respond.* Berkeley: University of California Press, 2009.

Balaji, Murali, and Henry Millstein. "Beyond Curry and Caliphs: How Advocacy in Education Has Shaped Hindu-Muslim Relations in the United States." *The Muslim World: Hartford Seminary* 107 (2017): 287–301.

Bald, Vivek. *Bengali Harlem and the Lost Histories of South Asian America.* Cambridge: Harvard University Press, 2015.

Barkan, Elliot R. "Race, Religion, and Nationality in American Society." Journal of American Immigration History 14 (1995): 41–64.

Barlow, Elizabeth. *Evaluation of Secondary-Level Textbooks for Coverage of the Middle East and North Africa.* Ann Arbor: Center for Middle Eastern and North African Studies; Tucson: Middle East Studies Association, 1994.

Barot, Rohit, and John Bird. "Racialization: The Genealogy and Critique of a Concept." Ethnic and Racial Studies 24 (2001): 601–18.

Barry, Colman J. *The Catholic Church and German Americans.* Milwaukee: Bruce Publishing Company, 1953.

Bassiouni, M. Cherif. *The Civil Rights of Arab-Americans: The Special Measures.* North Dartmouth: Arab-American University Graduates, 1974.

Bawardi, Hani. *The Making of Arab Americans: From Syrian Nationalism to U.S. Citizenship.* Austin: University of Texas Press, 2014.

Bayoumi, Moustafa. *How Does It Feel to Be a Problem?* New York: Penguin, 2008.

————. "Racing Religion." *New Centennial Review* 6 (2006): 267.

————. *This Muslim American Life: Dispatches from the War on Terror.* New York: NYU Press, 2015.

Bell, Derrick. "*Brown v. Board of Education* and the Interest-Convergence Dilemma." *Harvard Law Review* 93 (1980): 518–33.

Bellah, Robert N. "Civil Religion in America." *Journal of the American Academy of Arts and Sciences* 96 (1967): 1–21.

Belt, David. "How U.S. Social Conservatives Created Political Unity in Islam Fearmongering." Fuller Studio, 2016. https://fullerstudio.fuller.edu/u-s-social-conservatives-created-political-unity-islam-fearmongering.

Beydoun, Khaled. "Antebellum Islam." *Howard Law Journal* 58 (2014): 141–94.

————. "Between Indigence, Islamophobia, and Erasure: Poor and Muslim in 'War on Terror' America." *California Law Review* 104, no. 6 (December 2016): 1463–502.

———. "Between Muslim and White: The Legal Construction of Arab American Identity." *New York University Annual Survey of American Law* 69 (2013): 2–34.

———. "Islamophobia: Toward a Legal Definition and Framework." *Columbia Law Review* 116 (2016): 108. https://columbialawreview.org/content/islamopho bia-toward-a-legal-definition-and-framework.

Bjorck, Eric Tobias. *A Little Olive Leaf.* New York: William Bradford, 1704.

Blair, Alma R. "Haun's Mill Massacre." *Encyclopedia of Mormonism.* Provo: Brigham Young University Press, 1992. https://eom.byu.edu/index.php/Haun %27s_Mill_Massacre.

Blumenfeld, Warren J. "Christian Privilege and the Promotion of 'Secular' and Not-So 'Secular' Mainline Christianity in Public Schooling and in the Larger Society." *Equity and Excellence in Education* 39 (2006): 195–210.

———. "Christian Privilege in the United States: An Overview." In *Investigating Christian Privilege and Religious Oppression in the United States*, edited by Warren J. Blumenfeld, Khyati Y. Joshi, and Ellen E. Fairchild. Rotterdam: Sense, 2009.

Blumenfeld, Warren J., Khyati Y. Joshi, and Ellen E. Fairchild. *Investigating Christian Privilege and Religious Oppression in the United States.* Rotterdam: Sense, 2009.

Boaz, Danielle. "Practices 'Odious Among the Northern and Western Nations of Europe': Whiteness and Religious Freedom in the United States." In *Relating Worlds of Racism: Dehumanisation, Belonging, and the Normativity of European Whiteness*, edited by P. Essed et al., 39–62. New York: Palgrave Macmillan, 2019.

Bonilla-Silva, Eduardo. *Racism without Racists: Color-Blind Racism and the Persistence of Racial Inequality in the United States.* 3d ed. Lanham, MD: Rowman & Littlefield, 2010.

———. "Rethinking Racism: Toward a Structural Interpretation." *American Sociology Review* 62 (1997): 465–80.

Bowen, Patrick Denis. "The African-American Islamic Renaissance and the Rise of the Nation of Islam." University of Denver, 2013. https://digitalcommons.du .edu/cgi/viewcontent.cgi?article=1962&context=etd.

Brandeis, Louis D. "The Jewish Problem: How to Solve It." Speech to the Conference of Eastern Council of Reform Rabbis, April 25, 1915. https:// louisville.edu/law/library/special-collections/the-louis-d.-brandeis -collection/the-jewish-problem-how-to-solve-it-by-louis-d.-brandeis.

Brodkin, Karen. *How Jews Became White Folks and What That Says about Race in America.* New Brunswick, NJ: Rutgers University Press, 1998.

Boykin, William J., Henry F. Cooper, Fred Fleitz, Kevin Freeman, Frank J. Gaffney, Dan Goure, John Guandolo, Jim Hanson, Brian Kennedy, and Clare M. Lopez. *The Secure Freedom Strategy: A Plan for Victory over the Global Jihad Movement.* Washington, DC: Center for Security Policy Press, 2015.

Bulliet, Richard W. *The Case for Islamo-Christian Civilization.* New York: Columbia University Press, 2004.

Cainkar, Louise. "Fluid Terror Threat: A Genealogy of the Racialization of Arab, Muslim, and South Asian Americans." *Amerasia Journal* 44, no. 1 (2018), 27–59.

———. "Hijab as a Human Right: Hegemonic Femininity and Gender Policing." In *Arabs at Home and in the World*, edited by Karla McKanders. New York: Routledge, 2018.

———. *Homeland Insecurity: The Arab American and Muslim American Experience after 9/11*. New York: Russell Sage, 2009.

Cainkar, Louise, and Saher Selod. "Review of Race Scholarship and the War on Terror." *Sociology of Race & Ethnicity* 4, no. 2: 165–177 (2018).

Caner, Ergun, and Emir Fethi Caner. *Unveiling Islam: An Insider's Look at Muslim Life and Beliefs*. Kregel, 2002.

Carney, Zoe Hess, and Mary E. Stuckey. "The World as the American Frontier: Racialized Presidential War Rhetoric." *Southern Communication Journal* 80 (2015): 165.

Carpenter, J. Scott, Matthew Levitt, and Michael Jacobson. "Confronting the Ideology of Radical Extremism." *Journal of National Security Law and Policy* 3 (2009): 301–27.

Casanova, Jose. "Cosmopolitanism, the Clash of Civilizations and Multiple Modernities." *Current Sociology* 59 (2011): 252–67.

Cesari, Jocelyne. *Muslims in the West after 9/11: Religion, Politics and Law*. New York: Routledge, 2009.

Chan-Malik, Sylvia. *Becoming Muslim: A Cultural History of Women of Color in American Islam* (New York: NYU Press, 2018).

———. "Cultural and Literary Production of Muslim America." In *The Cambridge Companion to American Islam*, edited by Juliane Hammer and Omid Safi, 279–98. Cambridge: Cambridge University Press, 2013.

Cheah, Joseph. *Race and Religion in American Buddhism: White Supremacy and Immigrant Adaptation*. Oxford: Oxford University Press, 2011.

Cheng, Cindy I-Fen. *Citizens of Asian America*. New York: NYU Press, 2013.

Chomsky, Noam. *The Fateful Triangle: The United States, Israel and the Palestinians*. Chicago: Haymarket Books, 1983.

Cimino, Richard. "No God in Common: American Evangelical Discourse on Islam after 9/11." *Review of Religious Research* 47 (2005): 162–74.

Cohen, David S., and Krysten Connon. *Living in the Crosshairs: The Untold Stories of Anti-Abortion Terrorism*. New York and Oxford: Oxford University Press, 2015.

Cohen, John D. "The Next Generation of Government CVE Strategies at Home: Expanding Opportunities for Intervention." *Annals of the American Academy of Political and Social Science* 668 (2016): 124. https://doi.org/10.1177/0002716216669933.

Cole, David. *Enemy Aliens: Double Standards and Constitutional Freedoms in the War on Terrorism*. New York: New Press, 2003.

———. "The New McCarthyism: Repeating History in the War in Terrorism." *Harvard Civil Rights–Civil Liberties Law Review* 38 (2003): 24–26.

Conzen, Kathleen Neils, et al. "The Invention of Ethnicity: A Perspective from the U.S.A." *Journal of American Ethnic History* 12 (1992): 3–41.

Cook, Anthony E. *The Least of These: Race, Law, and Religion in American Culture*. New York: Routledge, 1997.

Corrigan, John, and Lynn S. Neal. *Religious Intolerance in America: A Documentary History*. Chapel Hill: University of North Carolina Press, 2010.

Cowan, Douglas E. "Theologizing Race: The Construction of 'Christian Identity.'" In *Religion and the Creation of Race and Ethnicity*, edited by Craig R. Prentiss, 112–23. New York: NYU Press, 2003.

Cremin, L. A. *American Education: The Colonial Experience, 1607–1783*. New York: Harper & Row, 1970.

Cubberley, Ellwood P. *Changing Conceptions of Education*. Boston: Houghton Mifflin, 1909.

Cunningham, Lawrence S. *An Introduction to Catholicism*, 22. Cambridge: Cambridge University Press, 2009.

Curtis, Edward E., IV. "Black History, Islam, and the Future of the Humanities beyond White Supremacy." Paper presented at the Duke University Franklin Humanities Institute, Feb. 16, 2016, https://humanitiesfutures.org/papers /black-history-islam-future-humanities-beyond-white-supremacy.

———. *Black Muslim Religion in the Nation of Islam, 1960–1975*. Chapel Hill, NC: University of North Carolina Press, 2006.

———. *The Bloomsbury Reader on Islam in the West*. London: Bloomsbury, 2015.

———. *The Columbia Sourcebook of Muslims in the United States*. New York: Columbia University Press, 2009.

———. *Islam in Black America: Identity, Liberation, and Difference in African-American Islamic Thought*. Albany: State University of New York Press, 2002.

———. *Muslims in America: A Short History*. Oxford: Oxford University Press, 2009.

———. "The Study of American Muslims: A History." In *The Cambridge Companion to American Islam*, edited by Juliane Hammer and Omid Safi. Cambridge: Cambridge University Press, 2013.

Dabashi, Hamid. *Brown Skins, White Masks*. London: Pluto Press, 2011.

Daouf, Sylviane A. *Servants of Allah*. New York: NYU Press, 1998.

Darwish, Nonie. *Now They Call Me Infidel: Why I Renounced Jihad for America, Israel, and the War on Terror*. New York: Penguin Random House, 1996.

Daulatzai, Sohail. *Black Star, Crescent Moon: The Muslim International and Black Freedom Beyond America*. Minneapolis: University of Minnesota Press, 2012.

Daulatzai, Sohail, and Junaid Rana. *With Stones in Our Hands: Writings on Muslims, Racism, and Empire*. Minneapolis: University of Minnesota Press, 2018.

Davis, David Brion. "Some Themes of Counter-Subversion: An Analysis of Anti-Masonic, Anti-Catholic, and Anti-Mormon Literature." *Mississippi Valley Historical Review* 47 (Sept. 1960): 205–24.

Detailed Information on the Immigration and Customs Enforcement: Office of Investigations Assessment, https://obamawhitehouse

.archives.gov/sites/default/files/omb/assets/omb/expectmore/detail/10002388
.2004.html.

Detroit Arab American Study Team. *Citizenship and Crisis.* New York: Russell
Sage, 2009.

Deuteronomy 25:19, I Samuel 15:3. https://www.bl.uk/treasures/gutenberg/donatus
.html.

Deutsch, Michael E., and Erica Thompson. "Secrets and Lies: The Persecution of
Muhammad Salah (Part I)." *Journal of Palestine Studies* 37 (2008): 51.

Disney, Lindsey R. "Associations between Humanitarianism, Othering, and
Religious Affiliation." *Social Work and Christianity* 44, no. 3 (Fall 2017), 60–74.

Dollinger, Marc. *Black Power, Jewish Politics: Reinventing the Alliance in the 1960s.*
Brandeis University Press, 2018.

Dudziak, Mary L. *Cold War Civil Rights: Race and the Image of American Democracy.* Princeton: Princeton University Press, 2011.

Duncan, Jason K. *Citizens or Papists? The Politics of Anti-Catholicism in New York,
1685–1821.* New York: Fordham University Press, 2005.

Dunn, Kevin M., Natascha Klocker, and Tanya Salabay. "Contemporary Racism
and Islamophobia in Australia: Racializing Religion." *Ethnicities* 7 (2007): 564,
567.

Dwight, Timothy. "The Duty of Americans, at the Present Crisis" [1798]. In
Political Sermons of the American Founding Era, edited by Ellis Sandoz. Carmel:
Liberty Fund, 1991.

Eisgruber, Christopher L., and Lawrence G. Sager. "Equal Liberty." In *Religion
and Equality Law,* edited by Nelson Tebbe, 241–72. New York: Routledge,
2013.

———. "Ten Commandments, Three Plastic Reindeer, and One Nation... Indi-
visible." In *Religion and Equality Law,* edited by Nelson Tebbe, 465–74. New
York: Routledge, 2013.

Elver, Hilal. "Racializing Islam Before and After 9/11: From Melting Pot to Islamophobia." *Transnational Law and Contemporary Problems* 21 (2012): 119, 174.

Emerson, Michael, and Christian Smith. *Divided by Faith: Evangelical Religion
and the Problem of Race in America.* New York: Oxford University Press, 2001.

Emerson, Ralph Waldo. *Selected Essays, Lectures and Poems.* New York: Penguin
Bantam Classics, 2006.

Emerson, Steven, dir. "Terrorists Among Us: Jihad in America," *PBS Frontline,*
1994.

Ernst, Carl W. *Introduction to Islamophobia in America: The Anatomy of Intolerance.* New York: Palgrave Macmillan, 2013.

Esposito, John L., and Ibrahim Kalin. *Islamophobia: The Challenge of Pluralism
in the 21st Century.* Oxford: Oxford University Press, 2011.

Everett, David, and Caleb Bingham. *Slaves in Barbary.* 1817.

Ewing, Katherine. *Being and Belonging: Muslims in the United States since 9/11.*
New York: Russell Sage Foundation, 2008.

Fahmy, Dalia. "The Green Scare Is Not McCarthyism 2.0: How Islamophobia Is

Redefining the Use of Propaganda in Foreign and Domestic Affairs." *Dialectical Anthropology* 39 (2015): 63–67.

Falwell, Jerry. *Listen America!* New York: W.W. Norton, 1980.

Feagin, Joe R. *The White Racial Frame: Centuries of Racial Framing and Counter-Framing*. New York and London: Routledge, 2013.

Feener, Michael R. *Islam in World Cultures: Comparative Perspectives*. Religion in Contemporary Culture Series. Santa Barbara: ABC-CLIO, 2004.

Feingold, Henry L. *The Jewish People in America: A Time for Searching: Entering the Mainstream*. Baltimore: Johns Hopkins University Press, 1992.

Feldman, Keith. *A Shadow over Palestine: The Imperial Life of Race in America*. Minneapolis: University of Minnesota Press, 2015.

Fields, Barbara J. "Ideology and Race in American History." In *Region, Race, and Reconstruction: Essays in Honor of C. Vann Woodward*, edited by J. Morgan Kousser and James McPherson, 143–177. New York: Oxford University Press, 1982.

Figueroa, Carlos. "Quakerism and Racialism in Early Twentieth-Century U.S. Politics." In *Faith and Race in American Political Life*, edited by Robin Dale Jacobson and Nancy D. Wadsworth, 56–79. Charlottesville: University of Virginia Press, 2012.

Finke, Roger, and Rodney Stark. *The Churching of America, 1776–2005*. New Brunswick, NJ: Rutgers University Press, 2005.

Finkelman, Paul. "The Crime of Color." *Tulane Law Review* 67 (1993): 2072–75.

Fisher, James T. *Communion of Immigrants: A History of Catholics in America*. New York: Oxford University Press, 2007.

Fluhman, J. Spencer. "An 'American Mahomet': Joseph Smith, Muhammad, and the Problem of Prophets in Antebellum America." *Journal of Mormon History* 34 (2008): 32, 43.

Flynn, Michael, and Michael Ledeen. *The Field of Fight: How We Can Win the Radical War against Radical Islam and Its Allies*. New York: St. Martin's Griffin, 2017.

Ford, Henry. "The International Jew: The World's Foremost Problem" [Digital reprint]. Dearborn: Dearborn Publishing Company, 1920, https://en.wikisource.org/wiki/The_International_Jew.

Forrell, George W. "Luther and the War against the Turks." *Church History* 14 (December 1945): 264.

Foxe, John. *Acts and Monuments of These Latter and Perillous Dayes*. 1563. In *Foxe's Book of Martyrs*, edited by Harold J. Chadwick. Newberry, Florida: Bridge Logos, 2001.

Fredrickson, George M. *Racism: A Short History*. Princeton, NJ: Princeton University Press, 2002.

Freedland, Michael. *Witch Hunt in Hollywood: McCarthyism's War on Tinseltown*. London: Aurum Press, 2009.

Friedlander, Jonathan. *Sojourners and Settlers: The Yemeni Immigrant Experience*. Salt Lake City: University of Utah Press, 1988.

Friedman, Alan. *Spider's Web: The Secret History of How the White House Illegally Armed Iraq.* New York: Bantam Books, 1993.

Froude, James Anthony. "Romanism and the Irish Race." *North American Review,* Dec. 1, 1879, 520–36.

Gabriel, Mark A. *Culture Clash: Islam's War on America.* Frontline, 2007.

———. *Islam And Terrorism: What the Quran Really Teaches about Christianity, Violence and the Goals of the Islamic Jihad.* Lake Mary: Charisma House, 2002.

Gans, Herbert J. "Toward a Reconciliation of 'Assimilation' and 'Pluralism': The Interplay of Acculturation and Ethnic Retention." *International Migration Review* 31 (1997): 877.

Garner, Steve, and Saher Selod. "The Racialization of Muslims: Empirical Studies of Islamophobia." *Critical Sociology* 41 (2015): 9–19.

Gergel, Richard. *Unexampled Courage: The Blinding of Sgt. Isaac Woodard and the Awakening of President Harry S. Truman and Judge J. Waties Waring.* New York: Sarah Crichton Books, 2019.

Ghanea, Nazila. "Religion, Equality, and Non-Discrimination." In *Religion and Equality Law*, edited by Nelson Tebbe, 95–108. New York: Routledge, 2013.

Ghanea Bassiri, Kambiz. *A History of Islam in America: From the New World to the New World Order.* Cambridge: Cambridge University Press, 2010.

———. "Religious Normativity and Praxis among American Muslims." In *The Cambridge Companion to American Islam*, edited by Juliane Hammer and Omid Safi, 208–27. Cambridge: Cambridge University Press, 2013.

Ghareeb, Edmund. *Split Vision: The Portrayal of Arabs in the American Media.* Washington, DC: American-Arab Affairs Council, 1983.

Gillum, Rachel M. *Muslims in a Post-9/11 America: A Survey of Attitudes and Beliefs and Their Implications for U.S. National Security Policy.* Ann Arbor: University of Michigan Press, 2018.

Gilmore, Ruth Wilson. *Golden Gulag: Prisons, Surplus, Crisis, and Opposition in Globalizing California.* Berkeley: University of California Press, 2007.

Glazer, Nathan, and Daniel P. Moynihan. *Beyond the Melting Pot: The Negroes, Puerto Ricans, Jews, Italians, and Irish of New York City.* South Yarra: Leopold Classic Library, 2016.

Goldstein, Eric L. "Contesting the Categories: Jews and Government Racial Classification in the United States." *Jewish History* 19 (2005): 79–107.

———. *The Price of Whiteness: Jews, Race, and American Identity.* Princeton: Princeton University Press, 2006.

Gomez, Lauren E. *Manifest Destinies: The Making of the Mexican American Race.* New York: NYU Press, 2007.

Gordis, David M., George Benedict Grose, Muzammil Siddiqi, and Benjamin Jerome Hubbard. *The Abraham Connection: A Jew, Christian, and Muslim in Dialogue.* Notre Dame: Cross Cultural Publications / Cross Roads Books of the Academy for Judaic, Christian, and Islamic Studies and Church and the World, 1994.

Gordon, Linda. *The Second Coming of the KKK: The Ku Klux Klan of the 1920's and the American Political Tradition*. New York: Liveright, 2017.

Gordon, Milton M. *Assimilation in American Life: The Role of Race, Religion, and National Origin*. Oxford: Oxford University Press, 1964.

Gordon, Sarah Barringer. "'Free' Religion and 'Captive' Schools: Protestants, Catholics, and Education, 1945–1965." *DePaul Law Review* 56, no. 4, Summer 207, 2007, 1177–220.

Gordon, Susan M. "Race, National Identity, and the Changing Circumstances of Jewish Immigrants in the United States." In *Faith and Race in American Political Life*, edited by Robin Dale Jacobson and Nancy D. Wadsworth, 80–102. Charlottesville: University of Virginia Press, 2012.

Gotanda, Neil. "Comparative Racialization: Racial Profiling and the Case of Wen Ho Lee." *UCLA Law Review* 47 (2000): 1689, 1692.

Gottschalk, Peter, and Gabriel Greenberg. *Islamophobia: Making Muslims the Enemy*. Baltimore: Rowman and Littlefield, 2008.

Green, Steven K. *Inventing a Christian America: The Myth of the Religious Founding*. New York: Oxford University Press, 2015.

———. "The Separation of Church and State in the United States." In *Oxford Research Encyclopedia of American History*. Oxford University Press, 2014: 7.

Greenwalt, Kent. "Freedom from Compelled Profession of Belief, Adverse Targeting, and Discrimination." In *Religion and Equality Law*, edited by Nelson Tebbe, 39–52. New York: Routledge, 2013.

———. Introduction to *Religion and Equality Law*, edited by Nelson Tebbe, 29–38. New York: Routledge, 2013.

Gregg, Gary. *The Middle East: A Cultural Psychology*. Oxford: Oxford University Press, 2005.

Grewal, Zareena. 2014. *Islam Is a Foreign Country*. New York: NYU Press.

Griggs, Khalid. "Fattah Islamic Party in North America: A Quiet Storm of Political Activism." In *Muslim Minorities in the West: Visible and Invisible*, edited by Yvonne Yazbeck Haddad and Jane I. Smith. Walnut Creek, CA: Altamira Press, 2002.

Gualtieri, Sarah. "Becoming 'White': Race, Religion and the Foundations of Syrian/Lebanese Ethnicity in the United States." *Journal of American Ethnic History* 20 (2001): 29–58.

———. *Between Arab and White: Race and Ethnicity in the Early Syrian American Diaspora*. Berkeley: University of California Press, 2009.

Guinier, Lani, and Gerald Torres. *The Miner's Canary: Enlisting Race, Resisting Power, Transforming Democracy*. Cambridge, MA: Harvard University Press, 2002.

Guir, William. *The Life of Mahomet: From Original Sources, Voices of India*. 1961, republished in 2002.

Haddad, Yvonne Yazbeck. "Arab American Christian Scholars and the Study of the Middle East in the U.S." Farhat Ziadeh Distinguished Lecture in Arab and Islamic Studies, 2010.

————. *Becoming American? The Forging of Arab and Muslim Identity in Pluralist America*. Waco: Baylor University Press, 2011.

————. *Not Quite American? The Shaping of Arab and Muslim Identity in the United States*. Waco: Baylor University Press, 2004.

Haddad, Yvonne Yazbeck, and Jane I. Smith. Introduction to *Muslim Minorities in the West: Visible and Invisible*, edited by Yvonne Yazbeck Haddad and Jane I. Smith, v–ii. Walnut Creek, CA: Altamira Press, 2002.

Haddad, Yvonne Yazbeck, Jane I. Smith, and John L. Esposito. *Religion and Immigration: Christian, Jewish, and Muslim Experiences in the United States*. Thousand Oaks: AltaMira Press, 2003.

Hafez, Farid. "Comparing Anti-Semitism and Islamophobia: The State of the Field." *Islamophobia Studies Journal* 3 (2016): 16–34.

Hamar Martinez, Jessica, Edwin I. Hernandez, and Milagros Pena. "Latino Religion and Its Political Consequences: Exploring National and Local Trends." In *Faith and Race in American Political Life*, edited by Robin Dale Jacobson and Nancy D. Wadsworth. Charlottesville: University of Virginia Press, 2012.

Hammer, Juliane. "Studying American Muslim Women: Gender, Feminism, and Islam." In *The Cambridge Companion to American Islam*, edited by Juliane Hammer and Omid Safi, 330–44. Cambridge: Cambridge University Press, 2013.

Hammer, Juliane, and Omid Safi. "Introduction: American Islam, Muslim Americans, and the American Experiment." In *The Cambridge Companion to American Islam*, edited by Juliane Hammer and Omid Safi, 1–14. Cambridge: Cambridge University Press, 2013.

Hammond, Phillip E. *Religion and Personal Autonomy*. University of South Carolina, 1992.

Haney Lopez, Ian. *Merge Left: Fusing Race and Class, Winning Elections and Saving America*. New York: The New Press, 2019.

————. *White by Law: The Legal Construction of Race*. 10th Anniversary ed. New York: NYU Press, 2006.

Hansford, Justin. "Jailing a Rainbow: The Marcus Garvey Case." *Georgetown Journal of Law & Critical Race Perspectives* 2 (2009), https://papers.ssrn.com/sol3/papers.cfm?abstract_id=1321527.

Harris, Cheryl I. "Whiteness as Property." *Harvard Law Review*, June 10, 1993, https://harvardlawreview.org/1993/06/whiteness-as-property/.

Harvey, Paul. "'A Servant of Servants Shall He Be': The Construction of Race in American Religious Mythologies." In *Religion and the Creation of Race and Ethnicity*, edited by Craig R. Prentiss. New York: NYU Press, 2003.

Herberg, Will. *Protestant–Catholic–Jew* [1955]. Chicago: University of Chicago Press, 1983.

Hernandez, Nimachia. "Indigenous Identity and Story: The Telling of Our Part in the Sacred Homeland." In *Religion and the Creation of Race and Ethnicity*, edited by Craig R. Prentiss, 61–84. New York: NYU Press, 2003.

Hickman, Jared. "Globalization and the Gods, or the Political Theology of 'Race.'" *Early American Literature* 45 (2010): 145–82.

Hicks, Rosemary B. "Religious Pluralism, Secularism, and Interfaith Endeavors." In *The Cambridge Companion to American Islam*, edited by Juliane Hammer and Omid Safi, 156–69. Cambridge: Cambridge University Press, 2013.

Higginbotham, Leon, Jr. *In the Matter of Color: Race and the American Legal Process*. New York and London: Oxford University Press, 1978.

Hill, Marvin S. "Carthage Conspiracy Reconsidered: A Second Look at the Murder of Joseph and Hyrum Smith." *Journal of the Illinois State Historical Society* 97, no. 2 (2004): 107–34.

Hill Fletcher, Jeannine. *The Sin of White Supremacy: Christianity, Racism, and Religious Diversity in America*. Ossining: Orbis, 2017.

Hirsi Ali, Ayaan. "How to Win the Clash of Civilizations." *Wall Street Journal*, August 18, 2020. https://www.wsj.com/articles/SB10001424052748703426004 575338471355710184.

Hitti, Philip K. *The Syrians in America*. New York: George Doran, 1924.

H.J.Res.49—Providing for Congressional Disapproval of the Proposed Direct Commercial Sale to Israel of Certain Weaponry and Munitions. 117th Congress (2021–2022). https://www.congress.gov/bill/117th-congress/house-joint -resolution/49/text?q=%7B%22search%22%3A%5B%22israel+arms+sale%22%5 D%7D&r=2&s=2.

Holmes, William F. "Whitecapping: Anti-Semitism in the Populist Era." *American Jewish Historical Quarterly* 63 (1974): 244–61.

Howell, Sally. "Laying the Groundwork for American Muslim Histories: 1865– 1965." In *The Cambridge Companion to American Islam*, edited by Juliane Hammer and Omid Safi, 45–64. Cambridge: Cambridge University Press, 2013.

Hsu, Madeline Y. *The Good Immigrants*. Princeton: Princeton University Press, 2015.

Hunter, James Davison. "The Culture War and the Sacred/Secular Divide: The Problem of Pluralism and Weak Hegemony." *Social Research* 76 (2009): 1307–22.

Huntington, Samuel. *The Clash of Civilizations and the Remaking of the World Order*. New York: Simon and Schuster, 1996.

———. "The Hispanic Challenge." *Foreign Policy* (March–April 2004): 40–46.

Hurd, Elizabeth Shakman. *Beyond Religious Freedom: The New Global Politics of Religion*. Princeton, NJ: Princeton University Press, 2015.

Hutchison, William R. *Religious Pluralism in America: The Contentious History of a Founding Ideal*. New Haven: Yale University Press, 2003.

Ibrahim, Nagwa. "The Origins of Muslim Racialization in U.S. Law." *UCLA Journal of Islamic and Near Eastern Law* 129 (2009).

"ICE Targets Immigrants from Muslim Majority Countries Prior to 2004 Presidential Election." Press release. Am.-Arab Anti-Discrimination Comm. & Yale Law School, Oct. 31, 2008.

Irving, Washington. *Mahomet and His Successors & Spanish Legends*. 1897.

Irwin, Lee. "Freedom, Law, and Prophecy: A Brief History of Native American Religious Resistance." *American Indian Quarterly* 21 (1997): 35–36.

Jackson, Sherman. *Islam and the Blackamerican: Looking toward the Third Resurrection.* New York: Oxford University Press on Demand, 2005.

Jacobson, Matthew Frye. *Whiteness of a Different Color: European Immigrants and the Alchemy of Race.* Cambridge, MA: Harvard University Press, 1998.

Jacobson, Robin Dale. "The Stranger among Us: The Christian Right and Immigration." In *Faith and Race in American Political Life*, edited by Robin Dale Jacobson and Nancy D. Wadsworth, 170–88. Charlottesville: University of Virginia Press, 2012.

Jacobson, Robin Dale, and Nancy D. Wadsworth, eds. *Faith and Race in American Political Life.* Charlottesville: University of Virginia Press, 2012.

Jamal, Amaney, and Liali Albana. "Demographics, Political Participation, and Representation." In *The Cambridge Companion to American Islam*, edited by Juliane Hammer and Omid Safi, 98–118. Cambridge: Cambridge University Press, 2013.

Jamal, Amaney, and Nadine Naber, eds. *Race and Arab Americans before and after 9/11: From Invisible Citizens to Visible Subjects.* Syracuse, NY: Syracuse University Press, 2008.

Jennings, Willie James. *The Christian Imagination: Theology and the Origins of Race.* New Haven: Yale University Press, 2001.

Jessup, Henry. *The Mohammedan Missionary Problem.* Philadelphia: Presbyterian Board of Publication, 1879.

Johnson, Sylvester A. *The Myth of Ham in Nineteenth-Century American Christianity: Race, Heathens, and the People of God.* New York: Palgrave Macmillan, 2004.

Jones, Orville Davis. "Sound the Tocsin of Alarm." *Economic Library* 3, no. 2. Indianapolis: Vincent Bros., 1892.

Jones, Robert P. *The End of White Christian America.* New York: Simon and Schuster, 2016.

———. *White Too Long: The Legacy of White Supremacy in American Christianity.* New York: Simon and Schuster, 2020.

Jones, Robert P., Daniel Cox, and Juhem Navarro-Rivera. *The 2012 American Values Survey: How Catholics and the Religiously Unaffiliated Will Shape the 2012 Election and Beyond.* Washington, DC: Public Religion Research Institute, 2012.

Joo, Thomas Wuil. "Presumed Disloyal: Executive Power, Judicial Deference, and the Construction of Race before and after September 11. *Columbia Human Rights Law Review* 34 (2002–3): 1, 28.

Joseph, Suad. 1999. "Against the Grain of the Nation—The Arab." In *Arabs in America: Building a New Future*, edited by Michael W. Suleiman, 257–71. Philadelphia: Temple University Press.

Joshi, Khyati Y. "The Racialization of Hinduism, Islam, and Sikhism in the United States." *Equity and Excellence in Education* 39 (2006): 211–26.

———. "The Racialization of Religion in the United States." In *Investigating Christian Privilege and Religious Oppression in the United States*, edited by Warren J. Blumenfeld, Khyati Y. Joshi, and Ellen E. Fairchild, 35–56. Leiden: Brill, 2009.

———. *White Christian Privilege: The Illusion of Religious Equality in America*. New York: NYU Press, 2020.

Jung, Moon-Kie. "The Racial Unconscious of Assimilation Theory." *Du Bois Review* 6 (2009): 375–95.

Kahera, Abel Ismail. "Muslim Spaces and Mosque Architecture." In *The Cambridge Companion to American Islam*, edited by Juliane Hammer and Omid Safi, 228–45. Cambridge: Cambridge University Press, 2013.

Kalkan, Kerem Ozan, Geoffrey C. Layman, and Eric M. Uslaner. "'Bands of Others'? Attitudes toward Muslims in Contemporary American Society." *Journal of Politics* 71 (2009): 1–16.

Kalmar, Ivan. "Race by Grace: Race and Religion, the Secular State, and the Construction of 'Jew' and 'Arab.'" In *Jews Color Race: Rethinking Jewish Identities*, edited by Efraim Sicher, 482–509. London: Berghahn Press, 2013.

Kamali, Sara. *Homegrown Hate: Why White Nationalists and Militant Islamists Are Waging War Against the United States*. Oakland: University of California Press, 2021.

Kang, Jerry. "Trojan Horses of Race." *Harvard Law Review* 118 (2005): 1498–506.

Kaplan, Dana Evan. *American Reform Judaism: An Introduction*. New Brunswick: Rutgers University Press, 2001.

Karim, Jamillah. *American Muslim Women: Negotiating Race, Class, and Gender within the Ummah*. New York: NYU Press, 2008.

Kearns, Erin, Allison Betus, and Anthony Lemieux. "Why Do Some Terrorist Attacks Receive More Media Attention Than Others?" *Justice Quarterly* 24 (2018): 985–1022.

Kerstetter, Todd M. *God's Country, Uncle Sam's Land: Faith and Conflict in the American West*. Champaign: University of Illinois Press, 2008.

Kessner, Thomas, and Betty Boyd Caroli. *Today's Immigrants, Their Stories: A New Look at the Newest Americans*. New York: Oxford University Press, 1983.

Khalidi, Rashid. *The Hundred Years' War on Palestine: A History of Settler Colonialism and Resistance, 1917–2017*. New York: Metropolitan Books, 2020.

Khan, Musarrat, and Kathryn Ecklund. "Attitudes toward Muslim Americans Post-9/11." *Journal of Muslim Mental Health* 7 (2012), https://quod.lib.umich .edu/j/jmmh/10381607.0007.101/--attitudes-toward-muslim-americans-post-911 ?rgn=main;view=fulltext.

Khatab, Sayed. *Understanding Islamic Fundamentalism: The Theological and Ideological Basis of al-Qa'ida's Political Tactics*. Cairo: American University in Cairo, 2011.

Kidd, Thomas S. *American Christians and Islam: Evangelical Culture and Muslims from the Colonial Period to the Age of Terrorism*. Princeton: Princeton University Press, 2008.

———. "'Is It Worse to Follow Mahomet Than the Devil?' Early American Uses of Islam." *Church History* 72, no. 4 (Dec. 2003): 766–90.

Kim, Claire Jean. "The Racial Triangulation of Asian Americans." *Politics and Society* 27, no. 1 (March 1999): 107–38.

Knebel, Fletcher. "Democratic Forecast: A Catholic in 1960." *LOOK* (March 3, 1959): 14–17.

Koshy, Susan. "Morphing Race into Ethnicity: Asian Americans and Critical Transformations of Whiteness." *Boundary* 28 (2001): 153–94.

Kumar, Deepa. *Islamophobia and the Politics of Empire.* Chicago: Haymarket Books, 2012.

Kundnani, Arun. *The Muslims Are Coming! Islamophobia, Extremism, and the Domestic War on Terror.* New York: Verso Books, 2014.

Lansing, Robert. *The Peace Negotiations: A Personal Narrative.* Boston, 1921.

Leiner, Frederick. *The End of Barbary Terror: America's 1815 War against the Pirates of North Africa.* Oxford: Oxford University Press, 2007.

Leonard, Karen. "Organizing Communities: Institutions, Networks, Groups." In *The Cambridge Companion to American Islam,* edited by Juliane Hammer and Omid Safi, 170–89. Cambridge: Cambridge University Press, 2013.

Levine, Amy-Jill. "Matthew, Mark, and Luke: Good News or Bad?" In *Jesus, Judaism, and Christian Anti-Judasim: Reading the New Testament after the Holocaust,* edited by Paula Fredriksen and Adele Reinhartz, 77–89. Louisville: Westminster John Knox Press, 2002.

Lewis, Bernard. *The Crisis of Islam: Holy War and Unholy Terror.* New York: Random House, 2004.

———. "The Roots of Muslim Rage." *The Atlantic,* Sept. 1990. www.theatlantic .com/magazine/archive/1990/09/the-roots-of-muslim-rage/304643/.

———. *What Went Wrong? The Clash between Islam and Modernity.* London: Weidenfeld and Nicolson, 2002.

Lichtman, Allan J. *Prejudice and the Old Politics: The Presidential Election of 1928.* Chapel Hill: University of North Carolina, 1979.

Lindsay, Hal. *The Everlasting Hatred: The Roots of Jihad.* Oracle House, 2002.

Lipset, Seymour Martin. "Blacks and Jews, How Much Bias?" *Public Opinion* 5 (July–Aug. 1987): 57–58.

Little, Douglas. *American Orientalism: The United States and the Middle East since 1945.* Chapel Hill: University of North Carolina Press, 2002.

Loring, Charles G. *Report of the Committee, Relating to the Destruction of the Ursuline Convent, August 11, 1834.* Boston: J. H. Eastburn, City Printer, 1834. https://collections.library.nd.edu/04f477d5b4/preserving-the-steadfastness-of -your-faith/showcases/33d9b247cb/the-burning-of-the-ursuline-convent.

Love, Erik. *Islamophobia and Racism in America.* New York: NYU Press, 2017.

Lowenstein v. Dept. of Homeland Sec, 09-2225-cv, 2d Cir. 2010. https:// www.courtlistener.com/opinion/179606/lowenstein-v-dept-of-homeland-sec.

Lyons, Jonathan. *Islam through Western Eyes: From the Crusades to the War on Terrorism.* New York: Columbia University Press, 2012.

Macedo, Stephen. *Diversity and Distrust: Civic Education in Multicultural Democracy.* Cambridge, MA: Harvard University Press, 2003.

Maghbouleh, Neda. *The Limits of Whiteness: Iranian Americans and the Everyday Politics of Race.* Stanford, CA: Stanford University Press, 2017.

Mahamdallie, Hassan. "Islamophobia: The Othering of Europe's Muslims." *International Socialism Journal* (2015). http://isj.org.uk/islamophobia-the-othering-of-europes-muslims/.

Mahmood, Saba. "Secularism, Hermeneutics, and Empire: The Politics of Islamic Reformation." *Public Culture* 18 (2006): 232–47.

Maira, Sunaina Marr. *The 9/11 Generation: Youth, Rights and Solidarity in the War on Terror.* New York: NYU Press, 2016.

———. *Missing: Youth, Citizenship, and Empire after 9/11.* Durham, NC: Duke University Press, 2009.

Mamdani, Mahmood. *Good Muslim, Bad Muslim: America, the Cold War, and the Roots of Terror.* New York: Pantheon, 2004.

Marable, Manning. *Malcolm X: A Life of Reinvention.* New York: Penguin Books, 2011.

Marable, Manning, and Hisham Aidi. *Black Routes to Islam.* New York: Palgrave Macmillan, 2009.

Marzouki, Nadia. *Islam: An American Religion.* New York: Columbia University Press, 2017.

Massad, Joseph A. *Islam in Liberalism.* Chicago: University of Chicago Press, 2015.

Mastnak, Tomaž. "Western Hostility toward Muslims: A History of the Present." In *Islamophobia/Islamophilia: Beyond the Politics of Enemy and Friend*, edited by Andrew Shryock. Indiana University Press, 2010.

Mathews, Basil. *Young Islam on Trek: A Study in the Clash of Civilizations.* New York: Friendship Press, 1926.

Mauleon, Emmanuel. "Black Twice: Policing Black Muslim Identities." *UCLA Law Review* 65 (2018): 1326–90. https://www.uclalawreview.org/black-twice-policing-black-muslim-identities.

"May Jews Go to College?" Editorial. *The Nation* (June 14, 1922): 708.

Mazur, Eric Michael. *The Americanization of Religious Minorities: Confronting the Constitutional Order.* Baltimore: Johns Hopkins University Press, 1999.

———. "Religion, Race, and the American Constitutional Order." In *Faith and Race in American Political Life*, edited by Robin Dale Jacobson and Nancy D. Wadsworth, 40–41. University of Virginia Press, 2012.

McAlister, Melanie. *Epic Encounters: Culture, Media, and U.S. Interests in the Middle East Since 1945.* Berkeley: University of California Press, 2001.

McCloud, Aminah. *African American Islam.* New York: Routledge, 2014.

———. "American Muslim Women and U.S. Society." *Journal of Law and Religion* 12 (1996): 51–59.

McConnell, Michael W. "Free Exercise Revisionism and the Smith Decision."

In *Religion and Equality Law*, edited by Nelson Tebbe, 195–240. New York: Routledge, 2013.

———. "The Problem of Singling Out Religion." In *Religion and Equality Law*, edited by Nelson Tebbe, 411–58. New York: Routledge, 2013.

McElwee, Sean, and Philip Cohen. "The Secret to Trump's Success: New Research Sheds Light on GOP Front-Runner's Stunning Staying Power." *Salon*, Mar. 18, 2016.

Meade, Edward R. "The Chinese Question." Paper presented at the Annual Meeting of the Social Science Association of America, Saratoga, Sept. 7, 1877. Charleston: Nabu Press, 2011.

Media Tenor International. "Coverage of American Muslims Gets Worse." n.d. http://us.mediatenor.com/en/library/speeches/260/coverage-of-american-muslims-gets-worse.

———. *A New Era for Arab-Western Relations—Media Analysis*. New York: Media Tenor, 2011.

———. "Openness for Dialogue Reached a New Low." *Annual Dialogue Report*, 2015. http://us.mediatenor.com/images/library/reports/ADR_2015_LR_WEB_PREVIEW.pdf.

Meer, Nasar. "Racialization and Religion: Race, Culture and Difference in the Study of Antisemitism and Islamophobia." *Ethnic and Racial Studies* 36 (2013): 385–98.

Melville, Herman. *White-Jacket; or, The World in a Man-of-War*. New York: Harper & Brothers, 1850.

Miles, Robert. *Racism*. New York: Routledge, 1989.

Miller, Judith. "The Challenge of Radical Islam." *Foreign Affairs* 72, no. 2 (Spring 1993): 43–56.

Mishra, Sangay. "Religion and Race: South Asians in the Post-9/11 United States." In *Faith and Race in American Political Life*, edited by Robin Dale Jacobson and Nancy D. Wadsworth, 170–88. Charlottesville: University of Virginia Press, 2012.

Moore, Kathleen. "A Closer Look at Anti-Terrorism Law: *American-Arab Anti-Discrimination Committee v. Reno* and the Construcion of Aliens' Rights." In *Arabs in America: Building a New Future*, edited by Michael W. Suleiman, 84–99. Philadelphia: Temple University Press, 1999.

———. *Al-Mughtaribun: American Law and the Transformation of Muslim Life in the United States*. Albany: State University of New York Press, 1995.

———. "Muslims in the American Legal System." In *The Cambridge Companion to American Islam*, edited by Juliane Hammer and Omid Safi, 138–55. Cambridge: Cambridge University Press, 2013.

Morey, Robert. *The Islamic Invasion: Confronting the World's Fastest Growing Religion*. Eugene: Harvest House, 1992.

Morris, Aldon. *The Origins of the Civil Rights Movement: Black Communities Organizing for Change*. New York: Simon and Schuster, 1984.

Morse, Samuel. *Foreign Conspiracy Against the Liberties of the United States*. Cambridge, MA: American and Foreign Christian Union from Harvard University, 1835. https://www.google.com/books/edition/Foreign_Conspiracy_Against_the_Liberties/J-LChYFcUf8C?hl=en.

Naber, Nadine. *Arab America: Gender, Cultural Politics, and Activism*. New York: NYU Press, 2012.

Nacos, Brigitte L., and Oscar Torres-Reyna. *Fueling Our Fears: Stereotyping, Media Coverage, and Public Opinion of Muslim Americans*. Lanham: Rowman and Littlefield, 2006.

Naff, Alixa. *Becoming American: The Early Arab Immigrant Experience*. Carbondale: Southern Illinois University Press, 1985.

———. "The Early Arab Immigrant Experience." In *The Development of Arab-American Identity*, edited by Ernest McCarus, 23–36. Ann Arbor: University of Michigan Press, 1994.

Nafisi, Azar. *Reading Lolita in Tehran: A Memoir of Books*. New York: Random House, 2003.

National Public Radio. "Capitol Insurrection Updates." February 2021. https://www.npr.org/sections/insurrection-at-the-capitol.

Netanyahu, Benjamin, ed. *International Terrorism: Challenge and Response*. New Brunswick, NJ: Transaction Books, 1981.

Neusner, Jacob. "Jew and Judaist, Ethnic and Religious: How They Mix in America." In *Religion and the Creation of Race and Ethnicity*, edited by Craig R. Prentiss, 85–100. New York: NYU Press, 2003.

Nguyen, Nicole. *A Curriculum of Fear: Homeland Security in US Public Schools*. Minneapolis: University of Minnesota Press, 2016.

Noll, Mark A. *God and Race in American Politics: A Short History*. Princeton: Princeton University Press, 2010.

Norris, Jesse J. "Explaining the Emergence of Entrapment in Post-9/11 Terrorism Investigations." *Critical Criminology* 27 (2019): 467–83.

Obama, Barack. Keynote Speech on Faith and Politics at the Sojourners/Call to Renewal, "Building a Covenant for a New America," June 26, 2006, Washington, DC, https://www.nytimes.com/2006/06/28/us/politics/2006obamaspeech.html.

Omi, Michael, and Howard Winant. "Concept of Race: Biological Reality or Social Construction?" In *A Reader on Race, Civil Rights, and American Law: A Multiracial Approach*, edited by Timothy Davis, Kevin R. Johnson, and George A. Martinez, 4. Carolina Academic Press, 2001.

———. *Racial Formation in the United States from the 1960s to the 1990s*. New York: Routledge, [1994] 2015.

Orfalea, Gregory. *The Arab Americans: A History*. Northampton: Interlink Publishing Group, 2006.

Osborne, Catherine. "Shoulder to Shoulder with American Muslims: What the Interreligious Community Is Doing to Combat Anti-Muslim Bigotry in America." *Journal of Ecumenical Studies* 51 (2016): 257–63.

Paddison, Joshua. *American Heathens: Religion, Race and Reconstruction in California*. Los Angeles and Berkeley: Huntington Library Press and University of California Press, 2012.

Paden, Catherine. "Political Advocacy through Religious Organization? The Evolving Role of the Nation of Islam." In *Faith and Race in American Political Life*, edited by Robin Dale Jacobson and Nancy D. Wadsworth, 189–206. Charlottesville: University of Virginia Press, 2012.

Painter, Nell Irvin. *The History of White People*. New York: W.W. Norton, 2010.

Panagopoulos, Costas. "Trends: Arab and Muslim Americans and Islam in the Aftermath of 9/11." *Public Opinion Quarterly* 4, no. 70 (2006): 608–24.

Park, Robert Ezra. *Race and Culture*. Glencoe: Free Press, 1950.

Park, Robert E., and Ernest W. Burgess. *Introduction to the Science of Sociology*. Chicago: University of Chicago Press, 1969.

Patel, Eboo. *Out of Many Faiths: Religious Diversity and the American Promise*. Princeton: Princeton University Press, 2018.

Peek, Lori. "Becoming Muslim: The Development of a Religious Identity." *Sociology of Religion* 66 (2005): 215–42.

———. *Behind the Backlash: Muslim Americans after 9/11*. Philadelphia: Temple University Press, 2011.

Peel, Roy V., and Thomas C. Donnelly. "The 1928 Campaign, an Analysis." *Journal of American History* 19 (1931): 456–57.

Pegelow, Thomas. "'German Jews,' 'National Jews,' 'Jewish Volk' or 'Racial Jews'? The Constitution and Contestation of 'Jewishness' in Newspapers of Nazi Germany, 1933–1938." *Central European History* 35 (2003): 195–221.

Pennock, Pamela. 2017. *The Rise of the Arab American Left: Activists, Allies, and Their Fight against Imperialism and Racism, 1960s–1980s*. Chapel Hill: University of North Carolina Press.

Pipes, Daniel. "The Muslims Are Coming! The Muslims Are Coming!" *The National Review* 43, no. 22 (Nov. 11, 1990). http://www.danielpipes.org/198/the-muslims-are-coming-the-muslims-are-coming.

———. "There Are No Moderates: Dealing with Fundamentalist Islam." *The National Interest*, 1995: 48–57.

Prashad, Vijay. "How the Hindus Became Jews: American Racism After 9/11." *South Atlantic Quarterly* 104 (2005): 583–606.

Prentiss, Craig R., ed. *Religion and the Creation of Race and Ethnicity: An Introduction*. New York: NYU Press, 2003.

———. "'Loathsome unto Thy People': The Latter-Day Saints and Racial Categorization." In *Religion and the Creation of Race and Ethnicity*, edited by Craig R. Prentiss, 124–39. New York: NYU Press, 2003.

Prideaux, Humphrey. *The True Nature of Imposture Displayed in the Life of Mahomet*. London, 1808.

Proceedings and Acts of the General Assembly of Maryland, Archives of Maryland 1704–1706. http://aomol.msa.maryland.gov/000001/000026/html/index.html.

Quran. Translated by Abdullah Yusuf Ali. 5th ed. Knoxville: Wordsworth Editions, 2001.

Qureshi, Emran, and Michael A. Sells. *The New Crusades: Constructing the Muslim Enemy.* New York: Columbia University Press, 2003.

Rana, Junaid Akram. "The Racial Infrastructure of the Terror-Industrial Complex." *Social Text* 34, no. 4 (2016): 111–38.

———. "The Story of Islamophobia." *Souls* 9 (2007): 153–57.

———. *Terrifying Muslims: Race and Labor in the South Asian Diaspora.* Durham: Duke University Press, 2011.

Rascoff, Samuel J. "Establishing Official Islam? The Law and Strategy of Counter-Radicalization." *Stanford Law Review* 64 (2012): 125–89.

Rauf, Imam Feisal Abdul. *Moving the Mountain: Beyond Ground Zero to a New Vision of Islam in America.* New York: Free Press, 2012.

Razack, Sherene H. *Casting Out: The Eviction of Muslims from Western Law and Politics.* Toronto: University of Toronto Press, 2008.

Reeve, W. Paul. *Religion of a Different Color.* Oxford: Oxford University Press, 2015.

Renteln, Alison Dundes. "A Psychohistorical Analysis of the Japanese American Internment." *Human Rights Quarterly* 17 (1995): 618–48.

Rich, Camille Gear. "Performing Racial and Ethnic Identity: Discrimination by Proxy and the Future of Title VII." *NYU Law Review* 79 (2004): 1134–270.

Richardson, Joel. *Antichrist: Islam's Awaited Messiah.* Enumclaw, WA: Winepress, 2006.

———. *The Islamic Antichrist: The Shocking Truth about the Real Nature of the Beast.* Los Angeles: WND Books, 2009.

———. *Mideast Beast: The Case of the Islamic Antichrist* [self-published], 2012.

Robertson, Pat. *The New World Order.* Nashville: Word, 1991.

Roediger, David R. *The Wages of Whiteness: Race and the Making of the American Working Class.* London: Verso, 2007.

———. *Working toward Whiteness: How America's Immigrants Became White.* New York: Basic Books, 2005.

Rowson, Susanna. *Slaves in Algiers, or a Struggle for Freedom* [1794]. https://quod .lib.umich.edu/cgi/t/text/text-idx?c=evans;idno=N21056.0001.001.

Runnymede Trust. *Islamophobia: A Challenge for Us All.* London: Runnymede Trust, 1997. https://www.runnymedetrust.org/companies/17/74/Islamophobia -A-Challenge-for-Us-All.html.

Saeed, Agha. "The American Muslim Paradox." In *Muslim Minorities in the West: Visible and Invisible,* edited by Yvonne Yazbeck Haddad and Jane I. Smith, 39–58. Walnut Creek, CA: Altamira Press, 2002.

Safa, Reza. *Inside Islam: Exposing and Reaching the World of Islam.* Frontline, 1996.

Said, Edward. *Covering Islam: How the Media and the Experts Determine How We See the Rest of the World.* New York: Pantheon, 1981.

———. *Orientalism.* New York: Vintage Books, 1978.

———. *The Question of Palestine.* New York: Vintage Books, 1992.

Said, Edward, and Christopher Hitchens, eds. *Blaming the Victims: Spurious Scholarship and the Palestinian Question*. New York: Verso, 1998.

Said, Edward W., Ibrahim Abu-Lughod, Janet L. Abu-Lughod, Muhammad Hallaj, and Elia Zureik. "A Profile of the Palestinian People." In *Blaming the Victims: Spurious Scholarship and the Palestinian Question*, edited by Edward Said and Christopher Hitchens, 235–96. New York: Verso, 1998.

Salaita, Steven. *Anti-Arab Racism in the United States: Where It Comes from and What It Means for Politics Today*. London: Pluto Press, 2006.

———. *Holy Land in Transit: Colonialism and the Quest for Canaan*. Syracuse: Syracuse University Press, 2006.

Saliba, Therese. "Resisting Invisibility." In *Arabs in America: Building a New Future*, edited by Michael W. Suleiman, 304–19. Philadelphia: Temple University Press, 1999.

Samhan, Helen. "Not Quite White: Race Classification and the Arab-American Experience." In *Arabs in America: Building a New Future*, edited by Michael W. Suleiman, 209–26. Philadelphia: Temple University Press, 1999.

Sarkar, Mahua. "Why Does the West Need to Save Muslim Women?" *Cultural Critique* 95 (2017): 244.

Satzewich, Vic. "Whiteness Limited: Racialization and the Social Construction of 'Peripheral Europeans.'" *Social History* 33 (2000): 271, 278.

Schildkraut, Deborah J. *Americanism in the 21st Century: Public Opinion in the Age of Immigration*. New York: Cambridge University Press, 2011.

———. "The More Things Change...: American Identity and Mass and Elite Responses to 9/11." *Political Psychology* 23 (2002): 514–19.

Schneiderman, Harry. "The Jews of the United States." *American Magazine* 91 (April 1921): 24.

Schultz, Kevin M. *Tri-Faith America: How Catholics and Jews Held Postwar America to Its Protestant Promise*. New York and London: Oxford University Press, 2011.

Secret Oath of the American Protective Association. Oct. 31, 1893. http://history matters.gmu.edu/d/5351 and http://www-personal.umd.umich.edu/~ppennock /doc-APA%20Secret%20Oath.htm.

Selod, Saher. "Criminalization of Muslim American Men in the United States." In *The Immigrant Other: Lived Experiences in a Transnational World*, edited by R. Furman and A. Ackerman, 48–61. New York: Columbia University Press, 2016.

———. *Forever Suspect: Racialized Surveillance of Muslim Americans in the War on Terror*. New Brunswick, NJ: Rutgers University Press, 2018.

Selod, Sehar, and David G. Embrick. "Racialization and Muslims: Situating the Muslim Experience in Race Scholarship." *Sociology Compass* 7 (2013): 646. https://doi.org/10.1111/soc4.12057.

Sha'ban, Fuad. *Islam and Arabs in Early American Thought: The Roots of Orientalism in America*, McLean: Acorn Press, 1991.

Shaheen, Jack. *Reel Bad Arabs: How Hollywood Vilifies a People*. Northhampton: Olive Branch Press, 2009.

Shams, Tahseen. "Visibility as Resistance by Muslim Americans in a Surveillance and Security Atmosphere." *Sociological Forum* 33 (2018): 73–94.

Shapiro, Edward S. *A Time for Healing: American Jewry since World War II*. Baltimore: Johns Hopkins University Press, 1992.

Sheehi, Stephen. "Duplicity and Fear toward a Race and Class Critique of Islamophobia." In *With Stones in Our Hands: Writings on Muslims, Racism and Empire*, edited by Sohail Daulatzai and Junaid Rana, 35–55. Minneapolis: University of Minnesota Press, 2018.

———. *Islamophobia: The Ideological Campaign against Muslims*. 2011.

Shryock, Andrew. *Islamophobia/Islamophilia*. Bloomington: Indiana University Press, 2010.

Silk, Mark. "The Abrahamic Religions as a Modern Concept." In *The Oxford Handbook of the Abrahamic Religions*, edited by Adam Silverstein and Adam Stroumsa, 80–81. Oxford: Oxford University Press, 2015.

Singh, Jasmine K. "'Everything I'm Not Made Me Everything I Am': The Racialization of Sikhs in the United States." *Asian Pacific American Law Journal* 14 (2008–9): 54, 65.

Smith, Marian. 2002. *Race, Nationality, and Reality: INS Administration of Racial Provisions in U.S. Immigration and Nationality Law since 1898*. Prologue Magazine of the National Archives 34, no. 2 (Summer 2002). https://www.archives.gov/publications/prologue/2002/summer/immigration-law-1.html.

Smith, Timothy L. "Religion and Ethnicity in America." *American Historical Review* 83 (1978): 1155–85.

Soni, Varun, "Freedom from Subordination: Race, Religion, and the Struggle for Sacrament." *Politics & Civil Rights Law Review* 33 (2005): 33–57.

Spellberg, Denise. *Thomas Jefferson's Quran: The Founders and Islam*. New York: Vintage, 2013.

Spencer, Robert. *The Politically Incorrect Guide to Islam (and the Crusades)*. Washington, DC: Regnery Publishing, 2005.

———. *Religion of Peace? Why Christianity Is and Islam Isn't*. Washington, DC: Regnery Publishing, 2007.

Stampnitzky, Lisa. *Disciplining Terror: How Experts Invented "Terrorism."* Cambridge: Cambridge University Press, 2013.

Stein, Stephen J. *Communities of Dissent: A History of Alternative Religions in America*. Oxford: Oxford University Press, 2003.

———. "Some Reflections on Will Herberg's Insights and Oversights." Special Issue: *The Fiftieth Anniversary of "Catholic, Protestant, Jew": Will Herberg's Book, Then and Now. U.S. Catholic Historian* 23 (2005): 13–23.

Stockton, Ronald. "Ethnic Archetypes and the Arab Image." In *The Development of Arab-American Identity*, edited by Ernest McCarus, 119–54. Ann Arbor: University of Michigan Press, 1994.

Stovall, Tyler. *White Freedom: The Racial History of an Idea*. Princeton, NJ: Princeton University Press, 2021.

Straus, Roger Williams. *Religious Liberty and Democracy Writings and Addresses*. Chicago: Willet, Clark & Co, 1939.

Strong, Josiah. *Our Country: Its Possible Future and Its Present*. New York, 1885.

Suleiman, Michael W., ed. *Arabs in America: Building a New Future*. Philadelphia: Temple University Press, 1999.

———. *The Arabs in the Mind of America*. Brattleboro, VT: Amana Books, 1988.

Sultan, Wafa. *A God Who Hates: The Courageous Woman Who Inflamed the Muslim World Speaks Out against the Evils of Islam*. New York: St. Martin's Press, 2009.

Swartout, R. R., Jr. "From Kwangtung to the Big Sky: The Chinese Experience in Frontier Montana." In *Montana Heritage: An Anthology of Historical Essays*, edited by R. R. Swartout Jr. and H. W. Fritz, 45–64. Helena: Montana Historical Society, 1992.

Tamimi, Azzam Islam. "Islam, Arabs, and Ethnicity." In *Religion and the Creation of Race and Ethnicity*, edited by Craig R. Prentiss, 167–80. New York: NYU Press, 2003.

Taras, Raymond. "'Islamophobia Never Stands Still': Race, Religion, and Culture." *Ethnic and Racial Studies* 26 (2013): 417–33.

Tebbe, Nelson, ed. *Religion and Equality Law*. New York: Routledge, 2013.

Tehranian, John. *Whitewashed: America's Invisible Middle Eastern Minority*. New York: NYU Press, 2010.

Theoharis, Athan. *Abuse of Power: How Cold War Surveillance and Secrecy Policy Shaped the Response to 9/11*. Philadelphia: Temple University Press, 2011.

Thomas, Jeffrey L. *Scapegoating Islam: Intolerance, Security, and the American Muslim*. Westport: Praeger, 2015.

Tocqueville, Alexis de. *Democracy in America* [1835]. Edited and translated by Henry Reeve. New York: D. Appleton & Co., 1899.

Turner, Richard B. "African Muslim Slaves and Islam in Antebellum America." In *The Cambridge Companion to American Islam*, edited by Juliane Hammer and Omid Safi, 28–44. Cambridge: Cambridge University Press, 2013.

Twain, Mark. *The Innocents Abroad*. Hartford: American Publishing Company, 1869. https://www.gutenberg.org/files/3176/3176-h/3176-h.htm.

Uddin, Asma T. *When Islam Is Not a Religion: Inside America's Fight for Religious Freedom*. New York: Pegasus Books, 2019.

U.S. Immigration and Customs Enforcement. "ICE Immigration Enforcement Strategy and Highlights 2." Jan. 2006. https://www.hsdl.org/?view&did=462257.

Volpp, Leti. "The Citizen and the Terrorist." *UCLA Law Review* 49 (2002): 19–33.

Wadsworth, Nancy D. "Ambivalent Miracles: The Possibilities and Limits of Evangelical Racial Reconciliation Politics." In *Faith and Race in American Political Life*, edited by Robin Dale Jacobson and Nancy D. Wadsworth. Charlottesville: University of Virginia Press, 2012.

———. "The Racial Demons That Help Explain Evangelical Support for Trump." *Vox*, April 30, 2018.

Wagner, William. *How Islam Plans to Change the World*. Grand Rapids: Kregel, 2004.

Warner, Stephen. "The Role of Religion in the Process of Segmented Assimilation." *Annals of the American Academy of Political and Social Science* 612 (2007). https://doi.org/10.1177/0002716207301189.

Washington, George. "Letter to the Jews of Newport." In *The Papers of George Washington, Digital Edition*, ed. Theodore J. Crackel. Charlottesville: University of Virginia Press, Rotunda, 2007. http://rotunda.upress.virginia.edu/pgwde/search-Pre06d132.

Wenger, Tisa. *Religious Freedom: The Contested History of an American Ideal*. Chapel Hill: University of North Carolina Press, 2017. https://doi.org/10.1177/0002716207301189.

West, Cornel. *Race Matters*. New York: Beacon Press, 1994.

Weyrich, Paul M., and William S. Lind. *Why Islam Is a Threat to America and the West*. Washington, DC: Free Congress Foundation, 2002.

Williams, Rhys H. "Civil Religion and the Cultural Politics of National Identity in Obama's America." *Journal for the Scientific Study of Religion* 52 (2013): 239–57.

Williams, Robert F. "'The Right of the People Shall Not be Violated': The Evolution of Constitutional Rights in New Jersey." *New Jersey History* 125 (2010): 40–47.

Winthrop, Robert C. "Governor Winthrop's Journal: June Meeting, 1872." *Proceedings of the Massachusetts Historical Society* 12 (1871–73): 233, 239.

Wong, Kam C. "The USA Patriot Act: A Policy of Alienation." *Michigan Journal of Race & Law* 12 (2006): 161–202. https://repository.law.umich.edu/cgi/viewcontent.cgi?article=1111&context=mjrl.

Wood, William. "It Wasn't an Accident: The Tribal Sovereign Immunity Story." *American University Law Review* 62 (2013): 1587, 1632–40.

Worrell, Mark P. "Signifying the Jew: Antisemitic Workers and Jewish Stereotypes during World War II." In *No Social Science without Critical Theory*, edited by Harry F. Dahms, 193–234. London: Emerald, 2008.

Wuthnow, Robert. *All in Sync: How Music and Art Are Revitalizing American Religion*. Berkeley: University of California Press, 2003.

Yang, Tseming. "Race, Religion, and Cultural Identity: Reconciling the Jurisprudence of Race and Religion." *Indiana Law Journal* 73 (1997): 119–85.

Young, Iris Marion. *Justice and the Politics of Difference*. Princeton: Princeton University Press, 2011.

Young, Mary E. "Indian Removal and Land Allotment: The Civilized Tribes and Jacksonian Justice." *American Historical Review* 64 (1958): 31–45.

Yousafzai, Malala. *I Am Malala: The Girl Who Stood Up for Education and Was Shot by the Taliban*. New York: Little, Brown, 2013.

Zarnowitz, Victor, and Geoffrey H. Moore. "The Recession and Recovery of 1973–1976." *Explorations in Economic Research* 4 (Oct. 1977). https://www.nber .org/system/files/chapters/c9101/c9101.pdf.

Zarrugh, Amina. "Racialized Political Shock: Arab American Racial Formation and the Impact of Political Events." *Ethnic and Racial Studies* 39 (2016): 2722–39.

INDEX

Note: page numbers in italics refer to figures. Those followed by *t* refer to tables. Those followed by *n* refer to notes, with note number.

AAAN. *See* Arab American Action Network

Abdullah, Zain, 16

Abraham, role in three Abrahamic religions, 193–94

The Abraham Connection (1994), 194

"Abrahamic Alternatives to War" (USIP), 195

Abrahamic national identity, 200; and Abrahamic dialogues, 194–95; and boundaries of Whiteness, redefinition of, 15, 22, 211; and colorblind discourse, 191, 200; government support of, when expedient, 195–97; groups working to establish, 194–95, 198; interfaith initiatives promoting, 193–200; Muslim American proponents of, 197; and Muslim-led anti-extremism campaigns, 199–200; parallels to earlier creation of Judeo-Christian identity, 195; peace movement and, 195–96; as potential replacement for Judeo-Christian identity, 15, 80, 211; as project to deracialize and depoliticize Muslims, 194, 198–99; rejection by young progressives, for failure to dismantle systemic racism, 15, 22, 191, 198–99, 200–208; resistance from con-

servative Jews and Christians, 80, 195; 9/11 attacks and, 194; support of some Muslims for, 22. *See also* assimilation by Muslims

Abraham Salon, 194–95

Abramson Family Foundation, 148

Absconder Program, 170, 175

Abstraction Fund, 146*t*–47*t*

Academy for Judaic, Christian, and Islamic Studies, 194

ACLU. *See* American Civil Liberties Union

Act Declaring Who Shall Be Slaves (1670), 36

ACT for America, 150, 151, 157, 164

Act to Prevent the Growth of Popery within This Province (Maryland colony), 52

Adams, John, 12

Afghanistan, US support of mujahideen against Soviets, 120, 124, 127, 128, 142, 255n113

African Americans: Christianization of, ineffectiveness in overcoming racial hierarchy, 76; conversions to Islam, Muhammad Sadiq and, 107–8; cultural and racial deficiencies, blaming of race rather than systemic

African Americans *(continued)*
racism for, 77; and Great Migration, 104; mass incarceration of, and Muslim support for prison reform, 206; Muslim, racialization *vs.* immigrant Muslims, 4, 16–17, 19–20; and religion in racialization, 19; White status as not available to, 28

Africans: Christian arguments for enslavement of, 29–30, 39–40; and curse of Ham, 19, 38–39; Muslim, as slaves, characterization as heathen savages, 88; as unfit for self-government, in White view, 40; White belief in inferiority of, 38–40

Ahmadiyya Movement, 107

Aidi, Hisham, 202

AIPAC. *See* American Israel Public Affairs Committee

Alan and Hope Winters Family Foundation, 146*t*–47*t*

Alba, Richard, 66, 68–69, 70

Albanian Muslims: immigration in early 20th century, 96; Mosques built by, 96

Ali, Muhammad, 111

Alien Land Law Act of 1913, 62

Alien Registration Act (Smith Act) of 1940, 86

Aliens Act of 1798, 75

Alsultany, Evelyn, 142, 145

Alt-Right movement, 143, 188, 202

American Center for Law and Justice, 152

American Civil Liberties Union (ACLU), 177

American Congress for Truth, 146*t*–47*t*

American Council Against Nazi Propaganda, 79–80

American dream: access to, dependence on racial-religious hierarchy, 190–91; achievement of, as goal of many immigrant Muslims, 200–201

American Enterprise Institute, 148

American Indian Religious Freedom Act (1978), 38

American Islamic Congress, 200

American Islamic Forum for Democracy, 146*t*–47*t*

American Israel Public Affairs Committee (AIPAC), 116, 165–66

Americanization movement, 64

American Jewish Committee, 47, 78–79

American Methodist Church, 76

American national identity: assimilation as historically essential to, 67; basis in English language, individualism, and capitalism, 11; Christianity as essential to, in Republican opinion, 167; claimed secularization of, 30; expansion to include Catholics, 28; expansion to include Jews, 28; as Judeo-Christian in post–World War II era, 27, 80–81; modern secular, as secularized Protestant norms, 30; necessity of changing, 22–23; in post–World War II era, exclusion of African American Protestants and Muslims from, 80; religious identity in, as racial project, 32; as shaped by Protestant settler colonialism, xenophobia, and anti-Black racism, 64; supposed incompatibility with Muslim practices, 20, 161, 166, 218n92. *See also* Whiteness; White status

American Party (Know Nothing Party), 57, 149

American Protective Association (APA), 56–57

The American Protestant Vindicator, 53

American Public Policy Alliance, 152, 157

Americans, real (White Judeo-Christian), Racial Muslims as perceived threat to, 6

American Values Survey, 141, 166

American way of life, as secularized Protestant norms, 30

America's Mosques Exposed! (film), 158

An Act to Repeal a Former Law Making Indians and Others Free (1682), 36

anti-Asian discrimination: expansion to peoples of Indian subcontinent, 62; laws banning immigration, 62; laws restricting legal rights, 62

anti-Black racism: blending with Orientalism, in racialization of Muslims, 111–12, 114; entrenchment within

Black-White paradigm, 87; merging with anti-Muslim racism after 9/11, 201; Obama and, 159–60; as part of American national identity, 64; targeting of, by coalition of young minority progressives, 203–4. *See also* racism

anti-Catholic discrimination: anti-democratic papal allegiance as concern, 46, 52, 53–54, *54*, 56, 71; and association of Catholicism with Islam, 53–54; conspiracy theories about plans to take over government, 56–57; Irish Catholics as particular focus of, 56, 57–58; before mid-19th century, 52–53; origin in European political conflict, 51; publications denouncing Catholics, 53, 57; similarity to current anti-Muslim discrimination, 52, 53, 55–56, 57; Spanish-American War of 1898 and, 55; theological basis of, 51–52; ties to foreign states as concern, 55; violence in, 55. *See also* racialization of Catholic immigrants

Anti-Defamation League, 78, 122, 143

anti-Mormon discrimination: removal of Brigham Young from governor's office, 59–60; violence in, 58. *See also* racialization of Mormons

anti-Muslim racism: Abrahamic national identity and, 197; after 9/11, Orientalism and Zionism funding, 127; complicating factors in analysis of, 15–18; inclusion of Muslim-appearing persons in, 64; and Islamophobia, relation between, 21; as justification for persecution of American Muslims, 170–71; merging with anti-Black racism after 9/11, 201; negative correlation with degree of contact with Muslims, 162; percentage of public expressing, 161–62; portrayal of Islam in, 21; public support for, 14–15; and racial violence, 186–88; similarities to anti-Black racism, 3–4; similarities to 19th-century anti-German discrimination, 75; similarity to anti-Catholic racism, 161–62; similarity to anti-Jewish, anti-Catholic

and anti-Mormon racism, 189; under Trump, 164–67. *See also* criminalization of Muslim identity after 9/11; Islamophobia; racialization of Muslim immigrants

anti-Semitism in America: discriminatory restrictions on Jewish immigrants, 50–51; Henry Ford and, 49–50; before late nineteenth century, 47; rapid decline with Jewish assimilation, 82–83; and trope of Jews as Christ killers, 46–47; violence in, 49. *See also* racialization of Jewish immigrants

APA. *See* American Protective Association

Arab American Action Network (AAAN), 173

Arab American organizations, leftist turn after Six Day War (1967), 120

Arab Americans: assimilation, dependence on White appearance and Christian faith, 70; lack of political clout in 1950s, 116; path to Whiteness, world events obstructing, 70

Arab Muslim world, five common negative perceptions of, 132

Arab nationalism: and association of Muslim identity with violent anti-Americanism, 103; and racialization of Muslims in US, 111; and US Middle East policy, 111; US opposition to, 118–19

Arab oil embargo (1973), and racialization of Muslims, 114

Arabs: association of Muslim identity with, 6, 31; depictions of, in mid-20th century US, 96, 114, 117; racialization of, 114–15; recognition of White status. political considerations in, 102–3; as term used to describe any Arab-looking people, 114; Zionist portrayals as bloodthirsty anti-Semites, 122

Al-Arian, Leena, 206

Al-Arian, Sami, 182–83, 206

Armenian immigrants: legal status as White as issue, 102; from Ottoman Empire, denial of White status to, 101–2

Army of God, 143, 202

Ashcroft, John, 174–75

Asian Americans: assimilation by, 63; as target of anti-Communist investigations, 86–87; transition to model minority, 63; White status as not available to, 28, 63. *See also* anti-Asian discrimination

Asians: restrictions on immigration of, 44–45; as unfit for self-government, in White view, 243n1. *See also* racialization of Asians

al-Assad, Hafez, 118, 119

assimilation, coercive: failure to force conversions from Judaism, Catholicism, and Mormonism, 77; immigration waves of mid-19th and early 20th centuries and, 67; and racialization of immigrant Muslims, 4, 7; US as society of, 4, 8, 68–69

assimilation theory, and permanent exclusion of Blacks, inability to explain, 69

assimilation to Anglo-Saxon Protestant norms: and America as coercive assimilationist society, 4, 7, 68–69; by Asian Americans, 63; by Chinese immigrants, concerns about viability of, 61–62; by Eastern and Southern European immigrants, 72; of "ethnic Whites," after switch from race to cultural ethnicity as marker of difference, 65, 66, 70–71; by German immigrants, in response to discrimination in World War, 75–76; as historically essential to American identity, 67; immigrants lacking, discrimination against, 11; Japanese Americans and, 63; Jewish immigrants before 1870s and, 47; levels of, in Racial Muslim typology, 7; by Mormons, 70; as not available to non-Whites, 67–68; permanent exclusion of Blacks from, 69, 70; pressure for, during World War I, 64; as price of White status, 83–84; as requirement throughout American history, 11; as unavailable to non-Whites and non-Judeo-Christians, 71, 75–76; variation across ethnic groups, 74

assimilation, by Catholics, 66–67, 70, 83–84; concerns about viability of, 54–56, 57

assimilation by Jews, 51, 66–67, 70; and class mobility, 82–83; early concerns about assimilability, 48, 49; and interfaith marriage, 82; and move to Conservative or Reform Judaism, 81–82; as price of White status, 78, 81; variations in degree of, 74

assimilation by Muslims: acceptance by many immigrant Muslims, 200–201; agreement with targeting of Religious Dissident Muslims as cost of, 200, 205; critical race theory on, 69; definitions and models of, 68–69; as ineffective for attaining full benefits of citizenship, 89; and Islamophilia, 205; multicultural version of, 68–69; secularization and Protestantization necessary for, 192; by Secular Racial Muslims, 7, 173; as seeking of Whiteness within existing racial hierarchy, 191; those rejecting, for failure to dismantle systemic racism, 15, 22, 191, 198–99, 200–208; as unavailable to religious, dissident, or non-White Muslims (segmented assimilation), 192–93, 201. *See also* Abrahamic national identity

Bachmann, Michele, 139, 157

Bail, Christopher, 144–45, 148

al-Bakr, Ahmed Hassan, 120

Baldwin, James, 67

Balfour Declaration, US opposition to, 114

Bannon, Steve, 164

Barbary Wars, 93–94

Barkan, Elliot, 68

Bayoumi, Moustafa, 5

Begin, Menachem, 195–96

Bell, Derrick, 19, 70, 87

Bellah, Robert N., 31, 84

Benedict, Ruth, 73

Benevolence International, 177

Bennet, John, 157

Beydoun, Khaled A., 99

BIA. *See* Bureau of Indian Affairs

"The Clash of Civilizations?" (Huntington), 129

"clash of civilizations" theory, 129–32; and anti-Muslim racism, 21; and calls to limit Muslim immigration, 48; Congress and, 130–31; Evangelicals' propagation of, 117, 130; Hiram's *Greek Slave* and, 95; influence on American culture, 130–32; liberals' rejection of, 164; in police training after 9/11, 179; promotion by Islamophobia industry, 146–47, 149; and purported Palestinian savagery, 120; and racialization of Muslims, 113, 130; similarity to racist tropes against Catholics and Jews, 129; and targeting of Muslim and Arabs in America, 131; Trump advisers' belief in, 164; and US treatment of Muslim immigrants, 113; and Western criticisms of Islam in late 20th century, 129

Clinton, William J. "Bill," 130

Coalition for Civil Freedoms (CCF), 206

coalition of young minority progressives challenging structural racism, 200–208; and alliance of Dissident Muslims with African American activists, 202, 206; and anti-Black racism, targeting of, 203–4; boost given to, by Trump White nationalism, 205–6, 209; destruction of systemic racism as goal of, 202, 204–5; ending of US imperialism as goal of, 204–5; groups included in, 202, 204, 208; and intercommunity racial biases, addressing of, 203–4; and Omar and Tlaib in Congress, 206–7; race-conscious approach to Islamophobia, 204–8; recognition of all forms of racism as intertwined, 205; rejection of colorblind assimilation paradigm, 202, 203, 204–5, 208; and US Middle East policy, opposition to, 204–5; and view of US as imperialistic, racist power, 202

Cohen, John, 185

COINTELPRO and COINTELPRO-BNHG, 111, 180

Cold War: end of, and replacement of Communism with Islam as US adversary, 115, 124, 128, 131; expansion of Whiteness to include Judeo-Christian identity in, 65, 81; US ideological separation from Soviets, and policies of inclusion, 63, 64; US mobilization of Arabs in, 119–20; US religious revival in response to Communism, 81; US rhetoric on freedom, campaign against racism necessitated by, 85–86; and US support for Israel, 119

Collins, Susan, 156

colonialism: British, justifications for, 91; and racialization of immigrant Muslims, 12. *See also* imperial ambitions of US

colorblind discourse: and Abrahamic national identity, 191, 200; rejection by coalition of young minority progressives, 202, 203, 204–5, 208

Columbus, Christopher, 35

Combating Terrorism Center, 143

Common Council For American Unity, 80

Common Sense (Paine), 12, 95

Communists in America: Jews and Asians as target of anti-Communist investigations, 86–87; and laws authorizing deportation of subversive non-citizens, 86

Concerned Women of America, 152–53

Congress: and "clash of civilizations" theory, 130–31; hearings on Muslim extremism, 156, 157–58. *See also* Omar, Ilhan; Tlaib, Rashida

Controlled Application Review and Resolution Program (CARRP), 176–77

Coolidge, Calvin, 42

Cordoba Initiative interfaith community center, opposition to, 162

Council Against Intolerance in America, 80

Council on American Islamic Relations (CAIR), 145, 149, 150, 187, 198

"countering violent extremism" (CVE) programs: Muslim-led, 199–200; Omar's criticisms of, 207; targeting of Radical Religious and Religious Racial Muslims, 185–86; Trump administration and, 186

Counterterrorism and Security Education Research Fund, 148
counterterrorism investigations, Muslims as primary targets of, 170
Crane, Charles, 114
Creativity Movement, 202
criminalization of Muslim identity after 9/11, 174–82, 209; abuses of Muslims overseas, 170; chilling effect of, 169, 181–82; and collective punishment of Muslims, 178–79; and "countering violent extremism" programs, 185–86; counterterrorism investigations targeting Muslims, 170; and equal protection doctrine, failure of, 3; and failure to consider social and political causes of radicalism, 185; and government interaction with Muslims through national security lens, 169; and heavy-handed surveillance and prosecutions, 174, 175–76, 179–82, 188; and immigration law, selective application of, 169–70, 173, 174–78, 188; impact on Muslim communities, 169; and intimidation of Religious Dissident and Religious Muslims, 120, 127, 172, 175, 176–77, 178, 181–84; and Islam as violent, oppressive non-religion, 89; and Islamic charities, government scrutiny of, 176–77; and Muslim Ban, 166–67, 177–78, 188, 197; and naturalizations of Muslims, delaying of, 176–77; public approval of, 170–71; and racial double standards in response to religious extremism, 14, 142–44, 169, 188, 202; racialization of Muslims and, 169, 170, 189; and racial violence against Muslims, 186–88; and registration laws for Muslims, 173; variation across Racial Muslim hierarchy, 171–74; and White nativist ideology, 89
The Crisis of Islam (Lewis), 129
critical race theory, on assimilation, 69
Cronkite, Walter, 125
Crusades, 90
CTSERF, 146t–47t
Cubberley, Ellwood P., 43

cultural racism against Muslims, as racialization of religion, 32–33
Curtis, Edward, 16
CVE. *See* "countering violent extremism" (CVE) programs
CVE Interagency Task Force, 185

Darwish, Nonie, 10, 146–47, 149
Daulatzai, Sohail, 206
Deady, John, 157
Dearborn Independent newspaper, 49–50, 50
Declaration of Proposals of the Lord, Proprietor of Caroline (1663), 36
demographic change, and potential change in White dominance, 211
Destroying the Great Satan (film), 164
De Witt, John L., 62
Dictionary of Races or Peoples (Dillingham Commission), 43
Dillingham Commission Report on Immigration, 43, 101
Diouf, Sylviane, 104, 105
dissident Muslim, as term defined in terms of mainstream politics, 10–11
Dobson, James, 139
Dominion Theology, 143
Donors Capital Fund and Donors Trust, 146t–47t, 148
Dow, George, 101
Downfall of Babylon (periodical), 53
Dow v. U.S. (1915), 100–101
Drew Ali, Noble, 108

Eastern and Southern European immigrants: assimilation of, 72; World War II as chance to prove loyalty, 72
Edwards, Jonathan, 11, 92
Egypt: alignment with Soviet Union, 119; and Arab nationalism, 119; and Suez Canal crisis, 119
Eisenhower, Dwight D.: "Back to God" campaign of, 81; and mobilization of Arabs in Cold War, 119–20; negative view of Arabs, 118–19
election of 2004, surveillance of Muslims prior to, 176
election of 2008, anti-Muslim rhetoric in, 157, 160

Franks, Trent, 157
Freedom Center, 146–47, 146t–47t
free exercise clause, applicability only to White Protestant sects, 29
Friends of Democracy, 79–80

Gabriel, Brigitte, 146–47, 149–51
Gabriel, Mark A., 149
Gaffney, Frank, 136, 148, 152, 153, 156, 160, 165
Garvey, Marcus, 107, 108
Gatestone Institute, 165–66
Geary Act of 1892, 62
gender, and racialization of Muslims, 17–18, 216n69
German immigrants: alliances with Jews, 79; arrival in US, 44, 53, 74; and assimilation, 47, 54–55; assimilation of, in response to discrimination in World War I, 75–76; Catholic, initial isolation of, 54–55, 74–75; characterization as lower-class Whites, 41, 42; destinations of, 54; discrimination against, in World War I, 75–76; reasons for leaving Germany, 74–75; White nativist backlash against, 75; and World War II, 63, 73
Ghost Dance, banning of, 37–38
Gingrich, Newt, 139–40
Giuliani, Rudy, 157
Glazer, Nathan, 77
Global Relief Fund, 177
Gohmert, Louie, 157
Gold, Harry, 87
Goode, Virgil, 155
"good Muslim, bad Muslim" frame, and Racial Muslim typology, 6–7
Gordis, David, 194
Gordon, Milton M., 68
government officials, support of Evangelical anti-Muslim views, 138–39
Graham, Billy, 118
Graham, Franklin, 138
Great Migration, 104
Great Seal of United States, addition of "In God we trust" to, 81
Greek Slave (Powers), 95
Greenglass, David, 87

Gregg, Gary, 132
Grose, George, 194
Guinier, Lani, 173, 191
Guir, William, 95
Gulf War, First: as clash of civilizations, 129; as "crusade," 128; and media portrayal of Muslims, 13; obstruction of Muslim path to Whiteness, 70; and opposition to Christian army on Muslim soil, 128–29; and racialization of Muslims, 114

Ham, curse of, 19, 38–39
Hamas, and First Gulf War, 128
Harlan, John Marshall, 62
Harris, Cheryl, 28, 209
Harvey, John, 35
hate crimes against Muslims, increase in, 186–88
Haun's Mill massacre (1838), 58
Hayari, Yahya, 109–10
Herberg, Will, 80, 81
Heritage Foundation, 148
Hezbollah, and First Gulf War, 128
Higby, William, 61
Hill, Margari, 203
Hill, Paul, 143
Hindu Indians, inclusion in anti-Muslim discrimination, 64
Hirsi Ali, Ayaan, 10, 148–49
Hitchock, Mark, 140
Hitler, Adolf, 79, 80
HLF. *See* Holy Land Foundation
Hollywood: and Catholic assimilation, 83; films on Holocaust, 117; and Jewish assimilation, 83
Holocaust: and establishment of Israel, 116; Hollywood films on, 117
Holy Land Foundation (HLF), 177
"Homegrown Threat of Violent Islamic Extremist Terrorism" (congressional hearing), 156
Homeland Security Act of 2002, 174
Hoover, J. Edgar, 110–11
Horowitz, David, 146–47, 146t–47t
Hossain, Mohammed, 181
House Un-American Activities Committee, 87

housing discrimination, Jewish immigrants and, 50

How Islam Plans to Change the World (Wagner), 130

Hungarians, low rating on US racial hierarchy, 42

Huntington, Samuel, 48, 129–30, 149

Hussain, Shahed, 181

Hussein, Saddam, 13, 127

Hutchison, Anne, 94

ibn Said, Omar, 105

ICE National Security Investigations Unit, 176

ICNA. *See* Islamic Circle of North America

Identity Europa, *150*

IMAN. *See* Inner City Muslim Action Network

Immigration Act of 1917, 62

Immigration Act of 1924, 43–44

immigration law: Asian immigrants, opening of borders to, 86; deportation of subversive non-citizens, 86; exclusionary, Christian arguments for, 210; national origin quotas, lifting of, 96; restrictions on non-White non-Christians, 85; selective application of, after 9/11, 169–70, 173, 174–78, 188

Immigration Restriction League, 43, 44

immigration waves of mid-19th and early 20th centuries, 40–45; calls to restrict Eastern and Southern European immigration, 43; and changed demographic of American cities, 41; ethnicity of immigrants in, 40; large number of non-English-speaking Eastern and Southern Europeans in, 40, 41; media portrayals of immigrants, 41; national origins of immigrants, 41; and need for coercive assimilation, 67; number of immigrants in, 40; and race-based immigration quotas, introduction of, 42; and scientific racism, 42; White nativist backlash against, 40–43, 45, 75. *See also* Catholic immigrants; Jewish immigrants

imperial ambitions of US: and creation of Racial Muslim, 89, 90; ending of, as goal of coalition of young minority progressives, 204–5; in Muslim-majority countries, and racialization of immigrant Muslims, 5, 7, 12–14, 17, 210–11

Indian Removal Act of 1830, 36

individualistic society, failure of Abrahamic national identity to address, 198

ING. *See* Islamic Networks Group

Inner City Muslim Action Network (IMAN), 204

In re Ahmed Hassan (1942), 102

In re Halladjian (1909), 102

In re Mudarri (1910), 100

In re Najour (1909), 100

Institute for Social Policy and Understanding, 205

insurgency, US reclassifying as terrorism, 123

Interfaith Conference of Metropolitan Washington, 194

interfaith initiatives: after 9/11, 80; of mid-20th century, and expansion of Whiteness to include Judeo-Christian identity, 78; as project to deracialize and depoliticize Muslims, 198–99; rejection by coalition of young Muslim progressives, 202, 208

Interfaith Network of New York, 194

interfaith programs: failure to address systemic racism, 198–99; in pursuit of Abrahamic national identity, 197–98

"The International Jew" (newspaper series), 48–50, *50*

internment of Arabs and Iranians, Reagan-era contingency plan for, 124

internment of Japanese Americans: justifications for, 62–63; parallels to discrimination against Muslims, 14; *vs.* treatment of other enemy nations' migrants, 63, 84–85

Inventory of US Government and Private Organization Activity Regarding Islamic Organizations as an Aspect of Overseas Activity (1957), 119–20

Investigative Project on Terrorism, 146*t*–47*t*, 148

Iran, CIA coup against Mossadegh in, 119

Iranian Americans: labeling of, based on actions of others, 14; surveillance and deportations of, during Iranian Revolution crisis, 125–26

Iranian Revolution: and designation of all Muslims as terrorists, 125–27; media portrayals of, 13; obstruction of Muslim path to Whiteness, 70; and public opinion of Iranians, *125*, 125–26; and racialization of Muslims, 114, 193; and US hostages, 125

Iraq: invasion of Kuwait, 128; nationalization of oil fields, 120; US support against Iran, 127

Iraq War: domestic investigations of Muslims prior to, 175–76; media justifications of US invasion, 135–36

Irish immigrants: alliance with Jews, 79; arrival of, 40, 74; assimilated, adoption of Black-White paradigm, 77; Catholic, nativists' fears about, 46, 51, 53, 57, 59; discrimination against, 57–58; ethnic groups within, 73; ethnic Whiteness awarded to, 66, 71; as mostly peasants, 54; opposition to, 56; on racial-religious hierarchy, 78; and sectarian violence, 55

Irving, Washington, 95

ISIS, Brides of, 17

Islam as violent, oppressive non-religion: and building of collective Christian identity, 90; and comparisons to Mormonism, 60; denial of status as religion, similarity to discrimination against Jews, Catholics and Mormons, 136–37; in efforts to stop mosque construction, 136; Evangelical Christians on, 137–41; in films of 20th century, 95; Flynn on, 164; history of American views on, 11–12, 89, 92–95; history of Western views on, 12, 90–92; Islamophobia industry spread of claim, 146–47, 149, 153; as justification for denying religious freedom to Muslims, 26, 30, 64, 153, 168, 211; as justification for European imperialism, 91; as justification for restrictions on Muslims, 166,

268n86; as justification for surveillance and targeting of Muslims, 145, 189; 19th century Protestant views on, 60; and post-9/11 criminalization of Muslim identity, 89, 91, 94, 211; public opinion on, 158–59; Republican politicians on, 157, 158; similarity of claims to justifications for segregation, 77

Islam Awareness Week, 197

Islamic Center of America, vandalism of, *171*

Islamic Circle of North America (ICNA), 145

Islamic civilization, Western criticisms of, in late 20th century, 129

The Islamic Invasion (Morey), 130

Islamicization of US, as goal of US Muslims: as claim of Islamophobia industry, 146, 151, 153, 164; Republican politicians on, 157–58

Islamic Networks Group (ING), 198

Islamic Society of North America (ISNA), 144–45, 149, 197

Islamophilia, 205

Islamophobia: American liberals' downplaying of, 209; and anti-Muslim racism, relation between, 21; and belief in Muslims susceptibility to radicalization, 185; and claimed incompatibility of Muslim and American cultures, 20, 161, 166, 218n92; criticisms of term, 21; in Democrats *vs.* Republicans, 158–59; factors leading to, 5–6; Former Muslims as validators of, 7, 10, 146–47, 148–51; intensification after 9/11, 202; introduction of term, 21; in liberals, 163–64; parallels to anti-Catholic nativism, 155, 156; parallels to McCarthyism, 157–58; systemic, and criminalizing of Muslim identity, 137; as systemic racism, 21; in Trump administration, 164–67. *See also* anti-Muslim racism

Islamophobia and Racism in America (Love), 5

Islamophobia industry, 145–53; books by, 148, 149, 151; claims of, 146, 149; and "clash of civilizations" narrative, promotion of, 146–47, 149; denial of Muslim religious freedom rights as goal of, 145–46; discrediting of those challenging racialization of Muslims, 151; domination of US narratives about Muslims, 148; efforts to destroy Muslim American civil society and leadership, 149; films by, 158. 156, 160, 164, 179; Former Muslims as validators of, 146–47, 148–51; funding sources for, 146*t*–47*t*, 147–48; grassroots protest groups, 150; growth after 9/11 attacks, 147, 148, 170; influence on Republicans, 154; on Muslim loyalty to US, impossibility of, 151; organizations funding, 146*t*–47*t*; Orientalist and Zionist ideology underlying, 147; and police training, 179; production of Islamophobia knowledge, 151–53; shaping of public opinion by, 144–46, 170; and Sharia law, activism against, 150, *150*, 152–53; similarity to Ku Klux Klan and Know Nothing Party, 149; similarity to McCarthyists, 151; testimony in congressional hearings, 156; training of law enforcement, 156; Zionists and, 165–66

ISNA. *See* Islamic Society of North America

Israel: demonization of Palestinian resistance fighters as Soviet proxies, 123–24; interfaith initiatives, and faith-washing, 199; justification of, and characterization of Muslims as violent and irrational, 13; labeling of opponents as anti-Semitic, 172; media portrayals of Israelis *vs.* Arabs, 117; Palestinian killing of athletes at Munich Olympics, 121; rights of Palestinians and, 12–13; and Six-Day War (1967), 116, 119, 120; and Suez Canal crisis, 119; war of independence, 117

Israel, establishment of, 115–18; events leading to, 12–13; as fulfillment of Christian prophesy, 117–18; Holocaust and, 116; justifications for, 116; number of Palestinians evicted in, 117; Palestinian opposition to, 115; parallels to

US taking of Native American land, 120; and racialization of Muslims, 114; US support for, 116, 117; Zionists' purchase of land in Palestine, 115. *See also* Zionism

Italian immigrants: arrivals of, 50, 51, 53; assimilated, adoption of Black-White paradigm, 77; dark-skinned, low classification on racial hierarchy, 72; discrimination against, 72–73; ethnic White status awarded to, 66, 71; initial isolation of, 54, 73; low rating on US racial hierarchy, 42. 43, 44, 78; as mostly peasants, 54; nativists' concerns about, 51, 53; and World War II, 63

Jackson, Andrew, 36

Jamal, Amaney, 5

Japanese American internment: justifications for, 62–63; parallels to discrimination against Muslims, 14; *vs.* treatment of other enemy nations' migrants, 63, 84–85

Japanese immigrants: assimilation of, 63; laws excluding migration, 62; loyalty to emperor, as concern, 63. *See also* anti-Asian discrimination

Jefferson, Thomas, 12, 94–95

Jessup, Henry, 94

Jewish immigrants: before 1870s, as educated and assimilated, 47; backlash against, 40–41, 44, 46, 47, 48–49; and changes in urban demographics, 48; classification as Black in South, 71; and Communist Party in America, 86; and conspiracy theories of threat to Protestant culture, 48–49; expansion of American identity to include, 28, 64; and Immigration Act of 1924, 44; and Jewish-Catholic alliances, 56, 78–79; justifications for persecution of, 48, 49–50; low rating on US racial hierarchy, 42–43, 44; number of immigrants, 40, 47; political clout in US, 116; public opinion on, slowness of change in, 79; and racialization of religion, 28; recategorization as ethnic rather than racial group, 73; and

Jewish immigrants *(continued)*
  religion in racialization, 19; as target
  of anti-Communist investigations,
  86–87; as threat to Protestant dominance, 47, 48–49. *See also* racialization
  of Jewish immigrants
Jewish immigrants, and achievement of
  White status, 28, 64, 65, 66, 70–71,
  78–79, 191–92; and assimilation to
  Anglo-Saxon Protestant norms, 78,
  81–83; denial of, to Jews from Ottoman Empire, 101–2; and disassociation
  from Blacks, 71–72; and entrenchment
  of Black-White dichotomy, 79; and
  legal but not social Whiteness, 40, 45,
  47, 65; lobbying for, 78–79
Jewish immigrants, assimilation of, 51,
  66–67, 70, 191–92; assimilability of,
  as concern, 48, 49; and class mobility,
  82–83; and interfaith marriage, 82; and
  move to Conservative or Reform Judaism, 81–82; as price of White status,
  78, 81; varying degrees of, 74
Jewish organizations, and anti-Communist investigations, 87
Jihad Watch, 146t–47t
JihadWatch blog, 156
Jim Crow laws, 103–4
Johnson, Lyndon B., 86, 118–19
Johnson, Sylvester, 39
Johnson v. McIntosh (1823), 36
Jones, Orville, 48
Judeo-Christian identity: Abrahamic
  national identity as potential replacement for, 15, 80, 211; as civil religion
  of America, 84; Muslim practices
  attacked as antithetical to, 133; as necessary prerequisite for American identity, 27; ongoing racism despite adoption of, 84–85, 88; in post–World War
  II era, 80–81; and switch from race to
  cultural ethnicity as marker of difference, 65, 66, 70–71; US failure to protect Jews in World War II as impetus
  for, 80; and US support for creation of
  Israel, 116, 118; Whiteness as not available to those outside of, 71. *See also*
  United States as White Judeo-Chris-

tian nation; Whiteness, expansion into
  European-heritage Judeo-Christian
  identity

Kazi, Nazia, 5
Kellogg, Miner Kilbourne, 96
Kennedy, John F.: and anti-Catholicism,
  57, 161–62; and Catholics' achievement
  of White status, 84; negative view of
  Arabs, 118–19
Ketron, Bill, 158
Khomeini, Ayatollah, 125
Kidd, Thomas, 92, 94, 117
Kim, Claire Jean, 63
King, Henry, 114
King, Martin Luther, Jr., 85
King, Peter, 156, 157
Kintner, Bill, 158
Know Nothing Party (American Party),
  57, 149
Koshy, Susan, 239n104
Ku Klux Klan: anti-immigrant violence
  by, 101; campaigns to boycott Jewish
  immigrant businesses, 50–51; Chris-
  tian roots of, as ignored by media,
  143; opposition to Jewish and Catholic
  immigrants, 40–41, 48–49, 55–56; reli-
  gious pluralism promoted by opponents of, 79–80; resurgence in 1920s,
  107; similarity to Evangelical Christians of today, 41; White Protestant
  supremacy as goal of, 41
Kumar, Deepa, 5

Lakota, 37
Langdon, Samuel, 92
Lansing, Robert, 114
Latinos: cultural deficiencies, blaming of
  group, not systemic racism, for, 77;
  inclusion in anti-Muslim discrimination, 64
law enforcement, Islamophobia industry's
  training of, 156
Lebanon, classification of Christian
  immigrants from, 95–97
Levant, classification of Christian immigrants from, 97–98
Lewis, Bernard, 129, 130

liberals, Islamophobia in, 163–64
Lieberman, Joseph, 156
The Life of Mahomet (Guir), 95
Limbaugh, Rush, 141
Lind, William S., 138
Lindsay, Hal, 140
Lipset, Seymour Martin, 191
literature: American, depictions of Muslims, 93–94; European, depictions of Muslims, 91
Lithuanian Muslims, immigration in early 20th century, 96
Los Angeles Eight, 124
Love, Erik, 5, 205
Luther, Martin, 94
Lynde and Harry Bradley Foundation, 146t–47t, 148
Lynn, Susan, 158
Lyon, Caleb, 60

Magnuson Act of 1943, 86
Mahomet and His Successors (Irving), 95
Maira, Sunaina, 197
Malcolm X, 108–9, *109*, 110
Mamdani, Mahmoud, 6–7
Manifest Destiny: establishment of Israel and, 117–18; as White Protestant notion, 35, 41
marker of differences, switch from race to cultural ethnicity as: and assimilation of "ethnic Whites," 65, 66, 70–71; and expansion of Whiteness into European-heritage Judeo-Christian identity, 65, 66, 70–71
Massachusetts Bay Colony, 35
Mastnak, Tomaž, 90
Mather, Cotton, 94
Mathews, Basil, 130
McCarran Act (Subversive Activities Control Act) of 1950, 86
McCarran-Walter Act of 1952, 86, 124
McCarthyism, 86
McVeigh, Timothy, 13–14, 131
Meade, Edward, 61
media: characterizations of Catholics, 55; coverage of Al-Qaeda before 9/11, 141–42; coverage of terrorism, lack of balance in, 142; Former Muslims'

appearance in, 10; hyperbolic depictions of Jews, 48; and Iranian Revolution, portrayal of Muslims in, 125; justifications for racial discrimination in, 72; justifications of US invasion of Iraq, 135–36; and low public opinion of Muslims, 13, 144–45, 170; portrayal of Israelis *vs.* Arabs, 117; portrayal of Mormons, 58; racial double standards in depictions of religious extremism, 142–44; and racialization of Muslims, 141–42
media portrayals of immigrants, in immigration waves of mid-19th and early 20th centuries, 41
Media Tenor, 142
MEF. *See* Middle East Forum
Melville, Herman, 35
Middle East: media coverage, lack of balance in, 142; Muslim states' agitation for independence after World War I, 111; oil reserves, control of, as US national security priority after World War II, 114, 118; restrictions on immigration from, 44–45; US client regimes in 1980s, 127; US hegemonic control, Arab opposition to, 118
Middle Eastern immigrants, disassociation from Black and Asian identity, 67–68
Middle East Forum (MEF), 131, 146t–47t, 151
Middle East Quarterly, 131
Middle Road Foundation, 146t–47t
Miles, Robert, 20
Miller, Judith, 131
Milton, John, 91
Ministry Act of 1693 (New York colony), 52
missionaries, negative portrayals of Muslims by, 92–93
MLI. *See* Muslim Leadership Initiative
The Mohammedan Missionary Problem (Jessup), 94
Montielh, Craig, 181
Moorish Science Temple, 104, 108, 110
Morey, Robert, 130
Morgan, Elaine, 158

Naber, Nadine, 5
Naff, Alixa, 97
Napoleon, 91
Nasser, Gamal Abdel, 110, 118, 119
National Conference of Christians and
    Jews (NCCU), 78, 80, 195
National Conference on Interfaith Youth
    Work (2003), 198
National Conference on Religion and
    Race (1963), 85
Nationality and Immigration Act of 1965,
    44–45
National Reform Association, 29
National Security Entry-Exit Registration
    System (NSEERS), 170, 175
national security laws, selective applica-
    tion to Muslims, 169–70
Nation of Islam (NOI): and Black nation-
    alism, 108; civil rights movement's
    rejection of militancy of, 110; conver-
    sion of most members to Sunni Islam,
    110; doctrines of, 108; founding of,
    104, 108; government investigations
    of, 110–11; growth of, 109; Malcolm
    X and, 108–9, 109; Moorish Science
    Temple as predecessor to, 108; Mus-
    lim immigrants' rejection of teachings,
    109–10; separatism of, 104; use of parts
    of Islamic doctrine, 108; on Whites as
    devils, 104, 108
Native Americans: Christian argu-
    ments for conquest and conversion
    of, 29–30, 35–38, 210; coerced conver-
    sions to Protestantism, 36–37; cul-
    tural deficiencies, blaming of group,
    not systemic racism, for, 77; denial
    of property rights to, 36; and free-
    dom of religion, 37–38; and Ghost
    Dance, banning of, 37–38; and Indian
    Removal Act of 1830, 36; Puritans'
    divine mandate to convert, 35; White
    status as not available to, 28
naturalization: limiting to Whites of good
    character, 98; of Muslims, delaying of,
    after 9/11 attacks, 176–77
Naturalization Act of 1790, 98, 100–101
NCCU. See National Conference of
    Christians and Jews

Nee, Victor, 66, 68–69, 70
Netanyahu, Benjamin, 123–24
"The New Islamist International"
    (Bodansky), 130–31
Newton D. and Rochelle F. Becker Foun-
    dation, 146t–47t, 148
New York Police Department (NYPD):
    counter-radicalization report, 185; sur-
    veillance of Muslims after 9/11, 179–
    80, 181–82
Nixon, Richard M., 121
NOI. See Nation of Islam
North American Interfaith Network, 194
North American Islamic Trust, 149
NSEERS. See National Security Entry-
    Exit Registration System

Oak Initiative, 139
Obama, Barack: and Abrahamic national
    identity, 196; attempted reset with
    Muslim worlds, 160; and birther
    movement, 138; claimed Muslim affili-
    ation of, 159–61; "countering violent
    extremism" programs under, 185;
    Evangelical Christians' criticisms of,
    138; religious faith of, 196; support for
    discrimination against Muslims, 14;
    theories of secret Muslim allegiance of,
    56; and "war on religion," accusations
    of, 161; White nationalists' distress at
    potential Black president, 159–60
Obsession (film), 160, 179
Odeh, Rasmea, 173
OFAC. See Office of Foreign Asset
    Control
Office of Foreign Asset Control (OFAC),
    183
Oklahoma City Bombings, early blaming
    of Muslims for, 131–32
Omar, Ilhan: Islamophobes' attacks on,
    155; and movement challenging struc-
    tural racism, 206–7; as Religious Dis-
    sident Muslim, 172, 207
Omar, Mohamed, 180
Omi, Michael, 30
Operation Boulder, 121
Operation Front Line, 176
Operation Liberty Shield, 175–76

Orange Day, 55
Organization of Arab Petroleum Exporting Countries (OPEC): media portrayals of, 13, 122, *122*; oil embargo (1973), 122, *122*
Orientalism: effect on Muslim identity, 137; and Islamophobia industry, 147
Orientalism, American: and Bush's harsh anti-Muslim policies after 9/11 attacks, 135; entrenchment of, 137; evolution in second half of 20th century, 132; grounding in European Orientalism, 113–14
Orientalism, and racialization of immigrant Muslims, 5, 6, 7, 12, 89, 90–92, 210–11; Middle East and North Africa as primary focus of, 17; use in excluding Muslims from religious freedom rights, 30
Orientalism, European: and US views on Muslims, 88, 92–95, 111–12; valuing of Arab culture in past only, 103
Ottoman Empire: citizens of, as unfit for self-government in US view, 99; immigrants from, denial of White status to, 101–2; number of (1860–1914), 246n67
Our Country (Strong), 53
outreach programs to Muslim communities: counter-radicalization programs, 185–86; national security focus of, 169

Pahlavi, Muhammad Reza (shah of Iran), 125
Paine, Thomas, 12, 95
Palestine: and Arab self-determination, US supporters and critics of, 114; British rule in, 115; Christian immigrants from, White status, as issue, 96–97, 98; US mission to (1919), 114
Palestinian Americans: activism, efforts to discourage, 131, 173, 182–83; labeling of, based on actions of others, 14; surveillance and attempted deportations of, 124
Palestinian resistance fighters: and "clash of civilizations" trope, 120; Israeli demonization as Soviet proxies, 123–24; media portrayal as violent and irra-

tional, 13, 120; obstruction of Muslim path to Whiteness, 70; Zionist portrayals as bloodthirsty anti-Semites, 122
Palestinian resistance fighters as terrorists (Palestinian terrorist trope), 120–21; extension to all Muslims, 125–27, 199; and surveillance and harassment of Arabs, 121, 122, 182–83
Palestinians: dehumanization by Zionism, 115; human rights of, as forbidden subject in interfaith initiatives, 199; Israel's ignoring of rights of, 12–13
Palin, Sarah, 160
Park, Robert Ezra, 68
Patel, Eboo, 198
Pawnee, 37
Pence, Mike, 196–97
Pennock, Pamela, 120
PENTTBOM investigation, 174
Pew Research, 159
peyote, and Native American religious freedom, 38
Pharis, Walid, 156
Pipes, Daniel, 131, 132, 151
Pledge of Allegiance, addition of "one Nation under God" to, 64, 81
Plessy v. Ferguson (1896), 62
police departments, Islamophobic training after 9/11, 179
Polish immigrants: low rating on US racial hierarchy, 43; Muslims, in early 20th century, 96
politicians, Islamophobic, 155–59; and congressional hearing on Muslim extremism, 156, 157–58; and legitimization of Islamophobic rhetoric, 158; Republicans and, 157–59; and US as White Judeo-Christian nation, 155
politicians, Muslim, Islamophobes' attacks on, 155
Pompeo, Mike, 165
Popular Front for the Liberation of Palestine, US surveillance of, 121, 124
Powers, Hiram, 95
Prager, Dennis, 155
President's Committee on Civil Rights, 85
Price, Charles S., 118

Prideaux, Humphrey, 91, 92
prison reform, Muslim support for, 206
progressives. *See* coalition of young minority progressives challenging structural racism
Project Nur, 200
Protestant-Catholic-Jew (Herberg), 80
Protestantism, ongoing domination of American culture, 29, 31; and Islam as deviance from Christian norm, 30; religious conservatives' support for, 30
Protocols of the Learned Elders of Zion, 48–49
public contact with Muslims: effect on views about Muslims, 162; low levels of, 163
public opinion: on degree of threat from radical Islamic terrorism, 161; effect of Islamophobia industry on, 144–46, 170; effect of media portrayal of Muslims on, 13, 144–45, 170; on Iranians, after Iranian Revolution, *125*, 125–26; on Islam as violent, oppressive non-religion, 158–59; on Jewish immigrants, slowness of change in, 79; on Muslims, correlation with degree of contact, 162; on Muslims, effect of Trump rhetoric on, 166; on Muslims, ongoing decline since 9/11, 170; percentage expressing anti-Muslim views, 161–62
Puritans: belief in Protestantism as pure Christianity, 35; divine mandate to convert Native Americans, 35; efforts to extirpate non-Puritan sects, 52; and religious freedom, 34–35

Al-Qaeda: and First Gulf War, 128; media coverage of, before 9/11, 141–42; and US support of Afghan mujahideen, 120, 124, 127, 142
Quayle, Dan, 127–28

race: definition of, 18–19; mid-20th century reclassification into three groups (Negroid, Mongoloid, Caucasian), 73; and religion, co-constitutive nature of, 5, 15–16, 22, 71, 209–10; separation of

concept from ethnicity in mid-20th century, 70–71, 73; in US, as defined by physical characteristics, 72. *See also* entries *under* racialization
racial bribe, 173, 189, 191
racial difference, as neither neutral nor stable, 209
racial hierarchy in America: biblical story of Noah's sons and, 39; and classification of immigrant groups, 71, 72–73; critical race theory on, 69; for European races, 42–43, 71; loyalty to, as condition of obtaining benefits of Whiteness, 77; mix of phenotypes and religion used in, 42; Muslims' low ranking on, 137; as part of founding structure, 26–27; and race-based immigration restrictions, 43–44; in racialization of immigrant Muslims, 4; as racial-religious hierarchy, 19; variation of freedom of religion across, 66; and World War II treatment of enemy nation migrants, 63. *See also* Black-White paradigm; racial-religious hierarchy in America
racialization: in America, control by White Christian elites, 30; and Christian theories of White domination, 30; definition of, 20
racialization of Arabs, as quintessential terrorists, 132
racialization of Asians, 61–63; characteristics attributed to Chinese, 61, 62; non-Christian religious faith and, 61, 63
racialization of Catholic immigrants, 28, 57–58; stereotypes and, 210; and systemic discrimination, 65. *See also* anti-Catholic discrimination
racialization of Jewish immigrants, 28, 46–51; characteristics ascribed to Jews, 47–48; hyperbolic physical depictions of Jews, 48; non-Christian religion and, 71; similarities to current racialization of Muslims, 46–47, 48, 50, 63; stereotypes and, 210; and systemic discrimination, 65
racialization of Mormons, 58–60; and comparison of Mormons to Muslims,

racialization of Mormons (*continued*)
60; supposed characteristics of Mormons in, 59; and systemic discrimination, 65, 210; as unfit for self-government, 59

racialization of Muslim immigrants: *vs.* African American Muslims, 4, 16–17, 19–20; after 9/11 terrorist attacks, 1–2, 6, 70, 114, 133–34, 135–37; and association of Muslim practices with savagery, 20; as based in earlier racialization of Native Americans and African Americans, 191; as bipartisan, 197; and "clash of civilizations" narrative, 113, 130; contribution of Western academics and journalists to, 114; and criminalization of Muslim identity, 169, 170, 189; and denial of Muslim religious freedoms, 26, 133, 153; effect of US relations with nation of origin in, 4, 113; European Orientalism and, 89; four factors in, 4–5, 11, 210–11; gender and, 17–18, 216n69; history of, 6; imperial ambitions of US in Muslim-majority countries and, 5, 7, 12–14, 17, 210–11; Islamophobia industry's discrediting of those challenging, 151; as justification for denying religious freedom, 26; leftist turn of Arab Americans after Six Day War (1967), 120; media and, 141–42; and non-applicability of religious freedom norms, 3–4; permanence of, as issue, 189; and racial double standards in response to religious extremism, 14, 142–44, 169, 188, 202; racial hierarchy in, 4; scholarship on, 5; seven crises central to, 114; similarity to past racialization of religious groups, 46–48, 52, 53, 55–57, 64, 65–66, 210; Trump and, 197; as unfit for self-governance, 169; and US public opinion on Muslims, 50; variation with international events, 133; White Protestant supremacy and, 4, 7, 11–12, 90, 210–11; xenophobia and, 4, 12, 90, 210–11. *See also* Orientalism, and racialization of immigrant Muslims; racial-religious hierarchy in America

racialization of Palestinians: as parallel to that of Native Americans, 117; as unenlightened barbarians, 118

racialization of religion in America, 20; control by White Christian elites, 30; founding as White Protestant nation and, 26; political functions of, 46; as understudied, 26; variation by religion's relationship with Protestantism and Whiteness, 28; variation with assimilation levels, 168; variation with historical circumstances, 167–68

racial minorities, increase in numbers and political influence of, and angst among conservative White Americans, 202

Racial Muslim identity: movement on racial-religious hierarchy, dependence on circumstances, 32; as obstacle to citizenship rights of Muslims, 87; permanent foreigner status of, 6, 211; range of ethnic and religious groups included in, 30–31, 88, 210

Racial Muslim identity, future of, 15, 211. *See also* Abrahamic national identity; coalition of young minority progressives challenging structural racism

Racial Muslim identity, social construction of: American empire and, 90; as blending of Orientalism and anti-Black racism, 111–12, 114; history of, 211; Orientalism and, 90; 9/11 terrorist attacks and, 1–2, 132; White Protestant supremacy and, 90; xenophobia and, 4, 12, 90, 210–11. *See also* racialization of Muslim immigrants

Racial Muslim typology, 6–10; and degrees of criminalization of Muslim identity, 171–74; as distinct from phenotype, 7; and "good Muslim, bad Muslim" frame, 6–7; as homogenizing social construct, 17; "religious" and "secular" in, as terms defined by dominant society, 10–11; and variation in discrimination, 4, 7. *See also* Former Muslims; Religious Dissident Muslims; Religious Racial Muslims; Secular Dissident Muslims; Secular Racial Muslims racial-religious hierarchy in America, 19; Abrahamic national identity's failure to dismantle, 15, 22; and access to American dream, 190–91; Asian Americans and, 63; cross-racial movement to destroy, 15; necessity of dismantling, 22–23

racial segregation, as more obvious under religious pluralism, 85

racism: government campaign against in Cold War, 85–86; as ongoing, despite expansion of Whiteness to include Judeo-Christians, 84–85, 88; as product of racialized social systems, 18–19. *See also* anti-Black racism; anti-Muslim racism

RACON, 110

radical Islam: as code for Religious Racial Muslims and Religious Dissident Muslims, 165; failure to consider social and political causes of, 185; public opinion on degree of threat from, 161; Western belief in Muslims susceptibility to radicalization, 185

al-Rahman, Ibrahima 'Abd, 105–6

Rana, Junaid, 206

Rapert, Jason, 158

Rauf, Feisal Abdul, 194

Reagan, Ronald, 124

Reed, David A., 101

Reeve, W. Paul, 59

relative valorization, 63

religion: hierarchical leadership in, Protestant concerns about, 52; and race, co-constitutive nature of, 5, 15–16, 22, 71, 209–10; as term, 18

Religious Dissident Muslims: agreeing to targeting of, as cost of assimilation for Muslims, 200, 205; alliance with African American activists, 202; assumed inassimilability of, 171; and coalition of young minority progressives challenging structural racism, 206; counter-radicalization programs aimed at, 185; criminalization of, after 9/11, 120, 127; discrimination against, as incentive for depoliticization and secularization, 8; govern-

ment targeting of, 169–70; high levels of discrimination against, 7, 8, 153–54, 171, 172, 175–78, 182–84, 214n22; as least likely to assimilate successfully, 192; marginalization in Abrahamic national identity, 198–99; Obama's criticisms of, 185; Omar and Tlaib as, 172, 207; race-conscious activism of, 204; as Racial Muslim type, 7; "radical Islam" as code for, 165; Secular Racial Muslims' complicity in criminalization of, 22; on systemic racism as foundation of anti-Muslim racism, 199; and US mass incarceration system, 206

religious extremism, racial double standards in responses to, 14, 142–44, 169, 188, 202

religious freedom: Americans' pride in, 153; as characteristic of free society, 34; constraints on, in early America, 53; definition of, 20; as historically restricted to White Protestants, 27, 29, 34–35, 63; Native Americans and, 37–38; as not equally available to all, 25; Puritans and, 34–35; variation across racial hierarchy, 66

religious freedom of Muslims: rights included within, 20; surveillance as violation of, 25

religious freedom of Muslims, denial of: due to classification of Islam as non-religion, 26, 30, 64, 153, 168, 211; due to racialization of Muslims, 3–4, 26, 30, 133, 153, 211; Evangelical Christians' support for, 25; as goal of Islamophobia industry, 145–46; as similar to African Americans and Native Americans, 211–12; as systemic racism, 21

religious identity: in American national identity, as racial project, 32; as racial marker, 5, 46

Religious Liberty and Democracy (Straus), 80

religious Muslim, as term defined by dominant society, 10–11

religious pluralism, as response to World War II Fascism and Nazism, 79–80

White Christian models for all Muslims, 9
securitization of Muslims, laws allowing for, 170
segregation: campaign against, 85, 86; laws enforcing, 103–4; White Christians' justifications for, 76–77
Sells, Cato, 37
Senate Committee on Homeland Security and Government Affairs, hearings on Muslim extremism, 156
separation of church and state: founders' agreement on, 28–29; groups lobbying to eliminate, 29
September 11 terrorist attacks, *134*; and anti-Muslim ideologues, new prominence of, 132; author's experience of, 1–2; Bush's harsh anti-Muslim policies following, 135; collective punishment of Muslims following, 178–79; and common negative perceptions of Muslim Arabs, 132; and Ground Zero Mosque, opposition to, 162, *163*; interfaith initiatives after 9/11, 80; and Islamophobia industry, growth of, 147, 170; Muslim efforts to prove loyalty following, 190; obstruction of Muslim path to Whiteness, 70; ongoing punishment of Muslim Americans for, 23; and public interest in Muslims, 148; and racialization of Muslims as violent extremists, 1–2, 5, 70, 114, 133, 135–37; and Racial Muslims, creation of, 1–2, 6, 22, 89, 111–12, 132; US refusal to recognize their own culpability in, 136. *See also* criminalization of Muslim identity after 9/11
settler colonialism in racialization of immigrant Muslims, 12
Sewall, Samuell, 94
Shaler, Nathaniel, 49
Shalom Hartman Institute, 199
Shariah: The Threat to America (Center for Security Policy), 152
Sharia law: conservative views on, 139–40; state anti-Sharia bills, *152*, 152–53, 157; US activism against, 150, *150*, 152–53, *167*

Shoulder to Shoulder Campaign, 194, 197–98
Sicilians, dark-skinned, low classification on racial hierarchy, 43, 72
Siddiqi, Muzammil, 194
Sikhs, inclusion in anti-Muslim discrimination, 64, 187
Simmons, Furnifold McLendel, 101
Sisterhood of Salaam Shalom, 198
Six-Day War (1967): Arab protests against land occupied by Israelis in, 120; and Israeli influence in US, 116; and racialization of Muslims, 114; and US support for Israel, 119
slavery: of Americans by Barbary pirates, 93; Christian arguments for, 39–40, 94, 210; forced conversions of Muslim slaves to Christianity, 95
slaves, African: Christianized, laws forbidding freeing of, 39; coerced conversion to Christianity, 39; distinction between Arab and Black slaves, 39–40, 105–6; educated Muslims among, 105–6; extinction of Muslim faith in, 106; origins of slaves, 104–5; percentage of Muslims among, 39, 104
Slavs, low rating on US racial hierarchy, 43, 44
Smith, Al, 56, 78, 155, 161–62
Smith, Joseph, 58, 59, 60, 210
Smith Act (Alien Registration Act) of 1940, 86
social hierarchies: race and, 209; religion and, 209–10. *See also* racial hierarchy in America; racial-religious hierarchy in America
social psychology view of racism, *vs.* structural racism, 19, 21
Social Science Association of America, 61
social structures, American, Protestantism's dominance of, 29
Society of Americans for National Existence (SANE), *146t–47t*, 152
Solomon, Job ben, 105
South Carolina, slavery law in 1690s, 39
Southern Christian Leadership Conference, 110
Southern Poverty Law Center, 188

Soviet Union, fall of, 115
Spanish-American War of 1898, 55
Spellberg, Denise, 12
Spencer, Robert, 156
Stampnitzky, Lisa, 123
stereotypes of Blacks, perpetuation by ethnic Whites, 77
stereotypes of Muslims, similarity to earlier stereotypes of Catholics, Jews, and Mormons, 169
Straus, Roger Williams, Jr., 78, 80
Strong, Josiah, 53
structural racism, 18–19; deracialization of structures, laws, and policies required to end, 19; and religion in racialization, 19; *vs.* social psychology view of racism, 19, 21. *See also* coalition of young minority progressives challenging structural racism
suburbanization: and Catholic assimilation, 83; and Jewish assimilation, 82–83
Subversive Activities Control Act (McCarran Act) of 1950, 86
Suez Canal: construction of, 91; crisis (1956), 119
Sultan, Wafa, 10, 146–47, 149
Supreme Court: on Fourteenth Amendment protections, 3; heightened scrutiny test for laws targeting minorities, 79; on laws barring Chinese immigration, 62; on Native Americans property rights, 36; on White *vs.* Caucasian classifications, 101
surveillance of Muslims: after 9/11, 174, 175–76, 179–82, 188; and intimidation of Religious Dissident and Religious Muslims, 182–84; lack of public outcry against, 2; legal challenge, approaches to, 2–3; media reports on, 2; Palestinian activists and, 121, 122, 124, 182–83; parallels to World War II surveillance of African American dissidents, 110; public support of, 170–71; similarity to McCarthyism, 124; as violation of religious freedom, 25
Sykes-Picot Agreement of 1916, 111, 115
Syria, Christian immigrants from: areas of settlement, 97; early immigrants,

assimilation of, 97; legal status as White as issue, 95–96, 97–98, 99–103, 247n94; number of immigrants, 97, 245n64; Syrian identity as product of US Immigration Service classifications, 97–98; White nativists' denigration of, 101
systemic racism: destruction of, as goal of coalition of young minority progressives, 202, 203–5; failure of Abrahamic national identity to address, 15, 22, 191, 198–99, 200–208; restrictions on Muslim religious freedom as, 21

Al-Tamimi, Ali, 184
Taylor, Edward, 94
television, and association of Muslims with terrorism, 145
terminology, 18–23
terrorism: American Muslim organizations condemning, media's weak coverage of, 144–45; conferences on, increase in 1970s, 123; definition of, 253–54n81; early study of, by uncredentialed "experts," 123; Paris attacks (2015), and violence against Muslims in response to, 187; US reclassification as act of war rather than crime, 123–24
terrorists: characterization as Cold War network controlled by Soviets, 123–24; designation of all Arabs as, 121
terrorists, designation of all Muslims as (Muslim terrorist trope), 125–27; Iranian Revolution and, 125–27; and rejection of justifiable political violence, 123; and surveillance and harassment of Arabs, 182–84
terrorists, designation of Palestinian resistance fighters as, 120–21; extension to all Muslims, 125–27, 199; and surveillance and harassment of Arabs, 121, 122, 124, 182–83
Terrorists Among Us (Emerson), 131–32
terrorist watch lists, 176
The Third Jihad (film), 156, 179
Thomas Jefferson's Quran (Spellberg), 12
Tito, Josip Broz, 119

Tlaib, Rashida: and Arab (Palestinian) terrorist trope, 207; career of, 207; Islamophobes' attacks on, 155; and movement challenging structural racism, 206–7; as Religious Dissident Muslim, 172, 207

Tobias, Eric, 94

Tocqueville, Alexis de, 29

Torres, Gerald, 173, 191

Troye, Edward, 96

The True Nature of Imposture Displayed in the Life of Mahomet (Prideaux), 91

Truman, Harry S.: focus on civil rights, 85–86; negative view of Arabs, 118–19; recognition of Israel, 13, 116

Trump, Donald J.: anti-Muslim policies of, 26; anti-Muslim rhetoric of, 166, 178; and birther movement, 138; boost given to coalition challenging structural racism, 205–6, 209; call to reduce immigration from non-European countries, 42; and Countering Islamic Extremism programs, 186; Evangelical Christian support for, 41; Islamophobia in administration of, 164–67; and Islamophobia industry, 147; and Muslim Ban, 166–67, 177–78, 188, 197; and Muslim Brotherhood, effort to criminalize, 172; and public opinion on Muslims, effect on, 166; and racialization of Muslims, 197; and racial violence against Muslims, 187–88; and rise of White nationalism, 202, 205, 209; support for discrimination against Muslims, 14

Turks, depictions of, in mid-20th century US, 96

Twain, Mark, 95

UNIA. *See* Universal Negro Improvement Association

Union of American Hebrew Congregations, 102

United States, as coercive assimilationist society, 4, 7, 68–69; failure to force conversions from Judaism, Catholicism, and Mormonism, 77; immigration waves of mid-19th and early 20th

centuries and, 67; and racialization of immigrant Muslims, 4, 7

United States, imperial ambitions of: and creation of Racial Muslim, 89, 90; ending of, as goal of coalition of young minority progressives, 204–5; in Muslim-majority countries, and racialization of immigrant Muslims, 5, 7, 12–14, 17, 210–11

United States as Christian nation, Christian groups asserting, 143

United States as White Judeo-Christian nation: demographic change and, 211; immigration law and, 174; US politicians on, 155–59. *See also* Judeo-Christian identity

United States as White Protestant nation: and Anglo-Saxon triumphalism, 26–27; and freedom of religion as limited to Protestant faiths only, 27; and Manifest Destiny, 35, 41; and racial hierarchy as part of founding structure, 26–27; and racialization of religion, 26

United States Capitol siege (January 6, 2021), 144, 186

United States Institute of Peace (USIP), 195

United States interaction with Muslim-majority lands: contradictory policies of early 20th century, 114; effect on racialization of Muslim immigrants, 4, 113; as minimal before World War II, 113; necessity of, in Cold War, 114

United States national identity. *See* American national identity

United States policy, Muslims disagreeing with, as suspect, 146, 153–54

United States v. Bhagat Singh Thind (1923), 101

United States v. Carolene Products Company (1938), 79

United States v. Cartozian (1914), 102

Universal Negro Improvement Association (UNIA), 107, 110

universities, quotas limiting Jewish admission, 51

USA PATRIOT Act of 2001, 170, 174, 183

USIP. *See* United States Institute of Peace

Vines, Jerry, 138, 149
violence by individual Muslims, Americans' blaming of all Muslims for, 13; as double standard, 14, 142–44, 169, 188, 202
Virginia, Third Charter of (1612), 36
Voices Against Radicalism, 200
Voltaire, 91

Wagner, William, 130
Wahabism, support for, as radical in US view, 172
Ward, Robert, 44
War on Terror: and collective vilification of Muslims, 164; and history of portrayals of Muslims as violent zealots, 91; liberals' support of, 164; parallels to anti-Communist investigations, 87; as racial project infused with religious animus, 87; and US mass incarceration of Muslims, 206; as war on Muslims, 188
Wars of Religion, and anti-Catholic discrimination in America, 51
Washington, Booker T., 71
Washington, George, 47
Washington v. Davis (1976), 3
Wenger, Tisa, 5, 37
Westmoreland, Lynn, 157
Weyler, Kenneth, 158
Weyrich, Paul, 138
What Went Wrong? (Lewis), 129
White Judeo-Christian nation, US as: demographic change and, 211; immigration law and, 174; US politicians on, 155–59
white man's burden, civilizing of Native Americans as, 36
White nationalism, intensification of: after 9/11, 202; under Trump, 202, 205, 209
White nativist groups: contemporary, Jews and Christians in, 80; religious pluralism promoted by opponents of, 79–80; rise of, 147
Whiteness: as Anglo-Saxon and Protestant, before mid-20th century, 65, 68;

change over time to secure Eurocentric Christian power, 209; expansion, goals of, 191; legal *vs.* social, immigrants and, 40; religious identity in shaping of, 5. *See also* citizenship, White identity necessary for; ethnic Whites
Whiteness, expansion into European-heritage Judeo-Christian identity, 65; and entrenchment of Black-White dichotomy, 79; and failure to force conversions from Judaism, Catholicism, and Mormonism, 77; and inclusion of Jews, Catholics, and Mormons, 64, 65, 66, 70–71, 78–80; interfaith initiatives and, 78; and ongoing racism, 84–85, 88; as response to Cold War competition, 65, 81; as response to World War II Fascism and Nazism, 65, 79–80; switch from race to cultural ethnicity as marker of difference and, 65, 66, 70–71; three factors in, 65
White Paper (May 1939), 115
White privilege: cross-racial movement to destroy, 15; necessity of dismantling, 27–28. *See also* coalition of young minority progressives challenging structural racism
White Protestant nation, US as: and Anglo-Saxon triumphalism, 26–27; and freedom of religion as limited to Protestant faiths only, 27; and Manifest Destiny, 35, 41; and racial hierarchy as part of founding structure, 26–27; and racialization of religion, 26
White Protestant supremacy, and racialization of Muslim immigrants, 4, 7, 11–12, 90, 210–11
White Racial Frame, 19, 69–70
White status: assimilation to Anglo-Saxon Protestant norms as cost of, 78; disassociation from Blacks as prerequisite for, 71–72, 77; Jewish achievement of, 191–92; loss of, after 9/11, 201; loyalty to American racial hierarchy as condition of obtaining, 77; Muslim achievement through assimilation, 201; as unavailable for African, Asian,

or Native Americans, 28; as unavailable to non-Whites and non-Judeo-Christians, 71

White status, Catholics' achievement of, 28, 64, 65, 66, 70–71; and assimilation to Anglo-Saxon Protestant norms, 83–84; and disassociation from Blacks, 72; and entrenchment of Black-White dichotomy, 79; and expansion of American Christian identity, 28, 64; Kennedy presidency as culmination of, 84; lobbying for, 79

White status, Jews' achievement of, 28, 64, 65, 66, 70–71, 78–79, 191–92; and assimilation to Anglo-Saxon Protestant norms, 78, 81–83; denial of, to Jews from Ottoman Empire, 101–2; and disassociation from Blacks, 71–72; and entrenchment of Black-White dichotomy, 79; and legal but not social Whiteness, 40, 45, 47, 65; lobbying for, 78–79

White supremacists: attacks on Muslims, 143; increasing violence by, 186; rise of, under Trump, 202, 205

Why Islam Is a Threat to America and the West (Weyrich and Lind), 138

Wilders, Geert, 158

William Rosenwald Family Fund, 146t–47t

Wilson, Woodrow, 42, 114

Winant, Howard, 30

Winthrop, John, 35

women, Muslim: and coalition of young minority progressives challenging structural racism, 202–3; and misogyny of Islam, interpreting Muslim

practices as evidence of, 20; oppression of, as claim of Islamophobia industry, 146, 148–49; secular liberals' belief in oppression of, 10

World Parliament of Religions (Chicago, 1893), 40

World Trade Center bombing (1993): and "clash of civilizations" trope, 131; and racialization of Muslims, 114

World War I: discrimination against German immigrants in, 75–76; and pressure to assimilate, 64

World War II: and Black nationalists' collusion with Japanese, 110; Eastern and Southern European immigrants chance to prove loyalty in, 72; surveillance of African American dissidents, 110; US failure to accept Jewish immigrants, effects on US policy, 80, 116; US ideological separation from Nazis, and policies of inclusion, 64, 79–80; US national security priorities after, 114

Wovoka, 37

xenophobia: and coercive assimilation, 4, 7, 68–69; and racial classification of Christian immigrants from Syria, 98; and racialization of Muslim immigrants, 4, 12, 90, 210–11

Yerushalmi, David, 152

Young Islam on Trek (Mathews), 130

Zhou Enlai, 119

Zionism: dehumanization of Palestinians, 115; and Islamophobia industry, 147. *See also* Israel, establishment of

Founded in 1893,
UNIVERSITY OF CALIFORNIA PRESS
publishes bold, progressive books and journals
on topics in the arts, humanities, social sciences,
and natural sciences—with a focus on social
justice issues—that inspire thought and action
among readers worldwide.

The UC PRESS FOUNDATION
raises funds to uphold the press's vital role
as an independent, nonprofit publisher, and
receives philanthropic support from a wide
range of individuals and institutions—and from
committed readers like you. To learn more, visit
ucpress.edu/supportus.

CPSIA information can be obtained
at www.ICGtesting.com
Printed in the USA
BVHW031941230122
626975BV00007B/360

9 780520 382299